Boundaries of Belonging

The 1947 Partition had a major impact on issues of citizenship and rights in India and Pakistan in the decades that followed. *Boundaries of Belonging* shows how citizenship evolved at a time of political transition and what this meant for ordinary people, by directing attention away from South Asia's Partition 'hot spots' – Bengal and the Punjab – to Partition 'hinterlands' of Uttar Pradesh and Sindh. The analysis, based on rich archival research and fieldwork, brings out commonalities, differences and the mutual co-construction of the 'citizen' in both places. It also reveals the way in which developments across the border, such as communal violence, could directly have an impact on minority rights in the neighbouring country. Questioning stereotypes of an 'authoritarian' Pakistan versus a 'democratic' India, Sarah Ansari and William Gould make a major contribution to recent scholarship that suggests the differences between India and Pakistan are overstated.

SARAH ANSARI is Professor of History at Royal Holloway, University of London.

WILLIAM GOULD is Professor of Indian History at the University of Leeds.

Boundaries of Belonging

Localities, Citizenship and Rights in India and Pakistan

Sarah Ansari

Royal Holloway, University of London

William Gould

University of Leeds

CAMBRIDGE
UNIVERSITY PRESS

CAMBRIDGE
UNIVERSITY PRESS

University Printing House, Cambridge CB2 8BS, United Kingdom

One Liberty Plaza, 20th Floor, New York, NY 10006, USA

477 Williamstown Road, Port Melbourne, VIC 3207, Australia

314-321, 3rd Floor, Plot 3, Splendor Forum, Jasola District Centre, New Delhi - 110025, India

103 Penang Road, #05-06/07, Visioncrest Commercial, Singapore 238467

Cambridge University Press is part of the University of Cambridge.

It furthers the University's mission by disseminating knowledge in the pursuit of
education, learning and research at the highest international levels of excellence.

www.cambridge.org
Information on this title: www.cambridge.org/9781316647172
DOI: 10.1017/9781108164511

First published 2020
First paperback edition 2022

A catalogue record for this publication is available from the British Library

Library of Congress Cataloging in Publication data
Names: Ansari, Sarah F. D., author. | Gould, William, 1973- author.
Title: Boundaries of belonging : localities, citizenship and rights in India and
  Pakistan / Sarah Ansari, William Gould.
Description: Cambridge, United Kingdom ; New York, NY : Cambridge
  University Press, 2020. | Includes bibliographical references and index. |
  Summary: "The 1947 Partition had a major impact on issues of citizenship
  and rights in India and Pakistan in the decades that followed"– Provided by
  publisher.
Identifiers: LCCN 2019010785 | ISBN 9781107196056 (hardcopy : alk. paper)
  | ISBN 9781316647172 (pbk. : alk. paper)
Subjects: LCSH: Citizenship–India. | Citizenship–Pakistan. | Civil rights–India.
  | Civil rights–Pakistan. | India–History–Partition, 1947. | India–Boundaries–
  Pakistan. | Pakistan–Boundaries–India. | India–History–1947- |
  Pakistan–History–20th century.
Classification: LCC DS480.842 .A57 2019 | DDC 323.60954/09045–dc23
LC record available at https://lccn.loc.gov/2019010785

ISBN 978-1-107-19605-6 Hardback
ISBN 978-1-316-64717-2 Paperback

They had left their cities but they carried their cities with them, as a trust, on their shoulders. That's how it usually is. Even when cities are left behind, they don't stay behind. They seize on you even more.   Intizar Hussain, *Basti* (1979), chapter 5

We are surrounded by places. We walk over and through them. We live in places, relate to others in them, die in them. Nothing we do is unplaced. How could it be otherwise?   Edward S. Casey, *The Fate of Place: A Philosophical History* (1997), p. ix

Contents

Figures

Acknowledgements

Writing a co-authored monograph that is not a chapter-by-chapter separation of India and Pakistan, but rather one which seeks to tie each state/place to the other throughout requires a particular kind of understanding between the authors. We feel that this book could not have been possible without a sense of mutual cooperation, assisted by the (sometimes excessively) easy-going nature of each writer. More importantly, it was also made possible by our long-term collaborations with a range of supporters and colleagues, and to them we extend our grateful collaborative thanks.

At an institutional level, the School of History, University of Leeds, and the History Department at Royal Holloway, University of London, have provided phases of research leave which have allowed us to finish off much of the research and writing required for this book. But, more broadly, the conceptual challenges of simultaneously writing about both places were only sustained in the long term by a large-scale research project grant provided by the Arts and Humanities Research Council (AHRC) between 2007 and 2010. *Boundaries of Belonging* is the ultimate long-term outcome of that project, entitled 'From Subjects to Citizens: Society and the Everyday State in India and Pakistan', which has spawned a whole range of other collaborations, networks and projects that have occupied us since then.

Much of the research material in this book was the product of long-term archival research stretching back over a decade and covering a number of different cities. We would like to thank the Nehru Memorial Museum and Library, New Delhi; the National Archives, New Delhi; the Uttar Pradesh State Archives, Lucknow; the Maharashtra State Archives, Mumbai; the Sindh Archives, Karachi; the Pakistan Institute of International Affairs, Karachi; the Institute of Sindhology, Jamshoro; the National Archives of Pakistan, Islamabad; the US National Archives at College Park, Maryland; the Asia Pacific Room of the British Library, London, which houses the India Office collections; the Centre of South Asian Studies, Cambridge; the Brotherton Library, University of Leeds; and the Emily Wilding Davison Library at Royal Holloway. We are also grateful for a small grant from the late Miss Isobel Thornley's Bequest to the University of London, which covered the cost of certain images included in our book.

Over the course of our joint enterprise, we have also depended upon the advice, support and friendship of a wide range of colleagues, mostly fellow historians but not only those limited to that discipline. For their assistance and advice on materials relating to our two chosen 'case studies' and also for listening to early drafts of chapters as presentations, we thank (in strict alphabetical order!) Sana Aiyar, Edward Anderson, Crispin Bates, Anjali Bhardwaj-Datta, Paul Brass, Stuart Carroll, Joya Chatterji, Cathy Coombs, Markus Daechsel, Santosh Dass, Antara Datta, Ayona Datta, Rohit De, Faizal Devji, Sarah Gandee, Jesus Garza-Chairez, Anindita Ghosh, Oliver Godsmark, Kevin Greenbank, Dan Haines, Tariq Jazeel, Justin Jones, Yasmin Khan, Elizabeth Leake, Stephen Legg, Eleanor Newbigin, Rosalind O'Hanlon, Steven Pierce, Ali Usman Qasmi, Pallavi Raghovan, Francis Robinson, Jonathan Saha, Uditi Sen, Farzana Shaikh, Ornit Shani, Taylor Sherman, Tom Simpson, Gurharpal Singh, Ian Talbot, Shabnum Tejani, Layli Uddin, Pippa Virdee, David Washbrook, Phil Withington, Andrew Wyatt, Vazira Zamindar and the organizers of the British Association of South Asian Studies in Cambridge, April 2016. For assistance in India, we would especially like to thank Ekta Gautam, Dakxin Chhara, Sunil Sonwane, Sandeep Pandey, Mudit Shukla, Mani Shankar Aiyar, Ram Advani, Patrick French and Shakti Sinha. Across the border in Pakistan, the same debt of gratitude goes to Sana Ansari, Aabida Ali, Lata Parwani, Nausheen Ahmad and Rafiq Safi Munshey, Babar Ayaz and Samia Khan, Masuma Hasan, Karamat Ali, Ghulam Muhammad Lakho and Gul Muhammad Umrani. Throughout, a range of professional and personal friendships have similarly helped to keep our joint enterprise afloat. For their good humour, intellectual debate around the book's themes and general encouragement, colleagues at Leeds and Royal Holloway not already mentioned would include Nir Arieli, Simon Ball, Manuel Barcia, Malcolm Chase, Kate Dossett, Shane Doyle, Simon Hall, James Harris, Will Jackson, Laura King, Graham Loud, Andrew Lunt, Andrea Major, and Michelle Ridge (at Leeds) and Evrim Binbas, Jason Brock, Justin Champion, Chi-Kwan Mark, Stella Moss, Penelope Mullens and Weipin Tsai, together with the many visiting academics from Pakistan who have spent time at Royal Holloway over recent years. Closer to home, a number of important friends and family members have provided moral support and/or feedback on the book, including Olivia Gould, Richard and Elizabeth Gould, Radu and Elena Harasemiuc, Alexandru Harasemiuc, Liz Gilston, Tariq Sadiq, Rajesh Jha, Irna Qureshi, Steve and Esther Cooper, Humayun, Akbar and Zafar, Rowan and Charlotte, Nasreen and Nayyar, Zufah and Zulkarnain, along with the rest of the extended Ansari-Girling-Machover-Waweru 'clan'.

Abbreviations

AICC	All-India Congress Committee, India
AIWC	All-India Women's Conference
APWA	All-Pakistan Women's Association
BC	Backward Classes
BL	British Library
DSO	District Supply Officer
FCO	Foreign and Commonwealth Office
GAD	General Administration Department
GCW	Gandhi's Collected Works
IAS	Indian Administrative Service
IOR	India Office Records, British Library, London
IPS	Indian Police Service
MEA	Ministry of External Affairs, India
MHA	Ministry of Home Affairs, India
NAI	National Archives of India, New Delhi
NDC	Ministry of Interior, Pakistan, Home Division National Documentation Centre
NMML	Nehru Memorial Museum and Library, New Delhi
NWFP	North-West Frontier Province
PHWA	Pakistan Hindu Welfare Association
PILER	Pakistan Institute of Labour Education and Research
PPP	Pakistan People's Party
PRODA	Public and Representatives Offices (Disqualification) Act
PSPE	Pakistan Special Police Establishment
PWD	Public Works Department
PWNG	Pakistan Women's National Guard
PWNR	Pakistan Women's Naval Reserve
PWVS	Pakistan Women's Volunteer Service
RSS	Rashtriya Swayamsevak Sangh
SC	Scheduled Caste
SCBA	Supreme Court Bar Association
SCF	Scheduled Castes Federation
SLRM	Sindh Land Reform Movement
SPE	Special Police Establishment (India)

ST	Scheduled Tribe
SWJN	Selected Works of Jawaharlal Nehru
TRO	Town Rationing Officer
UKHC	United Kingdom High Commission, Pakistan
UKNA	United Kingdom National Archives, Kew, London
UNO	United Nations Organization
UP	Uttar Pradesh (formerly the United Provinces)
UPSA	Uttar Pradesh State Archives, Lucknow
USNA	United States National Archives
VJSS	Vimukt Jati Sevak Sangh
WAF	Women's Action Forum
WIA	Women's Indian Association
WPB	Women's Protection Bill

Maps

Territorial structure of India and Pakistan. Boundaries: 1, Former Indian Empire; 2, Indo-Pakistan; 3, Provinces, Major States and Agencies; 4, Minor State; 5, Pakistan Provinces; 6, States adhering to Pakistan; 7, Indian Provinces; 8, States adhering to Indian Union; 9, States declared for independence or of doubtful status on October 1, 1947; 10, Foreign Possessions: 1, Diu, 2, Damão, 3, Goa (Portuguese); 4, Mahé, 5, Karikal, 6, Pondichéri, 7, Yanaon, 8, Chandernagor (French).

Map 1 Map of India and Pakistan

Map 2 Map of Uttar Pradesh (formerly the United Provinces)

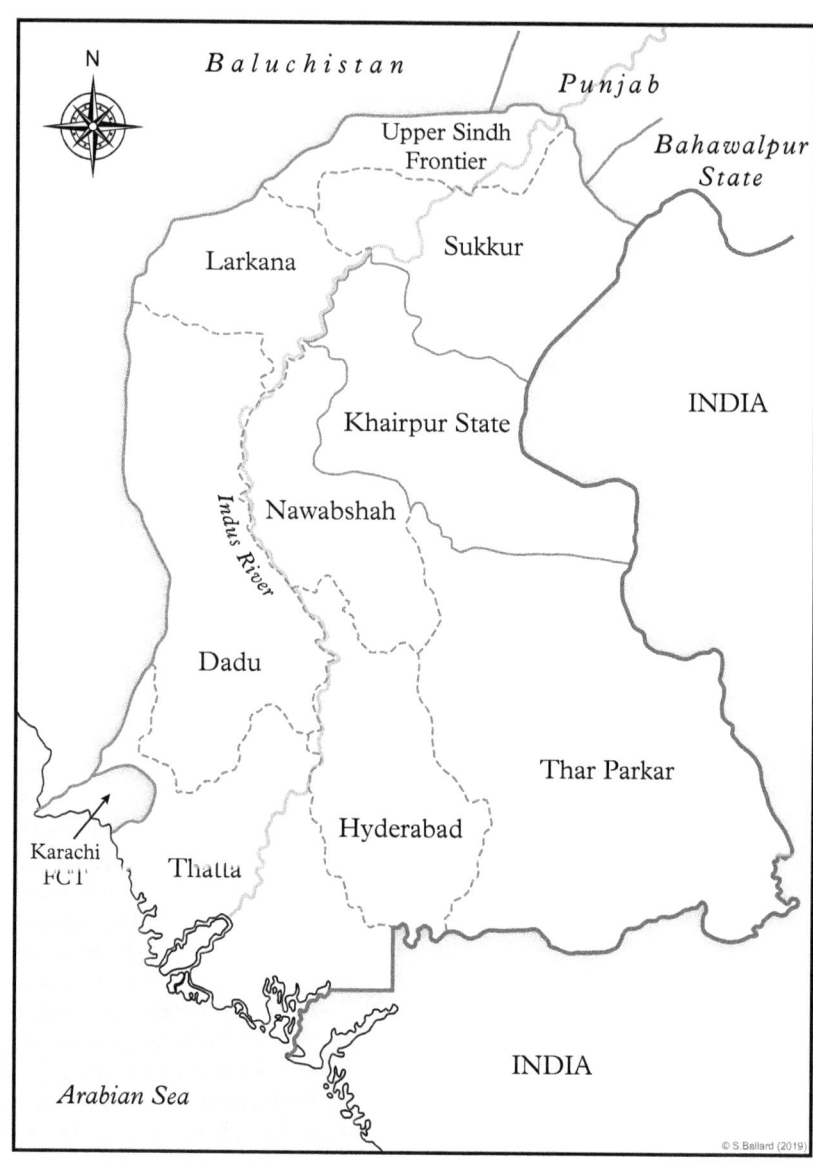

Map 3 Map of Sindh

Introduction

In March 1948, Mridula Sarabhai sent a report from Anandpur Sahib, Punjab, to India's first prime minister, Jawaharlal Nehru, Rameshwari Nehru and Lady Mountbatten. Sarabhai discussed how a group of Sikh women 'recovered' following abduction during Hindu-Sikh-Muslim violence had been transferred into the care of the Pakistan military. Sarabhai, the daughter of a powerful industrialist family of Gujarat and a key figure in the women's movement in India, had been tasked by the new Government of India to lead recovery operations for women abducted over the border during Partition violence. On three occasions, Sarabhai learned, this particular group of women had been 'handed back' to their 'abductors'. This practice, she claimed, was going on in more than one place in the border areas, and it was also suggested that the Pakistan military were 'making money through this scheme'.[1]

Partition – that is the division of British India into the separate states of India and Pakistan on 14/15 August 1947 – involved the massive transfer of people with perhaps as many as fourteen to sixteen million refugees eventually moving in opposite directions across the new border that was drawn up in the weeks leading up to Independence. The uncertainties, as illustrated by Sarabhai's report, bound up in what was the twentieth century's most significant exchange of populations (or alternatively forced migration) cannot, however, be easily explained as a simple narrative of victimhood. In the case of abducted women, many resisted the assumptions of the recovery operation based on its effect on their personal circumstances, with a number of first-hand accounts describing how women themselves refused to be 'saved', or to comply with the patriarchal assumptions of this particular population exchange.[2] Their

[1] 'Note on the visit to Anandpur Mela' 24/3/48 – to Jawaharlal Nehru, K. C. Neogy and Lady Mountbatten, Papers of Mridula Sarabhai, Reel 1, Nehru Memorial Museum and Library (hereafter NMML).

[2] This is explored in a number of case studies in Kamla Bhasin and Ritu Menon, *Borders and Boundaries: Women in India's Partition* (New Delhi: Kali for Women, 1998), and

agency meant that in some notable instances women identified as 'abductees' evaded recovery. On 1 March 1948, to give one example, Sushila Nayar and Gurbachan Singh acting as social workers reported to Nehru from Patiala that around 175 Muslim women had shown reluctance to leave their new homes or to be moved on from camps back to their original families.[3] Reportedly, around a quarter of these women directly resisted 'rescue' by running away from the recovery camp in which they had been housed.[4]

The often-forcible removal of people across newly drawn national boundaries highlights important dichotomies in the meaning of political independence in South Asia. On the one hand, there certainly existed a sense of powerlessness among many people who were directly subject to the vicissitudes of Partition. After all, the women of Anandpur Sahib and other places on both sides of the new border were 'recovered', whether they liked it or not, by the state authorities, both Indian and Pakistani, and so in many respects their individual freedom was denied. In the uncertain months and years that straddled British India's division, it was unclear how the supposed agents of each state were expected to act, and where the limits of their responsibilities for recovering citizens lay. But the predicament of abducted women did not represent a simple contradiction between powerlessness and agency. In practice, there was little consensus as to how the emerging rights of each state's new citizenry would be formed or framed in this period of significant political transition. The fate of India and Pakistan's recently created citizens was often determined either by high-level processes of intergovernmental negotiation or more precariously by the frequently arbitrary decisions made by local administrations, police officers and other government servants. Meanwhile, there were opportunities thrown up by this uncertainty – chances for individuals to shape and exercise their rights in new ways, and to take advantage of the ambiguities created by Partition and its accompanying movement of peoples on an enormous scale.

The idea of the citizen in both India and Pakistan was put together hurriedly and subject to change, not least because the geopolitical shape of postcolonial South Asia itself was decided in a matter of weeks. As late as March 1947, there was no absolute certainty that Partition should or would result from the decolonization of British India. Within the

---

similarly in Urvashi Butalia, *The Other Side of Silence: Voices from the Partition of India* (London: C. Hurst and Co., 2000), particularly chapter 4 'Women'.
[3] Jawaharlal Nehru to Sushila Nayar, 2 March 1948, *Selected Works of Jawaharlal Nehru* (hereafter *SWJN*), Vol. 5, p. 118.
[4] Jawaharlal Nehru to K. C. Neogy, 3 March 1948, *SWJN*, Vol. 5, p. 120.

gradually forming imagining of 'India' and 'Pakistan' that emerged out of discussions during and after the Second World War, there was always scope for alternative scenarios. In the fraught negotiations leading up to the transfer of power, and especially during the Cabinet Mission in the spring and summer of 1946, the separation of India and Pakistan was not regarded as inevitable. In fact, it is now well established that the 'father' of Pakistan – Muhammad Ali Jinnah – would have welcomed a solution short of absolute division, and that the Congress under Nehru accepted the prospect of Partition from March 1947, at least at the central level, as a lesser of many evils, and a means of preserving Congress's political authority.[5] The constitutional frameworks of postcolonial South Asia were also in large part the legacy of the same structure of colonial governance and so retained much that was similar after 1947: the provisions of the 1935 Government of India Act that had envisaged a federal system within a greater India eventually formed the basis of India's 1950 Constitution, and it similarly underpinned much of Pakistan's 1956 Constitution. But in the decades since Independence, India and Pakistan have come to be seen as very different places. Their subsequent evolution has taken them in apparently diverging political directions, with India often held up as a postcolonial 'success story' in contrast to Pakistan's reputation as a failing, if not failed, state. This oversimplification of their post-1947 histories has emphasized difference at the expense of recognizing commonalities at work across the region. This book is about how in the mutually interconnected social and political histories of these two new states we can find the messy realities of citizenship in each place. This is a history that includes the highest decisions of states as well as the politics of the streets, but it is a narrative that can only be complete if told in both places at once.

The historian of Germany Celia Applegate, in her exploration of regional histories in a European context, has argued persuasively for the need to 'regard the specificity of places as the outcome of social and cultural processes interacting with physical environments'.[6] Likewise, for sociologist Alan Warde, 'places are not automatic contexts for collective life but [are] created', and so can be regarded as 'resources to be manipulated in the creation, recreation and restructuring of the contexts in which people

---

[5] See Ayesha Jalal, *The Sole Spokesman: Jinnah, the Muslim League, and the Demand for Pakistan* (Cambridge: Cambridge University Press, 1985).

[6] Celia Applegate, 'A Europe of Regions: Reflections on the Historiography of Sub-National Places in Modern Times', *American Historical Review* 104, 4 (1999), p. 1181.

are made – or make themselves'.[7] Ignoring the spatial turn of the last couple of decades is no longer a realistic option for historians: to quote Doreen Massey, 'places' represent networks of complex associations that 'have over time been constructed, laid down, interacted with one another, decayed, and renewed. Some of these relations will be, as it were, contained within the place; others will stretch beyond it, tying any particular locale into wider relationships and processes in which other places are implicated too'.[8] Moreover, because people 'move and stop, settle, and move again … places are shifting and changing, always becoming through people's engagements – material as well as discursive – in, through and with them'. 'Place', therefore, 'is not where social relations simply take place, but an inherent ingredient of their modalities of actualization'.[9] In other words, rather than opposed to or disruptive of 'place', mobility – or movement – is an inherent part of how spaces are defined and operate,[10] and therefore central to the processes by which citizenship is also, imagined, constructed or contested.

Boundaries of Belonging responds to these conceptual insights regarding the significance of 'place' by centring its exploration of the impact of Independence on citizenship and rights in two specific localities – one Uttar Pradesh (UP), an Indian state after 1947, and the other Sindh, a province in Pakistan. Both were parts of British India that were less associated with the immediate upheavals of Partition as compared with the Punjab and Bengal, but which came to be hugely affected by its longer term consequences for Indian and Pakistani lives. Accordingly we use UP and Sindh – the focal points of our individual interests as historians of South Asia – as the common lens through which to investigate what 'belonging' came to mean more broadly in the recalibrated circumstances of the 1940s and 1950s. Crucially, our concentration on UP and Sindh allows us to explore the fallout from Independence and Partition from the perspective of two places that, on the one hand, were not physically divided, and, on the other, where the shifting status of local minority communities (which had become significant before 1947) proved to be critical to ideas about 'India' and 'Pakistan' moving forward.

[7] Alan Warde, 'Recipes for a Pudding: A Comment on Locality' *Antipode* 21 (1989), pp. 274–81.
[8] Doreen Massey, 'A Global Sense of Place', in *Space, Place and Gender*, ed. Doreen Massey (Minneapolis, MN: University of Minnesota Press, 2004), p. 120.
[9] Kostas Retsikas, 'Being and Place: Movement, Ancestors, and Personhood in East Java, Indonesia', *Journal of the Royal Anthropological Institute* 13 (2007), pp. 971–2.
[10] Tim Cresswell, *Place: A Short Introduction* (Oxford: Oxford University Press, 2004).

UP and Sindh – the former occupying much of the Ganges basin in north India, the latter straddling the Indus River further to the west – may appear on first inspection to have been separated during the colonial period by more than simply geographical distance. In particular, UP's location at the political heart of British India, for instance, contrasted markedly with Sindh's relatively peripheral position under the Raj. But by the early twentieth century both places could boast key centres of imperial activity. In 1911, accompanied by great pomp and ceremony, the political capital of British India transferred from Calcutta to New Delhi, on the border of UP, and the province had become a political thermometer for much of the rest of the country with its vast population, key party political figures and important cities. Karachi's rapid expansion meant that that by the First World War it was exporting more wheat than any other port in Britain's global empire and hence challenging Calcutta and Bombay for business.[11] There were also clear, if not necessarily acknowledged, parallels in terms of the communal patterns that existed in the two provinces. Both possessed influential minority communities, whose horizons (not simply political) had for a long time extended beyond the borders of their provinces.[12] Moreover, by the time of the Second World War, UP arguably represented a microcosm of India as a whole: the proportion of Muslims to the total population in UP, combined with pockets of (urban) dominance, more or less mirrored the overall situation in India. But Paul Brass's statement that UP Muslims (15 per cent of the population according to the 1931 Census) during the late colonial period 'constituted a cultural and administrative elite' with higher rates of change 'in several respects, including urbanization, literacy and government employment', could equally have been applied to Sindhi Hindus (c. 25 per cent), albeit with the addition of 'commercial' to their description.[13] With the rise of competing nationalist organizations over the course of the early twentieth century, and the emergence of religion as a source of conflict, these local communal realities endowed political developments taking place in both UP and Sindh with broader significance.

---

[11] Sarah Ansari, 'At the Crossroads? Exploring Sindh's Recent Past from a Spatial Perspective', *Contemporary South Asia* 23, 1 (2015), pp. 7–25.

[12] For more information on the trading activities of Sindhi Hindus that took them far from the province, see Claude Markovits, *The Global World of Indian Merchants 1750–1947: Traders of Sind from Bukhara to Panama* (Cambridge: Cambridge University Press, 2000); and Mark-Anthony Falzon, *Cosmopolitan Connections: The Sindhi Diaspora, 1860–2000* (Leiden: Brill, 2004).

[13] Paul R. Brass, 'Muslim Separatism in United Provinces: Social Context and Political Strategy before Partition', *Economic and Political Weekly* 5, 3/5 (January 1970), pp. 167, 169.

By the interwar period, UP's leading role in all-India politics had become well-established.[14] The province was now home to key movements that spanned the nationalist spectrum, including the Indian National Congress (the Nehru family famously had its base there), Hindu nationalism (the re-organized Hindu Mahasabha in Banaras in 1923 was headed by the Allahabad politician, Madan Mohan Malaviya) and Muslim political leadership (closely associated with Muslims living in the small towns or *qasbahs* of the province). UP spanned the 'Hindi' heartland of India, and its educational institutions, periodical publications and intellectual life were central to the crucial language debates of the late colonial period. It was in UP where early support for the Muslim League emerged in towns such as Aligarh, and it was UP Muslims who helped to drive the eventual claim of League politicians to speak for Muslims at an all-India level.[15] Another decisive development with far-reaching all-India significance were the knock-on political consequences generated by the decision of UP Congress politicians not to form a coalition with Muslim Leaguers there following the provincial elections of 1937. This move directly helped to set the scene for the increasingly separatist strategies of the latter at the all-India level.[16]

Meanwhile, as an outpost of Bombay Presidency, an increasing number of Sindhi Muslims during the early twentieth century grew more politically aware of their minority status within what they regarded as a Hindu-dominated administrative and political unit.[17] These concerns prompted discussion at the Round Table Conferences held in London in the early 1930s about whether Sindh should be removed from Bombay

---

[11] Gyanesh Kudaisya, *Region, Nation, "Heartland": Uttar Pradesh in India's Body Politic* (New Delhi: Sage, 2006).

[15] Francis Robinson, *Separatism among Indian Muslims: The Politics of the United Provinces' Muslims, 1860–1923* (Cambridge: Cambridge University Press, 1974). For a more recent (revisionist) exploration of separatist politics in the UP during this period, see Venkat Dhulipala, 'Rallying the *Qaum*: The Muslim League in the UP, 1937–1938', *Modern Asian Studies* 44, 3 (2010), pp. 603–40, in which he tests out the arguments and evidence that drive his *Creating a New Medina: State Power, Islam, and the Quest for Pakistan in Late Colonial North India* (Cambridge: Cambridge University Press, 2015). Another re-interpretation of the motives involved in Muslim separatist politics is provided in Faisal Devji, *Muslim Zion: Pakistan as a Political Idea* (London: C. Hurst & Co., 2013).

[16] Deepak Pandey, 'Congress-Muslim League Relations 1937–39: The Parting of the Ways', *Modern Asian Studies* 12, 4 (1978), pp. 629–54.

[17] For instance, see the case presented in M. A. Khuhro, 'A Story of the Suffering of Sind' (1930), in *Documents on Separation of Sind from the Bombay Presidency*, ed. with an introduction by Hamida Khuhro (Islamabad: Islamabad Islamic University, 1982), pp. 196–254. See also Sarah Ansari, 'Identity Politics and Nation-Building in Pakistan: The Case of Sindhi Nationalism', in *State and Nation-Building in Pakistan: Beyond Islam and Security*, eds. Roger D. Long, Yunus Samad, Gurharpal Singh and Ian Talbot (London: Routledge, 2015), pp. 285–310.

Presidency and turned into a separate province (which duly took place in 1936 in the wake of the 1935 Government of India Act). Supporters of Sindh's separation from Bombay deployed arguments that hinged (at least in part) on the 'logic' of its possessing a local Muslim majority, rehearsing (and perhaps contributing to) the League's later claims regarding Muslim-majority provinces en masse from 1940 onwards. Moreover, as Sindhis today still remind other Pakistanis, the first official resolution demanding the creation of 'Pakistan' was the one passed by the Sindh provincial assembly on 3 March 1943, its mover – G. M. Sayed (ironic in view of his later espousal of Sindhi nationalism) – arguing that Muslims in India were 'justly entitled to the right as a single separate nation to have independent national states of their own, carved in the zones in which they are in majority in the subcontinent of India'.[18] By 1947 – thanks to developments such as these – majority and minority communities in UP and Sindh alike had become increasingly sensitized both about their local position and in relation to the need (from their perspective) to protect their interests as the broader South Asian political landscape changed.

After Independence, UP and Sindh continued to play significant but different roles in the life of the new states of India and Pakistan. UP – as India's new 'Hindi heartland' and with the largest number of seats of any state in the Constituent Assembly, and later in the Lok Sabha – remained strategically placed at the hub of all-India politics and proximate to New Delhi as federal capital of the Indian Union. Its population, which was over 60 million according to the 1951 Census making UP by far and away India's biggest new state, endowed it with colossal political clout in relation to the nation-building politics of the late 1940s and 1950s.[19] Sindh, with the federal capital on its doorstep (Karachi was officially detached from the province in 1948 and turned into a federal territory), was also located in close proximity to the centre of power in Pakistan, though in practice many Sindhis felt that their province remained marginalized in political terms. From a population perspective, with only *circa* six million inhabitants in 1951, Sindh lagged considerably behind both East Bengal (42 million) and the Punjab (22.5 million). Like Bengalis, however, many Sindhis railed against what they regarded as the unfair dominance of Punjabis and *muhajirs* (Urdu-speaking migrants

---

[18] *Proceedings of the Sind Legislative Assembly*, Official Report, Vol. XVII, no. 6, Wednesday, 3 March 1943 (Karachi, 1943), p. 2, www.pas.gov.pk/uploads/downloads/Pakistan%20Resolution%20moved%20by%20G%20M%20Sayeed.pdf (accessed December 2018).

[19] Gyanesh Kudaisya, *A Republic in the Making: India in the 1950s* (New Delhi: Oxford University Press, 2017).

from India) within key institutions of the state such as the bureaucracy and the military, and for them, again like Bengalis, language became a particular bone of contention. With the introduction of the One Unit scheme in 1955, which merged the existing provinces in West Pakistan as a counterbalance to East Pakistan's numerical majority, the province's sidelining was further compounded, as was a growing sense of injustice among more nationalistically inclined Sindhis.[20] But these similarities and distinctions aside, what UP and Sindh most certainly did have in common after 1947 was the continuing presence of relatively sizeable religious minorities as well as considerable ongoing refugee traffic. Alongside members of minority communities who chose not to leave, UP became the destination of choice for large numbers of Sindhi Hindus, while Sindh (including Karachi) absorbed even greater quantities of migrants from UP. Sindh and UP, thus, found their own relationship transformed, thanks to these post–Partition demographic realities. As Vazira Zamindar has highlighted in her analysis of the content of contemporary cartoons in Karachi's Urdu-language press, refugees from UP who had taken refuge in cities in Sindh followed developments in their former home very closely from across the border.[21]

As one of the first multi-sited studies of its kind, *Boundaries of Belonging* also follows what Frederick Cooper has described for French Africa as a 'federal moment'. In it we explore postcolonial developments in the context of a possible larger set of processes related to South Asia's postcolonial history that are not based on 'automatic' assumptions of absolute separation after 1947.[22] As a consequence, our book deliberately refrains from revisiting developments in those former provinces of British India most usually associated with the traumatic end of empire in South Asia. Existing work on the main 'boundary' regions of the Punjab and Bengal, and later Kashmir, which were most obviously affected by Partition violence, have generated a picture of Independence as a

---

[20] Ansari, 'Identity Politics and Nation-Building in Pakistan'; Tariq Rahman, 'Language and Politics in a Pakistan Province: The Sindhi Language Movement', *Asian Survey* 35, 11 (November 1995), pp. 1005–16; Suranjan Das, *Kashmir and Sindh: Nation-Building, Ethnicity and Regional Politics in South Asia* (London: Anthem, 2004); and for a more general study that includes discussion of developments in Sindh, see Adeel Khan, *Politics of Identity: Ethnic Nationalism and the State in Pakistan* (London: Sage, 2004).

[21] Vazira Zamindar, *The Long Partition and the Making of Modern South Asia: Refugees, Boundaries, Histories* (New York: Columbia University Press, 2007), pp. 63, 87, 93.

[22] Frederick Cooper, *Citizenship between Empire and Nation: Remaking France and French Africa, 1945–1960* (Princeton: Princeton University Press, 2014).

moment of crisis, rehabilitation and border making. However, as we argue, some of the important 'hinterlands' of Partition were also affected by the impact of territorial division and population transfer, if less proximately, and so provide an effective context for examining broader meanings of Independence for Indian and Pakistani citizens. Moreover, the fact that UP and Sindh – entangled as they came to be with each another – cannot provide answers to every question about what being an Indian or Pakistani citizen meant during this period reinforces the necessity of looking beyond Partition's immediate 'hot spots' when assessing its longer-term consequences. UP – the key point of origin for Muslim migration to Pakistan in the years under scrutiny here – and similarly Sindh – the point of origin for many Pakistani Hindus who migrated to India from early 1948 onwards – may not have been physically cut in two as happened in the Punjab and Bengal, but these two particular places came to be intimately connected thanks to the pattern of migration flows between them that dragged on well into the 1950s. Both were also located in close proximity to where central state power was exercised, the federal capitals of Delhi and Karachi.

This approach also allows us to draw attention to how the 'state' in its different spatial guises operated on both sides of the new border, as well as what being a 'citizen' could signify for ordinary Indians and Pakistanis during a period of continuing flux and uncertainty. We explore how ideas and forms of citizenship in India and Pakistan were created by contingent processes of interaction between 'state' – its representatives and institutions – and 'society' – its citizens-in-the-making – in the decade after 1947. *Boundaries of Belonging*, therefore, is not principally concerned with the powerlessness of India and Pakistan's populations in the face of bureaucratic and police violence, but more with the ways that new or revised forms of citizenship and ideas about the rights of the citizen were articulated despite, or sometimes because of, violence and displacement. India and Pakistan today possess some of the world's most vibrant and diverse citizens' rights movements, which have emerged since the rise of political populism across the subcontinent in the 1970s. But many of their key themes and campaigns – work conditions, the cost of living, corruption, tribal and peasant rights – have deeper historical roots that relate directly to earlier moments in the definition of citizen rights in different parts of South Asia. At the same time, very often, these forms of activism have been obscured by larger, better-known or more accessible state-centred citizenship discourses. Such hierarchies are addressed by our exploration of the messy citizenship contexts of Partition, characterized by the struggles of relatively marginal communities to assert their rights.

This book accordingly sets out to move past explorations of 'formal' notions of the citizen that approach rights as something only 'transmitted' by law and constitutions.[23] Instead, it deliberately engages with everyday meanings of both citizenship and citizenship rights as these crystallized and – crucially – were contested in the two neighbouring countries. As well as narrating the apparent 'conferring' of rights from above, it explores ways in which ideas about rights were publicly circulated and how far these had an effect on early forms of legal activism. The creation and evolution of formal state-centred citizenship, and the particular entitlements and responsibilities that this status embodied, often stood in sharp contrast to vernacular ideas about citizen rights. The complicated link between these two levels of citizenship politics, we contend, sheds valuable light on tensions between belonging and exclusion, which we regard as the unfinished business of earlier nationalist struggles.

As part of our examination of the contested nature of citizenship in postcolonial South Asia, *Boundaries of Belonging* draws attention to the struggles for more inclusive citizenship that took place in both states, as marginalized groups to varying degrees excluded from 'citizenship in practice' sought to secure rights that they believed were due to them after 1947. That their demands for entitlements were often articulated in the vernacular – whether that of language, religion, caste, ethnicity or tribe – is significant for understanding what citizenship meant for ordinary people. The vocabulary of gender also entered the contemporary political equation as women similarly questioned – and challenged – what citizenship had really brought for them. Alongside formal efforts to establish notions of citizenship that squared with state-formulated priorities, 'hidden citizens' in both states appropriated the language of entitlement and rights to challenge asymmetries of power and exclusion that operated on both sides of the border.

None of these movements for rights in the late 1940s and 1950s made sense without some kind of reference to the idea of the state. In his famous 1991 article, Timothy Mitchell proposed that the idea of a boundary between state and society is simply an 'effect', namely an idea bound up with techniques of any particular political order.[24] Mitchell

---

[23] Joya Chatterji, *The Spoils of Partition: Bengal and India, 1947–1967* (Cambridge: Cambridge University Press, 2007), and Zamindar, *The Long Partition*.
[24] Timothy Mitchell, 'The Limits of the State: Beyond Statist Approaches and Their Critics', *American Political Science Review* 85, 1 (March 1991), pp. 77–96.

himself built on Philip Abrams's insight that the 'ideological' qualities of the state needed to be taken seriously in themselves.[25] These approaches to the state have a particular resonance for South Asia, and have been fruitfully explored by anthropologists for the contemporary period,[26] but as yet somewhat less so for the phase of transition to political independence itself. Without doubt, such treatments of the state (because they integrate social understandings of a state effect) need to be carefully historicized, taking account of how the state has been 'imagined' and debated at different levels of intensity over time and space. More recently David Gellner, when discussing life in South Asia's contentious northern borderlands, has drawn attention to the suggestion made by Abrams that students of the modern state should 'dispense entirely with "the state" as a category of analysis', but equally he cautions against wholeheartedly following this advice on the grounds that:

Today ethnographers everywhere are increasingly forced to think about the state because it intrudes, far more forcibly than it did seventy years ago, on the lives of the people they study ... People themselves are no longer content to view the state as a necessary evil. Increasingly they make demands of it and expect it to act positively to improve their lives. In the study of South Asia this has led to what might appear, at first glance, to be two contrasting trends: on the one hand, the study of the 'everyday state', how people actually interact with the state and what they expect from it ... and, on the other, following Abram's call, studies of the idea of the state, the 'state effect' as it has been called ... In fact, of course, the two kinds of study necessarily overlap ....[27]

In *Boundaries of Belonging*, we make the case for a historicized view of these same processes, in particular that the state mattered for most Indians and Pakistanis over the late 1940 and early 1950s, and their views on it were directly conditioned by the 'aftershocks' of decolonization itself. This unstable situation generated for many contemporaries a very specific historical sensibility: a notion of thinking both backwards and forwards in time, on the one hand involving reflection on past forms of colonial state control or repression, and, on the other, a series of forward-looking expectations linked to ideas of political freedom and

---

[25] Philip Abrams, 'Notes on the Difficulty of Studying the State (1977)', *Journal of Historical Sociology* 1, 1 (1988), pp. 58–89.

[26] See, most notably, Stuart Corbridge et al. (eds.), *Seeing the State: Governance and Governmentality in India* (Cambridge: Cambridge University Press, 2005); C. J. Fuller and Veronique Benei (eds.), *The Everyday State and Society in Modern India* (London: C. Hurst & Co., 2001); Thomas Blom Hansen and Finn Stepputat (eds.), *States of Imagination: Ethnographic Explorations of the Postcolonial State* (Durham, NC: Duke University Press, 2001).

[27] David W. Gellner (ed.), *Borderland Lives in Northern South Asia* (Durham, NC: Duke University Press, 2013), pp. 2–3.

responsibility. For this reason, the idea of the state, while being about local experience and contact, was also about imagining something in the process of realization, with an emphasis on achievement or failure. These perceptions were also informed by a sense of emergence from crisis. Concentrating on the immediate impact and fallout of 1947 itself means also concentrating on those whose recovery as citizens was also part of a political order: refugees, the displaced, the aforementioned abducted women and children who were theoretically separated from a state that acted upon them – a state that was presented as an autonomous set of institutions. But this sense of autonomy, it could be argued, was always a fiction that was itself created out of the conditions of the late 1940s.

The state in early post-Independence India and Pakistan therefore was not a uniform entity despite often being represented as such. Rather, it was a complex arrangement that worked through informal agents and appeared in different guises to different constituencies. Networks of formal and informal power, alongside neighbourhood and class structures, interacted with the state's various institutional levels and affected its appearance and its actions.[28] It was subject to conflicts between often competing social interests, which meant that its sway could be similarly unstable and unpredictable. The secrecy, for instance, surrounding the activities of state agents in contemporary India and Pakistan (such as the use of police informants) was established as a means of upholding the 'fiction' of a homogenous state that was presumed to act according to rules and principles, but which was ultimately arbitrary.[29] The division between what was explicit and what was hidden in this way developed out of a historically and spatially conditional set of variables in the exercise of power over the long-term transition to Independence.

Put another way, the very circumstances of Independence brought about certain forms of everyday state practices in the context of 'new' ideas about the public sphere and freedom, which together created a gulf between ideological state effect and its quotidian practices. Because this process evolved within a context of new ideas about rights, such rights were always imagined in relation to changing notions of space, across both conceptual and actual internal/external borders. The notion of an individual's citizenship rights in relation to the idea of the state,

---

[28] Fuller and Benei's *The Everyday State* sheds important light on the ways in which the large, amorphous and impersonal Indian State affected the everyday lives of its citizens, arguing that state and society merge in the daily lives of most, with the boundary between the two blurred and negotiable according to social context and position.

[29] Anastasia Piliavsky, 'A Secret in the Oxford Sense: Thieves and the Rhetoric of Mystification in Western India', *Comparative Studies in Society and History* 53, 2 (April 2011), pp. 290–313.

it could be argued, only made sense in a relative way to what they were/ had been/might be in a different jurisdictional space. What the state meant and how the rights of the citizen changed was shaped by the relational spaces of India and Pakistan, and epitomized by the close connections or movement between such regions as UP and Sindh in these early years.

But the concept of space is determined as much by social, conceptual and legal relationships as much as it is by physical ones.[30] In some places, frontiers and boundaries between particular spaces, especially those that divided nations, are extended into certain ideological constructions of the state too, and connect to other forms of social boundaries and differences. For example, the idea of 'Pakistan' in the North Indian state of UP encompassed at one and the same time: a state beyond India; a loyalty associated with a particular minority; a 'space of potential', such as 'potential' migration (the idea of the 'intending evacuee'); and a relational space that connected to the property and civic rights of individuals as well as to recent history itself. Across the border in what had become the Pakistani province of Sindh, 'India' similarly dominated the collective imagination. In turn, the relationship between these jurisdictional spaces (of 'Pakistan' in India and 'India' in Pakistan), being also imaginary, formed part of a public sphere of political commentary that had only recently emerged from forms of strong state censorship. The idea of a 'public sphere' has been taken up by historians of India in relation to new public forms of visual communication,[31] and perhaps most extensively language.[32] Our concept of the public, however, was strongly conditioned by the varied popular experiences of political freedom in India and Pakistan's early postcolonial years, not least because new freedoms from 1947 included those of expression. Historians working on the notion of the 'public sphere' in the very different historical context of pre-Revolutionary France have established how public opinion, and political references to it, worked to subvert the

---

[30] We might imagine this in terms of a 'cultural sociology of space', see Tim Richardson and Ole B. Jensen, 'Linking Discourse and Space: Towards a Cultural Sociology of Space in Analyzing Spatial Policy Discourses', *Urban Studies* 40, 1 (2003), pp. 7–22.

[31] See Sandra B. Freitag, 'South Asian Ways of Seeing, Muslim Ways of Knowing: The Indian Muslim Niche Market in Posters', *Indian Economic and Social History Review* 44, 3 (2007), pp. 297–331.

[32] Two prominent examples are Francesca Orsini, *The Hindi Public Sphere 1920–1940: Language and Literature in the Age of Nationalism* (New Delhi: Oxford University Press, 2009), and Veena Naregal, *Language Politics, Elites and the Public Sphere: Western India under Colonialism* (London: Anthem Press, 2002).

established authorities as a result of being suppressed or limited.[33] Early postcolonial Indian and Pakistani publics had only just emerged from colonial control and censorship, and so, from this perspective, the organs of the public – above all the print media – provided important opportunities for exploring changing views of the state, and the assertion of rights around it.

In *Boundaries of Belonging*, therefore, we maintain that new forms of public freedom in South Asia – though limited by the preoccupations of its successor governments with security in the late 1940s and early 1950s – created a vibrant public sphere of debate about the state, its responsibilities and what Indians and Pakistanis could expect of it. Again, this can be seen particularly vividly for this period in the press. Among the most important apparently autonomous state structures that these print media discuss are those of spatial borders on the one hand and those of the law on the other. Both are perceived as entities that contain a sum of many parts and yet appear to be abstract, formal frameworks. Overall, it was the process of negotiation of these structures, as well as the discussion of them, that ultimately created a sense of what the state was and where its power was located. This process of negotiation by India and Pakistan's new citizens was clearly multi-local – taking in the relative experiences of living in different places, or the discussion/debate about such intersecting local lives. This was the case at moments of mass movement (or when mass movement needed to be accommodated).

But we are cautious about overemphasizing mobility and so in addition examine how citizens' experiences can be very much situated in particular places, related to scales of jurisdiction and political power, from local, to regional, national and international. Here we take account of the work of Stephen Legg, who has suggested that 'an emphasis on scale [can serve] as a useful corrective to an overly networked emphasis on mobility, flows and transit across space'.[34] We also draw on Rajnarayan Chandavarkar's insight that the history of urban spaces cannot be taken out of their larger regional, national and international context, not least because of habitual movements of workers.[35] Everyday reflections on the state, although apparently related to the local context, are never in practice so

---

[33] James Van Horn Melton, *The Rise of the Public in Enlightenment Europe* (Cambridge: Cambridge University Press, 2001), in particular chapter 2 'Opacity and Transparency: French Political Culture in the Eighteenth Century', pp. 45–78.

[34] Stephen Legg, *Prostitution and the Ends of Empire: Scale, Governmentalities and Interwar India* (Durham, NC: Duke University Press, 2014), pp. 22–3.

[35] Rajnarayan Chandavarkar, *History, Culture and the City* (Cambridge: Cambridge University Press, 2015).

simply located but are also linked to broader notions of belonging and exclusion. The leverage that South Asia's citizens thought that they could exercise in the late 1940s and 1950s – for instance, with their local municipal corporation, or with an officer controlling a public utility in a particular *mohalla* (urban neighbourhood) – was both imagined and 'performed' across space and scale; and it was conceptualized in relation to other scales of the state, as well as to other spaces and places, both imagined and real.

Ted Svensson in his comparative study of the 'production' of post-colonial India and Pakistan has pointed to how, 'in the nascent years of Independence, notions of time and space became firmly intertwined within the boundaries of the nation state'.[36] The contours and agency of these two nation states in the making 'became possible and assumed their distinct shape on the basis of a performative 'naming' [... and] spatial notions [were] elevated to a position of cardinal significance within nation building and state formation'.[37] By profoundly altering 'notions of space ... and of time', particular 'representations of the state and identity markers, specific traits and behaviours gained legitimacy and authenticity at the expense of others'.[38] As a result, the event of Partition itself remained 'central to nation building and the delimiting of state identity in, as well as between, India and Pakistan', with narratives – as others have shown – continuing to unfold around this episode in both places to the present day.[39]

Accordingly, India and Pakistan's political cultures, though distinctive in key ways, have also exhibited entwined spaces of and for citizenship at moments of political transition. For us, these multi-local and multi-scalar everyday interactions played themselves out most obviously and directly in the context of post–Partition refugee rehabilitation, where negotiation with the state involved direct claims about properties and family histories in spaces that could now be on the other side of an international border. But this principle applied, to differing degrees, in a range of other negotiations, not least between citizens and the

---

[36] Ted Svensson, *Production of Postcolonial India and Pakistan: Meanings of Partition* (London and New York: Routledge, 2013), p. 19.

[37] Ibid.   [38] Ibid., p. 1.

[39] Ibid., p. 2; Tai Yong Tan and Gyanesh Kudaisya, *The Aftermath of Partition in South Asia* (London: Routledge, 2000), pp. 8, 29–77; Yasmin Khan, 'The Ending of an Empire: From Imagined Communities to Nation States in India and Pakistan', in *The Iconography of Independence: Freedoms at Midnight*, eds. Robert Holland, Susan Williams and Terry Barringer (London and New York: Routledge, 2010), pp. 47–56.

bureaucracy, something that is also reflected in contemporary practices around the everyday state.[40] This phenomenon of interacting with the local state, and discussing that interaction in the media, was heightened in our period as a result of the mass movements, dislocations and changes that occurred around Independence. Consequently, this forms one of the central themes of Chapters 2 and 3, wherein we explore the broad trajectory of developments playing out in our two specific contexts or places, UP and Sindh.

Our notion of the recently created Indian and Pakistani states is that these were entities that, in many respects, were only symbolically separated out from the social groups that they apparently served. To put it another way, as anthropologists of the 'everyday' have noted, they were 'porous' entities and the assumed boundary between them and society was a chimera or illusion.[41] The actions of ordinary Indians and Pakistanis had (and continued to have) consequences for what the state 'is'; and also what it 'does'. By extension, this lived reality affected (and affects still) the limits and possibilities of citizenship rights, for Indians and Pakistanis alike. Joya Chatterji has shown how the formal right of Indians and Pakistanis to hold their respective passports in the early 1950s was determined largely by *who* moved *where*, and *when* they moved, with this mutability eventually enshrined in citizenship legislation, namely Pakistan's Citizenship Act of 1951 (revised in 1952) and India's slightly later 1955 Citizenship Act. In relation to the latter, Chatterji describes it as a change from *jus soli* to *jus sanguinis* that was closely connected to how the return of Muslims to India – many of them coming back to UP from Sindh – was controlled.[42] We seek to extend Chatterji's argument here to consider how far the actions and movements of ordinary people not only affected how they claimed formal citizen's rights as holders of Indian and Pakistani nationality but in addition the ways in which substantive rights were negotiated over time. Citizens in both states undertook this process of negotiation unevenly and hierarchically. Yet because citizens' groups were, on the one hand, a material part of the state, and, on the other, embroiled in the process of its meaning and representation, the definitions and boundaries of rights could still be changed by 'movements of rights' as well as by the physical 'movements of migration'.

---

[40] Akhil Gupta, *Red Tape: Bureaucracy, Structural Violence, and Poverty in India* (Durham, NC: Duke University Press, 2012).

[41] Fuller and Benei, *The Everyday State and Society*, Introduction.

[42] Joya Chatterji, 'South Asian Histories of Citizenship, 1946–1970', *The Historical Journal* 55, 4 (December 2012), pp. 1049–71.

Arising from these contingent processes in which the state could assume quite different meanings to different groups of South Asian communities, as they migrated between different jurisdictions, there came to exist new and differentiated forms of citizenship. A useful additional conjectural framework in this respect is the one presented by James Holston who has explored how far marginal urban communities in Brazil, excluded from formal civic frameworks, have innovated alternative citizenship strategies. Holston's view of the Brazilian Constitution, which was based on the French *Declaration of the Rights of Man* and of the Citizen, is that it has historically enshrined legal inequality.[43] Unlike Brazil, such inequalities do not form part of India's 1950 Constitution, although, as we will explore in Chapter 6, there were categories of 'citizen' whose 'pariah' status came to be legally defined. In contrast, India's far-reaching 'Fundamental Rights' consciously sought to establish uniform and universal entitlements. Yet, these were in tension with other, historically structured levels of rights, derived from the colonial experience, which privileged particular community identities. India's Constitution (and constitutional negotiations) from the outset set up differentiated group rights on the basis of affirmative action for certain categories of disadvantaged citizen, based on caste, that are contained within its 'Directive Principles of State Policy' and 'Fundamental Rights'. Pakistan's more fluid constitutional arrangements were in some respects very similar and in others quite different. Like India, it inherited the legal tensions of the colonial period. But, in addition from 1956 onwards, the Pakistani Constitution differentiated formally between citizens – between Muslims and non-Muslims and between women and men – in terms of who could be head of state (only a male Muslim). Dichotomies in both India's and Pakistan's formal constitutional rights, created spaces for the sorts of auto-constructed urban citizenship assertions that Holston explores for Brazil. We explore these forms of popular politics throughout *Boundaries of Belonging*, and especially in Chapters 4 to 6.

In both India and Pakistan, 'liberal' notions of citizenship, prioritizing the rights of individual citizens, existed as perhaps the most powerful overarching agenda.[44] These played against differentiated rights set out for particular disadvantaged communities in some instances, and reinforced these in others. But they contained their own contradictions.

---

[43] James Holston, *Insurgent Citizenship: Disjunctions of Democracy and Modernity in Brazil* (Princeton, NJ: Princeton University Press, 2009).

[44] For a comparative discussion of 'Liberal', 'Communitarian' and 'Republican' notions of the citizen, see Michael Lister and Emily Pia, *Citizenship in Contemporary Europe* (Oxford: Oxford University Press, 2008).

Despite espousing the idea of 'universal' rights of the individual citizen, they were historically rooted in a racialized colonial past similar to that which had determined a modern politics of citizenship in states such as France and Britain.[45] Originating in a markedly different – European – context, they were predicated on hierarchies that valorized teleological, political and social 'development'. Their assumed universal applicability, in turn, was historically derived from the Eurocentrism that had sustained colonial power and presupposed the extension of northern hemisphere notions of secularism. In *Boundaries of Belonging*, we suggest that alternative, popular forms of citizenship assertion (sometimes communitarian) existed but that these did not always simply critique overarching liberal notions of the citizen. In fact, they more often evoked ideas of fundamental rights, while carving out particular spaces for further citizenship recognition. In this sense, as has been argued in works on colonial South Asia, alternative citizenship rights were not derived principally from extra-legal impulses.[46] It remained the case, however, throughout the immediate post-Partition years that alternative citizenship forms could be subordinated to and often hidden by state-centred 'universal' frameworks. While evoking some of these principles of the universality, vernacular rights movements during these years often defined themselves in relation to this hierarchy of subordination.

We have chosen to organize the following discussion both chronologically and thematically. This is because our aim is to look at India and Pakistan – and UP and Sindh – together as far as possible, drawing the post-Independence histories of both places into a joint exploration of the region more broadly. While there are inevitably distinctions between the developments or stories that we trace – rights as we have argued in this Introduction being always historically produced and so highly contextual in nature – our purpose is not to pit one location against the other. Since the very concept of rights in the national units of Pakistan and India was mutually interdependent and often based upon hastily conceived notions of nation state delimitation, studying both contexts through the same lens reveals more than the sum of its two parts. Each of our chapters threads together material drawn from both places, paying attention to

---

[45] Tony S. Juge and Michael P. Perez, 'The Modern Colonial Politics of Citizenship and Whiteness in France', *Social Identities: Journal for the Study of Race, Nation and Culture* 12, 2 (2006), pp. 187–212.

[46] Sukanya Banerjee, *Becoming Imperial Citizens: Indians in the Late-Victorian Empire* (Durham, NC: Duke University Press, 2010).

and acknowledging similarity and difference, as well as the fact that in neither India nor Pakistan has there been a single, all-encompassing narrative since 1947, whatever their official state ideologies may have wanted to communicate. Viewing them in the same frame not only allows common themes to be explored, it also facilitates what we identify here as powerful continuities between the pre- and post-Independence periods. Contemporary newspaper reports ('the first draft of history') represent a key set of primary sources underpinning our study, as are provincial-level archival records (though these are more straightforward to access for UP than in Sindh) and other official and non-official observations on the changing landscape of both places. As with any set of sources, whether primary or secondary, we have also faced the challenge of dealing with potential biases within our material, compounded by the mutual suspicions operating on both sides of the India-Pakistan border during these years. But we have sought to address this by acknowledging that it is contemporary perceptions, rather than necessarily 'hard truths', with which we are engaging. The same disclaimer applies to the fact that, unfortunately, the amount of 'evidence' relating to both case studies is uneven, with more gaps as far as developments in Sindh are concerned, as compared with what can be traced in UP. This reflects the unevenness of archival resources in different parts of South Asia, but we hope that we have found enough other ways to allow UP and Sindh to be explored alongside one another.

Chapter 1 begins by analyzing developments at the state level both before and after 1947, highlighting the figurative as well as the literal spaces and scales wherein relationships between state ceremony, power and the everyday were played out in the late 1940s and 1950s. By looking at the ways that state power was performed, the role of new and sometimes invented ceremonial traditions and the mundane but multifaceted interactions of ordinary citizens with their new states on different levels, the chapter explores how the Indian and Pakistani states projected themselves in the immediate post-Independence period, and their emphasis on patriotism and loyalty as criteria for belonging and citizenship.

Chapter 2 then explores how far the physical movement of people that was bound up in Partition shaped everyday meanings of 'citizenship' in places like Sindh and UP where huge competition for space and resources took place after 1947. From the outset, what we find is that ideas about citizenship in post-Independence India and Pakistan were intimately tied to the politics of movement. But this chapter also highlights that understandings of emerging citizenship were often shaped by the very material predicaments of migrants and minorities, which operated, and so often came to be viewed as, yardsticks of belonging and exclusion.

Chapter 3 extends this material perspective by focussing on urban centres in Sindh and UP and on key dynamics in the development of citizenship around the control of 'public goods' that emerged there. Following an exploration of the nature of urban politics in the late 1940s and early 1950s in our two regions, the chapter explores food and civil supply in relation to the politics of prices and price controls and to debates about food and civil supply administration. Supply and control of goods became a chief means in which ideas about citizens' relationship to the state interacted with civil supply problems and other scandals to become a point of public criticism in the press in both India and Pakistan. This chapter then turns to the popular discourses surrounding government corruption that emerged from these mechanisms around supply of goods and its administration, setting out the new postcolonial structures and organizations of 'anti-corruption' as these mechanisms developed in both UP and Sindh. Its examination of popular views of corruption includes how particular scandals developed in the press, and their broader meaning for ideas about citizenship rights. The chapter concludes by considering cross-border smuggling of material goods as an anti-state activity that raised direct questions about loyalty and belonging.

Chapter 4 considers processes involved in constitution-building in both states, as well as early Indian and Pakistani experiments with democratic elections. It explores how far the concept of 'citizen rights' that were encapsulated within these chimed with what ordinary Indians and Pakistanis believed their constitutional rights to be. Rather than assuming that the two states in constitutional terms moved in opposite directions, similarities as well as differences between the two sets of engagement are highlighted, demonstrating the range of quotidian readings of constitutional rights that emerged alongside the formal expressions of citizenship entitlement. In contrast to dominant approaches that view constitutions as canonical documents at the heart of processes of attempted consensus, we emphasize that constitutions in both India and Pakistan represented a process of conflict and contestation, which implicated ordinary subject/citizens, their experiences of governance and their multiple imaginaries of rights. By looking at various forms of active citizenship engagement, this chapter highlights how quickly popular politics in both Sindh and UP as well as more broadly in post-1947 India and Pakistan, came to be shaped by civic circumstances, such as debates about accessing public goods and what people perceived to be their entitlements as 'rights-bearing' citizens.

Finally, *Chapters 5* and *6* explore apparent contradictions bound up in Indian and Pakistani citizenship after 1947 in relation to marginalized groups living in UP and Sindh who, like their counterparts elsewhere, often found it difficult to fit into officially produced templates for citizenship. First *Chapter 5* traces the efforts of women's groups to establish their equal rights as citizens at a time of constitution-making and legal flux, highlighting the arguments and strategies that they pursued to make their case for fairer treatment. Then *Chapter 6* shifts the focus to (those whom we term) 'hidden citizens' – that is communities of people whose collective identities created problems in terms of acquiring the full benefits of citizenship. These included religious minorities (Muslims in India and non-Muslims in Pakistan), Dalits and the so-called criminal tribes (vimukta jatis), whose movement across national borders after 1947 raised repeated question marks with respect to 'where' and 'how' they belonged. These last two chapters do not assume that such minorities were necessarily denied citizenship rights in a formal sense, but instead investigate what could be the differentiated interpretation and administration of rights for them on the ground. It also examines different means by which they and other economically weak sections of local society sought to champion their 'group' rights, via legal activism, forms of political lobbying, the use of political mediation or acquiescence in official/formal means of extending constitutional guarantees.

By way of setting the scene for what follows in our chapters, we close our Introduction with the following extract from an article entitled 'India and Pakistan To-day', published in the British literary magazine *The Nineteenth Century* only a matter of months after Partition. Written by Sir Percival Griffiths, former colonial civil servant turned businessman,[47] who had visited India and Pakistan earlier that same year, it provides an impression (that was by no means unbiased) of the emerging relationship between the two new states. In it, Griffiths highlighted the uncertainties and mutual suspicion that he believed characterized interactions between India and Pakistan at this time, and which, as *Boundaries of Belonging* underlines, helped directly to shape official state policy towards, as well as more popular citizen perceptions of, each another. All the same, to understand developments in one place – India/UP – it is necessary to

---

[47] Phillip Mason, 'Obituary: Sir Percival Griffiths', *Independent*, 20 July 1992, www.independent.co.uk/news/people/obituary-sir-percival-griffiths-1534416.html (accessed December 2018).

appreciate what was happening in the other – Pakistan/Sindh – and vice versa. Partition may have produced two separate countries on 14/15 August 1947, but as our exploration of this key event's aftermath in the context of two particular localities suggests, India and Pakistan remained intimately, and often uncomfortably, bound together by a shared history and common challenges as they made the transition from colonial rule to postcolonial statehood side by side in the years that followed.

Having analyzed the internal problems of India and Pakistan, we now come to the more delicate question of the relations between the two Dominions ... Feeling between the two Dominions is extremely bitter and the bitterness permeates all classes of society. ... Each of these allegations and counter-allegations is discussed morning, noon and night in the house of every educated inhabitant of India and Pakistan, and in the process, as always happens when people brood over grievances, a bitterness out of all proportion to the magnitude of the causes is generated. It is also to be remembered that Pakistan genuinely believes that India intends to crush her if she can, and that, on the other side, many Hindus in India still consider that India should never have agreed to partition. Clearly all the elements out of which international quarrels develop are present here in a virulent form.[48]

---

[48] Sir Percival Griffiths, 'India and Pakistan To-Day', *The Nineteenth Century*, Vol. 143, no. 852 (1948), in FO 371/69729, UK National Archives.

1 'Performing the State' in Post-1947 India and Pakistan

On the first anniversary of Independence in August 1948, with tension mounting between India and Pakistan over the future of the Princely State of Hyderabad (Deccan) and its Muslim minority population,[1] the Indian Prime Minister Jawaharlal Nehru broadcast to the nation from the same spot in Delhi where he had delivered his 'Tryst with Destiny' speech twelve months before:

Free India is one year old today. But what trials and tribulations she has passed through during this infancy of her freedom. She has survived in spite of all the perils and disaster that might well have overwhelmed a more mature and well-established nation ... We have to find ourselves again and go back to [the] free India of our dreams. We have to re-discover old values and place them in the new setting of [a]free India. For freedom brings responsibility and can only be sustained by self-discipline, hard work and [the] spirit of a free people.

Nehru then concluded with the following impassioned 'call to arms':

Let us be rid of everything that limits us and degrades us. Let us cast [off] our fear and communalism and provincialism. Let us build up a free and democratic India where [the] interests of the masses, our people, has always the first place to which all other interests must submit. Freedom has no meaning unless it brings relief to these masses from their many burdens. Democracy means tolerance,

---

[1] For a detailed exploration of political developments taking place in Hyderabad (Deccan) before, during and after its incorporation within the Indian Union in 1948, and the issues that these raised for wider issues involved in how Indian citizenship was evolving at this time, see Taylor C. Sherman, *Muslim Belonging in Secular India: Negotiating Citizenship in Postcolonial Hyderabad* (Cambridge: Cambridge University Press, 2015). See also Taylor C. Sherman, 'The Integration of the Princely State of Hyderabad and the Making of the Postcolonial State in India, 1948–1956', *Indian Economic & Social History Review* 44, 4 (2007), pp. 489–516; Taylor C. Sherman, 'Migration, Citizenship and Belonging in Hyderabad (Deccan), 1948–1956', *Modern Asian Studies* 45, 1 (2011), pp. 81–107; Sunil Purushotham, 'Internal Violence: The "Police Action" in Hyderabad', *Comparative Studies in Society and History* 57, 2 (2015), pp. 435–66; and, for a contemporary assessment, Wilfred Cantwell Smith, 'Hyderabad: Muslim Tragedy', *Middle East Journal* 4, 1 (January 1950), pp. 27–51.

tolerance not merely of those who agree with us but of those who do not agree with us.[2]

As this attempt in the summer of 1948 to enlist fellow Indians in a 'war' to resolve some of the myriad problems caused by Partition underlines, all new regimes create, revive and mobilize political symbols – both material and rhetorical – as a means of consolidating power and simultaneously propagating visions of shared citizenship. Politicians and governments in Pakistan and India in the immediate post-Independence period followed distinctive strategies in their promotion of national iconographies and views of the ideal citizen.[3] But how these were recirculated – in different localities, by a range of different institutions and movements, and sometimes through the spontaneous response to them by 'crowds' – affected their meaning and impact over time. Furthermore, their transmission was far from passive thanks to the ways in which such symbols can themselves be transformed as a result of precisely this kind of circulation taking place at different social and spatial scales.[4] This opening chapter, therefore, begins our exploration of postcolonial citizenship by considering how far – for India and Pakistan during their early years – the process of 'making citizens' was also about consolidating the unitary state in ways that could often allow each country to emulate the other, despite contrasting contexts.

Following Independence and Partition, politicians supported by bureaucrats at the centre, whether they were located in the new capital cities of Delhi or Karachi, expressed a clear desire to manage or contain regional difference and to promote a strongly centralized unitary form of government. In this, irrespective of location, they were clearly influenced by their shared experiences of British rule and the political as well as the administrative structures that they had been bequeathed. And crucially, both encountered difficulties, at the state or provincial level, which highlighted the contingency of citizenship in the transition from colonial rule to independent government. But while India inherited most of its political, administrative, judicial and security structures largely intact, Pakistan was required to build a centralized state from the remains of provincial administrative structures, which in the case of the Punjab and Bengal had hurriedly been cut in two. This meant that in Pakistan

---

[2] Indian News Bulletin: '"The only war we want to fight, with all our might, is the war against poverty" says Pandit Nehru', 16 August 1948, FO371/69735 UK National Archives (hereafter UKNA).

[3] Srirupa Roy, *Beyond Belief: India and the Politics of Postcolonial Nationalism* (Durham, NC: Duke University Press, 2007).

[4] Benjamin Lee and Edward LiPuma, 'Culture of Circulation: The Imaginations of Modernity', *Public Culture* 14, 1 (2002), pp. 191–3.

(by comparison to India) the choices of unitary symbols were dependent on a more unstable – arguably artificial – balance of regional identities and likewise heavily influenced by the political circumstances at the moment of Independence alongside the wielding of the religious card, that is, Islam. In other words, Pakistan did not have as many 'ready-made' national histories on which to base the idea of a unitary independent identity as India did, and, as a result, in the words of Christophe Jaffrelot, 'Pakistan was born of a partition which over-determined its subsequent trajectory'.[5] The choice to pursue a unitary political system, and the symbols that accompanied this, therefore, had different outcomes for each country.

All the same, official government-driven attempts to propagate civic notions of national belonging could be contested at different scales, within formal institutions and in popular movements in both countries. For Pakistan, this involved, at one level, a tension between local (Punjabi) and migrant (*muhajir*) cultures that were dominant in the army, administration and politics, against demographically important regional identities, especially in East Bengal but also present in other provinces. In contrast, the idea of the Indian 'citizen' was more atomized given that country's greater size and resultant complexities, but equally, this process turned out to be no less about the consolidation of power around certain majoritarian symbols for the new regime.[6] For the Indian government, following Independence, it was not as if ideas of the nation had to be invented afresh as in Pakistan. Quite the opposite. The last century of colonial rule in the subcontinent had produced richly documented and highly contentious debates about 'Indian-ness' and the 'Indian people', from which the notion of 'Pakistan' itself had arisen as one dynamic, in terms of political representation[7] and the politics of identity.[8] However, when we focus specifically on *citizenship*, with all that this implied in terms of actual or anticipated constitutional rights, rather than the *nation state* as a whole, we can see that there were a range of

---

[5] Christophe Jaffrelot, *The Pakistan Paradox: Instability and Resilience* (London: Hurst, 2015), p. 1.

[6] Roy, *Beyond Belief*, chapter 1, argues that the state was the essential unifier, via a range of institutions of this vision.

[7] Francis Robinson, *Separatism among Indian Muslims: The Politics of the United Provinces' Muslims, 1860–1923* (Cambridge: Cambridge University Press, 1974), pp. 163–4.

[8] This is particularly the case when we consider the institutional basis of the 'Pakistan' movement, the Muslim League, which in key mobilizational phases of the early 1920s around the Khilafat balanced 'pan-Islamism' with Indian nationalism, in terms of two overlapping 'circles' of identity. See Mushirul Hasan, 'The Khilafat Movement: A Reappraisal', *Communal and Pan-Islamic Trends in Colonial India* (Delhi: Manohar, 1985), pp. 1–16.

contingent events, on occasion revolving around large-scale ceremonies, which complicated the symbols that each country used to reinforce its new national identity.

After 14/15 August 1947, South Asia's new postcolonial regimes quickly realized that opportunities had arisen to shape cultures of national identity together with citizenship values by connecting popular political symbols to state power. In India and Pakistan alike, this objective was pursued repeatedly in a series of staged ceremonial occasions, some of them serendipitous and others deliberately planned around the annual calendar marking such values as 'Independence' and the 'Republic'. This chapter accordingly takes as its starting point the impact of two key happenings – the deaths and subsequent funerals of Gandhi and Jinnah in January and September 1948, respectively. It explores their fallout in terms of the ceremonies that they triggered and locates them within the broader assortment of ceremonial processes that took place at a range of regional and political scales during this period, before considering ways in which India and Pakistan projected their authority vis-à-vis their citizens during these nation-building years. In particular, while this chapter's purview inevitably extends to more general developments as well, it focusses particularly on reactions in two specific places, namely the Indian state of Uttar Pradesh (UP) and the Pakistani province of Sindh, where issues connected with 'belonging' lay at the heart of much discussion about the evolving relationship between the postcolonial state and its citizens.

Personifying the Postcolonial State

An early pivotal moment for the new Indian government as far as the special use of symbolic nation-building ceremonies was concerned followed the demise of one of the masters of large-scale mobilization itself. On 30 January 1948, while at a prayer meeting in the gardens of Birla House in New Delhi, Gandhi came face to face with a Hindu extremist, Nathuram Godse, who shot him three times at point-blank range. In a real sense, the response to the murder provided India's new postcolonial regime with an opportunity to settle some political scores, but it also suggested, in a microcosm, how the use of commonly agreed national symbols could be interpreted and remoulded in multiple quotidian ways. Less than nine months later, with Jinnah's death from natural causes on 11 September, the new authorities in Karachi faced a similar challenge and reached similar conclusions.

In the weeks preceding Gandhi's assassination in early 1948, his efforts had shifted from Calcutta to Delhi where more and more Hindu and

Sikh refugees were arriving from the Pakistani province of Sindh, 'with their uncompromising bitterness towards the Muslims', and Delhi Muslims in large numbers were 'leaving their homes in the mixed localities of the city and concentrating themselves in those areas where Muslims had a preponderating majority'. Gandhi – in his efforts to restore 'communal peace' and 'keeping in remarkably close touch with Indian opinion' – campaigned for sufficient reconciliation between communities to allow 'Muslims to return in safety to their homes in Delhi and non-Muslims to Pakistan'.[9] When he broke what turned out to be his final fast on 18 January,[10] it was in response to receiving assurances from all communities in Delhi that Muslim life, property and religion would be both respected and protected. The press also pointed out the effects of the fast in Pakistan as well as among Muslim leaders in India.[11]

But in the first few hours, as the news of Gandhi's death spread, there was the fear that a Muslim might have been responsible. Violent reprisal attacks against Muslims consequently occurred in Lucknow and Bombay,[12] and military commanders all over India were told to stand by in case of an emergency in other cities.[13] Within the space of a few days, once it became known that the attacker was a member of the Hindu right-wing organization, the Rashtriya Swayamsevak Sangh (RSS), arrests took place, rounding up members of that militaristic organization and declaring it illegal.[14] This led to mass arrests in Allahabad and Kanpur, and popular attacks on the main RSS offices in the latter city.[15] Similar arrests were made of Hindu Mahasabha leaders.[16] The assassination thus provided state governments with an opportunity to maintain public order in response to the 'volunteer' organizations that dated from the war years and were still operating. Indeed, this was the context for the

---

[9] UK High Commissioner, New Delhi, Despatch 25, 4 February 1948, FO371/69729 UKNA.

[10] The Hindi newspapers of UP followed the fast in some detail; see 'Hindu-Muslim ekta ke liye Gandhiji ka anashan, desh tatha dharmke vinash ka ashaak darshak hone ki bajah mar jana accha. Prarthnake Pashchat Mahatma Gandhiki Ghoshna Congress tatha sarkarom mem bhrashtachaar se dukhi sabhi', *Aaj*, 16 January 1948.

[11] 'Gandhiji ke anashan se bharat-pakistan donon hi chintit', *Aaj*, 17 January 1948.

[12] UKHC, New Delhi, Opdom, First Half February 1948, IOR L/PJ/8/794 British Library (hereafter BL).

[13] A. C. B. Symon, 4 February 1948, 'The Assassination of Mahatma Gandhi and Liaquat Ali Khan', FCO371/69729 UKNA.

[14] See, for instance, 'Ban in Provinces: 50 Arrests in UP', *National Herald*, 5 February 1948.

[15] 'Kanpur mein Updrav aur curfew rashtriy svayansevak sangh aur jantaa mein sangharsh', *Aaj*, 4 February 1948.

[16] 'Bombay aur Puna mein giraftariyan hindu sabha ke netaon ke ghar par bhir ke hamle', *Aaj*, 3 February 1948.

passage of the 1948 United Provinces Maintenance of Public Order Bill, which sought to prevent the members of volunteer organizations from wearing any uniform or article of apparel that resembled in any way what was worn by the police or military called out to quell disturbances.[17] In UP too, to allay public fears, newspapers claimed to be able to provide detailed figures of arrests: in Lucknow it was reported that many of UP's RSS men had gone underground and that the government had decided to sequester their property. Reported arrests included those in Aligarh (twenty), Allahabad (eight), Bahraich (twenty), Budaun (eight), Ballia (five), Jaunpur, Lakhimpur (fifteen) and Meerut (twenty-five). In Hardoi, anti-Gandhi posters were found, while in Bara Banki the district organizer was charged for assaulting a Congressman and in Fatehpur five RSS members were arrested for distributing sweets in celebration of Gandhi's death.[18]

In the Constituent Assembly, India's first Home Minister and Deputy Prime Minister Vallabhai Patel fielded awkward questions about whether government servants could still belong to 'communal organizations' such as the RSS. His reply was that they were prohibited from political groups as well as from those 'which [tended] directly or indirectly to promote feelings of hatred and enmity between different classes or disturb public peace', although social welfare groups were exempted.[19] Patel himself, who had been seen as a leader with some sympathies for the Hindu Right of the Congress, also came under fire from a number of sources for apparently not taking sufficient care over the security linked to Gandhi's final prayer meeting. Overseas reporters closely monitoring these unfolding developments suggested that their repercussions might spread to Pakistan, where there was a danger of them stimulating a 'communal frenzy', given preaching by the Hindu Mahasabha and the RSS against Pakistan.[20]

Yasmin Khan has shown how Gandhi's funeral and the subsequent dispersal of his ashes to different parts of India operated as a key mechanism for the consolidation of Congress power together with the idea of the secular state.[21] However, in extending Khan's argument, it is clear

---

[17] 'The United Provinces Maintenance of Public Order (Second Amendment) Bill, 1948', Ministry of Home Affairs Judicial F 5/37/48 National Archives of India (hereafter NAI).

[18] 'Many RSS Men in UP Go Underground', *National Herald*, 6 February 1948.

[19] 'Question in the Constituent Assembly by Shri Damodar Swarup Seth Regarding the Joining of Communal and Social Organisations by Govt Servants', Ministry of Home Affairs Ests 15/18/48 NAI.

[20] 'Indian Reformer Is Shot at Point Blank Range by a Hindu Nationalist', *Manchester Guardian*, 31 January 1948.

[21] Yasmin Khan, 'Performing Peace: Gandhi's Assassination as a Critical Moment in the Consolidation of the Nehruvian Secular State', in *From Subjects to Citizens: Society and the*

Figure 1.1 Indian leaders carry the ashes of Mohandas K. Gandhi, Allahabad, 19 February 1948.
Photo by Bettmann/Getty Images

that quotidian responses to national symbols could often test these larger ideas on the basis of regional and local readings of India's past. Certainly, extraordinary scenes of public grief followed Gandhi's death, with one of UP's prominent newspapers including only one column on its front page as an expression of national shock and mourning, the day after the assassination.[22] A large-scale funeral in New Delhi was followed by a two-week official mourning and then the immersion of his ashes in the Ganges. The public reaction involved immense numbers of people, with reportedly more than a million congregating in the city of Allahabad alone (see Figure 1.1).[23] The political symbolism of this national event conveyed the tragedies of religious conflict (Gandhi had been killed at the hands of a Hindu extremist), and, by extension, the urgency of 'secularism' and the triumph of the Congress as its main champion.[24] This in itself was a powerful symbolic resource for Congress politicians, shortly following Independence, not least because the apparent threat of

Everyday State in India and Pakistan, 1947–1970, eds. Taylor Sherman, William Gould and Sarah Ansari (Cambridge: Cambridge University Press, 2014), pp. 64–89.

[22] 'Unmaad ki vedi par mana balidaan! Garib, ashaath, aur piditka sahara tut gaya rashtrapita mahatma Gandhi ki hatya hatyara jantadwara pakra gaya: Sara Bharat jagat shok santap aur chintagrast', *Aaj*, 1 February 1948.

[23] *The Times*, 13 February 1948. This number was also used by the British High Commissioner in Delhi.

[24] Khan, 'Performing Peace'.

both the right-wing of the Congress and right-wing parties such as the Hindu Mahasabha was still significant in the lead-up to the first national elections of 1951–2. Hindu traditionalists, including Purushottam Das Tandon who was successfully elected as Congress president in 1950, were in the ascendant as a result of the refugee crisis and the desire by some within the party to assimilate the right-wing RSS outfit (despite its ban following Gandhi's death) into the Congress Party organization itself.[25]

But it was the forms by which symbols of reconciliation and secularism were scaled both upwards and downwards which marked the extraordinary translatability of these events to a range of public contexts. As we will see later, local responses often challenged or subverted official narratives. Gandhi's death allowed the new Congress-led regime to consolidate its power – both at local and symbolic levels – in its strategic use of the state apparatus and in the strengthening of Nehru's executive authority.[26] The huge official funeral, which passed through the grand colonial spaces of Delhi, was witnessed by crowds lining the malls as its key audience in a specific set of Delhi-based rituals (see Figure 1.2). Khan shows how, in the aftermath of the funeral, there was a clamour for Gandhi's bodily remains.[27] Once Gandhi's pyre was lit on the evening of 31 January, Nehru had to issue orders to save throngs of people (the overall crowd numbered between 700,000 and one million) from falling into the fire.[28] At the specific location where the Mahatma had died, now considered by many to be a sacred site, people gathered up handfuls of the earth, leaving a large hole in the ground. Raj Ghat later became a memorial park for a range of other leaders – a sacred cremation space on the banks of the Yamuna, which related to Delhi's complex historical geography.[29] At the same time, the effect of Gandhi's passing was experienced in a multitude of other spaces. The UP press made a great deal of the international responses to the assassination.[30]

It was in the use of Gandhi's ashes that the spatial underpinnings of the new regime's secularism were most clearly demonstrated. Ashes were distributed from Delhi to all the states of India where they were scattered

[25] Bruce Graham, *Hindu Nationalism and Indian Politics: The Origins and Development of the Bharatiya Jana Sangh* (Cambridge: Cambridge University Press, 1990), pp. 19–22.

[26] Khan, 'Performing Peace', p. 68.   [27] Ibid., pp. 79–83.

[28] A. C. B. Symon, 4 February 1948, 'The Assassination of Mahatma Gandhi and Liaquat Ali Khan', FCO371/69729 UKNA.

[29] Mira Debs, 'Using Cultural Trauma: Gandhi's Assassination, Partition and Secular Nationalism in Post-Independence India', *Nations and Nationalism* 19, 4 (October 2013), pp. 635–53.

[30] 'Sara sansar stammit, London, Washington shok', *Aaj*, 1 February 1948; 'Videshon mein shok', *Aaj*, 4 February 1948.

Figure 1.2 People watching Mohandas K. Gandhi's funeral, Delhi,
31 January 1948.
Photo by Margaret Bourke-White/The LIFE Picture Collection/Getty Images

in local rivers, linking together the country's physical and political geography. This well-publicized network extended out from Delhi and,
importantly, was under direct Congress control and supervision. It
seemed far from coincidental that several of the locations set for receipt
of his ashes were areas of religious conflict – for instance, the Punjab in
the north-west and Hyderabad (Deccan) in the south.[31]

Ironically, shortly before his death Gandhi had as usual been protesting about matters that linked the local and quotidian to the national.[32]
Undertaking a fast for 'communal unity' in the context of the refugee

---

[31] Khan, 'Performing Peace', p. 77.
[32] 'Gandhiji ke anashan se bharat-pakistan donon hi chintit', *Aaj*, 17 January 1948.

problem in Delhi in early 1948 in response to communal tensions, he had set out the conditions for the breaking of his protest: the annual fair at the *dargah* (shrine) of the early thirteenth-century Muslim mystic Khawja Bakhtyar (also known as Qutbuddin Bakhtiyar Kaki), he argued, should be held, and Muslims ought be able to join it without fear; all mosques which in recent riots in Delhi had been converted into temples or residential accommodation needed to be returned to Muslims to become mosques again; Muslims should be able to move about without fear in formerly Muslim-majority areas of Delhi such as Karolbagh, Sabzimundi and Paharganj; Hindus should not object to the return of Muslims to Delhi; Muslims had the right to travel in railway trains without any risks; there should be no economic boycott of Muslims and the accommodation of non-Muslims in Muslim areas ought be left entirely to the discretion of the residents of those areas.[33]

As on many previous occasions, just before his murder Gandhi had successfully created publicity around a controversy that connected to high-level political struggles within the Congress Party and which had repercussions through India's entire polity. Official reports on Gandhi's motivation for fasting in early 1948, as related to India's Governor General Mountbatten, set out the former's annoyance at the policy of Patel towards Delhi's Muslims.[34] The external – British – interpretation was that the fast was as much designed to bring reconciliation between the two leaders as it was about the city's Muslim inhabitants,[35] and the controversy was even accompanied by positive reflections on Gandhi's motives in the Pakistani press.[36] Maulana Abul Kalam Azad, the leading Congress Muslim politician, also described how Patel remained 'indifferent' to the fasting, believing that these actions were directed at him, and as a result – Azad claimed – this affected local security arrangements for Gandhi in Delhi. Patel's apparent lack of concern came back to haunt him following the Mahatma's death. Gandhian politicians such as Jayaprakash Narayan and Prafulla Chandra Ghosh both held Patel publicly responsible for the lack of protection. Consequently, Gandhi's protests concerning the treatment of Muslims in India, together with his subsequent assassination, had a range of disciplinary repercussions for the Congress Party, and individual figures associated with it. There were knock-on consequences that filtered down to local Congress committees and to low-level administrators. Police, for instance, investigated those allegedly holding public meetings to celebrate Gandhi's death, with such

---

[33] *National Herald*, 18 January 1948.
[34] A. C. B. Symon, 25 January 1948, DO133/93 UKNA.   [35] Ibid.
[36] UKCOM, 'Reactions to Gandhi's Fast', 17 January 1948, DO133/93 UKNA.

events taking place in Gwalior and Jaipur where sweets were distributed;[37] and two *kanungos* (local revenue officers) in Ghaziabad district, B. K. Mathur Tahsildar and Anand Swarup, faced punishments for various misdemeanours, including the claim that they 'indulged in drinking wine on the night of Gandhiji's assassination'.[38]

Perhaps the most important quotidian significance of Gandhi's death was the range of implications that it had, on the one hand, for spontaneous popular protests around communal organizations and, on the other, for generating opportunities for local policemen and administrators to settle old as well as new scores. Exploring the spontaneous reactions that took place, we gain a sense of how ordinary citizens in urban UP and beyond identified with the larger symbols of national belonging. The news of Gandhi's death created shock across the city of Banaras, and both Hindu and Muslim shops simultaneously closed. All public employees took a day off.[39] Importantly, a similar spontaneous closure of shops also took place in Karachi, Sindh.[40] More directly, there was an attack by a large mob on the house of Veer Savarkar (Hindu Mahasabha leader) in the Dadar Mahim area of Bombay,[41] and a student demonstration in Lucknow in support of Gandhi and against the various organizations deemed responsible for his demise.[42] There were also local-level clampdowns on the Muslim National Guard and Khaksars, including community leaders who had held, for instance, the Chairmanship of the Bahraich Board.[43] In other centres in UP, opportunities were presented for assimilating RSS cadres into the Congress, with speakers at a meeting held by the president of the Lucknow Congress Committee suggesting that all (banned) RSS members should be absorbed into the Congress Seva Dal in each *mohalla* (urban neighbourhood).[44]

Clearly, as these instances collectively testify, the political moment created by Gandhi's assassination, alongside the very public ceremony of his funeral generated by the regime itself, allowed for new and spontaneous material interactions between citizens and the political process. In a very real sense, and in a way quite different to mass mobilizations in the colonial era, people involved in street politics were now able to

---

[37] Maulana Abul Kalam Azad, *India Wins Freedom: The Complete Version* (Delhi: Stosius Inc., 1988), pp. 243-5.

[38] 'Complaint against Shri Anand Swarup Supr. Kanungo Meerut', Revenue (B), Box 113, file 1029B/1950 UP State Archives (hereafter UPSA).

[39] 'Hamara Nagar: "Rashtrapita Gandhiji ki mrtyupar shok-sabha beniyabag mein shanivar ko 4 Baje"', *Aaj*, 1 February 1948.

[40] 'Pakistan mein Sarkari Chhutti: sara vaveshya bhi bandh', *Aaj*, 3 February 1948.

[41] *National Herald*, 2 February 1948; *Aaj*, 2 February 1948.

[42] *National Herald*, 3 February 1948.   [43] *National Herald*, 10 February 1948.

[44] *National Herald*, 9 February 1948.

engage directly with the political theories of Gandhism and Nehruvian secularism. In addition, the anticipation of fresh political freedoms, and the now poignant 'example' of Gandhi, had brought a heightened sense of how new governments were expected to operate: how, in particular, there was an acknowledged need to move away from the old bureaucratic approaches of British India.[45] Decolonization, in short, cultivated new public expectations that postcolonial regimes sought to channel and control, but which were exposed very clearly in such times of collective uncertainty.

Gandhi could not have died at a better time for the new regime under Nehru's leadership, for three significant reasons. First, developments just before his death represented a means for potentially bolstering the secular ideology of Nehru, something that he could use to confront the position of his rival, the more religiously conservative Patel. This would prove to be significant in the context of a renewed social and political conservatism evident in Indian Constituent Assembly debates of 1948–9 concerning refugees, women's rehabilitation and the hard line that was being urged in relation to Pakistan. Second, the specific timing of Gandhi's death, shortly after the already-fixed 'Independence Day' of 26 January (later to become 'Republic Day') that two years afterwards would be the date on which the Constitution was inaugurated, brought together two key memorial events. These directly served a politics of reconciliation and the idea of the rootedness of the Congress organization in the rights of the Constitution itself. Finally, while few were embarrassed to evoke Gandhi while he was alive, his death and accompanying 'loss' to India – at least for a time – provided another public opportunity to celebrate Gandhian values. This readiness was strongly reflected in contemporary press editorials. As *The Hindu* declared on 31 January 1948,

> ... let us face, as the Prime Minister exhorts us to do, all the perils that encompass us – and they are many and grave ... If we are true to Gandhiji's teachings, nothing must deflect us from considering all classes, castes and communities as children of the same mother, entitled to equal rights and – what is not less important – charged with equal responsibilities, all acting in harmony, earnestness and unison in the interest of the nation as a whole.[46]

But beyond local politics and street demonstrations, the force of Gandhi's murder lay in the effect it had on political debate and media

---

[45] The Hindi newspaper *Aaj*, for instance, printed a list of the times that Gandhi went to jail and his *Satyagraha* movements as an example, 'Bharat Pran Gandhiji ki jivan jhanki 1934 mein Puna mein bam dwara hatyaka vifal praytna', *Aaj*, 1 February 1948.

[46] 'Gandhiji', *The Hindu*, 31 January 1948.

commentaries. Gandhian ideas, especially given the violent and precipitate nature of his death, were represented as both universal and eternal in
a range of forums. Many reflected on his calls for political morality, such
as their use by a pamphleteer, Amar Nath Shastri, writing to Nehru in
1948 about Gandhi's passing as an explanation for state corruption,
together with the need for his memory to keep things 'clean'.[47] Others
complained about political selections to constituencies, either against
those who had made celebratory speeches when Gandhi had died,[48] or
in favour of those who claimed to have planned events in celebration.[49]
Gandhian ideas affected forms of public morality in other ways: in
Bombay in 1950, the local government refused to certify a cigarette
advertising film entitled *Ek Kash Ki Kahani* (A Story of a Puff) for
Cavender's Cigarettes. The film, censors argued, associated the father
of the nation with its propaganda to encourage smoking, especially as it
contained sequences with Gandhi's photograph, smokers in a cloth shop
and 'the anger of a mother-in-law' dispelled by the aroma of cigarette
smoke.[50]

Hence, the timing of Gandhi's death was a gift that could keep giving
for the Congress. Its anniversary each year neatly coincided with annual
Republic Days, allowing and encouraging public engagement to meld
the memory of this with a particular 'reading' of the Indian Constitution
itself. At an address at a public meeting on Sarvodaya Day at the Ramlila
Grounds, New Delhi, on 30 January 1950, Nehru's speech about the
Republic suggested to the audience that 'perhaps you may already be
aware of your rights – little more clearly than is necessary – but it is
equally necessary to know your responsibilities, otherwise a nation
cannot function'. Nehru deliberately phrased his call in terms of Gandhian notions of how unjust laws could be changed via a consensus

[47] 'Drive to check and ultimately eradicate corruption and bribe', by Amar Nath Sharma,
in Public 'Anti-corruption office efficiency. Suggestions regarding efficiency and anti-
corruption drive in government of Indian ministries', Home Public F 51/65/48 UPSA.

[48] In the Meerut constituency in March 1948, Balkrishna Sharma made such a complaint
against a rival, L. Bhagwat Prasad. See Balkrishna Sharma, to Pres. UPPCC, 24 March
1948, in 'Appeals against Sardar Teja Singh', AICC Papers, Election Files 4603/1951,
Nehru Memorial Museum and Library (hereafter NMML).

[49] 'Appeal against the decision of the UP congress PB rejecting Shri Chandra Bali Shastri
for the UP Assembly from Muhammadabad south dist Azamgarh', AICC Papers,
Election Files 4617/1951 NMML. Shastri claimed to have organized a huge party 'for
1000 Harijans' two weeks after Gandhi's death.

[50] Cinematograph Films, 'Ek kash ki kahani', General Administration Department
(hereafter GAD) 705/7(93)1950 UPSA.

Figure 1.3 A view of M. A. Jinnah's funeral, Karachi,
12 September 1948.
Photo by Dawn archive

between the will of the government and the will of the people,[51] something
that required not just the legal implementation of the Constitution but its
active connection to civic responsibilities.[52] Such connections allowed the
leadership to safely re-enact popular struggles with autocracy, which (via
reference to Gandhi) stood aside and above global materialism. Crucially,
too, they affected Nehru's own projected policy towards Pakistan, which
served a dual purpose of relative reconciliation on the international stage,
together with internal control of the Congress right wing: by speaking of
the 'panic and fear' of the Pakistani press, Nehru emphasized the need for
India not to resort to 'panic and fear' in relation to Pakistan.[53]

Across the border, like Gandhi's funeral, that of Jinnah held later the
same year in Pakistan's federal capital city of Karachi represented an
early 'ceremonial' opportunity for the embryonic Pakistani state to project itself (see Figure 1.3). News of Jinnah's death on 11 September

[51] 'Gandhian Ideals for the Nation', address at a public meeting in connection with
Sarvodaya Day on the second death anniversary of Mahatma Gandhi, Ramlila
Grounds, New Delhi, 30 January 1950. AIR Tapes, translated from Hindi. *Selected
Works of Jawaharlal Nehru* (hereafter *SWJN*), Vol. 14, Pt. 1, No. 7, pp. 261, 263.
[52] Ibid., p. 269.   [53] Ibid., p. 268.

1948 stunned Pakistan's new citizens. Although he did not die unexpectedly like Gandhi at the hands of an assassin, Jinnah had been growing steadily more unwell for some time – he had suffered from tuberculosis since the 1930s and then developed lung cancer. But awareness of Jinnah's declining health had been kept a closely guarded secret, and so his passing took most Pakistanis by surprise. Nor was this collective grief helped by the revelation that the ambulance transporting him from Karachi airport to his official residence had broken down en route, forcing him to wait at the side of the road for an hour before a replacement vehicle arrived. Jinnah's body was placed on public view at Government House where thousands visited to pay their respects. The enormous number of assembled mourners – a reported million people gathered in the city – who lined the three-mile-long funeral route the following day was credited with behaving in the main with admirable discipline, though, as one British High Commission report noted, 'the vast crowds who swarmed around the bier ... at one point completely disorganized the official programme'.[54] In an interesting and perhaps telling inversion of what had happened in India, British Pathé newsreel, which filmed the sea of people attending Jinnah's funeral, showed mourners scattering soil that had apparently been brought from 'all over the new nation' on his grave. In contrast to the nationwide *distribution* of Gandhi's ashes mentioned above, this ceremony materially and metaphorically sought to *connect* in symbolic fashion the country's constituent parts with its newly created political centre in Karachi.[55] Whereas the Congress had quickly realized the necessity to extend its authority outwards to other states in the lead-up to the first general elections in India, in Pakistan the problem was still one of the need or desire to centralize.

The Indian High Commissioner who attended Jinnah's funeral along with other members of the diplomat corps present in Karachi described events in detail to the authorities back in Delhi:

[Members of the diplomatic corps] turned up in full force, most of them in full morning dress with toppers. Jinnah lay on a low bed covered with a white sheet with a few rose petals strewn thereon. His face was bare, eyes closed and mouth open. I learn now that this was because he wore false teeth which according to Muslim custom are not buried with the body. The face showed acute and prolonged suffering, was horribly emaciated and shrivelled, and it looked as if the man had been dead a long while and not only the night before as given out. Zafrullah [Khan, Pakistan's Foreign Minister] was very composed. I thought

---

[54] UKHC, 'Pakistan: Monthly Appreciation of Events', No. 9 for September 1948, IOR L/WS/1/1599 BL.

[55] Khan, 'Performing Peace', pp. 81–5.

I detected even a faint smile flickering about his lips. He was the first to shoulder the bier. The procession itself numbered over a *lakh* [100,000] and was most orderly. Everyone was on foot. There were no women except Fatima Jinnah, Jinnah's daughter Mrs. Wadia, Lady Hidayatullah [wife of the Governor of Sindh] and Mrs. Tyabji, wife of the Chief Judge of the Sind Court.[56]

With government offices closed for three days, private businesses were not legally obliged to shut, but most chose to do so, though the spontaneity of shared grief was marred by the presence of roving bands of 'self-appointed enforcers' who reportedly caused unpleasant scenes, including setting fire to one of Karachi's principal restaurants.[57] On 22 October, the final act in Jinnah's mourning ceremonies (*chelum*) took place when a crowd estimated by observers at around 400,000 assembled near his burial place to pray and to listen to tributes from the country's top leaders.[58] The main focus of the speech by the new Governor General Khwaja Nazimuddin was the need for 'faith, unity and discipline if Jinnah's creation – Pakistan – was to reach fruition': 'the people', he advised, ought to 'scrupulously refrain from raising issues likely to create disruption or weaken authority and it was everyone's duty to join [the] armed forces and to subscribe to defence loans'.[59] On the occasion of Eid ul Azha, as part of the Hajj ceremonies, a few weeks later, Nazimuddin called on Pakistanis to dedicate themselves to 'the task nearest to the Quaid-i-Azam's heart – the establishment of a model Islamic state in Pakistan, a task requiring untiring effort, devotion to duty and a spirit of sacrifice',[60] and 'thousands [were said to have already made] pilgrimage

[56] Deputy High Commissioner, Karachi, to Ministry of External Affairs and Commonwealth Relations, New Delhi, 17 September 1948, MEA/2-1, 48 – Pak I (Vol. I), NAI. According to contemporary Indian sources, the view generally held in diplomatic circles was that the official story of Jinnah's death was not true and that Jinnah probably died in Quetta or on the plane, and that neither Liaquat Ali Khan nor Zafrullah Khan or any other 'bigwig' in Karachi knew of his death until after it had occurred. Both Liaquat and Zafrullah had been attending a function given by the French Ambassador in honour of the Pakistan delegation to the United Nations, and neither had apparently shown any traces of anxiety as reportedly 'Liaquat Ali was full of spirits and Zafrullah his usual cool self', ibid.

[57] Charles Lewis, US Chargé d'affaires (Karachi) to US Secretary of State, 15 September 1948, www.humsafar.info/doc_480915_us.php (accessed December 2018). The premises set alight were that of the Central Hotel, a sizeable establishment run along European lines, where the bar was open and people found to be drinking there. See Deputy High Commissioner, Karachi, to Ministry of External Affairs and Commonwealth Relations, New Delhi, 17 September 1948, MEA/2-1, 48 – Pak I (Vol. I) NAI.

[58] UKHC, 'Pakistan: Monthly Appreciation of the General Situation', No. 10 for October 1949, IOR L/WS/1/1599 BL.

[59] UKHC, Karachi, Opdom 85, 22–8 October 1948, IOR L/WS/1/1599 BL.

[60] UKHC, Karachi, Opdom 82, 8–14 October 1948, IOR L/WS/1/1599 BL.

to Quaid's grave'.[61] The reports by the Indian High Commission in Karachi, though they acknowledged that 'Jinnah's grave [had] become a place of pilgrimage for Muslims far and near', disputed the number of people visiting it on a daily basis. Rather, as Indian officials explained, enthusiasm was being 'kept alive by occasional free bus rides to the grave side, [and] by photographers being arranged to be in attendance when any one of importance visits the grave side to lay a wreath'. These photographs were then duly published in newspapers such as *Dawn*, giving visitors 'the satisfaction of not only seeing themselves ... but also offering proof of their loyalty to the State'.[62]

What the Indian High Commission, however, could confirm was the speed with which the land around the grave was cleared and levelled as part of the Pakistan government's plan to build a 'mosque, a replica of the Jumma Masjid in Delhi, an exquisite mausoleum over Jinnah's grave, a Dar-ul-Ulum [religious seminary] and an institute of technology' on the site. But while these schemes were given top priority, apparently placing other plans to build a new site for the federal headquarters in the vicinity of Karachi and a diplomatic colony into "'cold storage', the initial response from the public in terms of donating funds was described as disappointing:

[Syed Hashim] Raza, Administrator of Karachi called a public meeting in which the non-Muslims outnumbered the Muslims and the Parsis outnumbered the non-Muslims. It was given out that an announcement would be made as soon as Rs 10 *lakhs* had been collected. [But] as no announcement has so far been made, it may be presumed that even this paltry sum is not yet forthcoming.[63]

All the same, for local politicians, foreign dignitaries and ordinary citizens, the act of visiting the final resting place of the country's 'founding father' acquired enormous symbolic importance, with official and military ceremonies taking place there on special occasions. The first official act of the newly installed bishop of Karachi, for instance, was to visit Jinnah's grave in October 1948 to offer prayers and blessings.[64] As one visitor in 1950 commented in his private diary, there was a 'huge crowd there all the time, particularly on Thursday. His grave has become a place of pilgrimage. I saw a few people reading the Quran. They have

---

[61] 'No Bakr Id Joy This Year', *Dawn*, 16 October 1948.
[62] M. K. Kirpalani, Deputy High Commissioner for India in Pakistan, 'Fortnightly Report for second half of September 1948', 4 October 1948', MEA/2-1, 48 – Pak I (Vol. I) NAI.
[63] Ibid.   [64] *Dawn*, 7 October 1948.

turned it into a saint's shrine. At one stage there was even *qawwali*. But the Government of Pakistan has banned that'.[65]

In August 1949, with the first anniversary of Jinnah's death fast approaching, the authorities had to decide how the occasion was to be marked. People were requested 'to pay homage to the Father of the Nation and the Founder of the State' by participating in the largest possible number at a *fateha khawani* (condolence prayer meeting) to be held at his tomb and 'to bring with them their own copy of the Holy Quran for recitation'. A public meeting was also scheduled for the evening, to be addressed by Chaudhry Khaliquzzaman, chairman of the Muslim League, and other prominent personalities.[66] While the Quaid-i-Azam Relief Fund, set up to coordinate the various provincial, central and private refugee relief agencies, was intended to provide a lasting legacy of a more practical kind, the Pakistani authorities like their Indian counterparts took pains to prohibit any unauthorized use of Jinnah's name. As reports in the intensely patriotic Karachi newspaper *Dawn* explained in 1949, 'it [had] been observed that the hallowed name of the Quaid is being exploited by petty shopkeepers in Karachi. This tendency is objectionable unless official permission is obtained and all those shops who are using the Quaid-i-Azam's name without official permission are given time to stop doing so by the 1st of May 1949'.[67] This prohibition proved ineffective, however. Just a few months later, there were still reports of Jinnah's face appearing in advertisements for 'Pak' and 'Badshahi' *bidis* (cigarettes),[68] while in 1950, a disgruntled Karachi resident complained that

Although the Government have prohibited the use, association and display of Quaid-i-Azam's name and photo for purposes of business, advertisements etc., it is regretted that in actual practice these instructions are deliberately violated. Sometime ago I happened to see an advertisement in the city about Quaid-i-Azam Brand Pure Ghee. A medicine 'Jinnahspirin' is being openly sold. In certain cinema houses it has become a practice to display Quaid-i-Azam in pencil and chalk drawing with incorrect spelling of the leader's name. It is time that the authorities took serious view of such practices and punish the offenders.

---

[65] From *Auraq-i Paridshan*, Jamal Mian's *Sararnameh-i Pakistan*, entry for 29 August 1950, n.p.

[66] Office Memo No. 15/12/49 Public, 30 August 1949, Government of Pakistan, Ministry of the Interior, Home Division National Documentation Centre (hereafter NDC). It was also announced in 1949 that the government did not propose to hold any celebrations on Jinnah's 'official' birthday – 25 December – except to allow Pakistani flags to be flown on all government buildings, see Memo No. 15/11/49, 25 November 1949, Government of Pakistan, Ministry of the Interior, Home Division NDC.

[67] 'Shops Not to Be Named after Quaid-e-Azam', *Dawn*, 20 April 1949.

[68] *Dawn*, 30 September 1949.

We must show due respect to the founder of our State and even if his photo is to be displayed on the screen it must be one which is officially accepted by the Government.[69]

The same point was picked up by newspaper editors who reflected on the broader misuse of 'great names', citing with admiration Gandhi's opposition to cigarettes being named after him: as a *Dawn* editorial commented,

There has been an increasing tendency ... to name business concerns after Quaid-i-Azam. We can quite see that those who do it do so in order to seek blessing in their own way, from that great name, and thereby to make their wares attractive or acceptable to the customer. ... It is for the leaders and the Press of this country to explain this legislation [forbidding misuse of Jinnah's name] to the common people. There is much in a name: a great name has to be lived up to and not to be traded upon.[70]

In October 1951, following his own assassination, the body of Pakistan's first Prime Minister Liaquat Ali Khan was brought to Karachi from Rawalpindi and buried close to that of Jinnah, his funeral creating a second occasion for very public shared grieving on a massive scale:

thousands lined the streets of [the] capital to see his body brought from the airport. During the morning it lay on the veranda of his home in a casket heaped high with flowers. Mourners trudged slowly passed it. [In the] afternoon, 250,000 gathered in the polo fields where the coffin was brought for a state display before its burial. There it was laid on a gun carriage decked with flowers and drawn by Pakistan navy men thru [*sic*] the streets to the burial place.[71]

While this outpouring of national grief was more restrained than when Jinnah had died, the ceremonies associated with Liaquat's burial in the days and weeks that followed re-focussed the collective attention of the country's citizens on a site that had already become the emblematic centre of Pakistani national sentiment, and hence the symbolic terrain on which the state both performed and represented its new identity.[72]

Meanwhile in India, political advantages for the new regime continued to be drawn directly from Gandhi's death anniversaries. This was

---

[69] *Dawn*, 26 January 1950.   [70] Ibid.   [71] *Chicago Tribune*, 18 October 1951.
[72] The early 1950s witnessed lobbying to turn 16 October (the date of Liaquat Ali Khan's assassination) into a national Martyrs Day, when Pakistanis could pay homage not just to the murdered prime minister but to 'the thousands who gave their lives so that Pakistan might be created'. However, as one letter to *Dawn* added, 'It will not, however, be sufficient for the Government to just declare it a national holiday. It is the Government's duty to see that it is observed in a proper and befitting manner, and I am sure that the public will co-operate in every way'. See *Dawn*, n.d. August 1952.

particularly evident in the period leading up to India's first general elections in 1951–2 with supporters of the prime minister calling for Nehru to be seen as Gandhi's 'heir'. As we will explore in more detail in later chapters, Nehru derived considerable political mileage from this association when he confronted Tandon over the presidency of the Congress Party in 1951. As one national Indian newspaper put it, following the resignation of Tandon, the more 'secular' and 'Gandhian' leadership of Nehru suited him for this position: 'Congress opinion is agreed that today's decision of the AICC [All-India Congress Committee] to entrust Mr Nehru with full-fledged leadership of the Congress would have a tonic effect on Muslims and other minorities. It is also held possible that Muslims would join the Congress more readily and in larger numbers than under the presidentship of Mr. Tandon'.[73] However, once the Congress had firmly established itself following its successes in the first general elections, these kinds of references to Gandhi's legacy grew less frequent. Instead, at least in localities like UP, discussion revolved around a new generation of largely career politicians who no longer felt the need to pay the same degree of ideological lip service to the Mahatma.[74] Similarly, by the mid-1950s, commemorations for Jinnah in Pakistan had become more routine, with instructions in 1955 – the seventh anniversary of Jinnah's death – stating that a condolence prayer meeting (*fateha khawani*) would be held both at his *mazar* (tomb) and at the residence of his sister, Fatima Jinnah. But provincial governments were given strict orders that while they should put suitable arrangements in place, no public meetings were to be held 'under official auspice [*sic*], nor flags ... flown at half-mast'.[75]

Projecting the New State

When Pakistan and India came into existence on midnight on 14/15 August 1947, as was the case in many other states making the transition from colonial rule, their political leaders faced enormous mutual challenges as far as turning what had been a demand for political rights into a reality. In India, the transition to Independence ought to be viewed as a medium to long-term process, not least because notions of autonomy can be traced at least back to the framework under which Congress

---

[73] 'Reactions to Mr. Nehru's Victory in Congress', *Times of India*, 9 September 1951.
[74] William Gould, *Bureaucracy, Community and Influence in India: Society and the State, 1930s–1960s* (London: Routledge, 2011), pp. 153–4.
[75] 'Death Anniversary of the Quaid-e-Azam in 1955', Memo No. 15/23/55, 27 August 1955, Government of Pakistan, Ministry of the Interior NDC.

governments had held power in eight of British India's eleven provinces between 1937 and 1939. The period from the end of the Second World War, and especially following the elections of the winter of 1945–6, also signalled that the end of colonial rule was in sight. Yet while Partition refugees proved to be a consistent focus of public attention after August 1947, there was surprisingly little reflection in UP newspapers on the possible changes to the lives of most Indians that might have been brought about by these dramatic events in terms of new or anticipated democratic rights. Instead, when reflections on the meanings of 'Independence' did take place, they tended to be explored through the more murky lens of everyday problems – food supply, political problems, corruption and shortages. On the Pakistani side of the border, circumstances were by their nature more precipitate but also shaped by local considerations. For all the enthusiasm of those who at the stroke of midnight had found themselves 'Pakistanis', the reality of their new state meant very little to most people now living within its newly drawn-up frontiers. Despite the public celebrations that took place in Karachi to signal the official British handover, it was said that the vast majority of its new citizens 'scarcely realised that Pakistan had really come about'.[76] 'Pakistan' had after all been a rallying cry, envisaged – towards the later stages of the struggle to end British rule – first and foremost as a place that was *not* 'India'. Jinnah, when he had inaugurated Pakistan's separate Constituent Assembly on 11 August, referred to the creation of Pakistan as a 'supreme moment', and 'the fulfilment of the destiny of the Muslim nation'. But as contemporaries astutely recalled, while Independence celebrations were 'carried off with very scanty means and not in as perfect a manner as at Delhi … that never struck one as incongruous as it was improvised, Pakistan itself was being improvised'.[77]

Almost overnight, anything and everything that could be was re-labelled as 'Pakistan' or 'Pakistani': for many people there, just to hear the name of their country reportedly became a 'source of pride'.[78] From ministries to refugee rehabilitation boards to the railway, 'Pakistan' was added to their official designation. In due course, firms were advised to brand their products 'Made in Pakistan', so as to encourage 'patriotic'

---

[76] Comment by Wilfred Russell, cited in T. Royle, *The Last Days of the Raj* (London: Michael Joseph, 1989), pp. 171–2.

[77] Sahebzada Yaqub Khan, Delhi, 15 March 1997, quoted in Andrew Whitehead, *Oral Archive: India: A People Partitioned* (London: School of Oriental and African Studies, 1997, 2000), cited by Khan, 'The Ending of an Empire: From Imagined Communities to Nation States in India and Pakistan', *The Round Table* 97, 398 (2008), p. 47, http://dx.doi.org/10.1080/00358530802327845 (accessed December 2018).

[78] Keith Callard, *Pakistan: A Political Study* (London: Allen & Unwin, 1958), p. 270.

Pakistanis not to confuse them with foreign (Indian?) manufactures. And, day in and day out, the instruction to 'Patronise Pakistani Products' reverberated from public platforms and government speeches.[79] Acts as mundane as posting a letter turned into a way of projecting the same message. From October 1947, this required the use of former British India stamps overprinted with the word 'Pakistan', and franked with the slogan 'Pakistan *zindabad*' (Long Live Pakistan). It was not until July 1948 that the Pakistani authorities issued the country's first set of postal stamps. Produced to celebrate the first anniversary of Independence,[80] none of the four stamps, however, contained images that were directly connected with the eastern – Bengali – wing of the country: instead three depicted buildings in West Pakistan[81] while the fourth (apparently approved by Jinnah himself) was based on the crescent and star motif made familiar by the League's own flag, itself the template for Pakistan's national emblem (see Figure 1.4).[82]

India's own postal stamps showed an equal level of concern about territory and borders, especially vis-à-vis Pakistan. India's territorial claim to Kashmir was included on the 1950s' stamps depicting the map of India, where the whole province was included in cartographic representations, including the part beyond the 1948 ceasefire line.[83] India was less careful in the representation of its north-eastern boundaries, where, despite in effect 'annexing' Bhutan on maps from this time, it was suggested that 31,000 square miles of territory disputed with China lay 'outside' India. But Portuguese India, not absorbed within the Union until 1961, was incorporated in the maps of India on postage stamps in the 1950s.[84]

---

[79] *Dawn*, January 1950.

[80] These were printed in London because Pakistan still lacked the necessary presses, although there was confusion over what exactly was being celebrated as the date for Pakistani independence as given on these stamps as 15 (rather than 14) August 1947.

[81] The First Constituent Assembly Building in Karachi (formerly the Sindh Legislative Assembly), the entrance to Karachi airport, and the Lahore Fort gateway.

[82] In March 1948, it had been announced that the standstill agreement on postal arrangements would come to an end on the last day of that month. It was reported locally that India had proposed that ordinary mail between the two countries should be regarded as foreign mail, and hence that foreign rates should be charged instead of the existing internal rates. This would mean more than doubling the cost of ordinary letters as well as airmail rates. According to press reports, the Pakistan authorities wished to maintain the rates as the existing level but 'will, of course, have to follow India's lead'. See UKHC, Karachi, Opdom 26, 25–31 March 1948, IOR L/WS/1/1599 BL.

[83] By the late 1950s, India had made it illegal to import books with any maps that did not show Kashmir as part of India.

[84] Dudley Stamp, 'Philatelie Cartography: A Critical Study of Maps on Stamps with Special Reference to the Commonwealth', *Geography* 51, 3 (July 1966), pp. 192–4.

Figure 1.4 Muslim League National Guards with the Pakistani flag,
Karachi, December 1947.
Photo by Margaret Bourke-White/The LIFE Picture Collection/Getty Images

As far as currency was concerned, Pakistanis initially carried on using
British India bank notes and coins until April 1948, when the Reserve
Bank of India issued currency for use exclusively within Pakistan (that is,
without the possibility of redemption in India). Still printed by the India
Security Press in Nasik (in what was then the Indian state of Bombay),
the new banknotes were produced from Indian plates now engraved
(rather than overprinted) with 'GOVERNMENT OF PAKISTAN' in
English and its Urdu translation *Hukumat-i-Pakistan* added at the top
and bottom on the front only (see Figure 1.5).[85] This move, however,
unsurprisingly created considerable confusion at first, and so official

---

[85] The signatures on these bank notes apparently remained those of Indian banking and
finance officials.

Figure 1.5 A five-rupee currency note presented to M. A. Jinnah by the Ministry of Finance, 1 April 1948. Issued by the Reserve Bank of India, the note, stamped with Government of Pakistan (*Hukumat-i Pakistan*), operated as legal tender in the new state.

statements were needed to clarify that while the new bank notes were legal tender only in Pakistan, Government of India notes would continue to circulate for the foreseeable future.[86] Moreover, Pakistani and Indian rupees remained interchangeable up to 1949, when the two currencies finally went their separate ways after India but not Pakistan devalued its

[86] UKHC, Karachi, Opdom 26, 25–31 March 1948, IOR L/WS/1/1599 BL.

rupee and introduced new currency notes,[87] a move that contemporaries regarded as an opportunity for the country to pursue its own best interests regarding its currency status even if, in the short term, the shortage of Pakistani coins in circulation created local difficulties.[88]

One of the interesting inversions for India following Independence, and a topic that generated much media comment, was the role of administrative officers and policemen who had served the colonial regime and their 'transition' to a new democratic context. This changeover was critically important for all citizens given the fact that not only was the local bureaucrat or police officer the tangible face of the new 'state' but also one that had become especially palpable in the light of food and civil supply problems through the war years and thereafter. In early January 1948, the UP Governor Sarojini Naidu declared at the annual police parade at Lucknow that those who had fought for the freedom of the country were no longer simply *'badmashes'* (criminals) but rather *badmashes* 'in service of the country', whose duty was now to 'work as protectors of the people'.[89] There were plenty of general articles on the new spirit of service that ought to imbue the public servants' relations to the people.[90] In similar fashion, just over a week later, G. B. Pant, chief minister of the state (see Figure 1.6), addressed a conference of policemen in the city of Kanpur. In his speech he declared that 'The days when we detested the red turbans are over'. Pant proceeded to highlight the urgent need to fight bribery and corruption, instructing policemen to behave towards the people in the way that they would expect their fellow officers to behave with their own kinsmen elsewhere in the country: as he reminded them, 'Today, you are not merely policemen, but citizens of a free nation'.[91]

Nevertheless, there were plenty of instances, in UP at least, when complaints swiftly arose about the 'failed' administration of newly democratic India, which in the eyes of its critics had not fully made the

---

[87] In February 1949 new currency notes were introduced. Then in June 1949, pure nickel one-rupee Indian coins ceased to be legal tender in Pakistan; see UKHC, Karachi, Opdom 23, 3–9 June 1949, IOR L/WS/11600 BL.

[88] *Dawn*, 23 September 1949. As one press report pointed out, following Pakistan's decision not to devalue its rupee, coins of all value bearing pre-Partition stamps in the Sindh district of Badin were now being refused, with knock-on problems for trade thanks to the insufficiency of Pakistan-minted alternatives. See *Dawn*, 28 September 1949.

[89] 'Sarkar Aur Janta khitaab police-parade mein strimati Naidu ka Bhashan', *Aaj*, 7 January 1948; 'Work as Protectors of the People: Governor's Advice to the Police', *National Herald*, 6 January 1948.

[90] 'Sarkar Aur Sevak', *Aaj*, 9 April 1948.

[91] '"Imbibe Missionary Spirit": Premier Pant's Plea to Cawnpore Policemen', *National Herald*, 17 January 1948.

Figure 1.6 Govind Ballabh Pant, first premier/chief minister of UP.
Photo by James Burke/The LIFE Picture Collection/Getty Images

transition away from colonial governance. For instance, in the 'Reader's Forum' of Lucknow's *National Herald* newspaper, one G. Misra commented that the 'dawn of freedom' had been accompanied by a new menace in the district of Gorakhpur in the eastern part of UP – namely, the interaction between official and non-official. Misra gave the case of a particular magistrate, who was allegedly 'holding jurisdiction in many different areas' beyond his formal powers. 'These power hungry administrators', Misra concluded, 'are doing things which discredit the people's government and the Congress'.[92] As we will see in later chapters, the 'reconstruction' of the state administration to accommodate, in particular, the new demands of welfare, local government, land redistribution (*zamindari* abolition) and supply of goods often stimulated public debate about the role of minorities, migrants and refugees as far as public employment was concerned.

Unlike independent India that inherited the former headquarters of colonial power – New Delhi – together with a range of ready-made 'national' institutions already in place, the politicians and bureaucrats

[92] 'Reader's Forum', *National Herald*, 8 January 1948.

now running Pakistan faced the challenge of creating a whole set of new administrative structures. On the one hand, this infrastructure itself had to embody the 'state'; on the other hand, it was through this framework that the 'state' would have to operate, perform and reproduce itself on a day-to-day basis. At the federal level, a raft of replacement national institutions – ministries, commissions, committees – needed to be put in place, and quickly. Comparable trials and tribulations in terms of reconfiguring everyday administrative structures applied at the provincial level as well. Pakistan's biggest provinces (in terms of population) – East Bengal and West Punjab – had been parts of two larger units, namely united Bengal and the Punjab, themselves now divided in two. Hence, here too the local administration required extensive re-building. In the case of Sindh, though territorially unaffected by Partition, a large proportion of the province's non-Muslim government officials left for India in the months following Independence. And as was the case with India, the place of Princely States and tribal areas had yet to be resolved. It was much the same for municipalities and district boards, with their day-to-day operations disrupted by migration and displacement. Other explicitly 'national' bodies to be set up included a State Bank – regarded by the press as a necessary symbol of statehood – opened in Karachi on 1 July 1948 by Jinnah, who took the opportunity to call Pakistan's banking arrangements to be separated from those of India and also to conduct its banking in accordance with so-called Islamic ideals.[93] Meanwhile, against the backdrop of growing tension with India over Kashmir in 1948, the authorities established a Pakistan National Guard with the ambitious objective of training two million civilians, comprising both women and men, in the use of arms.[94]

In most of India, and particularly in locations such as UP, the Indian state was very closely associated with the principal vehicle of anti-colonial protest, namely the Congress that following Independence transformed itself from an all-embracing national *movement* into a political party. This association was, at one level, a by-product of colonial power itself: law and order and revenue collection as the principal logics of the colonial system were presided over and controlled by political administrators,[95] and at least in terms of party organization the Congress

[93] Branch offices of the new State Bank of Pakistan were opened in Lahore and Dacca; see UKHC, Karachi, Opdom 54, 1–7 July 1948, IOR L/WS/1/1599 BL.

[94] At a ceremonial parade of the PNG held in Karachi in May 1948, the turnout of the men's battalions was 'not impressive': the women, in contrast, were 'smart and keen, and attracted admiring and envious comment from their less active sisters among the spectators'. See UKHC, Karachi, Opdom 40, 13–19 May 1948, IOR L/WS/1/1599 BL.

[95] For a sense of how this worked through district administration, see David Potter, *India's Political Administrators 1919–1983* (Oxford: Oxford University Press, 1986).

necessarily mapped onto much of the same jurisdiction as had existed in the bureaucratic apparatus in the interwar period. Perhaps it was not so strange that power exercised locally involved a bureaucratic-political nexus in which Congress leaders exercised significant authority over local administrators. In effect, the Congress Party equalled the 'state' in the eyes of much of the population.[96] By way of parallel processes in Pakistan, there were complications generated by the fact that the state there, at least in period immediately following Independence, tended to be closely identified with another dominant political party, the Muslim League. To all intents and purposes, state and party were regarded by many Pakistanis (whether they liked it or not) as synonymous, and distinctions between the two extremely were blurred: in the words of Tai Yong Tan and Gyanesh Kudaisya, the League 'was expected to play a role similar to that of the Indian National Congress in India by providing the leadership and the organizational machinery to ensure and facilitate mass participation in the political structure'.[97] League politicians automatically assumed key roles both at the centre and in the provinces, dominating the federal Cabinet in Karachi, as well as providing a majority of the members of the Constituent Assembly also located in that city. Ministers and party officials combined their efforts to reinvigorate the League and engender 'solidarity and discipline in its ranks'.[98]

Under these circumstances, it was often hard in practice, whether in India or in Pakistan, to separate the state in terms of its administrative functions from those interests who claimed to represent it politically. We see this happening in UP, even though government servant rules were set up with the apparent aim of ensuring 'complete political neutrality' for government servants.[99] As we will explore in later chapters, public scandal frequently revolved around the misuse of political patronage towards civil servants and police officers, and the use of bureaucratic transfer. In Pakistan, corresponding patterns were evident, even after a ban on ministers holding party offices was included in the Constitution of the All-Pakistan Muslim League at the time of its formal establishment in February 1948.[100] Attempts to distinguish between the two were made

---

[96] For an exploration of how this worked in more detail, see Gould, *Bureaucracy, Community and Influence*, chapter 6.

[97] Tai Yong Tan and Gyanesh Kudaisya, *The Aftermath of Partition in South Asia* (London: Routledge, 2000), p. 204.

[98] UKHC, Karachi, Opdom 28, 1–7 April 1948, IOR L/WS/1/1599 BL.

[99] These were Rules 18, 19 and 20 of the Government Servant Conduct Rules. See Ministry of Home Affairs, File No. 25/59/52 – Ests. (A) NAI.

[100] This prohibition was later temporarily lifted in October 1950, only to be subsequently re-imposed.

trickier still by the fact that these same politicians often framed their rhetoric as if they were talking on behalf of the state, rather than the party to which they belonged. Leading Muslim Leaguer and 'Father of the Nation' – Jinnah – was transformed overnight into the state's supreme representative when he assumed the responsibilities of governor general at Independence, and then proceeded to juggle these duties alongside those of the head of the government, leader of the Muslim League and the office of president of the Constituent Assembly.

This high-level process of projecting the independent state often hinged on controlling information flows between India and Pakistan, whose relationship was poor from the start. In January 1948, the UP government issued a notification under the Maintenance of Public Order (Temporary) Act forbidding newspapers there from publishing any news item taken directly from Radio Pakistan in so far as these related to Kashmir, political matters or armed conflict.[101] To a great extent though, Radio Pakistan's reach was still very limited, prompting Pakistani politicians at federal and provincial level repeatedly to tour the country in person, in attempts to project the authority of the new state that they now represented as well as their own political interests. In April 1948, for instance, Jinnah – not long after his controversial visit to East Bengal where he drew criticism for his support for Urdu as the country's sole national language despite a majority of its citizens speaking Bengali – undertook a 'full and energetic' tour of the NWFP. There his speeches sought to hammer home the message that the 'anti-government' attitude that had so recently helped to remove a foreign (colonial) administration now needed to be replaced by discipline and a constructive approach towards solving Pakistan's social and economic problems.[102] Unity and discipline, he emphasized, were required 'if the difficult task of building Pakistan into [a] solid state was to succeed'. At a joint tribal *jirga* held against the backdrop of growing tension with India over disputed Kashmir, Jinnah assured assembled Pashtun chiefs that Pakistan, while not wishing to interfere with the internal freedom of their so-called tribes, would provide all possible assistance in educational, social and economic development: in return, he asked for tribal loyalty and assistance in national defence. The local press headlined the tour as a triumphal success, but other contemporaries reported a 'general sense of disappointment, in part thanks to excessive security restrictions and [also] partly to Jinnah's failure to appeal to rugged

---

[101] 'UP Ban on Publication of Pakistan Radio Reports', *National Herald*, 7 January 1948.
[102] UKHC, Karachi, Opdom 29, 8–14 April 1948, IOR L/WS/1/1599 BL.

Pathan humour – he ... usually spoke in English and kept at a distance from crowds'.[103]

Tours and ceremonial occasions shaped by various party political agenda took place at a local (state or provincial) level too. This has been explored at the level of high state ceremony in UP's main Congress-led projections of the nation, around flags, Independence Day and the politics of historical reconstruction and renaming.[104] However, the translation of some of these ideas at local-level perceptions of state power moved beyond the significance of region itself. In the UP city of Allahabad in January 1948, Acharya Jugal Kishore championed the Congress-linked volunteer movement, the Seva Dal, as an organization dedicated to service, self-sacrifice, simplicity, the promotion of national unity and improving the fitness and health of the Indian people through physical culture and training. In times of emergency, the idea was that the Seva Dal would act as a peace and relief brigade, as well as a 'School of Citizenship'.[105] In the Tehri district in the north-west of UP, a public meeting was held on 17 January 1948 to commemorate what local politicians described as 'Deliverance Day'. This anniversary marked the local taking over of law and order by the UP state government and was coordinated by a political-administrative combination of the veteran Indian Civil Service man B. D. Sanwal and Mahabir Tyagi, Congress politician and member of the UP Legislative Assembly for Dehradun. At the gathering in front of Tehri Jail, Tyagi made a speech saying that the officers of the UP government had come to 'serve the people who were now free'. The provincial government, he reported, had announced compensation to political sufferers, the refund of collective fines imposed on the people of the region, the release of political prisoners and freedom of speech and the press.[106]

In the Pakistani province of Sindh, in March 1948, equivalent grand-standing events were planned and delivered. The president of the Sindh Provincial Muslim League Yusuf Haroon, accompanied by Manzar Alam, the president of the States Muslim League who had migrated to the province from India, undertook the first visit since Independence by League office holders to some of Lower Sindh's smaller urban centres, including Thatta, Hyderabad and Tando Allahyar. Their official aim was

---

[103] UKHC, Karachi, Opdom 31, 15–21 April 1948, IOR L/WS/1599 BL.

[104] Gyanesh Kudaisya, *Region, Nation, "Heartland": Uttar Pradesh in India's Body Politic* (New Delhi: Sage, 2006), pp. 342–59.

[105] 'Congress Seva Dal Not a Military Body: Social Service the Goal, Says Jugal Kishore', *National Herald*, 23 January 1948.

[106] 'Deliverance Day Observed in Tehri: People Welcome UP Govt Officers', *National Herald*, 21 January 1948.

to 'create an awakening among the masses for the reorganization of the Pakistan Muslim League on a representative basis', but the majority of Haroon's time was taken up with addressing complaints about shortages of necessary goods and accusations of corruption in the administration. Even shrouds were apparently difficult to obtain, triggering the suggestion that the authorities should at least provide cloth for the dead even if they could not do so for the living. As one newspaper correspondent asked, 'Where is the utopia you promised us after the establishment of Pakistan? We have won our independence but can you honestly say that this has made any difference [to] the lot of the common man?'[107]

For many Pakistanis, Jinnah more than anyone or anything else – as reactions to his death discussed above have suggested – symbolized the new state: his rhetoric along with his physical being were both constitutive and representative of Pakistani identity, and hence Pakistan itself. Indeed, Jinnah's way with words equipped those running the new state with a rich repository of useful nation- and state-building resources. By the early 1950s, the authorities had launched an official Pakistani emblem that featured Jinnah's most famous saying. Green in colour, and incorporating a crescent and a star, this symbolic shorthand for the state signified Pakistan's ideological foundation – Islam – while its shield, divided into quarters and showing the country's major crops at this time – cotton, wheat, tea and jute – pointed to the agricultural base of its economy. The surrounding floral wreath, which alluded to traditional Mughal art forms, emphasized Pakistan's Indo-Muslim cultural heritage. Finally, the scroll supporting the shield contained three Urdu words – نظم ،اتحاد، ایمان – that read (from right to left) 'iman-ittihad-nazm'. Translated as 'Faith, Unity, Discipline' – virtues invoked by Jinnah both before and after Independence – these were turned into Pakistan's official guiding principles, which, emblazoned on hillsides and public monuments, came to acquire pride of place alongside Jinnah's own portrait as a physical embodiment of Pakistan's identity and political reality. While their exact ordering has triggered an ongoing debate, in practice, Jinnah himself prioritized them differently in different speeches. In 1950, a letter writer in Dawn suggested that, echoing the Statue of Liberty in New York, 'the Pakistan Government should construct in memory of our beloved Quaid-i-Azam, a huge structure on the Oyster Rocks in Karachi harbour, just off Clifton, visible miles away to the incoming ships and the planes as well. If possible the words "Unity, Faith and Discipline" may be inscribed on it, and brilliantly lighted at night'.[108]

---

[107] Dawn, 23 March 1948.
[108] UKHC, Karachi, Opdom 51, 24–30 June 1948, IOR L/WS/1/1599 BL.

Both India and Pakistan quickly produced national flags, either as adaptations of older ones or largely new, inspired by those of the parties that spearheaded the recent struggles for Independence. India's was based on the Congress's Swaraj flag, but with the spinning wheel replaced by the Ashoka Chakra or eternal wheel of law. The gradual production of this flag linked back to the 1931 Karachi Congress, which had passed a resolution on the flag, and the requirement for it to be 'officially acceptable' to the Congress. It was from this point that the issue of the 'communal' significance of its colours was perhaps most strongly and openly debated, with potential designs that were totally saffron eventually being abandoned for the tricolour: white representing Christian communities, green representing Muslims and saffron Hindus. The flag encapsulated debates about the material and symbolic role of Gandhi's constructive nationalism: In 1931, it had been made of home-spun cloth, with an image of the spinning wheel placed at the centre. By the time of Independence, the full image of a spinning wheel had been replaced by a martial sign of the conquering warriors of Ashoka – the *Dharma Chakra* – the wheel of cosmic order. When this replacement was proposed in July and August 1947, Gandhi expressed a sense of disappointment and concern that the spinning wheel had been lost.[109] However, typically he took the opportunity at a prayer meeting to turn his dismay into the positive point that 'the country should have only one flag and everyone should salute it'. For Gandhi, the significance of the flag also surpassed simple questions of demographic symbolism and denoted ideas of belonging for minorities, particularly Muslims: before Independence, it had made him 'very happy to hear that in the Constituent Assembly both Choudhry Khaliquzzaman[110] and Mohammad Sadullah[111] saluted the flag and declared that they would be loyal to the National Flag. If they mean it, it is a good sign'.[112] And just before Independence, Pakistan's incoming government adopted a flag very similar to that used by Muslim League, which had itself drawn inspiration from flags associated with the Sultanate of Delhi, the Mughal

[109] See, for instance, his piece in *Harijanbandhu*, 3 August 1947, reproduced in *Gandhi's Collected Works* (hereafter *GCW*), Vol. 96, pp. 151–3.
[110] Chaudhry Khaliquzzaman (1889–1973), a prominent Muslim League leader from UP, remained in India until November 1947 when he migrated to Pakistan, succeeding Jinnah as president of the Muslim League in 1948.
[111] Muhammed Saadulah (1885–1955) was the prime minister of Assam prior to Independence. In 1940 he was a member of the Muslim League Executive Committee that met in March at Lahore to draft the Lahore or 'Pakistan Resolution'. He was elected to the Constituent Assembly of India in 1947 and later became a member of its Drafting Committee. He did not migrate to Pakistan.
[112] 'Speech at a Prayer Meeting', New Delhi, 22 July 1947, *GCW*, Vol. 96, p. 113.

Empire and the Ottoman Empire, with the green representing Islam and the country's Muslim majority while its white stripe symbolized religious minorities and minority religions. In the centre, the crescent and star – traditional symbols associated with Islam – denoted progress and light respectively.

National anthems took longer to be approved. With the handover of power looming, government officials in Bombay, for instance, had requested confirmation regarding what tune to play on 15 August 1947. On 11 August, they received the following reply: 'In connection with the celebrations of the "Independence Day", all collectors are informed that "God Save the King" should not be played or sung on the 15th August [but] there will no objection to "Vande Mataram"[113] being played or sung if so desired'. Though the chief secretary to the Political and Services Department of the Government of Bombay promised that 'orders regarding the new national anthem [would] be issued in due course', it took until January 1950 before India's official choice – *Jana Gana Mana* – was adopted by the Constituent Assembly. Indeed, it is not clear what was sung officially at the intervening Independence Day celebrations of 1947–49. Pakistan faced its own musical headache when it came to finalizing its own national song. At the direct invitation of Jinnah, a first set of words was penned in 1947 by Jagannath Azad, a Punjabi Hindu, Urdu poet and scholar of Iqbal's poetry.[114] Interviewed much later (in 2004), Azad recalled the circumstances under which he had been asked to write Pakistan's national anthem:

In August 1947, when mayhem had struck the whole subcontinent, I was in Lahore working in a literary newspaper. All my relatives had left for India and for me to think of leaving Lahore was painful. My Muslim friends requested me to stay. On August 9, 1947, there was a message from Jinnah Sahib through one of my friends at Radio Pakistan Lahore. He told me 'Quaid-i-Azam wants you to write a national anthem for Pakistan' ... I asked my friends why Jinnah Sahib wanted me to write the anthem. They confided in me that 'the Quaid wanted the anthem to be written by an Urdu-knowing Hindu'.[115]

---

[113] Written as a poem by Bankim Chandra Chattopadhyay in 1875, and later composed as a song by Rabindranath Tagore, *Bande Mataram* ('Mother I bow to thee') was adopted as India's national song in January 1950, its first two verses having been adopted as the National Song of India by the Congress Working Committee in October 1937.

[114] Shortly after writing the national anthem, Azad (1918–2004) migrated to India, where from 1977 to 1980 he was professor of Urdu and head of the Urdu Department at the University of Jammu.

[115] See http://defenceforumindia.com/forum/threads/debate-over-hindu-writing-paks-1st-anthem-continues.5636/ (accessed December 2018). See also Raza Rumi, *Delhi by Heart: Impressions of a Pakistani Traveller* (New Delhi: Harper Collins India, 2013) for another version of this comment by Azad shortly before his death.

In December 1948, in the wake of Jinnah's death, for reasons that are not clear other than the Pakistani authorities' likely desire for something written by a Muslim,[116] a search was started for a replacement anthem, and a National Anthem Committee was set up, comprising politicians, poets and musicians and initially chaired by the Information Secretary. Progress, however, proved to be slow. Following the first foreign head of state visit (by President Sukarno of Indonesia) in January 1950, when there had been nothing available to be played, renewed urgency was attached to the search. Members of the public now started to worry about Pakistan's embarrassing lack of an anthem. As one letter writer to *Dawn* pointed out: 'We want to sing our National Anthem full-throated and we – men, women and children – would like to stand-to-attention when its tune is played by our military band'.[117] Others agreed:

The National Anthem of a great country always represents the virility, ambition and spiritual urge of its people. After our religion it is one single factor which is capable of reinforcing our morale even in the worst circumstances. It can also be used to discipline our people whether they are students or workers in field or factory. It is a pity that although this is the third year of our existence the authorities have not so far been able to release the tune and the wordings of our National Anthem.[118]

In 1950, the Committee eventually gave the go-ahead for music by Ahmed G. Chagla (approved the previous year) to be performed during a state visit by the Shah of Iran in March, and then the following August the Ministry of Information and Broadcasting officially approved new lyrics – written by the well-known poet Hafeez Jullundhri and chosen from over 700 submissions – with the complete anthem broadcast publicly for the first time on Radio Pakistan that month.[119]

Pakistan, like India and other states that had won their freedom from colonial rule, evidently needed to remind its citizens that they belonged to a qualitatively different kind of political arrangement than had existed in the past. National days, parallel to those devised in India, represented one relatively straightforward way of getting this message across. Hence,

---

[116] It is likely the fact that Azad had migrated to India where he initially became a government official was an additional factor. In 1948 Azad joined the Government of India's Ministry of Labour as editor of *Employment News*. A few months later he was appointed as assistant editor (Urdu) with the Ministry of Information & Broadcasting's Publications Division.

[117] *Dawn*, 14 June 1950.   [118] *Dawn*, 17 June 1950.

[119] Suroosh Irfani, 'Pakistan: Reclaiming the Founding Moment', *Viewpoints Special Edition: The Islamization of Pakistan, 1979–2009* (Middle East Institute: Washington, DC, 2009), p. 15, https://www.mei.edu/sites/default/files/publications/2009.07.Islamization%20of% 20Pakistan.pdf (accessed December 2018).

14 August – Pakistan's Independence Day – became a key date in the annual calendar, when politicians and public were encouraged to celebrate the anniversary of Pakistan's creation. In addition, 23 March – Pakistan Day – conveniently marked both the passing of the 1940 Lahore (or 'Pakistan') Resolution and later when the first Constitution came into effect in 1956. Jinnah's official birthday – 25 December – was turned into a public holiday, as, from 1949 onwards, was the annual commemoration of his death (11 September). On these state occasions, politicians at national and provincial level issued suitably stirring messages via official press releases and through the media, with Radio Pakistan playing an important role as its reach expanded over the course of the 1950s. Though Jinnah was too unwell to speak directly to crowds gathered in Karachi to celebrate Independence Day in August 1948, his words of patriotic encouragement were relayed to by Liaquat Ali Khan, and then dominated newspaper headlines the following day:[120] as Jinnah reminded Pakistan's new citizens, the establishment of the country was 'a fact of which there is no parallel in the history of the world. It is one of the largest Muslim States ..., and it is destined to play its magnificent part year after year, as we go on, provided we serve Pakistan honestly, earnestly and selflessly'.[121]

But despite the specific rhetoric involved, Pakistan's first anniversary celebrations were very like those taking place in India a day later, though perhaps rather more clearly focussed on military technology – a military tattoo, and a fly-by which dropped leaflets on the crowd (also officially and conveniently estimated at 200,000), followed the official summaries of the past year. Speeches focussed much more markedly on the adversity facing Pakistan from 'enemies' (viz. India), and the main reference to Pakistan's future related to the establishment of a government operating 'on Islamic principles' of equality, fraternity and social justice.[122] With tension mounting over India's policy towards the Princely State of Hyderabad (Deccan), Pakistani newspapers reported on Liaquat's reference to how enemies had 'conspired to paralyze the new state and how Pakistan had bravely weathered the storm', on the existence of a 'Sikh

---

[120] *Dawn*, 15 August 1948.
[121] *Ibid.* For more discussion of the early role played by the All Pakistan History Conference. in helping the Pakistani state to shape a historical narrative that could strengthen the argument for a distinct Muslim identity after Partition, see Ali Usman Qasmi, 'A Master Narrative for the History of Pakistan: Tracing the origins of an ideological agenda', *Modern Asian Studies*, doi: https://doi.org/10.1017/S0026749X17000427, Published online: 18 October 2018.
[122] R. R. Burnett, Acting High Commission to Pakistan, Despatch 223, 18 August 1948, DO 133/106 UKNA.

conspiracy', the alleged conspiracy to destroy important papers and records, and the 'presence of a certain element whose cult is to spread discord'.[123]

According to contemporary observers, with little visible progress in terms of reorganizing the city's administration, the Karachi authorities found themselves with their 'hands full' when it came to mounting the first anniversary celebrations: 'The much heralded Refugee Rehabilitation Finance Corporation so far appear[ed] to have achieved nothing at all', as one observer commented.[124] But refugee welfare remained a dominant theme on these state occasions, exploited by official rhetoric as well as challenged by the government's critics. Time and again, the Pakistan government scheduled its release of information on refugee rehabilitation to coincide with the anniversary of Independence, taking the opportunity to outline the progress that it claimed was being made together with ambitious future projects intended to address any continuing problems.[125] In his 1953 Independence Day speech, Prime Minister Mohammad Ali Bogra announced a scheme for the resettlement of some 43,000 refugee families in the federal capital, and appealed for public donations to help with the costs involved.[126]

It was not just anniversaries of key moments in the creation of Pakistan that offered opportunities to enact and, in the process, reinforce the official identity of the new state. While members of Pakistan's Constituent Assembly were finding it extremely hard to agree on what a 'Muslim state' would actually mean in practice, the religious calendar provided additional collective occasions for the authorities to exploit. In 1948, Liaquat and his colleagues were 'lavish' in their exhortation to the public to observe the month of fasting in the manner 'befitting the largest State of Islam'.[127] In the run-up to Ramadan (the Muslim month of fasting) that year, the prime minister took the step of issuing an official injunction

---

[123] *Dawn*, 15 August 1948.

[124] UKHC, Karachi, Opdom 69, 29 July–5 August 1948, IOR L/WS/1/1599 BL. The Refugee Rehabilitation Finance Corporation (RRFC) was set up in March 1948 for the specific purpose of resettling refugees by advancing loans to them for various purposes. It was authorized 'to grant loans to refugee shopkeepers, cottage industry workers, artisans, agriculturalists, whether working individually or with a cooperative society or a company formed for that purpose'. It could also grant loans to provincial governments 'for undertaking cooperative schemes for refugee rehabilitation'. In 1953, it had a working capital of thirty million rupees subscribed by the Pakistan Government. See US Embassy, Despatch 976, 'The Refugee Problem in Pakistan', 28 April 1953, 890D.411/4-2853 United States National Archive (hereafter USNA).

[125] 'Refugee Rehabilitation', US Despatch 67, 3 August 1954, 890d.411/8-354 USNA.

[126] UKHC Review of Events in Sind, Karachi and Baluchistan, No. 17, 11–24 August 1950, DO 35/5300 UKNA.

[127] UKHC, Karachi, Opdom 53, 1–7 July 1948, IOR L/WS/1/1599 BL.

to Muslims to observe the fast in practice as well as in spirit: a move that caused a British observer to comment cynically that 'this Islamic fervour on the part of Pakistan officials who, privately, and in some cases publicly also, are but moderate observers of the Quranic injunctions, is probably designed to steal the thunder of the Mullahs'.[128] The state authorities also made use of religious festivals – in particular Eid ul-Fitr at the end of Ramadan and Eid ul-Azha (that marked an important stage in the annual Hajj) – to deliver public messages about Pakistan's identity as well as its progress, whether past, present or future. In August 1947, shortly after Independence, Jinnah used the occasion of Pakistan's first Eid celebrations to remind its new citizens that

No doubt we have achieved Pakistan, but that is only yet the beginning of an end. Great responsibilities have come to us, and equally great should be our determination and endeavour to discharge them, and the fulfilment thereof will demand of us efforts and sacrifices in the cause no less for construction and building of our nation than what was required for the achievement of the cherished goal of Pakistan. The time for real solid work has now arrived, and I have no doubt in my mind that the Muslim genius will put its shoulder to the wheel and conquer all obstacles in our way on the road, which may appear uphill.[129]

A couple of years later, the Prime Minister's Eid message in July 1950, though less dramatic, promised an early imposition of a (long-awaited by some) refugee tax.[130] Refugee interest groups welcomed Liaquat's assurance, but they also cautioned his administration against becoming 'remote from those whose will it embodies': while the state might want to impress outsiders with what Pakistan had achieved since Independence, 'we cannot mould their judgement by pomp and pageantry'.[131] On the same day in Karachi, some 200,000 worshippers offered their Eid prayers in the open space surrounding Jinnah's *mazar* (tomb): 'From all parts of the city since early morning ... crowds converged on the ground ... thousands had to line themselves up on the road for the prayers ... After the prayer was over nearly every Muslim from the congregation visited the resting place of the Father of Nation, the Quaid-i-Azam, and paid homage to his memory'.[132]

---

[128] UKHC, Karachi, Opdom 54, 1–7 July 1948, IOR L/WS/1/1599 BL.

[129] See http://m-a-jinnah.blogspot.co.uk/2010/03/first-eid-in-pakistan-18th-aug-1947.html (accessed December 2018).

[130] For details on the introduction of a tax bill intended to raise additional revenue for the relief and rehabilitation of refugees, see statement by Dr Mahmud Hussain, Deputy Finance Minister, in 'Facts and Figures on Refugee Relief and Rehabilitation', 19 October 1950, 890.D.411/10-1950 USNA.

[131] 'Transmitting Editorial on Refugee Tax', 25 July 1950, 890d.411/7-2550 USNA.

[132] *Dawn*, 25 September 1950.

Anniversaries and national days, however, could prove to be a double-edged sword by also creating space for critics of government to air their dissatisfactions: in Pakistan in 1950, while 'the din of Independence Day oration was still echoing', a *Civil and Military Gazette* editorial bluntly observed that '[a]t present, the League is, for the vast majority of the population, a name and not a particularly well-sounding name'.[133] In 1954, following a growing split between the party and the federal government, a group of Muslim League supporters turned the official Independence Day gathering in Karachi into a very public demonstration against the incumbent Prime Minister Mohamad Ali Bogra and his administration. The political atmosphere on the eve of this particular anniversary was undeniably tense. While the East Bengal governor had just prorogued the Legislative Assembly in Dhaka to prevent the provincial – United Front – ministry from being overthrown, students in Karachi were demonstrating in support of President Nasser in Egypt with a citywide strike planned for 16 August. Meanwhile, the Muharram season had reached its climax – significant, bearing in mind local Sunni-Shia friction – and, in addition, refugees and non-refugees in Karachi were hugely divided over the local police force.[134]

India's national celebrations could likewise prove to be ambiguous state occasions, which in the years following Partition quickly moved beyond the apparent muted optimism of the first celebration of August 1947, covered elsewhere.[135] Whereas the authorities celebrated the new Republic in style, the Independence Day celebrations of 1948–50 were notably restrained and in some senses even 'gloomy' according to external observers. Just as in Pakistan, these events represented deliberate acts of political theatre, which attempted to maintain the rhetorical upper hand in the light of rising public dissatisfaction and accusations against the new authorities. There was certainly much to play for in the run-up to India's first general elections, which partly explains this approach. However, to a great extent, the muted festivities of the early post-Independence years reflected a period of deeper attempted official control of political opposition. In 1948, the Government of India tried to make it clear that Independence Day should not be treated as a moment for festive celebration, but instead as a day of remembrance for the Father of the Nation (Gandhi). Consequently, the attempted pattern

---

[133] Monthly summary of political events in Pakistan – August 1950, 6 September 1950, 790D.00/9-650 USNA.

[134] See Sarah Ansari, 'Police, Corruption and Provincial Loyalties in 1950s Karachi, and the Case of Sir Gilbert Grace', *South Asian History and Culture* 5, 1 (2014), pp. 54–74.

[135] Kudaisya, *Region, Nation, "Heartland"*.

was not one of a celebratory holiday, but ceremonies that revolved around flag hoisting, and police or military parades. The occasion involved a guard of honour composed of a contingent of the Royal Indian Navy and of the Royal Indian Air Force.[136] Visits accompanied by homage were paid to the site of Gandhi's funeral pyre at Raj Ghat, after which Nehru raised the Indian flag on the Red Fort, in front of a crowd estimated to be around 200,000. Nehru's speech expressed the need for the public to pursue 'truth and toleration' and to root out the 'communal virus' from the nation.[137] He also appealed once more to public servants to 'identify themselves with the needs of the people'.[138]

Patel's speech in Delhi on this first anniversary, in contrast, was more explicit in suggesting the means by which public ceremony could be used to restrain popular protest: his speech discussed political unrest in nearby Malaya, Indochina and Burma, and translated this discontent into the need for India to exercise public discipline, even if this required denying 'the people, from time to time, a certain degree of personal freedom'.[139] The deputy prime minister enthusiastically hailed the fact that the largest area of territory for over a thousand years had been integrated into the entity of India – a barely veiled reference to the ongoing integration of the Princely States. In a more subtle fashion, Patel also associated the citizen's 'duty to neighbours' with the centrality of 'loyalty to the state' and the need to oppose 'divided loyalties'.[140] Much of the press meanwhile allowed itself greater scope to celebrate achievements – the Damodar Valley Scheme, the Hirakud and Bhakra Dams, for instance, were proudly mentioned by the *Hindustan Times*. Hindi and Urdu dailies, such as *Hindustan* and *Hind Samachar* (East Punjab) and *Navashakti* and *Rashtravani* (Bihar), even asked the UK High Commissioner for messages of congratulations to include in their special 'Independence Day' issues.[141] Indian newspapers on the left, conversely, focussed on a critique of continued poverty, repudiated pledges and – perhaps most importantly – the idea that 'Civil Liberty' had been 'the first casualty of Freedom'. Such press coverage reflected, more strongly, a great deal of the popular response to the first two years of Independence, manifested

[136] 'Mahatma's Ideals on Greatness', *The Statesman*, 16 August 1948.
[137] A. C. B. Symon, Acting High Commissioner, Despatch 123, 4 September 1948, DO133/106 UKNA.
[138] 'Mahatma's Ideals on Greatness', *The Statesman*, 16 August 1948.
[139] A. C. B. Symon, Acting High Commissioner, Despatch 123, 4 September 1948, DO133/106 UKNA; 'Sardar Patel's Appeal for Co-operation', *The Statesman*, 16 August 1948.
[140] 'No Room for Divided Loyalty in India', *The Statesman*, 16 August 1948.
[141] For instance, Jagat Narain to Sir Terence Shone, 30 July 1948, DO133/106 UKNA.

in journalistic comments about rising prices, the scarcity of essential goods and problems of administration. The reference point here was the recent public security legislation that targeted – alongside communal organizations – leftist groups. This hesitant mood continued during the years that followed, with content usually linked to ongoing problems of the year in question. In 1950, public speeches made a point of the importance of restraining the 'degeneration' of public and commercial life. Here again, it was Patel who expressed this sentiment most directly: 'Our public life seems to have degenerated into a fen of stagnant water' was how he referred specifically to the Congress Party's 'lax' discipline as compared to its pre-Independence days.[142] Significantly, even Nehru chose this moment to comment specifically on the menace of black marketeers and continuing problems involved in refugee rehabilitation.[143]

Just as the new regimes in India and Pakistan changed the nature of state ceremony, there were efforts to adapt the material iconography of urban spaces. But here too, the political symbolism of postcolonial iconoclasm was complicated by local responses to such changes. As Paul McGarr's exploration of shifting relations between India and Britain in the decades following Independence has argued, the politics of statues in India from the mid-1950s formed part of 'a broader dialogue between central and state governments, political parties, the media and the wider public on the legacy of British colonialism in the subcontinent': to a great extent, removing colonial-era statues represented 'a significant, and perhaps necessary, step in the creation of a new "imagined" community'.[144] At the same time, the decision to remove such reminders of the recent colonial past, whether in India or Pakistan, was often quite specific in its historical readings, with statuary and place names relating to, for instance, the 1857 Mutiny-Rebellion being targeted with particular urgency. The statue of the nineteenth-century Viceroy Lord Lawrence, who had led 'loyal' troops to recapture Delhi in 1858, was in consequence removed from the Mall in Lahore at the end of August 1950.[145] Similarly on 14 May 1957 – the one hundredth anniversary of the uprising – Nehru delivered a speech in the Lok Sabha suggesting that British-era statues could be divided into three categories: first, those that were offensive to national dignity; second, those possessing historic

---

[142] UKHC, New Delhi, Opdom 16, for period 2–16 August 1950, Part 1, Telegram, DO133/106 UKNA.
[143] Ibid., Part II Savingram, DO133/106 UKNA.
[144] Paul M. McGarr, 'The Viceroys Are Disappearing from the Roundabouts in Delhi: British Symbols of Power in Post-Colonial India', *Modern Asian Studies* 49, 3 (2015), p. 790.
[145] R. R. Burnett to Maclennan, 4 September 1950, DO133/106 UKNA.

significance and, finally, those that were merely artistic. Overall, in most parts of India there were few powerful voices arguing for the position that monuments from the British period were 'offensive to national dignity'. In fact, significant lobbies existed by now that were in favour of restoring and maintaining historical artefacts, pictures and statuary. All the same, in a number of cases (which were, importantly, contingent on moment and context), statues, other monuments and cemeteries were desecrated, defaced, destroyed or removed by crowds and focussed popular movements. Agitation also centred on the removal of statues of Queen Victoria from key public places, including one that was located in front of the Council Hall in Bombay. Other memorials could trigger more direct popular reaction. Cemeteries became particular targets for this. The total number of cemeteries taken over by April 1948 was 812 across India, 254 of which had been abandoned by 1959. Over 300 of the remainder had to be closed, and there were reports of sites being desecrated especially when they were located in remote areas.[146]

The justification for changes in statuary could be more direct at the level of state governments, with the public meaning of such figures being openly discussed. Hence, in response to the centenary anniversary of the 1857 Mutiny-Uprising, the Bombay authorities appointed a committee the following February to examine the issue of how and whether to retain statues. This team was tasked with identifying, among other things, which statues were 'offensive to Indian sentiment from the point of view of either the uprising of 1857 or other Indian national movements'.[147] While its members decided that 'none were offensive', they also recommended their gradual removal and replacement with 'statues and monuments which are more in consonance with the sense of patriotism and nationalism which has developed since the attainment of independence in 1947'. Ultimately, in the view of the committee, it was 'necessary that such links which publicly and prominently remind us of our past bondage and which militate against us our ever developing sense of nationalism should be gradually done away with'.[148]

---

[146] Note to Wickson, 6 February 1959, 'Disposal or Retention of Pictures and Statues of the British Era in India', DO133/150 UKNA.

[147] *Report of the State Committee Appointed to Examine the Question of the Retention in Public Places of Statues of the British Period and Other Relics* (Bombay: Govt. of India Press, 1961), p. 2.

[148] Ibid., p. 3. Rather than being melted down, some of these statues ended up in unusual places. Maharashtra had seventy-five overall and there was a suggestion in September 1961 for an 'open-air museum' for them. Others were removed from UP in 1957, where it was alleged that some found their way into the courtyards of government servants; see VCM, 20/2/59 UKNA. When a wealthy American collector, Mr Givelber of Cleveland, Ohio, later wanted to purchase some of the old colonial statues, the Home Department

A familiar desire to sweep away the past – for comparable symbolical reasons – was reflected in the civic planning that went into renaming thoroughfares across the subcontinent. In the case of Karachi, its Municipal Corporation announced in April 1949 that it was considering a scheme to call the city's principal roads after prominent Pakistani leaders, while, for 'the convenience of the public', the smaller streets and lanes that ran off them would just be numbered. In 1951, the first part of this plan was realized, when in February the Karachi Municipal Advisory Committee 'accepted amidst applause' the report of the ten-man subcommittee, which, 'yielding to a long-felt public desire', had recommended replacing English names with more appropriate 'local' alternatives. Of the thirty-three major roads and streets involved, seven would commemorate important Hindu leaders, while the remainder were to celebrate Pakistan's Muslim identity.[149] Karachi's Administrator, Syed Hashim Raza, meanwhile, appealed for public cooperation to popularize Urdu, calling for it to be used instead of English for name-plates and boards on buses, shops, offices, banks and other premises in the federal capital.[150] Not all residents of the city approved of these changes, however. As one disgruntled Karachi correspondent explained,

I am not impressed by the City Fathers' selection of names for Karachi streets. I want to ask them why they prefer long names, sometimes longer than the roads themselves. I won't shrug my shoulders if they stress the historical or national importance of these names. The first criterion in selecting a name should be its brevity. Why not rename a few roads (if possible all) as 'Red Rose, Lilly White, Jasmine Wild', etc. I am sure many would join with me when I say that Red Rose Road sounds better than, say, Khan Sahib Chaudhry Qadruatullah Road, which it is difficult to utter in one breath or even two.[151]

Conclusion

The political symbolism bound up in annual national events such as India's 'Independence Day' linked official and 'sanitized' readings of its anti-colonial past with ideas of a future democratic governance. In a similar fashion, the Pakistani authorities, whether on secular state

of India sought the advice of the UK government. Other statues turned up in unusual places – for instance, when the water level dropped in the Ambajheri tank in Nagpur in 1961, a statue of Victoria was found in the bottom; see R Courts to the High Commissioner for the UK, New Delhi, 29 December 1961, DO133/150 UKNA. The nine-foot marble edifice was subsequently whisked away and leaned up against a local Public Works Department *godown*; see J. R. G. Wythers to Guy, 11 December 1961, DO133/150 UKNA.
[149] *Dawn*, n.d. February 1951.   [150] Ibid.   [151] Ibid.

occasions or religious ones, sought to emphasize crucial differences between the past and the present, while holding out promises for the future. But as demonstrated by contemporary reactions in locations such as UP and Sindh, this was not a symbolism over which the authorities in either Delhi or Karachi had total control. Colonial officialdom had never presupposed any kind of political or cultural unity across what was British India. As an Indian 'Empire', it had served the interests of rulers to encourage regional differentiation, downplay the idea of a 'unified' India and, not least, uphold many of the particular privileges of the Princely States. From the perspective of Delhi after August 1947, this legacy, combined with the fact of Pakistan's creation, made it all the more important to early postcolonial publicists to reiterate the interconnectedness of the new state's regions, and not just by talking about a single nation. The demographic audiences for the 'idea' of India had to be emotionally connected – via cultural and historical symbols that traversed the spaces separating them – and brought into dialogue through processes of political enactment. The same priorities applied as far as Pakistan's authorities were concerned, where the rationale for its separate creation in August 1947 had to be continually reinforced as a way – at least in theory – of stressing what its people shared, whether or not they were Muslims and wherever they lived.

What this chapter's exploration of developments in the context of UP and Sindh, and cities such as Delhi and Karachi, has highlighted is that at first these representations built upon clearly defined agents – from government servants and politicians to pamphleteers, artists and architects – all of whom proved to be tacit in their role.[152] But they were later disrupted, and sometimes re-appropriated, by groups who were using them in a range of different localities and often for their own purposes.[153] Indeed, this combination of state-driven and quotidian vision reveals a great deal about the day-to-day differentiated spatial responses to citizens' identity. They highlight just how far symbolic communication could be a fragile and contingent phenomenon, in which the relationship between different places could and did make a difference.

Moreover, as we have suggested through our focus on Sindh and UP, these efforts – shaped and directed by politicians and civil servants in the two capital cities located in close proximity – took place in a variety of

---

[152] Joanne Roberts, 'From Know-How to Show-How? Questioning the Role of Information and Communication Technologies in Knowledge Transfer', *Technology Analysis and Strategic Management* 12, 4 (2000), pp. 429–43.

[153] Keith Axel, 'Anthropology and the New Technologies of Communication', *Cultural Anthropology* 21, 3 (2008), pp. 354–84.

hyper-textual, material and performative ways, meeting and responding (to varying extents) to localism, and sometimes being informed by it, as symbolic ideas circulated across the 'spaces' now occupied by the Indian and Pakistani states. But, as it turned out, these means of symbolic communication, precisely because they were spatial, could not simply be rhetorical. In independent India, they had to take into account that there were linguistically and culturally varied 'publics',[154] which also helped to build and bolster notions of civic belonging around diverse ideas of the past. Precisely because these ideas circulated regionally, culturally and socially, they could be reformed and transgressed in the process, and consequently develop into a wide range of other political symbols with potentially insurgent effects. Over in Pakistan, the situation had a somewhat different gloss. Rather than diverse ideas of the past feeding into what it now meant to belong as an 'Indian', the process there hinged on an assumed 'common past', that of the subcontinent's Muslims, which was deployed to construct a sense of belonging in the present. Accordingly, state representatives as well as interest groups and individuals in Pakistan tended to emphasize that, despite the distances separating its constituent parts and peoples, all were now involved in the shared enterprise of constructing a 'nation' out of its component elements, irrespective of whether or not they actually shared the same religious identity. Nonetheless, on both sides of the post-1947 divide, citizenship ideas in practice were made more 'vernacular', and shaped if not necessarily reconfigured, by popular engagement with the idea of 'citizenship', whether this was propelled from below or directed from above.

---

[154] Michael Warner, *Publics and Counterpublics* (Cambridge, MA: MIT Press, 2002).

2 People on the Move
Refugees and Minorities in Uttar Pradesh and Sindh

Newspaper columns published in *Dawn* by Pakistan's leading female journalist of the 1940s and 1950s, Zeb-un-Nissa Hamidullah,[1] provide a vivid sense of the frustrations experienced by many people living in Karachi as it swelled in size from c. 350,000 inhabitants in 1947 to nearly 1.5 million just five years later. The following commentary – produced in May 1952 just as the Muslim month of fasting (Ramadan) was beginning, with temperatures soaring and water in short supply – drew attention to the routine trials and tribulations that the city's inhabitants were experiencing in the early 1950s:

We could talk about the water shortage. Yes we've got something there. Something that could work us into an emotional frenzy especially when we remember the daily little irritations due to lack of sufficient water even for a daily bath. We could talk about the housing problem. A topic as old as yesterday and as young as today. In Karachi at least. We could point out that nothing, or so little as to be insignificant, has been done to ease the situation for the average man. ... We could. But we won't. Enough is enough and the heat is almost more than we can bear today without adding to it.[2]

Chapter 1 has explored how ideas, promises and agendas originating in the nationalist movements of the first half of the twentieth century shaped not only the policies of independent governments in South Asia but also the kinds of demands that their new citizens made of them. At the same time, as post-Independence developments in localities such as UP and Sindh remind us, the modus operandi of many institutions involved in what people thought of as the 'state' did not change, or changed very little, during the years under scrutiny here.

---

[1] Born to a Bengali father and English mother in Calcutta and married into a Punjabi family, Zeb-un-Nissa [Zaibunnisa] Hamidullah (1918–2000) had started writing for newspapers, including Bombay's *The Illustrated Weekly of India*, before Independence. Her 'Thru' a Woman's Eyes' column in *Dawn* (later renamed 'Between Ourselves' and extended to cover broader issues) made her Pakistan's first female political commentator.
[2] 'Thru' a Woman's Eyes', *Dawn*, 26 May 1952.

There were both structural and contingent reasons for this continuity: crucial administrative and executive functions of government (from trad-itions and hierarchies in the public services and policing to mundane forms of bureaucratic writing and procedure) remained largely intact across South Asia following the British departure. In India, the postco-lonial administration was quickly integrated into the parallel functions of the dominant political party – the Congress – which allowed for an array of semi-formal political functions in the work of the local state alongside political leaderships at national as well as provincial level. In Pakistan, where the Muslim League at this time still enjoyed a dominance that belied its strength on the ground, the administration alongside the army served as the only properly established structure of governance in the early period following Independence, and even then, at a federal and at a more local level, it faced a huge test in terms of piecing together an integrated bureaucratic structure out of former provincial arrangements.

The lingering aftershocks of the Second World War also allowed for continuities. Wartime rationing and requisitioning introduced in British India (which had continued after the conflict had ended in 1945) had stretched the colonial bureaucracy to its widest extent to date, while, at the same time, exposing new weaknesses and opening up fresh oppor-tunities to identify and critique political and administrative 'corruption'. The more general limitations of the everyday postcolonial state from poor planning to deficient implementation and uneven access to resources, enlarged the rhetorical space in which essential issues, such as citizenship, could be raised and discussed.[3] In addition, these debates were often configured strongly around what was imagined to be happening in *other* places (i.e. across the new border), principally as an outcome or legacy of the physical movement of peoples before, during and following Partition.

Political freedoms associated with Independence brought with them throughout the subcontinent a heightened consciousness as to how governments were expected to operate after 14/15 August 1947. In particular, there was often popular support for the idea that the new authorities needed to move away from – even reject – the old bureau-cratic approaches of British India. The demise of colonial rule had raised hopeful expectations that things would be run differently in the future. This anticipation was further amplified by the mass migrations that 'bookended' Independence and their impact on individuals, wider

---

[3] William Gould, Taylor C. Sherman and Sarah Ansari, 'The Flux of the Matter: Loyalty, Corruption and the "Everyday State" in the Post-Partition Government Services of India and Pakistan', *Past & Present* 219, 1 (2013), pp. 237–79.

society and the workings of the state. Decolonization, or the end of empire, in short, cultivated new public expectations, and this anticipation transformed rapidly as the two new postcolonial regimes established themselves, both internally and also in relation to each other. Absolutely central to this political adjustment were popular ideas about national and regional 'belonging', which in both India and Pakistan now translated into a fundamental tension in the form of a dichotomy between the promises of democratic change on the one hand and the realities of how the bureaucracies running them continued to operate on the other. At the same time, while the wheels of government often turned in much the same way as they had done in the late colonial period, the theoretical reach of the independent state into areas of development, welfare and local political change raised levels of public expectation enormously.

Independence, however, did not change the fact that, as before 14/ 15 August 1947, most Indians and Pakistanis continued to experience and perceive 'government' in terms of the lower-level officials who manned bureaucracies, and with whom they came into direct contact. This continued to be so even where the expressed objectives of these functionaries had allegedly changed according to the rhetoric of political leaderships at the centre, whether this was Delhi or Karachi.[4] In this regard, there existed in practice spatial and conceptual disjunctures between what India's and Pakistan's new citizens 'heard' in their leaders' speeches – relayed to them in the press or by word of mouth – and what they experienced first-hand at the level of the province, district or city and town where they lived. At a public meeting held in Lahore in August 1949, for instance, Liaquat Ali Khan asserted that everyone in Pakistan had the same right 'to be provided with food, shelter, clothing, education and medical facilities', implying that the state recognized its responsibilities for providing the run-of-the-mill necessities of life.[5] In a similarly paternalistic vein at a public meeting in New Delhi at the end of January 1948, Liaquat's Indian counterpart Jawaharlal Nehru had presented the 'raising of three hundred and forty or fifty million people, raising them economically, certainly raising them educationally' as a major national problem.[6]

But, just as under colonial rule, the provision of basic services remained chiefly in the hands of provincial or state-level government

---

[4] Akhil Gupta, *Red Tape: Bureaucracy, Structural Violence, and Poverty in India* (Durham, NC: Duke University Press, 2012), pp. 81–2.
[5] *Pakistan Times*, n.d. August 1949.
[6] Address at a public meeting in connection with Sarvodaya Day, New Delhi, 30 January 1950, *Jawaharlal Nehru Collected Works*, Vol. 14, p. 284.

departments. While public health, education and labour legislation were coordinated by the central authorities, it was still provincial or state ministries that set the all-important prices for – and when necessary (as often happened during the post-1947 years) rationed – essential food grains, sugar and other commodities in short supply.[7] Equally, government officials working at the local level – such as district magistrates and police superintendents – retained primary responsibility for the routine maintenance of law and order. Hence, 'to the ordinary man Government truly [began] with the provincial administration and its local representative'; it was there that 'the machinery of law and order, of taxation, of flood control and irrigation' started to operate, for while 'the bureaucratic apparatus functions impersonally, the character of the provincial ministry [could] make a real impression on the popular imagination', in effect distinguishing the 'machine' from its 'operator'.[8] This chapter is accordingly explores these tensions and the ways in which they played out, often in an interrelated cross-border manner, in the different spaces and jurisdictions of India and Pakistan, and in particular, from our perspective, in Sindh and UP.

As our Introduction has already suggested, there could be variations between different states/provinces in relation to their respective central authority, with the result that Indian and Pakistani citizenship often tended to be 'imagined' in terms of geographical and jurisdictional spaces and distances. Just as this could be the case *within* India and Pakistan (for instance, in the relationship between UP and Delhi or that between Sindh and Karachi), a similar spatial relationship also existed *between* India and Pakistan. Put another way, though the locality determined the representatives of the state with whom citizens came into contact, the nature of these dealings was frequently discussed and acted upon in relation to understandings of what was happening (or perhaps what people thought was happening) elsewhere, whether on their side of the border or across it. As Arjun Appadurai has emphasized, local communities tend to be formed in ways that are 'relational and contextual', as opposed to stemming from some inherently 'scalar or spatial' characteristics.[9] In the 1940s and 1950s South Asia, this was more than just thinking about Indian or Pakistani identity as a mirror of the 'other' country: public opinion could equally be conditioned by more localized

---

[7] Richard Symonds, *The Making of Pakistan* (2nd ed., London: Faber & Faber, 1950), pp. 180–1.

[8] Keith Callard, *Pakistan: a Political Study* (London: Allen & Unwin, 1957) p. 268.

[9] Arjun Appadurai, 'The Production of Locality', in his *Modernity at Large: Cultural Dimensions of Globalization* (Minneapolis: University of Minnesota Press, 1996), pp. 178–9.

reactions to people arriving from other places or others leaving their families and goods behind – population movements, the presence of refugees in the cities of northern India and West Pakistan (particularly in UP and Sindh) and the thorny issue of evacuee property. It is with these themes that this chapter is concerned.

Refugee Rehabilitation and the Predicament of Minorities

The movement of people across the border between India and Pakistan was not simply one of the most extraordinary instances of human movement in the twentieth century because of its scale. Though a definitive total is impossible to provide thanks to the massive demographic confusion that Partition produced, an estimated fourteen to sixteen million people sought to cross the hastily delineated borders in what remains arguably the largest migration in history. In the north-west, the Grand Trunk Road together with the railway built alongside it became major arteries along which huge numbers of these refugees travelled. Further south, people crossed the Rajasthan border into and out of Sindh or travelled by ship between the port cities of Bombay and Karachi. In divided Bengal, refugees also moved in both directions across the new Indo-Pakistan frontier, though the pattern of migration here was qualitatively different to its western counterpart on account of the more porous nature of this border.[10] Across North India, in both the east and the west, people were on the move during the months surrounding Independence, and this movement continued to ebb and flow in the years that followed.

What marks this enormous human movement out from other comparable mass migrations, apart from its size, are two other features. First was its coincidence with the creation of two independent countries, which meant that the movement, displacement and rehabilitation of migrants became an integral part of the wider process of formal citizenship definition.[11] Second, and perhaps of greater significance for our discussion, were the ways in which not only movement but anticipation of movement conferred on people the status of belonging and generated ideas about rights. So, before an individual or family had even decided or started to

---

[10] For a study of the rich literature that has been spawned through the historical imagination of Bengali-speaking writers in West Bengal and Bangladesh through issues of homelessness, migration and exile, which highlights how the Partition of Bengal in 1947 has thrown a long shadow over memories and cultural practices there, see Debjani Sengupta, *The Partition of Bengal: Fragile Borders and New Identities* (Cambridge: Cambridge University Press, 2015).

[11] For the clearest study of this process to date, see Joya Chatterji, 'South Asian Histories of Citizenship, 1946–1970', *The Historical Journal* 55, 4 (December 2012), pp. 1049–71.

migrate from either India or Pakistan, they could be marked out as potential citizens of the other, and hence no longer living in the right place or deemed to possess the rights that came with being categorized as either Indian or Pakistani. This presumption did not only exist in government ordinances – rapidly constructed to deal with the exchange of populations – it was also embedded in wider public political discourse. Clearly a product of the massive refugee rehabilitation process, it was linked to the pressing need to solve the problem of property and property rights, such as how to decide what happened to the homes and other buildings owned by those assumed to have transferred their loyalties across the border, whether or not they had actually left. The implications surrounding the idea of 'intending evacuees' were far-reaching. On the one hand, conceptual connections were made between India's and Pakistan's jurisdictional spaces and the notion of the citizen in both countries. On the other, associated ideas of 'minority loyalty' were also in tension, if not contradiction, with the unfolding rights of citizenship contained within the constitutional documents of both India and Pakistan as these materialized in the decade following Independence.

In exploring these processes, historical focus has been on the main regions of refugee movement and settlement, especially around the main cities in divided Punjab and Bengal, which has brought its own limitations. As Gyanendra Pandey emphasized more than two decades ago in his pioneering exploration of developments in Delhi in 1947–8, the city did 'not represent all of India'. For him, it made 'no sense to try to speak of India as a whole in any summary way'. Rather his focus on one locale, he argued, allowed him 'to speak in relatively concrete terms, ... because – for a variety of reasons – Delhi reflected in concentrated form several tendencies that were at work in other parts of the subcontinent too in 1947'.[12] In the years since Pandey justified linking the local with the national, and in the process highlighted the wider significance of Delhi's transformation into a 'refugee-istan', extensive research has been conducted on the nature of Partition migration and associated 'Relief and Rehabilitation' efforts in relation to how this upheaval affected the former British India provinces of the Punjab and Bengal in particular.[13]

---

[12] Gyanendra Pandey, 'Partition and Independence in Delhi: 1947–1948', *Economic and Political Weekly* 32, 36 (6–12 September 1997), p. 2262.

[13] See, for instance, Vazira Zamindar, *The Long Partition and the Making of Modern South Asia: Refugees, Boundaries, Histories, Cultures of History* (New York: Columbia University Press, 2007); Ravinder Kaur, *Since 1947: Partition Narratives among Punjabi Migrants of Delhi* (New Delhi: Oxford University Press, 2007); Uditi Sen, 'Refugees and the Politics of Nation Building in India, 1947–1971' (unpublished PhD dissertation, University of Cambridge, 2009); and Haimanti Roy, *Partitioned Lives: Migrants, Refugees, Citizens in*

But both UP in India and Sindh in Pakistan remain less well-known localities in this respect, despite offering rich opportunities for exploring Indo–Pakistani interactions in this period.

Both regions were pivotally important to the politics of refugees. UP, after all, was the key point of origin for some of the most influential Muslim migrants to Pakistan as well as large numbers of Urdu-speaking refugees (known as *muhajirs*) who headed for the province of Sindh where Pakistan's capital city Karachi was located. Moving in the other direction, Sindhi Hindus were certainly among the best-organized migrants to make their new homes in UP. While UP was not required to accommodate the same quantity of refugees as Indian Punjab, its status as arguably India's politically most important constituent state-unit (and certainly its largest in terms of population[14]) meant that it provided a highly symbolic 'test area' for how refugee rehabilitation might be effective more generally. Likewise, while Sindhi Muslims were marginalized within Pakistan's new political establishment, the fact remained that Karachi was now the federal capital and so many of the broader debates about refugees and matters concerning their relief and rehabilitation centred on this city and its hinterland. In other words, though their shares of the overall refugee population may have been smaller in numerical terms than those of the Punjab and Bengal, UP and Sindh provided the major contexts within which many of the anxieties generated by Partition later came to be discussed and played out.

When exploring the massive range of documents generated by Partition, what is immediately striking are the extraordinary and complex connections between the rapidly changing decisions of government and the lives of those either migrating or living in areas of mass migration. At the same time, as other historians have noted,[15] available written sources reveal a vast but important dichotomy between government statements and resolutions – the rhetoric of the central governments of India and Pakistan (and indeed their provincial or state governments too) and the reality on the ground. One of the most important instances of this dichotomy surrounded post-Partition reconstruction, and, in particular,

India and Pakistan, 1947–1965 (New Delhi: Oxford University Press, 2012). The last is a focussed study of developments relating to the two Bengals in the wake of Independence and Partition.

[14] According to the 2011 Indian Census, UP's population of 199,281,477 represented 16.49 per cent of the population of the country as a whole and it was the largest Indian state in terms of population. See www.census2011.co.in/states.php (accessed December 2018).

[15] See, for instance, Yasmin Khan, *The Great Partition: The Making of India and Pakistan* (London: Yale University Press, 2007).

the idea of relational minority safeguards. Indeed, this issue had lain at the very root of some of the earliest negotiations surrounding the division of British India into two or more separate independent countries. Sometimes referred to as the 'hostage theory', the idea that each new dominion would trade the safeguards of its minorities with the other was part of the Muslim League's fundamental strategy and found a place in the 1940 Lahore (or Pakistan) Resolution.[16] After Independence, this understanding was formalized in the India–Pakistan agreement of 19 April 1948 at the Inter-Dominion Conference held in Calcutta, according to which each was required to protect its own minorities. In implementing minority safeguards, the agreement presupposed that the important areas of contention in minority-rights protection would lie in the actions of local officers, recommending that:

The two dominions and their provincial governments shall declare and make it widely known to their officers and other employees that any government servant proved to have been guilty either of dereliction of duty in protecting the lives and properties of the members of the minority community, or of directly or indirectly ill-treating the members of the minority community, or showing prejudice against the minority community in the discharge of duties, shall receive exemplary and deterrent punishment.[17]

It detailed how adequate steps should be taken to remove discrimination in the grant of export licenses and railway priorities, or to remove the tendencies towards economic boycott. It also dealt with the issue of refugee property and of refugees, which by early 1948 had revealed itself as a problem that was unlikely to be resolved without some kind of coordination of this kind.[18]

The influx of refugees to UP from places that would later become Pakistan had begun on a large scale from as early as the end of February 1947. The first rush went to Saharanpur (a major railway junction) and Dehradun, and many were accommodated in *dharamshalas* and *gurdwaras*. The pressure on the city of Hardwar in the north-west of what was still then called the United Provinces was particularly heavy, resulting in a need for the Rampur camp to make space, by the end of 1948, for thousands of extra individuals. By June 1947, 5,000 refugees had already arrived, triggering instructions to Town Rationing Officers (TROs) and

---

[16] Ayesha Jalal, *The Sole Spokesman: Jinnah, the Muslim League and the Demand for Pakistan* (Cambridge: Cambridge University Press, 1985).

[17] 'Each Dominion to Protect Its Own Minorities – Abolition of Barriers against Food Movements Recommended – India Pakistan Agreement at Calcutta', *National Herald*, 20 April 1948.

[18] Ibid.

to District Refugee Officers to manage the newcomers. Over the summer of 1947, the inflow rapidly increased. In August 1947, 45,000 arrived, and in September another 70,000, inflating the total to around 200,000 by the end of that month. The peak month proved to be January 1948, when 74,000 crossed over. By April 1948, the total had reached around 450,000. This mass migration of displaced persons into UP led directly to the promulgation of an ordinance for the registration of refugees,[19] a process that had the effect of actually encouraging further migrants who perceived this move as a means by which provinces would take responsibility for rehabilitation. Eventually, as well as those formally recognized as refugees, an additional 150,000 'unregistered' new arrivals made their way there.[20]

The situation on the ground in Sindh turned out to be very similar in terms of scale, if not timing; refugees only started arriving there in sizeable numbers in the run-up to Independence. But in July 1948, the Pakistan–Sind Joint Refuge Council reported that more than 700,000 Muslim refugees had entered the province since the previous August. Nearly 75 per cent of these had congregated in Karachi, while the remainder were mostly to be found in Sindh's larger towns, with only a small proportion – some 60,000 – in the countryside.[21] By 1951 (the time of Pakistan's first national census), with communal disturbances in northern India adding another influx of around 80,000 refugees, Karachi's population had more than doubled to just over one million.[22] This expansion was generating a myriad of practical problems in a city not designed to accommodate such numbers: according to a statement issued in August 1950 by Pakistan's Ministry for Refugees and Rehabilitation,

the entire administrative machinery, whether in respect of sanitation and public health or water supply or housing [has been] put out of gear. What makes the problem still more complicated is that this surplus is not static, but is continually and rapidly increasing.[23]

In India, in contrast to the pronouncements made by politicians at the centre, there was little discussion of active measures at the state level to

[19] 'Resume of the Activities of the Refugee Department' in 'Refugee Standing Committee Proceedings', Relief and Rehabilitation, Box 23, File 341/48 UPSA.
[20] Ibid.
[21] K. R. Sipe, 'Karachi's refugee crisis: the political, economic and social consequences of partition-related migration' (unpublished PhD, Duke University, 1976), p. 252.
[22] Ibid., pp. 134–7.
[23] 'Statement by Refugee Minister on Refugee Problem', 10 August 1950, 890D.411/8-1050 United States National Archives (hereafter USNA).

protect minorities or to implement the reciprocal aspects of the agreement even in the local legislative assemblies. With the return to India in March 1948 of a sizeable number of Muslims who had initially left UP during the Partition violence, Mahavir Tyagi, a member of the right wing of the UP Congress,[24] issued a press statement in Lucknow. For Tyagi, Hindus from Pakistan continued to possess the right to take refuge in North India. They had not been, he argued, a willing party to Partition. On the other hand, as a secular state, while India might have a 'duty' to Muslims, evidently there was 'no space for all of these [returning] people'. Therefore, for Tyagi, Pakistan should either cede to India some districts of the Punjab to provide that badly needed extra space or agree to rehabilitate some of these returning Muslims.[25] Tyagi's call for action was representative of both a popular response among some Indians to Pakistani migrants[26] and a powerful section of the central and provincial government of the time.[27] It was a position also taken in the context of the dissolution of the main political party of the Muslims in UP – the Muslim League – as we will see later in this chapter.

Official messages that addressed the issue of refugees, however, were more cautious and proved to be much the same in Pakistan as well as India. State-level and provincial authorities, on both sides of the border, released carefully tailored publicity at regular intervals about what was being done for refugees,[28] especially where property acquisition and redistribution was complicated by the more informal, and sometimes illegal, activities of refugee societies and associations.[29] In an article published in the press under the banner heading 'More than 20,000 Refugees Already resettled in UP', the UP Rehabilitation Minister Govind Sahai, for instance, announced in early January 1948 that more than 20,000 refugees had already been settled in his particular state

---

[24] See William Gould, *Hindu Nationalism and the Language of Politics in Late Colonial India* (Cambridge: Cambridge University Press, 2010), chapter IV.

[25] 'India Bound Movement of Muslims: Tyagi's Warning to Government', *National Herald*, 12 April 1948.

[26] This sentiment was expressed in the Hindi press's reaction to the return migration of 'disappointed' Muslims, see 'Pakistan Musulmanon ka ghar', *Aaj*, 3 January 1948.

[27] India's first Home Minister, Vallabhai Patel, as we saw in Chapter 1, had also famously expressed the need for Muslims to demonstrate their loyalty to the Indian state.

[28] See, for instance, the Proceedings of Relief and Rehabilitation Committees, in 'Construction of Small and Pucca Shops in Parts of Lucknow', Relief and Rehabilitation, Box 40, File 213/49 UPSA. These files discussed amounts budgeted for rehabilitation but without a discussion of the results of such expenditure or its relative scale.

[29] Secretary of the Lahore Refugee Society, Agra – Dewan Hukum Chand to Chief Secr. UP, 'Construction at Agra', 14 January 1952, Relief and Rehabilitation, Box 45, File 13 (6)/51 UPSA.

alone. During the following year, or so he claimed, the UP government looked set to spend Rs. 2 *crores* (20 million) on rehabilitation, and he proceeded to outline the various schemes that it had inaugurated, arguing that 20,000–25,000 of the new arrivals had successfully secured industrial employment.[30] The UP government similarly publicized the extent to which it went to establish a separate colony for refugees in Allahabad, adding that it would advance Rs. 1.5 *lakhs* (150,000) to support further schemes of this kind.[31] Radha Kant, UP's Director of Resettlement and Employment, reported in mid-April 1948 that thus far 150,000 ex-servicemen and civilians had been registered with employment exchanges and 28,000 provided with employment. Likewise, 2,650 refugees had been absorbed into the services.[32] As 'a step towards ameliorating the hardship of refugees', the UP government relaxed the maximum age limit by four years to twenty-seven for the civil service judicial branch examination.[33] Given the scale of the problem – there were around 600,000 refugees present in UP by mid-1948 – these initiatives were relatively limited in scope. It took until July 1948 for a Rehabilitation Finance Administration to come into existence, and housing remained in short supply, with the UP authorities themselves admitting that about 300,000 refugees (or 60,000 families) would not be accommodated by formal rehabilitation in housing.[34]

It was much the same story in Sindh – albeit with its own local twist on developments – which experienced a complex combination of political and economic knock-on effects of movement on this massive scale. While the volume of migrants heading to the province was considerably smaller than either the numbers going to West Punjab or to East Bengal, their local impact was disproportionately boosted by the fact that Karachi, Pakistan's new capital, was located there.[35] By September 1947, the city contained some 10,000 refugees, the majority housed in three huge camps, and so – with tensions rising – the provincial authorities that month passed the Sind Maintenance of Public Safety Ordinance, ostensibly to protect minority interests.[36] In actual fact, the legislation served

---

[30] *National Herald*, 12 April 1948.   [31] Ibid.   [32] *National Herald*, 18 April 1948.
[33] 'Another Concession to Refugees', *National Herald*, 16 April 1948.
[34] 'Resume of the Activities of the Refugee Department' in 'Refugee Standing Committee Proceedings', Relief and Rehabilitation, Box 23, File 341/48 UPSA.
[35] It should be noted that while Karachi was detached from the province of Sindh in 1948 and turned into a separate Federal Capital Territory, it remained the biggest urban centre in the locality, and hence acted as a magnet drawing refugees to this part of Pakistan. See Sarah Ansari, *Life after Partition: Migration, Community and Strife in Sindh, 1947–1962* (Karachi: Oxford University Press, 2005), chapter 1.
[36] 'Promulgation of Sind Maintenance of Public Safety Ordinance 1947', Despatch 206, 23 September 1947, 845F.00/9-2347 USNA.

only to heighten minority concerns, and the number of non-Muslims seeking to leave for India rocketed upwards. Some 50,000 registered with local Congress organizations for travel assistance, provoking reactions that ranged from claims that this was all part of 'a well organised plan to cripple Pakistan' to the solemn reiteration of earlier promises to protect the place of minorities within the new country.[37] Sindh Chief Minister M. A. Khuhro, however, adopted a particularly hard line, publicly denouncing the desire of Hindus and Sikhs to leave and threatening that if they chose to go then they would be allowed to take very few possessions with them.[38] Following a relatively rare outbreak of communal violence in January 1948 involving migrants arriving in and leaving the city, the exodus picked up momentum, drawing in up-country Hindus as well as others based closer to Karachi and prompting steps by the provincial authorities to stem the outward flow: confidential orders were issued allowing non-Muslims to leave only if they were in possession of a special permit from their district magistrate and could produce income tax certificates to prove that they had no outstanding public debts.[39] These moves proved futile, and by March more than 50,000 a week were departing by sea for Indian ports, while others made the trip by train.[40]

Meanwhile, official publications boldly proclaimed the efforts being expended by the Pakistani authorities, at the centre and at a provincial level, to deal with the refugee crisis. In Sindh, as elsewhere in Pakistan, the way in which the authorities approached and handled space for migrants was inevitably influenced by the broader administrative and political framework within which these processes took place. An All-Pakistan Joint Refugees Council was established at the end of 1947 to synchronize the undertakings of its provincial counterparts. A central ministry coordinated provincial refugee rehabilitation efforts, while the Quaid-i-Azam Relief Fund provided a centralized structure for coordinating the various provincial, central and private relief agencies that had mushroomed since Independence.[41] Another initiative was the Pakistan Refugee Rehabilitation Finance Corporation, set up in 1948 with Rs. 1

---

[37] 'Refugee Problem in Pakistan', Despatch 141, 22 September 1947, 845.00/9-2247, USNA. 'Refugee Situation in Pakistan', Despatch 177, 13 October 1947, 845F.00/10-1327 USNA.

[38] The Chief Secretary to the Sindh government even resigned in protest at Khuhro's very public contradiction of earlier assurances that the rights of minorities would be respected, see Despatch 29, 15 September 1947, 845F.00/9-1547 USNA.

[39] UK High Commission Opdom 8, 15–21 January 1948, IOR L/WS/1/1599 British Library (hereafter BL).

[40] Despatch 244, 18 March 1948, 845.00/3-1848 USNA.

[41] 'Facts and Figures on Refugee Relief and Rehabilitation', 19 October 1950, 890D.411/10-1950 USNA.

crore to invest. Among the refugee projects helped in different parts of Sindh were those involving refugee shoemakers (who had clustered in the newly constructed Nazimabad district of Karachi), glass-bangle produces (from Firozabad in western UP) and migrant blanket-makers in Sukkur.[42] Attempts to set up cottage industries that might provide female refugees with sources of income also attracted much press coverage together with the moral backing of prominent Pakistani women such as Fatima Jinnah and Raana Liaquat Ali Khan. The effectiveness of these rehabilitation efforts, however, was often disputed by contemporaries, some with their own axes to grind. In April 1949, for instance, the then central minister for refugees and rehabilitation, Khwaja Shahabuddin, accused the Sindh provincial administration of obstructing his rehabilitation programme, claiming that

in certain areas, Government officials and local people intentionally put spanners across the progress of rehabilitation work. In many districts and talukas, local officials [have] cold-shouldered the refugees and shown much indifference in making allotments, thereby causing a lot of unrest among refugees ... The refugees are anxious to be able to stand on their own legs, but this is not possible unless they are given their due.[43]

Corresponding propaganda about refugee rehabilitation in UP was reasonably effective given the evident problems of nationally organized rehabilitation attempts undertaken during this same period. Indeed, the view from Delhi was far from rosy: on 5 January 1948 the police resorted to using tear gas to disperse a crowd of refugees who had recently arrived from West Punjab and which had gathered in Khari Baoli to take forcible possession of houses in Phatak Habish Khan vacated by Muslims.[44] In April 1948, the reported scenes at Chandni Chowk of increasing numbers of street hawkers, and overcrowded properties, were supplemented by Nehru's announcement that the city could not possibly absorb any more refugees and that the country had already taken in five *lakhs* since Partition.[45] These words of caution echoed statements by Khuhro in Karachi who earlier that year had already sought to limit – on the grounds that 'for every one Hindu that [*sic*] has left, two Muslims have come in'[46] – the arrival of further incomers.[47] But the combination of events at these two scales of nation and province contributed to calls to

[42] 'Development of Industries', Despatch 46, 8 July 1950, 890D.19/7-850 USNA.
[43] *Dawn*, 22 April 1949.   [44] Ibid.
[45] 'Delhi Overflowing with Refugees. City Can Take No More', *National Herald*, 6 April 1948.
[46] *Dawn*, 18 January 1948.
[47] For more details, see Sarah Ansari, 'Partition, Migration and Refugees: Responses to the Arrival of *Muhajirs* in Sind after 1947', in *Freedom, Trauma, Continuities: Northern India*

seize and make use of empty properties for incoming refugees in both places. Consequently, ministries across North India were given great public support for policies of evacuee property acquisition. This was perhaps most starkly emphasized in a newspaper article arguing for the allotment of the (empty) house of Jinnah to a refugee, which premised that equivalent large houses had been left vacant in Karachi and allotted to incoming migrants.[48]

It was this context – the problems of using property and space for rehabilitation, and a public awareness that the 'refugee situation' appeared increasingly chaotic – that contributed to the problematic and uneven shape of citizenship rights for UP's remaining Muslim communities. And this took place whether or not they had any connection to Pakistan or had any intention to migrate there. Simply being Muslim in parts of North India, and in most instances living in Muslim neighbourhoods where some families may have left (especially in cities and often for reasons of security) undermined presumptions that they should be automatically viewed as full rights-bearing citizens. As we will see below and in other chapters, despite the nature of uniform rights granted in India's Constitution, this situation created an unevenness in citizenship that required some groups to volunteer expressions of loyalty and to assert rights. For others, such rights were automatic and hence invisible. This contingency and unevenness or rights conferral was to have extensive implications for how other groups protected and promoted their rights, especially for groups whose situation placed them on the margins of majoritarian expectations of the citizen. At one level, the supposition about individual, family and community intentions of Muslims in North India was a product of the rehabilitation crisis. The drive to accommodate Hindu and Sikh migrants from Pakistan became tangled up with the identification of 'intending evacuees' to Pakistan, which was both a formal and informal categorization. However, in juxtaposing official with popular and organization-based documents, the predicament of UP Muslims (like Muslims in India more generally) was also moulded by changing political circumstances, and the expression of public opinion about minorities.

Disputes associated with the vexed question of refugee rehabilitation raised questions about where the loyalties of minorities lay, as testified by lengthy discussions in Pakistani and Indian newspapers alike.[49] Complex negotiations over evacuee status in which the letter of the law could be

---

and Independence, eds. D. A. Low and Howard Brasted (Armidale: Sage, 1998), pp. 91–105.
[48] *National Herald*, 4 April 1948.   [49] *Dawn*, 13 June 1952.

arbitrarily applied on the ground led to a particularly precarious position for minorities, and especially those viewed as potential migrants. In Indian states such as UP, this position changed over time, and particularly hardened in the late summer of 1948, following the reverse migration of Muslims back to India: in August 1948, the UP Refugee Department responded by suggesting that the words of the UP Evacuees Administration of Property Act 1948, viz., 'or intending to depart' should replace the existing 'or is preparing to depart', and that its coverage should be stricter so as to include those Muslims who had returned after leaving on temporary permits.[50]

But such problems did not exist in a vacuum in either country. The public sphere of discussion about refugees contrasted the movement and the plight of refugees. In Indian newspapers, the large-scale traffic of refugees from Sindh[51] was placed directly alongside reports on the restrictions of sales of Muslim property. To take just one instance, in Saharanpur in West UP the district magistrate issued an order in April 1948 restricting Muslims from selling or letting to a non-Muslim any property, whether movable or immovable, situated within the district except under prior permission from the district magistrate. The order was set out in highly legalistic language, being reported as 'under Section 144 Cr PC'.[52] The personal experiences of refugees were also juxtaposed against the allegedly harsh treatment of evacuees leaving Pakistan for India, and the possibility of retribution by search officers of Muslims. Such articles and reports delved into the very personal world of migrants' everyday 'personal effects' in the search by officers for arms.[53]

This public sphere of debate about refugees and migrants on the two sides of the border had its starting point in inherent assumptions that each country had about the other. In reporting on refugee issues, the Indian press commonly commented on the situation in Pakistan as part of a trans-Hindu idea of community sympathy. For Pakistani newspapers, Muslims in India were equally members of a bigger transnational community of believers, and by implication potential Pakistanis. Reports in India at the end of December 1947 showed how the Karachi Congress

---

[50] 'Memorandum of the First Meeting of the Prov Legislature for the Refugee Department', 30–31 August 1948, in 'Refugee Standing Committee Proceedings', Relief and Rehabilitation, Box 23, File 341/48 UPSA.

[51] '3000 Non-Muslims Being Evacuated from Sind Every Day', *National Herald*, 10 April 1948. See also, 'Tees hazaar hindu sharannarthee ke Karachi mein sthiti gammir', *Aaj*, 2 January 1948.

[52] *National Herald*, 10 April 1948.

[53] 'Searches of Persons Leaving Sind', *National Herald*, 7 January 1948.

Committee was alarmed about what it viewed as the indiscriminate allotment and requisitioning of houses under the Rent Control Act and the 'wrongful making over' of running business concerns to Muslim refugees under Pakistan's Rehabilitation Ordinance. The Congress Committee had apparently 'condemned the fact that Hindus have to stay in their own houses locked up for fear of their appropriation'; and denounced 'the omnibus form that has to be filled', which asked about their income tax, value of property and reasons for why they should not be ejected.[54]

The problem of accommodating refugees, and its attendant public discussion, had its effect too on provincial governments. In India, it pushed the UP government towards a hard policy vis-à-vis ambiguous cases of Muslim evacuee property in certain instances, although this was sometimes encouraged by central policies. By the summer of 1949, official policy in UP, influenced by the centre, was to not allow individual members of families to hold onto properties when the rest of the family had migrated; if Muslims had, while in Pakistan, acquired property there, they should be assumed to be evacuees from India, even if they had returned.[55] By then, the issue of temporary permits to Muslims who wished to 'return' to India were used as a mechanism for marking them as 'intending' and eventually permanent 'evacuees'. Officers in the central government advised provinces like UP on how to expedite the control of their properties:

... we want to be fair in the administration of the law. We have no intention of penalising the Muslim nationals of India. But the Pakistan Muslims cannot be treated leniently. If the District Officer, after making summary enquiries, is morally convinced that a person is an evacuee as defined by the law, that person's property must be taken over . We do not want long drawn out legal proceedings, and have, for that reason, cut out all interference by the courts. If we ourselves start entrusting the administration of the law not to administrators, but to judicial officers, we shall be defeating the purpose of the Ordinance. Apart from peculation and corruption that will spring up, proof will be exceedingly difficult ... We can't allow people to just turn up and claim that they are not evacuees but loyal Indian citizens, as has happened in Delhi. If he is not here, he cannot turn up, and that is the best proof of his being an evacuee and his property being evacuee property.[56]

[54] 'Karachi Hindus Internees in the Homes: Terror of Forcible Occupation', *National Herald*, 1 January 1948.

[55] Notes from the discussion by Shri R. P. Varma with the Custodian General, Relief and Rehabilitation (A), Box 41, File 553/49 UPSA.

[56] V. D. Dantyagi to Bhagwan Sahay, 'Administration of Evacuee Property in UP', 27 August 1949, Relief and Rehabilitation, Box 41, File 552/49 UPSA.

There were, however, two further complications in UP, which illustrated the gulf between formal policy and quotidian realities. On the one hand, the practical implementation of evacuee property ordinances meant discrimination towards claims on the basis of religion – with Muslims being automatically required to *prove* that they were not evacuees. A notification was established, preventing sale of properties, which clearly targeted Muslims. Here there was clear disagreement in the Central government between two secretaries, V. D. Dantyagi and C. N. Chandra, on how this should be interpreted. The latter took a relatively liberal approach as we will see below. In contrast, Dantyagi suggested to provincial governments that 'notifications may be issued under this Section prohibiting transfers of immovable property without the prior consent of the Collector in areas where a good deal of Muslim property is situated'. Permission could certainly be granted by the Collector as a matter of course where the seller was a non-Muslim. But where the seller was a Muslim it was necessary 'to investigate the facts ... to see whether the sale is being effected with a view to migrate to Pakistan or transfer the sale proceeds to that Country'.[57] Such an approach was, however, ultra vires of section 298 of the (then) Constitution Act, which stated that no distinction could be made between various nationals on the ground of religion or place of birth and so forth. These particular observations, ironically, were made in a file entitled 'issue of notification banning transfer of immovable property of *Muslims* [italics added]'.[58] On the other hand, in truth, the administration of property, its sale and claims to its possession was extraordinarily messy and open to abuse. The UP Custodian of Evacuee Property summed up the difficulties of implementing what he termed a 'fair' approach:

From the administrative point of view it is quite impossible to subject the entire population of the United Provinces to the rigours of section 26 notification which will require every person transferring immovable property to obtain a certificate from the District Magistrate. Floodgates of corruption will be opened, there would be endless cases of delays and the public already harassed with the interference of State in so many aspects of life will consider all this another source of harassment.[59]

As this comment suggests, there certainly was scope to get around the changing rules on evacuee property, particularly since proceedings under

---

[57] V. D. Dantyagi to Chief Secretaries to Provincial Governments, 'Issue of Notification Banning Transfer of Immovable Property of Muslims', 26 July 1949, Relief and Rehabilitation Department, Box 40, File 514/49 UPSA.

[58] Note of 21/9/49, 'Issue of Notification Banning Transfer of Immovable Property of Muslims', Relief and Rehabilitation Department, ibid.

[59] Note of 22 September 1949, ibid.

the evacuee property ordinance were not declared as 'judicial' and therefore often under the executive authority of individual officers. Moreover,
such was the scale of work involved that, by mid-1949, the Refugee
Department in UP reported that it was unable to cope, with some
officers reportedly unable to understand the provisions of the UP Land
Acquisition (Rehabilitation and Refugees) Act of 1948.[60] Reports from
refugee organizations and their sponsors poured in to the authorities,
for instance from the Sindhi Panchayat in western UP, alleging that
Muslims were continuing to dispose of property 'illegally'. Meanwhile,
the district magistrates of areas not originally included in the notification of control of properties also called for inclusion, suggesting that the
personal views and opinions of individual administrators could deter-
mine the scope and reach of the policy and its effects on Muslims. For
instance, J. N. Goel, Budaun's district magistrate, argued that there
were 'many Muslim properties' in his district and that many of the
families had 'connections in Pakistan'.[61] Naturally, it was possible for
those with the right connections then to influence the mind of officers.
C. N. Chandra, secretary to the Government in Delhi, described one
such process:

a practice appears to have grown up in some places of the parties to an enquiry
under the evacuee legislation bringing letters either from office holders or well-
known public organizations or from other highly placed gentlemen, addressed
to the officer holding the enquiry or an officer to whom an appeal from the
decision of the enquiring officer will lie, containing statement of fact or
expressions of opinion having a direct or indirect bearing on the subject
matter of the enquiry. Although in most cases the writers of these letters
themselves possibly do not mean it, there can be little doubt that the party
who secures such letters wants them to influence the judgement of the officer to
whom they are addressed.[62]

Equally, the plight of new refugees in some of the major UP towns did
not necessarily fit neatly into existing rehabilitation plans. In early 1950,
observers, such as Prakashvati Sood from Meerut, reported that newcomers were often not welcome, since they were held responsible for
disturbing the 'peace and business' of the town.[63] Refugees often

---

[60] 'Staff PLAO Lucknow', Relief and Rehabilitation, Box 20, File 299 (5)/48 UPSA.
[61] J. N. Goel, district magistrate and deputy custodian, Budaun District to Secretary to
Government, R and R (a) UP, 18 August 1949, Relief and Rehabilitation Department,
Box 40, File 514/49 UPSA.
[62] C. N. Chandra, Secretary to Government of India to Chief Secretaries All Prov.
Governments, 12 September 1949, ibid.
[63] 'Standing Committee – Relief and Rehabilitation Dept., 5th Meeting on September 30
1950', Relief and Rehabilitation, Box 54, File 154/50 UPSA.

attempted to negotiate rents down, the construction of houses through cooperative societies was not very successful, refugee loans were being 'misused'[64] and when facilities and settlements began to fill up in western UP, there was a general resistance on the part of refugees to move to districts in the east of the province.[65]

The same kind of official announcements about policies towards refugee rehabilitation were issued in Pakistan, though often rebutted by groups representing refugee interests, whose complaints were given publicity in the pro-refugee press. Numerous instances dating from the late 1940s provide an indication of the extent of frustration there with the state's failure to accommodate refugee demands. In many of them, the position of the refugees concerned was framed in relation to non-Muslims whether the latter had left for India or remained in Pakistan. Accommodation there, as in UP, was a recurrent source of complaint: as one report complaining about the allotment of evacuee property in Karachi asserted, 'Thousands of premises have been vacated by Hindu evacuees since January 6th [1948]. But the officers of the Rehabilitation Department and the rent controller have been evading to allot them [sic] to the refugees and the government servants', resulting in 'Hardships to Refugees'.[66] And when property had been allotted, grievances did not necessarily cease. In 1949, the Hyderabad district magistrate informed refugees under his jurisdiction that they were 'not liable' to pay the arrears of the electricity charges due from their allotted property's former Hindu occupants: 'In connection with the representation made by the present Muslim occupants of the Hindu evacuee houses, that the Hyderabad (Sind) Electric Supply Company were recovering arrears due from the evacuee Hindus, from them, Government have declared such recoveries unlawful'.[67] The same went for employment. Under a headline that asserted that 'Muslims [are] still being replaced by Hindus in Sind Schools', refugees in Larkhana, Upper Sindh, pointed out the 'glaring instance' of its Government High School: 'In this institution 23 Muslim refugee teachers had been appointed of which only three are left. All the remaining have been replaced by Hindu teachers who have been imported back to Sind, many without their families'.[68]

---

[64] Ibid.
[65] 'Proceedings of the Meeting of the Standing Committee, Relief and Rehabilitation Department, Council House, Lucknow, September 3, 1949'.
[66] *Dawn*, 9 March 1948.   [67] *Dawn*, 10 April 1949.   [68] *Dawn*, 23 October 1948.

Representing Refugees/Demonizing Minorities

For those with the financial, organizational or social connections, there were certainly means by which new arrivals in India or Pakistan could further their interests. Among other strategies, the plight of refugees was, as others have shown in different contexts,[69] represented to higher echelons of government by deputations of refugee organizations in both India and Pakistan. For instance, in the first week of January 1948, a deputation of refugees from Lucknow travelled to meet Patel in Delhi to present a range of demands, which included complaints about the inadequacy of government loans for starting small businesses.[70] Deputations were also an effective way of drawing attention to the difficulties faced by refugees in Pakistan as well as highlighting what they expected of the state and its representatives. Karachi, as home to the federal authorities, was the main centre of this activity, and a steady stream of deputations made their way to the offices and homes of leading politicians located there. In late April 1948, for instance, a group of representatives of the Jamiat-i-Muhajireen in Pakistan, headed by the leading refugee cleric Maulana Shabir Ahmad Usmani, handed over a detailed memorandum on refugee problems to the prime minister. Apart from wanting to be recognized as the 'sole refugee organization for Pakistan' that would advise on 'all activities of the Government in connection with the refugees', it demanded that the entire complement of houses, land, shops and other property left by Hindus be reserved for refugees, who would also take the place of Hindus in representative bodies, from local district councils to the highest legislature of the land. In response, Liaquat Ali Khan assured the deputation's members that their recommendations and suggestions would be given full consideration by his government.[71]

Local community groups likewise often made their feelings known through written petitions. In July 1952, residents of the Pakistan Housing Colony in Karachi did precisely this when they submitted an impassioned memorandum to the Pakistani prime minister drawing his attention to deplorable conditions prevailing there. As this explained, if no effective measures were taken by the authorities immediately, then some 13,000 refugees would be forced to leave their new homes: 'Walls and

---

[69] See, for instance, Zamindar, *The Long Partition*; Uditi Sen, 'Dissident Memories: Exploring Bengali Refugee Narratives in the Andaman Islands', in *Refugees and the End of Empire: Imperial Collapse and Forced Migration during the Twentieth Century*, eds. Panikos Panayi and Pippa Virdee (London: Palgrave Macmillan, 2011), pp. 219–44; Uditi Sen, *Citizen Refugee: Forging the Indian Nation after Partition* (Cambridge: Cambridge University Press, 2018).

[70] *National Herald*, 8 January 1948.   [71] *Dawn*, 1 May 1948.

roofs [had] started cracking soon after they were built because of rotten material used by the company responsible for construction. ... There [had been] no arrangements so far for construction of sanitation' and the colony was 'developing fast into a new slum'.[72]

But responses varied in terms of the vocal support from politicians that such petitions secured. In Pakistan, during the years immediately following Independence, the central government was dominated by politicians who had played a leading role in the pre-August 1947 Muslim League and often hailed from places that now lay in India thanks to Partition. Their sympathies at least often tended to lie with refugees and their representatives. It was a different situation at the provincial level, such as in Sindh where ministries fluctuated in terms of their support for central policies on refugee resettlement and rehabilitation. This stance was epitomized by the reluctance of the then chief minister of Sindh Khuhro to accept large numbers of refugees sent southwards from West Punjab in 1948 to relieve pressure on resources there. Later, his administration attempted to deter new refugees from UP from crossing the Indian border in 1952–3.[73]

In UP, meanwhile, the support of politicians for refugee organizations, like those that were active in Sindh, could be linked to underlying ideas and presumptions about emigrants (by and large Muslims) and specifically their place within 'national culture' and Indian citizenship. Central to this process was the dissolution, by May 1948, of the UP Muslim League Parliamentary Board; the end of separate electorates on the basis of religious community and the push by some of the UP Congress leadership, encouraging Muslim leaders to effect a change in 'attitude' of their rank-and-file constituencies.[74] However, this process of 'attitude' change took place in palpable ways around the movement of people across the border and their appeal to the leadership. A crucial figure in this respect was P. D. Tandon, leading politician on the right wing of the Congress. As a leader who linked province to centre (he later became president of the Congress and was a rival to Nehru in 1949–50), Tandon operated as a focal point for the publicity surrounding refugees. For Tandon, assimilation into a high caste majoritarian view of national culture ultimately foregrounded what he believed to be the 'problem' of Pakistan. Tandon, therefore, made for an ideal figure to patronize and support organizations such as the All India Refugee Association (AIRA), a Sindhi-dominated lobbying body active in UP that was headed by

---

[72] *Dawn*, 1 July 1952.   [73] Ansari, 'Partition, Migration and Refugees'.
[74] Gyanesh Kudaisya, *Region, Nation, "Heartland": Uttar Pradesh in India's Body Politic* (New Delhi: Sage, 2006), pp. 362–6.

Choitram P. Gidwani.[75] The AIRA developed out of refugee agitations for compensation, especially via evacuee property, and was galvanized by movements such as the 'Evacuee Property Day' and direct lobbying of the Prime Minister's Office. It regarded Tandon as a prime supporter, and, according to Gidwani, while 'the rehabilitation policy of the Government' was critiqued as 'totally inadequate', Tandon provided hope.[76] The AIRA also sought Tandon's help in rent disputes,[77] and in preventing the recovery of income tax demands issued on Sindhi refugees by the Pakistani authorities.[78] Indeed, Tandon's stance on refugees and Muslim properties was a fundamental dynamic of his dispute with Nehru himself, and the AIRA spared no ire in denouncing Nehru as a man whose 'culture' was Muslim and who showed too much open 'appeasement' of Pakistan.[79] In 1950, the Sindhi Hindu Refugee Panchayat, based in Durgapur Camp, Jaipur, wrote to Tandon for help in preventing Muslims from selling and mortgaging properties in Rajasthan. The Panchayat provided lists of Muslim government servants who had retained properties but migrated, or who had 'deceived refugees'.[80] In 1950, Tandon presided over the All India Refugee Conference in Delhi, at which Gidwani complained of the inadequacy of refugee loans, suggested that evacuee property laws had failed to prevent a 'drain of crores of rupees from India to Pakistan' and charged the Jamiat-ul-Ulama with agitating against the ordinance. Gidwani summed up his list of accusations with the doubt that 'elements returning to India [in the main from Sindh] who have breathed the poisonous atmosphere of Pakistan will ever remain loyal to our country'.[81]

---

[75] Gidwani, who hailed from Mirpurkhas in Lower Sindh, had been president of the Sindh Provincial Congress prior to Independence, and hosted Subhas Chandra Bose on the latter's visit to the province in 1935, just before it separated from Bombay Presidency. See Sidney Sawyier, 'Dail Gidwani – An Odyssey of His Own', *Sindishaan* 6, 4 (October–December 2007), pp. 14–24.

[76] Choitram P. Gidwani, All India Refugee Association to Tandon, 15 January 1951, Tandon Papers, File 183 National Archives of India (hereafter NAI).

[77] Choitram P. Gidwani, All India Refugee Association to Tandon, 23 July 1952, Tandon Papers, File 301 NAI.

[78] Statement of the Displaced Income-tax Payers' Association, New Delhi. Draft Resolutions of the All India Refugee Conference, 29–30 July 1950, Tandon Papers, File 301 NAI.

[79] All India Refugee Conference, 29–30 July 1950, General Comments on the Resolutions, Tandon Papers, File 301 NAI.

[80] From representatives of the Sindhi Hindu Refugee Panchayat, Jaipur, Durgapur Camp, Gopaldas H. Ladhani, Congress Social Worker, to Tandon, 29 January 1950, Tandon Papers, File 301 NAI.

[81] Speech of Dr. Choithram P. Gidwani, Chairman Reception Committee, All India Refugee Conference, Delhi, 29–30 July 1950, Tandon Papers, File 134 NAI.

Other correspondents to Tandon requested help in acquiring evacuee property, such as one P. R. Kishanchand – a self-declared 'man of status' – also originally from Sindh, who wanted assistance with acquiring a shop in Kanpur in 1952;[82] or the District Refugee Corporation in Jhansi that sent a letter of complaint about a rationing officer (B. R. Sharma) and the inadequacy of his call for tenders for evacuee properties.[83] This led to a host of other smaller colonies of displaced persons seeking Tandon's help, including the poorly provisioned Lajpatnagar Panchayat Settlement near Delhi that requested a training or work centre.[84] Supporting Hindu refugee organizations so visibly also meant that Tandon became a forum of partisan complaints about alleged 'Muslim' brutality. His private papers are littered with accounts of such excesses, suggesting that even had he wanted a balanced account of the violence, he was unlikely to have received it.[85] In extension of this patronage, Tandon was targeted by members of the RSS calling to be reinstated in government service following the ban on the organization triggered by Gandhi's assassination, including one missive from a Sindhi migrant looking for work and help for his son who had been jailed as an RSS member.[86] In another appeal letter, contrasts were drawn between the apparent 'tolerance' being shown to 'Pakistani' Muslims as compared to what RSS loyalists were receiving.[87] Others contacting Tandon sought support for their complaints against Muslim government servants in Delhi and UP.[88] Later, Tandon even provided a sympathetic voice for the likes of Baburao Patel, a columnist who wrote a strongly anti-Muslim critique of the Pakistani documentary *Josh-i-Jehad* (The Passion of Religious Crusade) that appeared in *Film India* in March 1952.[89]

Being made Speaker of the UP Assembly in 1948 did not deter Tandon from publicly expressing his views in official settings. If the Socialists supported the language of Hindustani (that incorporated many

---

[82] P. R. Kishanchand to Tandon, 19 December 1952, Tandon Papers, File 128 NAI.
[83] District Refugee Cooperative Society to B. R. Sharma, TRO cum R and R Officer, 9 January 1950, Tandon Papers, File 119 NAI.
[84] Lajpatnagar Panchayat Statement, n.d., Tandon Papers, File 301 NAI.
[85] For instance, Statement of S. S. Bhasin, of district Campbellpur, 22 August 1947 (at present taking shelter under the roof of Arya Samaj, Old Hospital Road, Jammu), Tandon Papers, File 29, NAI. This letter described Hindu deaths near Wazirabad.
[86] L. H. Ajwani, Prof. of English, Sind College, Karachi to Tandon, 21 November 1947, Tandon Papers, File 29 NAI.
[87] S. No. 734, S. C. Sharma, Tundla to Tandon, 24 July 1950, Tandon Papers, File 28 NAI.
[88] 'The responsible citizens of Ghaziabad' to Tandon, 21 September 1947, Tandon Papers, File 29 NAI.
[89] Baburao Patel to M. I. Quadri [*sic*], 24 March 1952, Tandon Papers, File 11 NAI.

Urdu words associated with UP Muslims),[90] he claimed in one public declaration in the spring of 1948, this meant that they backed the Muslim League's Two-Nation theory, which he held responsible for India's Partition. The country's salvation, for Tandon, lay instead in everyone having 'one culture and civilization'. Muslims, therefore, he believed, had to 'own the Indian culture and civilization like they have done in China'. Tandon's view of Hinduism, however, was largely assimilationist and in some ways not dissimilar to the late colonial Hindu revivalist organization, the Arya Samaj in UP. Partition, Tandon told the UP Assembly in 1948, was due to the past sins of Hindus and if they did not open the doors of Hinduism to Muslims, they would experience even worse grief.[91] Earlier at an open session of the Hindi Sahitya Sammelan held in Bombay in December 1947, and attended by among others V. D. Savarkar (former leader of the ultra-nationalist Hindu Mahasabha), Tandon had suggested that there was still an attempt to satisfy Muslims in relation to the national language, and that in the past that British had encouraged the idea that Muslim culture was different. At that same meeting, Seth Govind Das argued that while Muslims were voicing their loyalty to the Indian Union, they continued to follow the same old policy; if they did not want to show loyalty, then they should go to Pakistan.[92]

But it was not just the likes of Tandon and (famously) Patel[93] who picked up on and ran with the theme of Muslim (dis)loyalty in the years following Independence. Demand for loyalty in post-Independence India was a political device. G. B. Pant, in a January 1948 election meeting at Lucknow's famous Aminuduallah Park, proposed that 'if the Muslims persisted in their old ways, a Hindu raj would be inevitable'. Put another way, if Muslims desired to be one with non-Muslims, he

---

[90] For a brief survey of the immediate post-independence promotion of Hindi and the deliberate marginalization of Urdu in UP among ministerial figures including G. B. Pant and Sampurnanand, see Kudaisya, *Region, Nation, "Heartland"*, pp. 368–80. The promotion of Hindustani related to a section of the Hindi Sahitya Sammelan in the late colonial period, who favoured the idea of a national vernacular which embraced vocabulary drawn from Urdu. This group opposed those in the Sammelan, such as Tandon and Sampurnanand who argued for a 'pure' and more sanskritized Hindi. See Francesca Orsini, *The Hindi Public Sphere 1920–1940: Language and Literature in the Age of Nationalism* (Delhi: Oxford University Press, 2009).

[91] 'Maintain Ethical Standard in Elections: Speaker Tandon's Plea', *National Herald*, 20 April 1948.

[92] 'Sammelan Demands Hindi in Devanagri as Lingua Franca', *National Herald*, 1 January 1948.

[93] References to Patel's comments in Lucknow and an accompanying cartoon of him shaking a Muslim whose mouth has been padlocked can be found in *National Herald*, 8 January 1948.

argued, they should vote for the Congress candidate, reiterating the well-established mantra of Muslims having to prove their loyalty and how ultimately they could win over the goodwill of the majority by honestly supporting the Congress.[94] This sort of rhetoric undoubtedly could have an effect on the ground. In Shahjahanpur during district board elections, for instance, Damodar Swarup Seth maintained that villagers were threatened with imprisonment, if they dared to vote for socialists: according to him 'there appeared to be an organized effort in every district by the district authorities through the police and other agencies to threaten the Muslims as a whole that they would be sent to Pakistan if they failed to vote for the Congress candidates'.[95] Unsurprisingly, the General Secretary of the Hindu Mahasabha in Kanpur, Ashutosh Lahiri, contended in a public speech in early 1948 that the loyalty of Union Muslims was still in doubt:[96] and in Bijnor 'it was said that if the Muslims did not vote for the Congress, they would be considered disloyal to the Government', while a parallel situation was reported in Gorakhpur.[97]

The same line of questioning took place in relation to where – territorially – the loyalty of minorities in Pakistan lay after August 1947, amplified by high-profile scandals exposing the allegedly 'treacherous' or anti-state actions of influential or well-placed individuals. In late September 1948, the personal assistant to the then Sindh Chief Minister Pir Ilahi Bux was detained by Karachi Airport Customs as he was about to leave for India by the afternoon Indian National Airways flight to Delhi. Once he had been handed over to the police, reports alleged that Pasaram had been carrying with him confidential documents relating to trucks, motor cars, jeeps, important bridges and other strategic positions that required special defence measures in the province.[98] At a public meeting held in the city's Eidgah Maidan after Friday prayers the following day, a number of refugee speakers – with their own complaints as far as the Sindh political setup was concerned – described the provincial government as the patron of fifth columnists, corrupt officials and murderers, and called upon the federal authorities to take over Sindh's administration immediately.[99] Letters in that day's *Dawn* newspaper also expressed concerns about non-Muslims in other strategic posts in the wake of the Pasaram scandal: 'If Indian Government can make it a matter

[94] 'Vote for Congress Candidate to Prove Your Bona Fides': Pandit Pant's Plea to City's Muslim Electorate', *National Herald*, 8 January 1948.
[95] *National Herald*, 25 April 1948.
[96] 'No Change in Attitude of Union Muslims', *National Herald*, 9 January 1948.
[97] *National Herald*, 19 April 1948.
[98] 'Hindu PA of Sind Premier Arrested at Drigh Road', *Dawn*, 1 October 1948.
[99] 'Taking over of Sind Administration by Centre Demanded', *Dawn*, 5 October 1948.

of policy not to post non-Hindus at key posts, why can't we?', asked one correspondent.[100] *Dawn*, famously pro-refugee and (on the whole) loyal supporter of the central Pakistani authorities, periodically published other reports of non-Muslim officers apparently decamping at short notice to India, along the lines of 'Mr. Govind Ram, Mukhtarkar, at Sukkur, who was entrusted with the distribution of cloth to flood sufferers, it is learnt, suddenly absconded to India on September 2, taking with him a large number of government papers'.[101] This kind of negative coverage prompted at least some Sindhi Hindus to seek to pledge their loyalty publicly to Pakistan. As one such deputation, in its written memorandum presented to the governor of Sindh that same month, explained:

We want to be assimilated in the Pakistan State in a way so that we may cease to be regarded as a minority and live a free and honourable existence [... we] should be permitted to sail in the same boat with the majority so as to sink or swim with them.[102]

Marking Evacuees: Property and Its Control between India and Pakistan

The pivotal 'goods' that underpinned both refugee rehabilitation and the uncertain status of evacuees was property, both housing and business. In UP, much of the tension was linked to property being forcibly removed from Muslim hands, whether its owners had permanently migrated to Pakistan or not.[103] In contrast, in Sindh the problem in late 1947 and early 1948 – from a minority standpoint at least – lay in individuals not being permitted to dispose of property as they wished prior to their scheduled departure to India. But in both localities, as we have already begun to see, property represented a vital transmission mode in the interaction between government action (in the form of ordinances and other legislation) and popular ideas of an individual's 'constitutional' rights.

In UP, there was a fairly rapid turnover of legislation from the 1948 UP Evacuees Administration of Property Act, which applied to sixteen

---

[100] Ibid.
[101] 'Hindu Officer Absconds with Sind Government's Papers and Rs. 70,000', *Dawn*, 26 October 1948.
[102] 'Sind Hindus Pledge Loyalty to Pakistan', *Dawn*, 26 October 1948.
[103] For explorations of what this confiscation meant in relation to people's lives, see Zamindar, *The Long Partition*, and Khan, *The Great Partition*.

districts in the western part of the state,[104] to the 1949 United Provinces Administration of Evacuee Property Ordinance and then the central Administration of Evacuee Property Act of 1950. The 1949 Ordinance, passed early that year, widened the definition of 'intending evacuee' compared with the preceding 1948 Act. By 1949, the designation had expanded to cover the following categories: first, someone who might have left or might leave the Indian Union even without the fear of communal disturbances for any place in Pakistan; second, a person who resided in Pakistan and who was unable personally to manage or supervise his/her property or whose property was being managed by an 'unauthorized person': and third, an acquisition of any interest in property in Pakistan, irrespective of where the person resided. Most notably, the jurisdiction of the civil courts was barred for objections against the authorities' decisions; courts could not question the legality of their actions and rights of appeal were considerably restricted.[105]

These executive powers were particularly noteworthy given that the 1949 Ordinance prevented the sale of properties without the approval of the state government, with special focus on Muslims who had to seek the permission of a district magistrate (who acted as deputy custodians). In practice, this measure proved to be a very rough instrument for dealing with the wide array of possibilities surrounding evacuee property. In 1952, an Administration of Evacuee Property Amendment Bill was passed, which liberalized the terms on which some evacuee property could be restored and which, critically, omitted chapter IV covering 'intending evacuees'.[106] Furthermore, this omission was itself, some contemporaries claimed, part of a wider attempt being undertaken by the Government of India to settle Pakistan's objections to this categorization of Muslims.[107] However, it led to a protest reaction from V. G. Deshpande of the Hindu Mahasabha and others in Congress itself, including Sucheta Kripalani, who believed that refugee organizations should have been consulted.[108] In due course, further amendments followed in 1953, 1956 and 1960, intended to overcome various practical problems in its implementation, including the recovery of rents and

---

[104] The districts were Dehradun, Saharanpur, Jhansi, Meerut, Muzaffarnagar, Bulandshar, Aligarh, Mathura, Basti, Nainital, Agra, Mainpuri, Etah, Moradabad, Bijnor and Garhwal.

[105] Enclosure V 'The United Provinces Administration of Evacuee Property Ordinance 1949', in 'Third Meeting of the Standing Committee', Relief and Rehabilitation, Box 12, File 235/49 UPSA.

[106] D. R. Kohli to all State Governments, 17 May 1952, '1950 Evacuee Property Act', Relief and Rehabilitation, Box 35, File 756 UPSA.

[107] Note of N. Sharma, 6 September 1952, ibid.   [108] *The Pioneer*, 6 November 1952.

damages from occupants of properties (Section 10A), the separating out of the interests of evacuees from non-evacuees with interests in a property (Section 10(2)) and the recovery and return of property 'wrongly declared' as evacuee property (Section 27).[109]

There was a substantial difference between the provisions of both the Ordinance and the Act, and their implementation, however. A great deal of power and initiative was ultimately handed down to each locality – files in the UP archives on the 'Standing Committee' set up to provide advice on refugees are surprisingly thin. In addition, while the government could only pay for staff and other costs involved in dealing with evacuee property issues from rents received from evacuee property itself,[110] officials evidently proved quite ineffective in securing rents, and were as a consequence faced with repeated protests from refugee organizations (as testified by the letters sent to Tandon, discussed earlier). Over and above everything else, any compensation for properties lost by evacuees was not settled due to the failure of India and Pakistan to agree on a settlement (particularly in relation to provisions set out in the Karachi settlement of January 1949) throughout the early 1950s.[111] Many Partition migrants found themselves literally at the mercy of (failed) bilateral agreements.

Equally, given the complex nature of the evacuee property rules, there were practical ways for migrants to evade the loss of property. In June 1948, officials in UP, as compared with other Indian states, were more urgently attempting to find accommodation for refugees. This resulted from the return of UP Muslims who had originally sought refuge in Pakistan but now wanted to resume their old lives – together with their former properties and jobs – in India. The authorities identified that in fact many Muslim owners had left houses in possession of relatives or friends,[112] and were also protected via connections to local administrators; therefore, as Govind Sahai, a UP minister, explained at the time:

They have no use for these vacant houses but are only keeping a semblance of occupation with the sole objective of preventing the allotments of these houses to

---

[109] '1950 Evacuee Property Act', Relief and Rehabilitation, Box 35, File 756 UPSA.

[110] 'Resume of the Activities of the Relief and Rehabilitation Department, Uttar Pradesh', 'Second Meeting to Advise on Refugees', Relief and Rehabilitation, Box 62, File 41/49 UPSA.

[111] 'Statement by Shri Ajit Prasad Jain, Minister for Rehabilitation on recent negotiations with Pakistan on Evacuee Property', '1950 Evacuee Property Act', Relief and Rehabilitation, Box 35, File 756 UPSA.

[112] Bhagwat Prasad Singh, Secretary of the Congress Committee, Nagina, to Govind Sahai, UP Parliamentary Secretary, Lucknow, 14 July 1948, 'Requisitioning of Building Lying Vacant for the Purpose of Housing Refugees', Relief and Rehabilitation, Box 1, File 265/1948 UPSA.

the refugees. Apart from ordinary houses many big and palatial buildings are thus held up from being utilized. Some Hindus – big house owners – have also adopted the same tactics. Local officials are also at times helpless to prevent such mischief on account of personal contacts ... I feel that the indignation of refugees over this matter has now come to such a pitch that an explosion might be expected any moment.[113]

The administration for evacuee property was headed by a 'Custodian' for each Indian state. In UP, the first official appointed to this post was Raghunath Prasad Varma, a member of the judicial branch of the PCS, with district magistrates acting as his 'deputies'. However, the key bureaucrats involved in ascertaining and preparing lists of evacuee property were TROs. It was significant that these officers were also involved in the control of rationing, food and civil supply around which there were a range of corruption scandals.[114] They were then in turn supported by an extensive field staff.

Whether or not individual officers did act in a corrupt manner (and there were many times when this happened), or how far influence was brought to bear on them, the reality was often less important than the belief that this behaviour was *thought* to be taking place. Such rumours created expectations that alternative informal approaches should be used. Varma's instructions around properties, for instance, suggested the importance of hearsay and speculation, as the following 1949 directive indicated: 'there have been transfers of evacuee property on a rather extensive scale and that such transfers still continue to be effected. While it is possible that these reports are very much exaggerated ... still I am to impress on you the necessity of taking suitable measures to check such transfers, if they are taking place in your district'.[115] As this guidance suggests, misappropriation by officers was tacitly known about, and so to prevent corruption, field staff were required to deposit an equal amount to the rents they received on a typical day from tenants of evacuee property.[116] The Director of Cottage Industries in the UP, who had the authority to distribute loans and controlled goods to refugees, boasted, 'In distributing this controlled material (iron and steel), this office has

[113] Note of Govind Sahai, 1 June 1948, in 'Requisitioning of Building Lying Vacant for the Purpose of Housing Refugees', Relief and Rehabilitation, Box 1, File 265/1948 UPSA.
[114] For more discussion on this theme, see Chapter 3.
[115] Shri Raghunath Prasad Varma, Custodian, Evacuee Property to all District Magistrates, 26 July 1949, in 'Instruction Regarding Taking Over and Preparation of Lists of Evacuee Property', Rehabilitation and Relief (A), Box 2, File 501/49(A) UPSA.
[116] Sri Manmohan Kishan, Asst. Secretary to the Govt. of India to all Part 'A', 'B' and 'C' States, 'Collection of Rent of Evacuee Property through Field Staff – Instructions Regarding', 29 October 1951, Relief and Rehabilitation, Box 23, File 308/1951 UPSA.

earned a fair name and it has been rarely that the allottees have been found guilty of black-marketing and the like offences'.[117]

Then again, migrants to UP who were unable to access property via normal channels could also take advantage of complex rules, delays and uncertainties in the evacuee property administration. In reality, the allotment of properties to refugees was regularly anticipated by squatting or forcible occupation. In reply to a UP government circular of early January 1949, the Allahabad district magistrate pointed out that whereas no houses had been requisitioned up to that point, refugees in local towns had already taken possession of twenty-six properties that had previously belonged to Muslims.[118] Perhaps not unexpectedly, seizing property illegally, especially houses supplied with facilities, was viewed as preferable to waiting for allocated housing. The city of Kanpur had an extensive programme of tenement building for refugees – 2,200 single-roomed and 600 double-roomed tenements and 500 shops, to be paid for from a total budget of around Rs. 10,000 million.[119] However, the reality was less positive: as a deputation from the Friends Colony Association in Kanpur to the UP government in August 1954, following completion of the housing complex, complained, the rent of 'A type quarters' (allegedly the tenements of the highest quality) was very high even though there was no electricity supply, tenants had to deposit three months' rent in advance, there was no outer compound wall for security and no proper drainage for flats on the first floor.[120]

In Sindh, the problems of implementation were not always identical in nature. But as we will see below, in terms of how citizens interacted with the local state, there were some important similarities around how rumour informed social behaviours, especially concerning supposed administrative corruption. In the view of its critics there, the proposed Economic Rehabilitation Bill that was under discussion in 1948 fell far short of expectations. In February 1948 (before the city of Karachi had

---

[117] 'Rehabilitation Brochure – Letters Issued to DMs etc.' Relief and Rehabilitation, Box 447, File 467/50(a) UPSA.

[118] Bhagwan Sahay to Dwarka Prasad Singh, district magistrate, Gorakhpur, 23 August 1948, Relief and Rehabilitation, Box 1, File 265/1948 UPSA.

[119] To make a comparison with other cities in UP, Kanpur's was an ambitious building programme. One hundred tenements and forty-eight shops were built in Saharanpur and fifty houses and forty-eight shops were built in Lucknow. S. R. Das, IAS to the Secretary to the Government of India, Ministry of Rehabilitation, New Delhi, 14 March 1952, in 'Construction by state PWD for displaced persons in Kanpur 1952–53', Relief and Rehabilitation, Box 2, File 143 (5)/52 UPSA.

[120] Deputation of Friends Colony Association, Swaroop Nagar, Kanpur, 25 August 1954, in 'Construction by State PWD for Displaced Persons in Kanpur 1952–1953', Relief and Rehabilitation, Box 2, File 143 (5)/52 UPSA.

been detached administratively from Sindh in April that year), the Sindh Legislative Assembly (SLA) debated the difficulties involved in the economic rehabilitation of the province's swelling refugee population, with Hindu members rejecting the Sindh government's attempt to regulate retrospectively the buying and selling of evacuee property, and in particular empowering rehabilitation officers to intervene to decide whether or not such transactions were valid. Much of the discussion revolved around the term 'bona fide', and its possible replacement with what those advocating the amendment preferred as a more precise reference – namely 'according to the law in force and for adequate consideration' – which in their view would reduce the discretion, and potential discrimination, available to government officials. As one Hindu member of the Assembly Holaram H. Keswani maintained, 'A person should have his right of ownership even though he is living in a foreign country. He must have the right of selling his property, and that property can be sold freely through his own attorney or by his coming over here according to the law of the land ... [which] is being absolutely destroyed here'. In addition, 'to penalize the transfers so far made by persons who have migrated or even by persons who have not migrated and who want to remain here' would put 'impediments' in the way of people 'who are migrating from Sind and are anxious to sell their property in the open market'.[121]

According to another SLA minority member, Sirumal Vishindas, the declared policy of the government had always been to persuade Sindhi Hindus to remain, but

if anybody wants to go away, they shall give him all facilities. Therefore those persons who want to sell the property in the open market should not be prohibited from doing so and no impediment should be placed in their way ... the case of the Hindus who want to go is absolutely pitiable. Their moveable property cannot be sold ... anybody who sells the moveable property is put in jail.[122]

Vishindas then proceeded to detail the problems faced by minorities in his hometown of Larkana in Upper Sindh: 'You do not allow them [non-Muslims] to sell their property and pay their debts and go away ... you ask them to leave the property in the hands of Government Officers, but you do not permit them to discharge their debts'.[123] In response, chief minister Khuhro dismissed complaints of possible official interference as exaggerated. More generally, the debate in the SLA revealed different

---

[121] 'Discussion on Bill No. IV of 1948 – Economic Rehabilitation Bill', 6 February 1948, *Sindh Legislative Assembly Debates*, Vol. III, Book No. 3 (Karachi: Government of Sind Press, 1948), pp. 3–32.
[122] Ibid.   [123] Ibid.

interpretations of the role of rehabilitation officers during this uncertain transition time For the bill's critics, these officers were likely to create problems for migrating Hindus by refusing to accept the validity of transactions. As far as its supporters were concerned, trusting the officials involved was essential; as one argued,

> I do not think that the Rehabilitation Officer who will be in charge of these affairs will be a lunatic person. He will be a man of common sense and he will act in a proper manner as a responsible officer and he is sure not to cancel any sale or exchange transaction arbitrarily ... So we must leave it to the discretion of the officer.[124]

Evacuee property in Sindh and UP alike came to be viewed in the press and by members of the local administration as an area of potential bureaucratic misappropriation. In April 1950, disciplinary proceedings against government servants in UP exposed instances of bureaucrats profiting from loopholes in evacuee property, such as one Ram Bojharat Singh, a supervisory *kanungo*, who was alleged to be in the possession of the *sir* land of Nawab Nasiruddin Khan, an evacuee.[125] And there was habitual suspicion within the Indian central government that some Muslims had returned under false names so as to try to enter the railway services.[126] But the impact of this situation fell harder on particular targets: Muslim government servants who remained in UP throughout had found themselves under closer than normal scrutiny from the outset, but this was reinforced and further complicated after March 1948 when significant numbers of Muslims who had originally migrated to Pakistan came back to India, and for the most part, took up (or attempted to take up) posts in the lower civil services in states such as UP. In June 1948, one month before a permit system was introduced to restrict the movement of people between India and Pakistan in July, Indian CID reports warned of what was described as

> a whispering campaign going on here against the movements and activities of those who have returned from Pakistan. Reports reveal that there has been a gradual dwindling of correspondence emanating from Pakistan and one of the reasons for this decrease is that a courier system may have been adopted ... Moreover a large number of people who are still in service in the Indian Dominion or engaged in business or other occupations have sent their families to Pakistan. Cases have occurred of government servants going on leave and staying away in Pakistan and

---

[124] Ibid.
[125] C. P. Gupta, Deputy Commissioner to Commissioner, Lucknow and Faizabad Division, 'Faizabad, Efficiency. Compulsory Retirement of the Official after Completing the Service of 25 Years or Attaining the Age of 50 on the Grounds of Efficiency', 27 April 1950, Revenue B, Box 121, File 1082B/1948 UPSA.
[126] Government of India, Ministry of Home Affairs, 'Verification of Character and Antecedents of Candidates under State Employment', 10 August 1950, Appts Box 295, File 1947/321 UPSA.

not returning in due time while others try to seek jobs in Pakistan by clandestine methods while those guilty of offences such as embezzlement, especially among the lower ranks, e.g. constables, run away to Pakistan to escape the penalty of the law ... All of these factors have the result that the general public are beginning to doubt the loyalty of Muslims to the Indian Union.[127]

Drilling down to the world of individual government servants and their families, as Vazira Zamindar has done, reveals that this situation was rarely one of just the relationship between employee and employing authority.[128] Importantly, it was also complicated by the predicament of families divided by the new political arrangements. Once the controls on movement were firmly in place on both sides of the border, government servants who may have had family members located or re-located across it were placed under special scrutiny in both India and Pakistan. K. P. Bhargava, for instance, later wrote to all heads of department in UP that

prima facie there is a presumption against those employees who continue to keep their families in Pakistan in spite of the fact instructions issued over a year ago that such action would convey the impression that their interests lie in another country and that their continued loyalty could not be relied on especially in times of emergency. Government servants who keep their families in Pakistan will frequently require leave to go and visit them. They may also constitute a potential source of communication or leakage to undesirable and unfriendly quarters of information ... which is vital to the security of the country.[129]

'Suitable departmental action' was proposed for anyone who refused to repatriate family members, and 'family' could cover any kind of dependant. There were, of course, many government servants and police officers who were willing to comply but who were, perversely, prevented from doing so by the very rules put in place to restrict movement. This personal conundrum was exacerbated by the bureaucratic hurdles required to make claims as an evacuee, through – in India – the Ministry of Relief and Rehabilitation, rather than directly to the UP authorities.[130] Hence, Kumari Hamida Begum, daughter of constable Zahir Alam, and Mushahid Husain, son of constable Shahid Husain of Dehradun, migrated to West Pakistan during the disturbances in the western part of UP in the early 1950s. As required, the two constables

---

[127] B. N. Jha to Secretary to Government of India, 'Restriction on the Movement of People between the Indian Union and Pakistan and Vice Versa', 26 June 1948, Home Police, Box 6, File 211/1948 UPSA.

[128] Zamindar, *The Long Partition*.

[129] K. P. Bhargava to all H of D, Principal Heads of Officers, 'List of Persons in Govt Service Who Have Gone or Who Intend to Go to Pakistan', 9 March 1950, Police Dept., Box 392, File 899/47 UPSA.

[130] S. P. Advani to Chief Secr. to Gov., UP, 'Verification of Claims of Evacuees', 19 January 1950, Revenue B, Box 181, File 224B/50 UPSA.

were asked to bring their children back. But they failed to do so because they were unable to get permits for the permanent resettlement of their children in India. When this transfer was finally arranged through the auspices of the Relief and Rehabilitation Department, the system of passports had been enforced and their family members found themselves unable to obtain the necessary new form of travel documentation.[131]

That this element of suspicion surrounding government servants came to affect especially lower cadres of the civil services in UP was also indicative of how widespread and arbitrary questions of loyalty could become. For instance, Mohammad Mobin Khan, a UP *kanungo*, was slated for disciplinary action partly for his alleged 'lethargy' but also because 'his son-in-law who formerly lived in Aligarh has gone to Pakistan. Although he says that he has no touch with him, yet his loyalty to the Indian Dominion cannot be said to be beyond doubt'.[132] Given this kind of situation, and fearing the negative backlash of a suspected connection to Pakistan, many Muslim government servants attempted to slip away quietly, but in the process were accused of secretly plotting to migrate. This was the dilemma for Syed Masoodul Haq, a criminal record keeper from Jaunpur who sent in his resignation from Bombay and whose 'loyalty' was consequently in doubt. It was a similar outcome for Massom Haider, assistant at the Government Central Girl's School in the same district: in April 1951, the Collector of Jaunpur wrote, 'The migration of his wife and mother six months before clearly shows that he was planning secretly to migrate to Pakistan. He could have resigned while working in tahsil [*sic*] and then migrated from India. Instead he adopted a secret mode for reasons best known to him'.[133] In other instances, Muslim government servants were branded as culpable in corrupt actions – in August 1948, for instance, the UP government followed up on a number of Muslim constables who had 'decamped' to Pakistan after allegedly embezzling money in the vicinity of Meerut and Lucknow.[134] Such activities were perceived to be fairly widespread in UP at this time, and supported by public discussions on the subject of Muslim (dis)loyalty in the vernacular press.[135]

[131] C. K. Srivastava, Dept. Super. of Police, UP, to Dept. Secr. to Gov. UP Home Dept. (Police), 'List of Persons in Govt Service Who Have Gone or Who Intend to Go to Pakistan', 13 October 1952, Police Dept., Box 392, File 899/47 UPSA.

[132] 'Efficiency. Compulsory Retirement of the Official after Completing the Service of 25 Years or Attaining the Age of 50 on the Grounds of Efficiency', Revenue B, Box 121, File 1082B/1948 UPSA.

[133] 'Restriction on the Movement of People between the Indian Union and Pakistan and Vice Versa', Revenue B, Box 181, File 224B/50 UPSA.

[134] Note of Lal Bahadur, Home Police, Box 6, File 211/1948 UPSA.

[135] See for instance, 'Musulmano par vishwaas na kare', *Aaj*, 12 January 1948.

The relationship between divided and increasingly distant – metaphorically if not physically – places again occurred around the issue of government servants. In early January 1948, India's High Commissioner to Pakistan, Sri Prakasa visited Lucknow to explore the possibility of the absorption of officials in Pakistan who were desirous to serve in the UP administration. These were mostly Hindus, appointed by the British in what local reports described as 'a system of divide and rule' and who wanted 'their services to be transferred, and with them their provident fund money and other privileges'.[136] In April 1949, a central claims organization was set up both in India and Pakistan to receive claims for pensions, provident funds, leave salary and security deposits from provincial and state government officials and employees working for local bodies who had migrated. The idea was that each central government after receiving the claims would forward them to the other government for verification and acceptance.[137] But, as it turned out, the transfer of funds and other privileges was slow and unwieldy. By November 1950, salary and provident fund claims of Muslims who had migrated to Pakistan had still not been completely processed, and the authorities were asked to expedite them. In the meantime, the relevant monies had been withdrawn and kept in a 'suspense' account, along with those of other government servants.[138] On both sides of the new border, then, Partition and the challenges it posed, created opportunities for some in government service and made the position of others precarious.

Conclusion

This chapter has highlighted the effects of population transfer on the working of, and perceptions concerning, early promises of citizenship in both India and Pakistan, primarily through the lens of developments taking place in UP and Sindh and in relation to the flux that characterized this period. As Joya Chatterji has argued, formal rights of citizenship were determined by this movement of refugees between India and Pakistan immediately following Independence: the timing and nature of

---

[136] 'Absorption of Pakistan Officials in UP: Sri Prakasa's Reported Mission in Lucknow', *National Herald*, 3 January 1948.

[137] 'Instructions Regarding Verification of Claims of Those Government Servants Who Migrated to Pakistan', Letter from Officer In-Charge, Central Claims Organization, Ministry of Rehabilitation, Government of India, New Delhi, 23 January 1950, Irrigation Department, Box 12, File 111/1950 UPSA.

[138] R. S. Das to J. Nigam, Secr. to Gov., Revenue Dept., 'Arrears Claims of Pay of Shri Abdul Aziz Khan, Partition Amin, Bareilly, now in Karachi (Pakistan)', 25 November 1950, Revenue (C), Box 20, File 95C/1950 UPSA.

the various controls on movement, the implementation of the permit system and then its replacement with a system of passports, she contends, occurred as a response mechanism, especially with respect to the re-migration of Muslims from Pakistan back to India (there was hardly any movement of this kind in the other direction).[139] But, as this chapter has explored, the discussion of minority and refugee rights, from a relational perspective, also gradually came to define more nuanced and substantive notions of citizens' rights. These were generated, on the one hand, by a comparable political milieu in different localities, in which ideas of the 'refugee' and 'minority' were gradually changed by the commonplace experiences of dealing with property, family movement, occupational benefits and other forms of collateral against the backdrop of Partition. On the other hand, these notions were also fashioned and refined by a public sphere of discussion in which events in Pakistan were reported in India and vice versa.

The fluid and fluctuating links between Pakistan and India – as epitomized by continuing connections between people moving from one to the other and sometimes back again, and the movement of information (or misinformation) in both directions – were general as well as particular, with specific reporting, for instance, on each country's refugee policy or on decisions taken across the border to promulgate anti-corruption legislation.[140] Some of the most important interactions in the public space created by this media revolved around *popular reflections* on national and local governance, as much as on the interaction of formal institutions. Notions of citizenship, and more particularly what being a citizen entailed in practice, came to be based on certain exclusions. The latter – often exemplified by individual members of minority communities deemed to be in the wrong place – were formed by the material predicament of refugees and/or minorities that defined notions of belonging in India and Pakistan. And as we have sought to highlight here, they were shaped as well by the cross-border interaction of knowledge about new citizens caught up in local politics of belonging in UP and Sindh.

---

[139] Chatterji, 'South Asian Histories of Citizenship'.
[140] 'Pakistan Ordinance to Fight Corruption', *National Herald*, 7 January 1948.

3   Citizens and the City
From People on the Move to the Movement of Goods

In December 1947 T. T. Krishnamachari,[1] Madras member of the Indian Constituent Assembly, raised the following question:

Will the Honourable Minister for Relief and Rehabilitation be pleased to state whether the Government are aware that ships bringing refugees from Karachi have been detained under the orders of the Government of Pakistan, and if so for what reasons?

Krishanmachari went on to ask whether or not the Indian government knew that refugees boarding these ships were closely searched – on one occasion reputedly for nearly fourteen hours – before being permitted to embark. In response, Minister K. C. Neogy explained that no ships had been detained under any orders of the Pakistan government, though vessels carrying refugees from Karachi did have to spend about a day at the wharf for disembarkation and embarkation purposes as well as to allow for the completion of the necessary paperwork formalities. This meant that refugees on their way to India were regularly and closely searched by both the Sindh police and Pakistani Customs, with this process usually taking around six hours. In one instance, however, 'when the Customs had finished their search and the passengers' luggage had been stored in the hold, the Sind police objected that the search by the customs was not sufficient. All the luggage was taken out of the hold and searched a second time by the police. On this occasion, the search took about fourteen hours' (see Figure 3.1).

Neogy then explained that the Indian authorities had already raised the matter with their Pakistani counterparts, and both had agreed that there should be no search of refugees' baggage in either India or Pakistan. This decision, however, had not been implemented immediately in Karachi where the local police had ostensibly wished to continue checking whether unauthorized firearms, merchandise in bulk and goods whose

---

[1] Tiruvellore Thattai Krishnamachari (1899–1974), popularly known as 'TTK', was the Indian Finance Minister from 1956-8.

Figure 3.1 Non-Muslim refugees leaving Karachi by sea,
December 1947.
Photo by Margaret Bourke-White/The LIFE Picture Collection/Getty Images

export had been banned by Sindh authorities were being taken to India
by the departing refugees. All the same, following repeated representations to the Pakistan government, the Indian High Commissioner was
now able to report that there had been 'considerable improvements' in
the matter of searching with fewer than than 10 per cent of bags being
actually opened and inspected.[2]

Krishanmachari's question in India's Constituent Assembly together
with clarification provided by the minister responsible for overseeing
refugee affairs points to the significance attached not just to people but
also to material things crossing (or perhaps not crossing) the line of
division established in August 1947. And in the years that followed, what
might be described as the material fallout from Partition came to figure
prominently in people's everyday lives, particularly in urban centres that
were hugely affected by the influx and departure of refugees, and where

---

[2] 'Boundary Commission Awards Punjab and Bengal and Disturbances Arising
Therefrom', 3 November–31 December 1947, DO133/61 UK National Archives
(hereafter UKNA).

access to immovable evacuee property became a key issue. In localities such as UP and Sindh – much more so than other former British Indian provinces affected by Partition-related migration such as the Punjab and Bengal – the majority of refugees arriving there after August 1947 headed for towns and cities. In the case of Sindh, while a sizeable number of rural refugees were transferred from West Punjab by the central Pakistani authorities in 1948, most people coming from India gravitated towards the province's urban centres. Likewise, many of its inhabitants traveling in the other direction left behind predominantly urban lifestyles.[3] It was much the same story in UP where cities and towns swelled in size thanks to the arrival of displaced persons from what had become Pakistan, including a substantial Sindhi component.

Importantly, in UP and Sindh in the late 1940s and 1950s, the scale of the disruption caused by Partition-related migration generated new forms of public critique, both from those seeking new homes and among those not directly displaced. It is these criticisms of the state that manifested around a range of resources and goods which form the central focus of this chapter. As Chapter 2, an enduring topic of complaint during the early post-Independence years focussed on the difficulties involved in securing accommodation, a place to live. Inevitably there could be variations on this theme. Sometimes the authorities – whether at the local or at the national level – were not doing enough; sometimes they were criticized for not leaving sufficient opportunity for people to pursue their own initiatives.[4]

Consequently, there was considerable uncertainty and competition connected with what happened to immovable evacuee property – that is, houses and other buildings associated with people who had either migrated, or were expected to migrate, and whose status as a result had become ambiguous, both in the eyes of the state and as far as local communities were concerned. To those who lost out in what was often a fierce contest over scarce resources, the decisions of rehabilitation officials regarding the allocation of evacuee property could appear arbitrary at best, and corrupt at worst. Personal connections at the disposal of those with the right networks (or social capital) were often credited with making a noticeable difference to how successfully someone emerged from this process of competitive readjustment to their new surroundings.

---

[3] Sarah Ansari, *Life after Partition: Migration, Community and Strife in Sindh, 1947–1962* (Karachi: Oxford University Press, 2005).

[4] Refugee expectations of the state are discussed in Ian Talbot, 'Punjabi Refugees' Rehabilitation and the Indian State: Discourses, Denials and Dissonances', *Modern Asian Studies* 45, 1 (2011), pp. 109–30.

However, as we argue in this chapter, the process of securing property was just one part of a much larger discussion about the movement and control of goods and services – a situation compounded by the upheavals of Partition and also related to longer term changes taking place during and since the Second World War years.

Concentrating in particular on urban centres in present-day Sindh and UP, this chapter discusses two key dynamics involved in the development of citizenship that connected with this control of 'public goods'. In its first section, it explores the theme of food and civil supply, in relation to both the politics of prices and price controls and debates about food and civil supply administration. After tracing the comparative regimes of civil supply in India and Pakistan and their effect on urban politics, it then highlights the extent to which supply and control of goods – a major issue during what was perceived on both sides of the border as a time of austerity – became an important means through which ideas about citizens' relationship to the state were articulated and played out. In particular, we investigate ways in which civil supply problems became a point of public criticism in the press in both UP and Sindh, and how scandals or problems involving this public good were frequently discussed and debated by Indians and Pakistanis in a similar fashion.

This chapter's second section moves on to consider the popular discourses surrounding government corruption, which emerged from the mechanisms involved in the supply of goods and their administration. It sets out the new postcolonial structures and organizations of 'anti-corruption' as these had developed following the end of the Second World War, and discusses a number of cases of anti-corruption investigation dating from the post-Partition period in both our regions of India and Pakistan. This examination of popular views of corruption extends into a discussion of how particular scandals developed in the press, and their broader meaning for ideas about citizenship rights, concluding with consideration of cross-border smuggling as an 'anti-national' problem in the early 1950s.

Politics of Price Controls and Rationing

In early September 1948, the Indian authorities banned the entry into India of the English-language Karachi newspaper *Dawn* , on the grounds of (what was described as) its consistent violation of both the spirit and the letter of the Inter-Dominion Agreement that the two governments had reached five months earlier in Calcutta. From an Indian perspective, under the terms of that agreement, the press had been directed 'not to indulge in propaganda against either Dominion', nor 'to publish exaggerated versions of news of the character likely to inflame or cause fear or alarm [the] population'. *Dawn*, it was alleged, had been 'indulging in scurrilous propaganda against the Dominion of India' and 'wholesale vilification' of its 'major communities and ministers'. The time had come to clamp down and prevent copies of it from crossing the border into India.[5]

In reality, as the content of newspapers being published at the time in UP and Sindh underlined, there was equally huge dissatisfaction with developments closer to home. There was a direct and material connection between the outcomes of Partition, the 'refugee problem' and a range of other urban complaints in both localities throughout the late 1940s and early 1950s. Vazira Zamindar has shown in relation to the city of Karachi during this period just how quickly refugee interest groups exploited any suspicion that the local authorities might be ignoring possible abuses, using the law courts to highlight when and how the system was allegedly manipulated in favour of those with all-important connections in the right places.[6] The same situation existed in Delhi and the cities of UP. The public services that came under fire from urban dwellers, who frequently sent complaining letters to the editors of local newspapers, ranged from the provision of electricity and water to public transport facilities, the rationing of vital everyday commodities and bureaucratic abuse.[7] Whether living in what had become independent Pakistan, or across the border in India, citizens across South Asia faced a similar set of challenges when it came to negotiating life in their changed surroundings. In these urban contexts, hastily organized movements to represent the rights of urban dwellers appeared: across towns and cities of UP monster petitions and complaints emerged regarding the introduction of new municipal rules or taxes. In January 1948, for instance, the Lucknow Municipal Board received some 13,000 protests in response to the introduction of new house and water tax assessments that were intended to raise around Rs. 500,000 for the local authorities.[8]

Historians of popular movements in a range of different contexts, including South Asia, have argued that apparently spontaneous protests

[5] 'Dawn's Entry Banned into India', *Indian News Bulletin*, 6 September 1948, FO371/69735 UKNA.
[6] Vazira Zamindar, *The Long Partition and the Making of Modern South Asia: Refugees, Boundaries, Histories* (New York: Columbia University Press, 2007) see chapter 4, 'Economies of Displacement'.
[7] Sarah Ansari, 'Everyday Expectations of the State during Pakistan's Early Years: Letters to the Editor, *Dawn* (Karachi), 1950–1953', *Modern Asian Studies* 45, 1 (2011), pp. 159–78.
[8] 'Lucknow Municipal Board', *Aaj*, 11 January 1948; 'Objections against Municipal Levy Tax', *National Herald*, 12 January 1948.

often come about as a result of a sudden transition in standards of living, or local religious observance, or expectations of the local state.[9] In particular, from the outbreak of the Second World War, a range of urban protests had erupted in undivided India triggered by the issue of commodity prices that were artificially raised thanks to the control of supply, movement and cost of goods introduced by the wartime control regime.[10] This reaction was by no means unique to South Asia, but as a result of the man-made Bengal famine of 1943, the governance of supply here was critiqued with particular urgency. The combination of factors that led to the death of around three million people in Bengal has been extensively explored by scholars of famine who have also explained the specific consequences of the disaster in that province.[11] However, given what we now know about the human-made effects of the famine, the governance structures (of which Bengal was a part) had wider resonance in the operation of a complex array of civic scandals and protests against them. As we will argue below, these structures of governance around supply were important not merely or even principally as instruments for the control of goods. Rather they were social networks which themselves illustrated the unbounded and ambiguous nature of the local state in an array of different (but inter-related) towns and cities across the region.

Rationing and other state-imposed controls had such a big effect on India and Pakistan's post-1947 urban populations partly because of the perception of, and partly because of the effect of, rapid changes in policy. The most important result of this process was its impact on prices, something that became most evident during the first year following Independence. Rationing and the movement of goods stimulated heated public debate in the provincial assemblies, in selection of candidates for elections at all levels, and in newspapers and public speeches at this time. So, for instance, in early January 1948, C. B. Gupta, the UP Minister for Food and Civil Supplies, announced the imminent implementation of 'decontrol' from 1 February, arguing that 'few could resist' the appeal being made by Gandhi for decontrol. Rationing, Gupta further

---

[9] See, for example, the descriptions of social conflicts in Gyanendra Pandey, 'Encounters and Calamities: The History of a North Indian *Qasba* in the Nineteenth Century', in *Subaltern Studies III: Writings on South Asian History and Society*, ed. Ranajit Guha (Oxford: Oxford University Press, 1984), pp. 231–70.

[10] See William Gould, *Bureaucracy, Community and Influence: Society and the State, 1930s–1960s* (London: Routledge, 2011), pp. 121–30.

[11] Lance Brennan, 'Government Famine Relief in Bengal, 1943', *The Journal of Asian Studies* 47, 3 (1988), pp. 541–66; M. Mufakharul Islam, 'The Great Bengal Famine and the Question of FAD Yet Again', *Modern Asian Studies* 41, 2 (2007), pp. 421–40; Paul R. Greenough, *Prosperity and Misery in Modern Bengal: The Famine of 1943–1944* (New York: Oxford University Press, 1982).

explained, would only remain in place for residents of the six largest towns in UP,[12] for those who earned Rs. 100 or less, and for categories of industrial and railway workers, refugees living in camps and towns then under rationing, inmates of jails and hospitals and members of the police force. However, public reports on this policy also pointed out how, as had been the case in Bengal in 1943, it was the anticipation of a change in policy that directly led to hoarding. In this circumstance, it was the expectation of decontrol (rather than control) that produced the holding back of goods.[13] Hoarding, or at least accusations about it, also sharply increased in April 1948, albeit under somewhat different circumstances. Now, due to the spike in prices, the UP government announced that it was considering the re-imposition of controls on cloth. This need was partly prompted, the authorities argued, by the entry of newcomers – refugees – into the cloth trade. In order to prevent either hoarding or the slowing down of deliveries to the market, local merchants were to be offered incentives to make sure that their cloth reached anxious customers.[14]

The fluctuation between 'control' and 'decontrol' was itself used as a political rallying cry in the months after Independence, when it turned into a means of expressing, and rejecting, a colonial legacy. Hence, following an announcement that decontrol would begin to take effect from March 1948, UP's first Finance Minister K. D. Paliwal in a speech delivered in the small city of Ora – located between Kanpur and Jhansi – claimed that the controls would be consumed in the 'sacred flames' of forthcoming Holi celebrations. Here were clear opportunities aplenty to articulate an anti-colonial message, and Paliwal, among others, argued that controls had been forced upon them as a legacy of the British Raj: 'The people have to bear with them and bravely face the acute shortage created as a result of the war'.[15] Such posturing linked well to Gandhi's own recent public declarations pointing out the damaging effects of state control, as demonstrated in his January 1948 speech in Delhi when he suggested that *khadi* should be seen as the 'livery of freedom' and not subject to controls.[16] Yet, the uncertainty of a situation in which policy could be rapidly changed within a matter of days undoubtedly fuelled public distrust. When the UP government stayed its decision to

---

[12] These were Lucknow, Kanpur, Allahabad, Banaras, Meerut and Agra.
[13] 'Food Rationing in UP to Go: Mr. C. B. Gupta Announces Decision', *National Herald*, 8 January 1948.
[14] *National Herald*, 22 April 1948.
[15] 'Further Decontrol by Holi', *National Herald*, 2 January 1948.
[16] 'Control Blesses the Rich and Curses the Poor: Gandhiji Says Monopolies Must Go at Once', *National Herald*, 7 January 1948.

decontrol thirty-eight towns in the surplus areas at the start of January 1948,[17] this then led to huge protests in major cities elsewhere in India as well as in UP itself. In Bombay and Patna the same month, Trade Union Congress-led 'anti-decontrol day protests' were organized, driven by claims that decontrol was not in the interests of workers and the middle classes because it led to the sudden rise in important commodities like sugar.[18] In Lucknow, representatives of the Textile Workers' Union, the MES Workers' Union, the UP Electric Supply Workers' Union, and the Electric and Sanitary Workers' Union condemned decontrol, on the grounds that it would worsen the living conditions of the 'common man', make prices soar and aid employers to increase their profits.[19]

In Pakistan, despite the central government producing two apparently balanced budgets in 1947–8 and 1948–9, the economy came under increasing pressure very quickly, with inevitable knock-on effects on people's everyday lives. 'Austerity' was the catchword of the times (see Figure 3.2). Shortages of basic food items – rice in East Bengal and wheat in the West Pakistani provinces – and other essential commodities, such as cloth, resulted in the re-introduction of wartime price controls and periodic rationing (see Figure 3.3). Under these circumstances, hoarding and black market trading increased sharply, posing a stark challenge to the ability of the state to manage the distribution of goods that were in such short supply. As contemporary press reports underlined, rationing was a source of frequent disquiet:

A large section for Karachi ration card holders again have been given a paltry four *chhatanks*[20] of sugar for the whole month of March. In January he was promised the restoration of his original 12 *chhatanks* of sugar the following month, but there was an acute sugar famine during the first 15 days of February. On the arrival of sugar ships in Karachi the scarcity was removed. But the ration shops were still doling out only 4 *chhatanks* of sugar per person in March. There have been reports of bad distribution in Karachi as people living in Preedy quarters, Plaza Quarter and Ramaswami area have not received their ration at all. Although no sugar ration was distributed to Karachi hotels, restaurants, canteens and coffee houses in February [the Civil Supplies Department] could not explain how most of the city restaurants were able to serve their customers with plentiful amounts of sugar last month.[21]

Ration cards represented an enduring feature, and headache, of daily life: As another 1948 report explained,

---

[17] 'Grave Food Position May Force UP Govt to Revise Decontrol Policy', *National Herald*, 3 January 1948.
[18] 'Anti De-Control Day Protests in Bombay', *National Herald*, 6 January 1948.
[19] *National Herald*, 9 January 1948.   [20] 1 *chhatank* = c. 50 grams.
[21] 'Sugar Ration for March only Four Chhataks [*sic*]?', *Dawn*, 11 March 1948.

FIFTH ANNIVERSARY EXTRA

Figure 3.2 Cartoon capturing the austerity policies of the Pakistan authorities in the early 1950s. Placard slogan reads 'AUSTERITY PARADE', while the sash on the marcher taking the salute reads: 'THE PAKISTANI CONSUMERS', *Dawn* (Karachi), 14 August 1952.

Mr. J. G. Kharas, Director of Civil Supplies Karachi has issued a statement informing the people of about a week's notice (till October 11) to hand in any bogus ration cards or risk prosecution on being checked. House to house checks would be introduced after the above date. No action will be taken against any cards handed in during the period before this date.[22]

All this meant that 'supply' together with 'rationing' were key refrains in debates about the limits of social consumption in UP and Sindhi towns and cities. This in turn affected public discussions of urban class and the problems of how to negotiating housing and rents. In UP, for

---

[22] 'Drive against Bogus Ration Cards to Begin on October 11', *Dawn*, 2 October 1948. Elderly Pakistanis who had lived through the Second World War and the period following it continued to refer to grocery shops as 'ration stores' well into the twenty-first century.

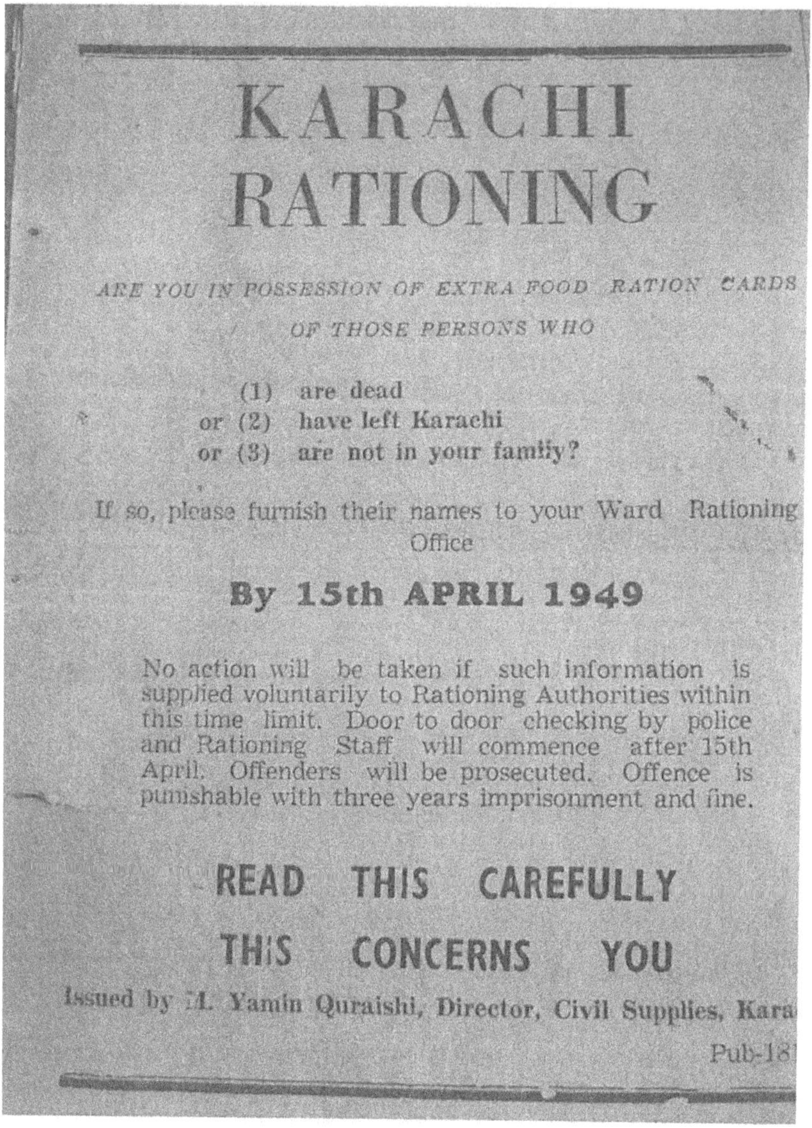

KARACHI RATIONING

ARE YOU IN POSSESSION OF EXTRA FOOD RATION CARDS

OF THOSE PERSONS WHO

(1) are dead
or (2) have left Karachi
or (3) are not in your family?

If so, please furnish their names to your Ward Rationing Office

By 15th APRIL 1949

No action will be taken if such information is supplied voluntarily to Rationing Authorities within this time limit. Door to door checking by police and Rationing Staff will commence after 15th April. Offenders will be prosecuted. Offence is punishable with three years imprisonment and fine.

READ THIS CAREFULLY

THIS CONCERNS YOU

Issued by M. Yamin Quraishi, Director, Civil Supplies, Kara

Pub-18

Figure 3.3 Rationing notice (*Dawn*, Karachi), 1949.

instance, in January 1948 the idea was mooted that the construction of luxury homes, costing Rs. 50,000 or more, would be banned in the state, under a scheme which the local authorities proposed to enforce so as to ensure an 'equitable distribution of building materials to members of the middle classes'. Quotas of cement fixed locally were to be the mechanism involved, and so in discussion of the necessary legislative provisions in the UP Legislative Assembly, speakers debated how 'these days' lower-middle-class houses were identified as costing no more than Rs. 15,000 while those of the upper middle classes cost around Rs. 30,000 or slightly more. The number of houses to be constructed in each district would be fixed by government and quotas of building materials allotted to applicants through the drawing of lots by district magistrates.[23] Such discussions took place against the backdrop of wider conversations on housing problems that had surfaced in newspapers, especially in relation to industrial cities such as Kanpur, where urban workers combined to protest against the idea of unfair privileges built into the rationing system.[24]

The debate often revolved around the everyday challenge of dealing with the local administration when it came to housing and rents. For instance, two acts – the Municipal Act of 1900 and the Rent Control and Eviction Act – governed the erection and letting out of new buildings. The former required plans to be submitted in quadruplicate to the municipal board for approval, a process that often took months and needed to be chased up. Then the application would be passed on to the Public Works Department, which was also notoriously slow in making its decisions. As the *National Herald* reported, 'One is fortunate if, at long last, through the "good offices" of a friend of one of the clerks, one is able to get the inner machinery moving and finally have the plan passed'.[25] The next headache was getting permits from the District Supply Officer for bricks, iron and cement. The municipal board, 'after sleeping over the plan for months, will suddenly awaken and send the house owner an assessment for the house and water tax ... and then he starts to receive bills for taxes on a building that is still under construction'. Next a citizen would have the Rent Control and Eviction Act showered upon him or her. This would make it necessary to write to a Rent Controller about when the building could be occupied, 'who would then allot the premises to a needy person who is reliable ... but invariably they would turn up then leave, or sublet, or pass it over to a relative'. To get the rent assessments, a builder would again have to 'loosen his purse', and there would be more weeks or months before the rent itself started to materialize.[26]

---

[23] *National Herald*, 6 January 1948.
[24] 'Hamara Nagar', *Aaj*, 5 January 1948; 'Housing in Kanpur', *National Herald*, 13 April 1948.
[25] *National Herald*, 6 September 1951.   [26] Ibid.

Urban differentiations of this kind were furthermore driven by considerations of local corruption. Frequent protests about the corrupt activities of lower-level officials testified not just to the extent of malpractice, but also to the everyday frustrations that it caused on both sides of the new border. Karachi, the nerve centre for Pakistan's industry, commerce and finance, was transformed into 'a place where money pours from all directions [providing] temptations for the government servants who exercise a great deal of power and patronage. The businessman is all too willing to oblige in consideration of large profits which he can derive from undeserved concerns'.[27] Public frustration was as palpable in urban Sindh as it had become in UP: as one Pakistani critic of changes in 1951 to the local system of charcoal rationing – an absolutely essential everyday commodity in early 1950s' Karachi – complained,

The gist of the whole order is that a consumer instead of registering his card in the shop of his choice is compelled to go to the shop of his particular area, which means that those favourite shop-keepers who on account of their own faults, and or bad dealing, were left out by the public have been rewarded for their bad dealings by the department. ... the mere fact that the shopkeepers would know that there is no competition and the customer has no other option but to come to them will lead to corruption [but] the only answer which the authorities can give to this is that there will be official supervision and that we feel is not excuse enough.[28]

Prices and controls were, thus, significant reflections of the commonplace experiences of Independence and civic culture, often articulated via reflections on and comparisons with the recent colonial past and the continued interaction with government servants under what many Indians and Pakistanis were coming to see as a neocolonial system. This was a repeatedly rehearsed public description of how the 'ordinary citizen' was forced to interact with government, with corruption a key dynamic linking the complaints of the public and the everyday to higher-level stings, notions of social responsibility, and also hierarchy and power.[29] Housing and social expenditure were singled out as areas of dispute and debate, where the acquisition of wealth by particular urban communities was blamed for reinforcing the complex of corruption, both in terms of practices and perceptions. Corruption in civil supplies was habitually presented in the press and by politicians as socially

---

[27] 'Role of Public Service in Pakistan', *Times of Karachi*, 14 August 1953.
[28] *Dawn*, 14 December 1951.
[29] See, for example a discussion of this in 'Bhrashtachar nivarak vibhag', *Aaj*, 30 January 1948.

hierarchical, and hence socially divisive.[30] Gandhi in his same January 1948 'livery of freedom' speech delivered in Delhi captured these popular concerns when he raised the issue of the regular trade in petrol permits. A person, he alleged, could earn Rs. 10,000 by selling his permit, yet 'the ordinary Indian' saw the cost of everything else go up as a result.[31]

The issue of just how much cement could be allocated for large buildings was made particularly poignant in UP cities given the periodic discovery of large-scale misappropriation of supply across the state. UP's largest industrial centre Kanpur again provides a good example of this kind of official corruption. A large proportion of the cement allocated to different public bodies and individuals in the state was claimed during 1947 by the Kanpur Development Board. One of the Board's officers (who was subsequently and conveniently transferred to Delhi) suspected that these allocations had been sold in the black market.[32] In early 1948, police raided the Board's offices where they found registers of cement sold to its contractors, with the latter reportedly selling cement that had been given to them for specific works in connection with the former's building schemes on the black market.[33] Contractors involved in this cement scandal were arrested and several thousand tons of cement retrieved from their *godowns* (warehouses).[34] Moreover, it was significant for public views of corruption that officers themselves were often found to be directly complicit. Again in Kanpur and during the same month, the Town Rationing Officer (TRO) conducted a surprise raid on the Etawah Bazar area rationing office, which resulted in the detection of the issue of a large number of cloth coupons on non-existent ration cards.[35] However, Kanpur was not the only city where these kinds of activities came to light: a similar supply scandal around the rationing officers erupted in Azamgarh in early 1948.[36] The District Supply Officer (DSO) and the Assistant DSOs of Allahabad were suspended after serious allegations relating to cement and petrol permits,[37] while a further twenty-five were arrested by Bareilly's TRO for trying to export food grains from the town in contravention of UP's Food Grain Movement Order.[38]

---

[30] 'Hamara Nagar', *Aaj*, 5 April 1948.   [31] *National Herald*, 7 January 1948.
[32] 'Inquiry into Cement Misappropriation: Cawnpore Police Make Surprise Raids and Seize Records', *National Herald*, 6 January 1948.
[33] 'Cawnpore Development Board Office Raided: Huge Quantity of Cement Believed Sold in the Black Market', *National Herald*, 5 January 1948.
[34] *National Herald*, 9 January 1948.   [35] *National Herald*, 7 January 1948.
[36] 'Hazaron Bundle Sut Baramad', *Aaj*, 3 January 1948.
[37] *National Herald*, 10 April 1948.   [38] *National Herald*, 6 January 1948.

Crucially, corruption in civil supplies produced discourses that increasingly centred on the relationship between what was happening in the cities of UP and Sindh and other urban spaces, both nationally and internationally. This connection between different urban spaces emerged not least because such activities involved movement of goods and trade, which also linked into political networks in multiple localities. To take one – representative – case, twenty-five *maunds* of rationed food grains were seized in Lucknow on 7 January 1948 at the city station there. The wagon had been booked by Mr. Ahmad Khan, a subinspector of police in Shahjahanpur who was coming to Lucknow on leave in preparation for retirement.[39] On a much bigger scale, the UP government moved to cancel the licences of about 400 steel fabricators across the province in December 1947, and directed district magistrates to closely scrutinize the old lists and recommend afresh the names of those concerns that could be considered genuine claimants to a steel quota.[40]

Networks of supply corruption spread to spaces further afield, directly as well as conceptually. Alongside frequent discussions of local supply corruption in the press in early 1948 were reports on larger-scale scandals in other places: UP newspapers, for instance, reported the prosecution of S. C. Mitter, a former Director of Industries Bengal and Controller of Supplies, Government of India, alongside six others on charges of accepting, and conspiracy to accept, illegal gratification relating to the procurement of war materials from Bengal to UP.[41] References were also made to the 'cloth famine' of 1943–4, when textile magnates likely to benefit from proposed decontrol were publicly criticized: these business interests, which back in 1943 had 'thrived as never before at a time when the people suffered [and] never allowed a Tariff Board to examine their cost of production', were 'today expected to be honest and friends of the people'.[42]

Nevertheless, the wealthy were not always the obvious target of criticism in this changing critique of corruption. In other contemporary reports, we find that often a notion of social chaos, created by the influx of refugees, was deployed as a reason to explain the growth of corruption and unfair advantage: as one Indian newspaper report put it, 'Hawkers and refugees throng the recognised shops and buy outright whatever stock is made available for sale. The result of this confusing situation is

[39] *National Herald*, 8 January 1948 (1 *maund* = c. 37 kilos).
[40] 'Government Order Review of Steel Fabricators' Lists', *National Herald*, 6 January 1948.
[41] Alleged Acceptance of Bribes: Case against Bengal Official Opens', *National Herald*, 8 January 1948.
[42] 'Who Gains from Cloth Decontrol?', *National Herald*, 10 April 1948, Magazine Section.

that there is widespread corruption, and large profits made in transaction, go neither to the manufacturer nor to the public revenues through taxation'.[43] Corruption and anti-corruption thus became a theme for civic association in ways that intersected different urban localities, via the supply of moving goods.

Rather like the hagiographies of 1930s anti-colonial leaders, tales of heroic anti-corruption crusaders, who struck at the roots of the everyday forms of graft, became popular. One such figure in UP was a district magistrate by the name of B. D. Sanwal. The local and divisional railway authorities were reported to have refused to cooperate with Sanwal in his energetic drive against corruption. In one incident, three bags of salt belonging to the Doon Salt Syndicate Dehradun were lying unrecorded in the railway goods office, but when the district magistrate sent for relevant goods office records, the stationmaster refused to comply. The divisional superintendent of railways at Moradabad also refused to take action on Sanwal's request to halt the transfer of goods office staff who were wanted by the authorities in connection with an anti-corruption investigation.[44] Sanwal was also noted for his work in Mussoorie where, as district magistrate, he was credited with organizing 'the speedy rehabilitation' of former Muslim evacuees returning to the district and their buildings.[45]

Over the border in Sindh, similar processes were at work. Corruption and public reactions to it dominated public imaginations. In 1947 Karachi as well as being Pakistan's new capital was home to Sindh's Legislative Assembly and also, at least initially, the headquarters of the provincial administration. However, less than a year after Pakistan's creation, Karachi was formally separated in terms of administration from the rest of the province. In its new guise as a Federal Capital Territory, covering a little over 2,000 square kilometres, control shifted from provincial into central hands in May 1948. This move divided the Pakistani state – from the perspective of many living in Karachi – into two tiers. On the one hand, federal ministries and other bodies based in the city juggled all-Pakistan responsibilities. On the other, a combination of provincial and municipal-level officials were tasked with addressing complaints on matters ranging from food supplies and housing shortages to

---

[43] *National Herald*, 22 April 1948.   [44] *National Herald*, 6 January 1948.
[45] 'Rehabilitating Muslim Evacuees in Doon', *National Herald*, 6 April 1948. While most UP Muslims who were deemed to have migrated to Pakistan did not return to their former homes, there were cases of individuals who made their way back to India usually for a combination of personal and employment reasons. See Zamindar, *The Long Partition*, for individual examples of this return migration.

educational provision, bus routes and refuse collection.[46] General executive authority was exercised by the office of the Chief Commissioner, whose jurisdiction extended to control over prisons, police and local bodies (such as the Karachi Municipal Corporation or KMC), while sanitation and the maintenance of roads were among the main tasks of the Corporation. With so many of Karachi's new residents expecting considerably more from the local authorities than the latter could deliver, it is not surprising that people habitually complained about the service they were, or were not, receiving. By the summer of 1948, just a year after independence, Karachi – like other urban centres in Sindh – faced huge problems in terms of how to absorb its hugely swollen number of inhabitants. Water and sewerage arrangements had quickly proved inadequate to cope with their needs. There was a marked deterioration in municipal cleanliness, public health services, roads and transport facilities, and so in July 1948 the KMC was dissolved on the grounds of poor administration as well as alleged corruption.[47]

Complaints about poor service being provided by local state representatives, however, persisted. Time and again, people living in Karachi and other urban centres in Sindh aired their concerns, whether in relation to communal water taps that ran dry, or, alternatively, about insufficient support from officials when too much water in the form of monsoon rains caused havoc for refugees living in shanty-style temporary accommodation. In 1950 flooding caused by severe monsoon rains sparked three weeks of demonstrations outside the homes and offices of federal ministers and Muslim League leaders, prompting calls for 'more action' and 'less oratory'.[48] Similarly, 1953 witnessed considerable anxiety, and public protest, over Karachi's inadequate water supply that threatened acute shortages in the forthcoming dry season. There were also ominous signs that the city's sewers, constructed for a much smaller urban population, were close to breaking point.[49] In 1954 a number of refugees were

---

[46] At the time of independence, Karachi possessed a relatively recently created Municipal Corporation: with a mayor, a deputy mayor and seventy-three councillors (of whom sixty-five were elected by ballot; the composition of its board reflected the population of a city that, before 1947, had been made up of c. 50 per cent Hindus, 40 per cent Muslims and 10 per cent including Christians, Parsees, Buddhists and Jews. In 1950, in line with the increase in the city's population, the number of councillors was expanded to 100, of whom 96 were to be elected by ballot.

[47] The KMC remained suspended until January 1954, with its normal business under the control of a government-nominated British Municipal Commissioner (R. A. F. Howroyd).

[48] 'Recent Developments in Refugee Rehabilitation in Karachi and West Pakistan', US Embassy Despatch, 4 August 1950, 890D.41/8-450 USNA.

[49] UKHC Fortnightly Reports, dated 16–29 December 1952, 10–23 February 1953, 17–29 June 1953, DO35/5300 UKNA.

killed and many more injured during heavy rains that caused a wall to collapse on their shacks in the Pakistan Industrial Fairground, prompting fresh outbursts of what were by now well-rehearsed criticisms of the city authorities. On repeated occasions, the city's *Dawn* newspaper captured much of this frustration at the deficiencies of the everyday state. Its comments published in 1952 in response to an ongoing wider campaign to upgrade Karachi's status to a full-fledged province highlight the infuriation:

A government should be judged on its beneficial activities and not on surplus budgeting. In present day democracy a national government is expected to give to the citizens a minimum standard of educational facilities, medical help, health care, sanitary condition of life, speedy justice and law and order. The present set-up has miserably failed to do so due to Karachi being deprived of a voice in its own administration.[50]

But the presence within one city of competing sources of government authority – federal and municipal – often led to problems, particularly in relation to the allocation of scarce resources like land for housing. In one case, a group of refugees were permitted in 1948 to start building on a plot of land apparently on the written orders of the then Collector of Karachi. In 1949 the Ministry of Health and Works allotted four blocks of land to the Pakistan Employees Cooperative Housing Society (PECHS), one of which happened to include the – by now – constructed 'Khudadad Colony'. It took until August 1951, following 'a long silence', before the Administrator called a meeting with the Deputy Secretary of the Ministry for Health and Works, the Collector and a PECHS representative to discuss the problem. Instead of regularizing the colony as its inhabitants had been expecting, however, the Administrator simply ordered a further survey to establish if accommodation had actually been constructed. As one of its residents complained, 'Our houses are *pucca* ones and cost ... more than half a crore of rupees, which include[d] expenses incurred in connection with construction of three big mosques, levelling of uneven land after tollsome [*sic*] labour, erection of water stands and cost of water pipe line etc'. For people like this former refugee, the first priority of the authorities should have been to 'relieve us of our mental agony'.[51]

Pakistan, unlike India, failed to hold a general election during this period. While polls were conducted periodically at provincial level, where their results could produce political shockwaves (as in East Bengal in 1954 when the ruling Muslim League was ousted by an opposition

[50] 'Case for Karachi Province II', *Dawn*, 26 April 1952.   [51] *Dawn*, 8 December 1951.

United Front victory), this meant that Pakistani voters lacked the same potential means of redress – a democratically elected national parliament – as their Indian counterparts. Accordingly, in the absence of representative institutions through which citizens could – directly or indirectly – air their grievances, newspapers like *Dawn* (in English) and *Jang* (in Urdu) offered valuable outlets for the public's irritation. Moreover, Karachi was home to a large proportion of the newspapers published in Pakistan, testifying to the city's status as the federal capital and its importance as the main centre for political comment and criticism. In letter after letter written to their editors, inhabitants of Karachi poured out their exasperation at what they viewed as the prevailing administrative inefficiency, as illustrated by the following critical correspondence that appeared on *Dawn*'s pages in early 1952:

The Economy Committee has recently submitted its second interim report making recommendations to the Government for the eradication of general inefficiency in the Central Government Departments. But one cause of this inefficiency does not appear to have been touched anywhere in its first or second report. [It] is that the officers, superintendents and more than 80% in the Government departments are those who were recruited in war-time to the Central Government services as Third Division Clerks and they have been promoted in Pakistan to the posts of Assistants In-charge, Superintendents, Administrative Officers, Assistant Controllers, Directors etc. Due to [their] lack of higher education. ... they are incapable of expressing their views properly in the English language. They generally waste their valuable time in preparing rough drafts and notes in pencil. Such drafts are invariably amended, revised or re-written by the approving authorities. To remove the root of inefficiency, it is suggested that the Central Secretariat may be advised by the Economy Committee to ban the promotions of matriculates over graduates to the higher posts beyond the posts of Assistants irrespective of their length of service. This will not only increase the efficiency in the Central Government departments but will also give an impetus for higher education.[52]

These kinds of publicly expressed grievance provide valuable insights into what Pakistanis in the late 1940s and early 1950s believed to be the rights and duties of citizens. For an office-holder of the All-Pakistan Barbers' Association, who firmly disassociated himself from a demonstration by 'foot-path' barbers protesting at the authorities' rehabilitation plans, solving difficulties by 'the most peaceful and legal means [were] the attributes of the citizens of a free and democratic state like Pakistan'.[53] Similarly, when firewood sellers in the city were ordered at extremely short notice to vacate their shops and move to the newly constructed suburb of Lalukhet (later renamed Liaquatabad following

---

[52] *Dawn*, 6 January 1952.   [53] *Dawn*, 15 December 1951.

Liaquat Ali Khan's assassination in 1951), they claimed that, though it would take them years to re-establish their businesses afresh, 'We have to obey the government and carry out its order and cooperate with it, but at the same time [we] request the authorities to appreciate our difficulties'.[54] In this, the recourse of organizations to local protest against the everyday state, in the face of governments' actions in cities, could be seen in similar ways in both UP and Sindh,[55] The relationship between citizen and the state was, after all, a reciprocal one, as such requests as these testify.

The frustration experienced by ordinary people during Pakistan's early years, like those of their counterparts in India, is revealed in the writings of Majeed Lahori, a journalist and poet who – following his move to Karachi after independence – became a well-known columnist ready and willing to raise more widely held concerns through the medium of wit and satire. In 1948 he began writing a column entitled '*Harf o Hikayat*'[56] that appeared in the Sunday edition of the Urdu-language *Jang* newspaper (for which he wrote on a regular basis until his death in 1957). As his poem 'Beggary was forbidden but … !' illustrates, Lahori always took the side of the underdog, filling the role of 'a tribune of the people which no other Pakistan artist had the courage or talent to attempt … he accurately expressed the embittered feelings of the general public [with] targets located amongst those whom the Pakistan movement [had] carried to power: bureaucrats, politicians, black-marketeers, allotment-grabbers, the ladies of APWA[57] and the Shia community':[58]

> Get for me a building, get for me a bungalow,
> Get for me a printing house, get for me a factory,
> Get for me a petrol pump or cinema,
> If not a bus, then at least a bus stand.
> Get for me in the name of the nation, Oh giver,
> It will be kind of you.[59]

[54] *Dawn*, 25 December 1951.
[55] 'Hamara Nagar – hazaron parishan 5 ghante tak bina pani ke', *Aaj*, 11 April 1948.
[56] *Harf o Hikayat* = disputing or complaining conversation.
[57] The All-Pakistan Women's Association (APWA) was set up just after Partition by the wife of Prime Minister Liaquat Ali Khan, Raana Liaquat Ali.
[58] 'Death of Pakistan Political Satirist', 12 July 1957, 890d.41/7-1259 USNA. As pointed out in this US report, Lahori's criticisms of Shias would have been understood by 'the average Pakistani' to be targeted at persons of the highest rank in Pakistan and not the small bazaar merchants belonging to this sect of Muslims.
[59] *Jang*, 14 April 1957.

Corruption and Anti-corruption

'Corruption' and 'anti-corruption', just as in the late colonial period, were inescapable features of the political landscape in both India and Pakistan after 1947. In virtually identical language, politicians in both countries now urged government servants to ensure that their conduct conformed to the new 'cleaner' spirit of independence and democracy. In Pakistan, this was epitomized by Jinnah's oft-quoted instruction to gazetted officers in Chittagong during what turned out to be his controversial visit to East Bengal in early 1948. After reminding them that 'those days are gone when the country was ruled by the bureaucracy', he emphasized that 'You do not belong to the ruling class; you belong to the servants. Make the people feel that you are their servants and friends, maintain the highest standard of honour, integrity, justice and fair play'.[60] The following October, while Pakistanis were still coming to terms with Jinnah's death, the country's Finance Minister, Ghulam Mohammad, reinforced the message that rooting out corruption would 'strengthen Pakistan'.[61] A very similar sentiment was expressed across the border. UP's chief minister in the first years after independence, G. B. Pant used much the same rhetoric when he spoke of the need for clean administration to accompany the political freedoms of independence. In a speech to police officers in Kanpur in early 1948, he declared that 'the days when we detested the red turbans [colonial policemen] are over'. In discussing the need to fight bribery and corruption, 'policeman should behave towards the people just as they would expect police to behave with their own kinsmen in different parts of the country'. Today, he argued, officers were not merely policemen, but citizens of a free nation.[62]

For many Pakistanis and Indians, therefore, visible 'anti-corruption' mechanisms were integral to the way that the new state sought to distance itself from what many of them viewed as its 'corrupt' colonial predecessor. There was pressure on those who represented it, whether politicians, elite civil servants or petty officials, to fulfil their responsibilities to Pakistan's and India's citizens – their 'public' – in fair and honest ways. Maladministration in a range of forms was no longer acceptable, at least according to the rhetoric of politicians, at both

---

[60] 'Address to the Gazetted Officers of Chittagong', 25 March 1948, www.humsafar.info/480325_doy.php (accessed December 2018).
[61] *Dawn*, 7 October 1948.
[62] '"Imbibe Missionary Spirit": Premier Pant's Plea to Cawnpore Policemen', *National Herald*, 17 January 1948; See also, 'Police Kartashya', *Aaj*, 6 January 1948.

national and local levels: and bureaucrats, like their politician counterparts, were expected to operate honestly when discharging their duties.
But the challenge of negotiating bureaucratic procedures together with
the impact of day-to-day shortages of essential goods meant that ordinary
members of the public who wished – to take just two common instances –
to obtain a license to sell controlled goods or a new ration card often
found themselves engaging in some form of corruption. The result was
that 'many civil servants found themselves in a position of considerable
power. They could influence the commercial fortunes of private individuals by granting licences, awarding contacts or allotting refugee property.
Owing to the shortage of staff such officials often operated without
effective supervision or control'.[63]

The authorities in both new countries likewise signalled early on their
public determination to address the problem of corruption within
the federal and provincial administrations. In 1947 both Constituent
Assemblies passed Prevention of Corruption acts, making corrupt activities into a special crime. In 1948 in Pakistan, the (now) federally
controlled Special Police Establishment (SPE), which had been set up
in 1942 across British India to investigate rampant corruption in government departments, was officially renamed as the Pakistan Special Police
Establishment (PSPE), and charged with rooting out 'illegal gratification' in all its various forms. As Fazlur Rahman, Pakistan's Federal
Minister for the Interior at the time, explained, 'The functions of the
Special Police Establishment are to investigate and bring up for trial cases
of bribery and corruption involving transactions with the Central and
Provincial Governments'.[64] Previously responsibility for addressing these
crimes had fallen under provincial jurisdiction, but this new agency was
intended to supplement and reinforce the efforts of ordinary provincial
police forces: no one would be considered above the law and 'even a
Minister in Pakistan had no claim to special protection'.[65] Likewise in
India, the SPE continued its work after Independence as an organization
at the centre, but its functions were very thinly spread. While lip service
was paid to the idea of regionally linking offices, with branches located in
Calcutta, Shillong, Ranchi, Puri, Jubbelpore, Delhi, Bombay and
Madras, its sanctioned strength in 1948 remained a mere 139 constables

---

[63] Keith Callard, *Pakistan: A Political Study* (London: George Allen & Unwin, 1957),
p. 298.
[64] Fazlur Rahman, 8 March 1948, *Constituent Assembly (Legislature), Debates*, 1948, Vol. I,
p. 320.
[65] UKHC Opdom 14, 12–18 February 1948, IOR L/WS/1/1599 BL.

with 70 posts to be filled over the following years.[66] In reality, therefore, the SPE faced stiff resistance in its investigation activities from government departments across India where systematic corrupt practices remained well-entrenched.[67]

Another comparable early signal of intent in Pakistan was the Public and Representatives Offices (Disqualification) Act of 1949 (PRODA), which provided the means for impeaching 'persons judicially found guilty of misconduct in any public office or representative capacity or in any matter relating thereto'.[68] This measure arguably represented the most widely publicized achievement of Pakistan's first Constituent Assembly.[69] It empowered the governor general as well as provincial governors to refer any charges of misconduct in public office to the courts or to a special judicial tribunal, with the penalty for being found guilty set as personal disqualification for up to ten years. By also permitting members of the public to submit allegations – providing that five people supported them and could lodge a deposit of Rs. 5,000 – this legislation made politicians and government servants, in theory at least, accountable to ordinary Pakistanis. In practice, PRODA came to be used as a way of putting political pressure on government ministers, either by opposition politicians or the central authorities themselves, resulting in – as one contemporary described it – an 'epidemic' of such petitions in the early 1950s.[70]

By contrast, India did not introduce the same legislative infrastructure as that set up by PRODA in Pakistan. The outcome was a similar political milieu in terms of an anti-corruption competition between political leaders and their associated administrators, but fewer available mechanisms with which to prosecute malpractice. Accusations of prosecution against government servants were certainly covered by the Anti-Corruption Act and also a complex series of government servant rules and procedures (albeit rules which operated their internal social hierarchies): the Civil Services (Classification, Control and Appeal) Rules; the Punishment and Appeal Rules for Subordinate Services; the UP Disciplinary Proceedings (Administrative Tribunal) Rule; the UP Public

---

[66] 'Question in the Constituent Assembly by Prof. N.G. Ranga', Ministry of Home Affairs, SPE, File 12/5/48 NAI.

[67] Gould, *Bureaucracy, Community and Influence*, pp. 113–4.

[68] *Gazette of Pakistan*, 9 July 1949.

[69] Pakistan's Constituent Assembly passed forty-four pieces of legislation between March 1948 and September 1954, aimed at amending or supplementing the 1935 Government of India Act and the Indian Independence Act of 1947.

[70] M. H. Gazdar, April 1952, *Constituent Assembly (Legislature) Debates*, 1952, Vol. I, p. 1455.

Services Commission (Limitation of Functions) Regulations; and the Government Servants' Conduct Rules to name but a few.[71] As far as politicians were concerned, mutual accusations were usually played out with renewed vigour around election times.

These important distinctions between Pakistan and India reflected, in large part, the difference following Independence between a place (Pakistan) where the bureaucracy managed to retain and increase power in the polity as a whole, and another (India) where a successor party ruled through mostly decentralized bureaucratic structures. Whereas most political corruption scandals in India were contained by the structures of the Congress organization and party discipline exercised by the All-India Congress Committee (AICC), the situation in Pakistan was rather different. For India, political corruption scandals featured heavily both in the correspondence that flowed between provincial and central Congress organizations and, likewise, in the local and national press.[72]

By contrast, in the early 1950s in Pakistan, we find a number of high-profile judicial inquiries, with four former provincial chief ministers all disqualified from political office for varying lengths of time. One of the first to fall foul of PRODA was M. A. Khuhro who – having been dismissed as chief minister of Sindh in 1948 on the grounds of 'maladministration, gross misconduct relating to his duties and responsibilities, and corruption' – was charged the next year under PRODA regulations. Following his dismissal, a local newspaper editorial praised Khuhro's successor, Pir Ilahi Bakhsh for his 'honest' admission that 'the contagion of corruption had so enveloped the whole of the province [Sindh] that its effect is discernible in every nook and corner', and consequently his 'determination to eradicate it with a firm hand'. The new premier's promise not to interfere in the provincial government services, which the editorial viewed as 'a hindrance to good administration' that prevented 'Public Servants from giving their best to the state', was similarly welcomed.[73] Pir Ilahi Bakhsh stressed his Ministry's good intentions, claiming that before he and his Cabinet colleagues had even set foot in their offices within the Sindh Secretariat they had sworn an oath in the presence of leading refugee cleric Maulana Shabbir Ahmad Usmani to remain 'scrupulously honest and devote themselves to the service of the people', waging 'a Holy War against corruption and [making] an all-out effort to eradicate the evil'.[74] Later on, in 1951, following Khuhro's official rehabilitation and reinstatement as Sindh's

---

[71] Gould, *Bureaucracy, Community and Influence*, pp. 116, 119.
[72] See, for instance, 'Congress mein Bhrastachar', *Aaj*, 25 January 1948.
[73] *Dawn*, 5 May 1948.   [74] Ibid.

premier, he was once again dismissed, on this second occasion with c.60 charges of corruption levied against him.[75] Though these were rejected towards the end of the year, yet another PRODA petition was then filed against him, this time by a 'group of private citizens' supported by opposition factions within Sindh's highly factionalized political establishment, and he was disqualified from holding office for a further six years.[76] Finally, in 1958 Khuhro was sentenced to five years for alleged black market activities, involving the illegal selling of an imported, and very expensive, Chevrolet car. All the same, this outcome did not dent his popularity among many Sindhis who took the line that it was unfair for Khuhro to be singled out for hard treatment when many others involved in the same activity remained at liberty.[77] But as this example suggests, although the practices (and, indeed, the rhetoric) of corruption and anti-corruption were not dissimilar on both sides of the border, it is clear that in Pakistan, unlike India, the executive power of the bureaucracy and the patterns of political rivalry provided effective licences for the regime in power to remove officers and ministers on the basis of that rhetoric.[78]

There were also important disparities at the local level, not least because of the varied developments of anti-corruption mechanisms in the former provinces of British India. Under the Congress regimes of the late 1930s, UP and Bihar had set up their own anti-corruption committees.[79] By 1946, this had resulted in the formation of district anti-corruption committees, which were subsequently reformed and developed through the late 1940s and into the early 1950s.[80] In 1955, they were further enhanced through the acquisition of a formal constitution of membership including the requirement that they contain members of the state legislature, a representative of the Bar Association and five nominated non-officials.[81] In Pakistan following Independence, anti-corruption departments were also established at the provincial level.

---

[75] 'Disruption in the Sind Provincial Government', 15 December 1951, 790D.00/12-1551 USNA.

[76] US Embassy Despatch 959, 29 January 1953, 790d.00/1-2953 USNA.

[77] See 'Impressions from a Trip to Sind and Multan', 30 March 1959, 790d.00/3-3059 USNA.

[78] See Ilyas Chattha, 'Competitions for Resources: Partition's Evacuee Property and the Sustenance of Corruption in Pakistan', *Modern Asian Studies* 46, 5 (2012), pp. 1182–211, for a discussion of the part that the redistribution of evacuee property played in the institutionalization of corruption in Pakistan, with particular reference to West Punjab.

[79] Gould, *Bureaucracy, Community and Influence*, pp. 105–11.

[80] 'Measures to Fight Corruption: Pant's Discussion with District Committees', *National Herald*, 16 April 1951.

[81] 'District Anti-Corruption Committees', Home Police (A), Box 76, File 402/55 UPSA.

In East Bengal, this move led to over 6,000 cases being registered in 1948–9 (of which about only one-third eventually produced convictions).[82] In Sindh, supported by his force of anti-corruption police officers, wide powers were given to that province's Anti-Corruption Commissioner in an attempt to bring about a much-heralded thorough 'clean-up' of the provincial administration. These powers included suspending any officer belonging to any department when charged with corruption, as well as ordering departmental inquiries as and where necessary. The Sindh provincial authorities were also supposed to consult with their Commissioner when making appointments and confirming or promoting officers. By the early 1950s, the federal government had promulgated further anti-corruption legislation. The 1953 Civil Services (Prevention of Corruption) Rules now meant that a Pakistani government official could be presumed guilty if he had 'a general and persistent reputation' for corrupt practices, and if his lifestyle, or that of his family, was not in line with his 'visible means'.[83] A corresponding pattern of developments was repeated in other parts of the country. A 1950 report on Pakistani Punjab, for instance, claimed that the machinery of day-to-day administration had become noticeably less efficient: 'water mains are not repaired, the post is slow and incompetent, canal bank roads are no longer properly maintained, and in a number of other ways standards are still falling'. 1951 saw a further rise in corruption at the lower levels, with increases complaints about *bhai-bandi* (nepotism) and 'oppression' by subordinate officers.[84]

No doubt, the fallout from these provincial, national and cross-border scandals and punishments had a direct effect on everyday discussions of corruption on the streets of cities in UP and Sindh. In the case of UP, food procurement and supply controls connected debates in its legislative assembly to problems of administrative enforcement and the operating of black markets. In April 1951, for instance, the Minister for Food and Agriculture, K. M. Munshi, publicly decried a situation in which the enforcement of hoarding and black marketing laws for food grains was ineffective, due to the inability of state governments, based on a popular mandate, to implement such laws, and because of the corruption in the administration of such systems on the part of administrative

---

[82] This was in addition to the 5,485 cases processed through normal police procedures. See Nurul Amin, 23 March 1949, *Official Report of East Bengal Legislative Assembly*, 1949, Vol. III.

[83] Mohammad Ali, 24 September 1953, *Constituent Assembly (Legislature), Debates*, 1948, Vol. II, p. 204.

[84] UK Deputy High Commissioner, Lahore Despatch, 6 July 1950, UKNA; UK Deputy High Commissioner, Lahore Despatch, 9 February 1951, DO35/3186 UKNA.

staff.[85] But at a more mundane level, for many ordinary Indians and Pakistanis living in localities such as UP and Sindh, corruption remained an inescapable fact of everyday life, made all the more difficult by the reality that the guardians of law and order – the police – were themselves often culpable. As one early 1948 *Dawn* report, under the headline 'He came... He saw... He suspended', explained:

Karachi's Superintendent of Police went out in plain clothes on Wednesday morning to seek the truth in the public complaint about the prevalence of corruption in the police force. Strolling up Harding Bridge[86] he saw two police constables on duty stopping over-loaded camel carts and allowing them to pass after taking bribes. He walked up to the constables and revealing his identity suspended them on the spot.[87]

A similarly persistent theme running in many of UP's Hindi-language newspapers at the same time was reportage on city-based protests against the police in places such as Kanpur and Agra. In particular, this included numerous letters of complaint and articles relating to corruption among inspectors on the railways.[88] Here, the specific grievances highlighted, on the one hand, systematic corruption in the movement of goods, and, on the other, the harassment of ordinary citizens as they attempted to carry out the everyday but extremely frustrating task of booking a train ticket.[89]

Corruption – or the need to curb it – entered nearly all aspects of life, criss-crossing and, in the process, entangling public and domestic spheres on both sides of the border. Just as the notion of citizenship embraced certain ideals about the family, so ideas about anti-corruption implicated the 'roles' or responsibilities of women. In April 1951 in fifteen UP cities, plans were set up for an All-India Women's Food Council, as a means of 'mobilizing the Indian housewife to fight the food battle' and countering problems of hoarding. As well as joining in this fight, the campaign promoted the idea that a good proportion of the country's food needs could actually be covered by careful husbanding in the home and that women should pledge to forego one day's cereal ration per week and prepare food from non-rationed food items.[90]

A similar link between citizen-centred anti-corruption and 'women's duties' was reflected in the writings of Zeb-un-Nissa Hamidullah. Her

---

[85] 'Extension of Grow More Food Scheme', *National Herald*, 7 April 1951.
[86] Harding Bridge linked Karachi port and the Haji Camp to the city's main Secretariat quarter.
[87] *Dawn*, 5 March 1948.
[88] 'O T railway bhrashtaachaar band ho, 5 January Gorakhpur mein Virodh sabha', *Aaj*, 6 January 1948.
[89] 'Railway ke bhrashtaachaar ka Virodh', *Aaj*, 20 January 1948.
[90] 'Food Crisis and Women', *National Herald*, 16 April 1948.

columns, entitled 'Thru a Woman's Eyes', which appeared in *Dawn* from the beginning of 1948, covered topics that ranged from how to handle the in-laws to impassioned calls to Pakistani women to cast aside 'bad habits' and fulfil their duties, not just as wives and mothers, but – equally importantly – as citizens of the newly created Pakistan, which needed their help just as much as that of their fathers, husbands and sons. Accordingly, as in the following piece dating from July 1948, she repeatedly admonished them for their own 'corrupt' behaviour, and for turning a blind eye to the misdemeanours of others, and in the process summed up much of the rhetoric as well as the reality of the post-Partition years:

There is a great deal of complaint of bribery and corruption in our State today: not that these evils have come with the establishment of Pakistan (for they were very conspicuous during the British reign as well) but because we are shocked and pained when we find our Muslim brothers indulging in such activities. Although men who accept bribes or are guilty of gross dereliction of duty, are justly condemned by every right thinking individual, I consider that the wife of such a man is often the real culprit and deserves the blame for all that her husband may do. ...

There are wives, I wish their number were as few as we would like to believe, who think their husbands are very clever fellows if they can make some money on the quiet. In fact they sometimes call their husbands foolish for not taking sufficient 'advantage' of the position they occupy. [They] encourage their husbands to take bribes, and save their consciences by saying that everyone does such things. Such wives are insulting their womanhood and the power it gives them. The women of Pakistan have often voiced their love for their country and their desire to serve it. Many of them complain that they are not provided with sufficient opportunities to be of service. ... A woman must strive to keep her husband content and thereby make it easy for him to be honest. In her children she must instil a perfect uprightness of character and a hatred of corruption. A woman who accomplishes these tasks to the best of her ability has done the greatest service to the State.[91]

Meanwhile, there were other problems of supply corruption that shaped wider notions of social (in)justice. Smuggling was one such illicit activity, with local newspaper columns frequently reporting on efforts to tackle it, such as when, to take one everyday instance, '32 bales of [illegally imported] fine cloth' were seized in the UP city of Kanpur in April 1948.[92] Smuggling, on the one hand, represented a direct challenge to state authority – in particular its ability to exercise control over the new borders that divided Indian and Pakistani territory and across which movement was becoming increasingly regulated – but, on the other, the

[91] *Dawn*, 6 July 1948.
[92] *National Herald*, 4 April 1948; 'Hamara Nagar', *Aaj*, 8 April 1948.

very act of publicizing official efforts to clamp down on this 'menace' added useful weight to the state's authority. The difference in value between the Indian and Pakistani currencies, thanks to the devaluation of the Indian rupee in 1949, pushed up the profits to be made by smuggling across – from Pakistan into India – what remained in practice a porous border. Moreover, the element of corruption associated with smuggling meant that it could easily assume an anti-national character, and often, though not always, culprits were assumed to be working in the interests of the other country, even when economic factors were more likely to have been the principal driving force. Hence, the illicit cross-border transfer of goods represented a source of particular disquiet during the early post-Independence years, highlighting the instability of the physical boundaries that separated 'belonging' from 'not belonging'.

In Pakistan, non-Muslim government officials were often blamed for involvement in smuggling, either accused of turning a blind eye or of offering active support to smugglers. They consequently attracted a disproportionate share of the blame, and not just in East Pakistan where a highest proportion of Hindus had continued to live after August 1947. In reports on anti-smuggling initiatives in West Pakistan that were issued frequently throughout the late 1940s and early 1950s, individuals belonging to minority communities were often the main target of criticism, whether implicit or explicit: As one 1948 report put it,

The racket of smuggling precious food grains from Jaisalmer state to Sind continues unabated. There has been a slight check in these activities for some time due to increased government vigilance. However they are now renewed due to the help of Mr. Ramchand Advani, Deputy Collector and Sub-Divisional Magistrate who has always been notoriously anti-Muslim and has a long list of unhappy deeds to his credit. Whenever any camels and food grains are intercepted both camels and food grains are returned to the smugglers under the influence of Mr. Ramchand.[93]

Smuggling raised challenges for both governments, with the series of Inter-Dominion agreements signed by India and Pakistan between late 1948 and early 1950 revealing how important but also how difficult resolving the complicated economic fallout from Partition was proving to be, particularly during a time when essential commodities were in short supply.[94] In 1949, we see this reality reflected in the suggestion of drastic measures as the way to check food smuggling from Sindh, which included declaring a ten-mile (later in practice five-mile) strip of land

---

[93] 'Foodgrains Smuggling to Jaisalmer Continues', *Dawn*, 11 October 1948.
[94] 'Relations between the British Commonwealth and the Governments of India and Pakistan, 18 June 1948–21 June 1950', DO133/91 UKNA.

along the Indo–Pakistan border as a prohibited area and the introduction of a compulsory levy on the total produce of local *zamindars*, regarded by urban-based commentators as the main culprits. As a spokesman for the Sindh authorities responded, 'until and unless the smuggling of food grains [was] declared as high treason by the Pakistan Government and drastic measures were not taken', this 'evil' would not be eradicated: 'The inforcement [*sic*] of auxiliary forces on the border to check the smuggling is no solution. The officials should be very hardworking and without favour'.[95] To compound matters further, according to press reports, there were as few as 55 head constables stationed along the 700-mile border of West Pakistan with India 'to fight the food-smuggling menace', but even so by July officials were claiming somewhat prematurely to have halted the smugglers' trade completely.[96]

The following year, against the backdrop of the ongoing Indo-Pakistan exchange rate dispute,[97] a mounting number of reports about smuggling generated another spike in public alarm. Even though a recently signed trade agreement between Delhi and Karachi had – in theory at least – legalized the transfer of a number of formerly smuggled goods – such as tobacco, cigarettes and betel nut products – contemporaries observed that the trade imbalance (in favour of India, at least this was how it looked to Pakistani commentators) along with continuing shortages of essential products such as wheat and rice would keep commodity trafficking channels open for the foreseeable future.[98] In response, the authorities argued that the decision not to devalue the Pakistani rupee – blamed by critics for a slump in the price of agricultural goods – was designed to benefit the consumer, and they reinforced the official line that 'apart from causing a national loss to the country, smuggling is a corrupt practice. The Government propose to meet this threat firmly and if anybody is found indulging in this nefarious activity however high he may be, he would be dealt with firmly under the law'.[99]

In 1952, popular anxiety about smuggling in Pakistan reached a new peak. Newspapers alleged that large-scale smuggling of food grains was continuing across the Sindh–India border with massive quantities of

---

[95] *Dawn*, 1 April 1949.   [96] *Dawn*, 28 April 1949; *Dawn*, 1 July 1949.

[97] 'Policy Statement Prepared in the Office of South Asian Affairs', 9 October 1950, 780.00/10–1750, Foreign Relations of the United States, 1950, The Near East, South Asia, and Africa, Vol. V, https://history.state.gov/historicaldocuments/frus1950v05/d99 (accessed December 2018).

[98] In 1949, the Sindh authorities took steps to encourage the production of betel products to feed the demand of refugee *paan* eaters for these vital ingredients. *Dawn*, 13 October 1949.

[99] *Dawn*, 1 September 1950.

commodities in short supply being stored in secret granaries in cities such as Sukkur in Upper Sindh before being trafficked out of Pakistan to India. By now smugglers – commonly alleged in the press to be Hindu traders – were the country's 'Enemy no 1',[100] and smuggling was repeatedly tagged as anti-national involvement.[101] *Dawn* in January 1952, for instance, reported on the confiscation by anti-smuggling staff of 4,000 *maunds* of top-quality wheat while crossing the Sindh border. The smugglers in this case were alleged to be 'Hindu banyas', though in passing it did also mention that three Muslims had been arrested.[102] As some contemporaries pointed out, prevention held the key to solving the problem, for 'a potential wrong-doer', or so they believed, would be deterred not by 'the severity of punishment but [by] its certainty'. Moreover, commentators highlighted the complex set of interests involved in this 'nefarious business'. This included *zamindars* with their large estates and hence large surpluses of food grains, who were said to operate hand-in-hand with wealthy and enterprising traders, camel cart drivers who actually transported the grain to India, the border police without whose active cooperation large-scale smuggling was simply not possible and last but not least the bankers and money-changers who arranged for payment in Pakistan rupees: 'Which of [these] categories involved in the smuggling business is an efficient and honest border police officer likely to catch first?'. Rather than just focussing on how to punish offenders if or when they were apprehended, critics of the authorities instead called for the introduction of a Food Grains Control Act, border patrols with special police 'equipped with portable wireless, fully armed with modern weapons' and networks of informers located in suspect areas. Crucially, they called for the creation of the necessary 'socio-political consciousness (or public opinion) in the mind of the peoples against anti-social offences in general and smuggling in particular'.[103]

In April 1952, coinciding with severe shortages of food and other essential items, the Pakistan Constituent Assembly issued instructions for 'all-out war' to be declared against smugglers, with central and provincial authorities permitted to frame special laws including preventative detention in order to fight the menace – deemed a rampant threat to the security of the state – more effectively.[104] The resulting crackdown bolstered the mandate of Pakistani officials to act as primary protector of the dividing line that separated their country from its neighbour. The response, however, was mixed, and not everyone supported the new policies. Muhammad Sadiq Chaudri, of the 'Sind Cotton Growers and

---

[100] *Dawn*, 27 January 1952.   [101] *Dawn*, 11 April 1952.
[102] *Dawn*, 12 January 1952.   [103] *Dawn*, 4 February 1952.
[104] *Dawn*, 16 April 1952.

Abadgars Association' in Hyderbad, among others, offered a rather different explanation for the problem:

We have been for past few years been hearing from the high and low that Pakistan is surplus in food. This propaganda had lulled us into a sense what ultimately turned out to be false security. The bubble has burst and hunger stalks the land. The apologist is, however, even now busy in proclaiming that Pakistan is really not deficient in food and the present calamity is due to bad harvest and smuggling. ... The Government is to blame because while a show of procurement was made no real procurement took place. ... We are one people, one government and have one aim. The Government can surely take the public into its confidence and the public will cooperate wholeheartedly.[105]

Conclusion

In both India and Pakistan in the first few years following Independence, a great deal of public debate concerned the control, supply and movement of goods. And the matter of food and civil supply became the material basis for imagining the responsibilities but also broader development of the citizenry in places such as UP and Sindh. This was important, not least because of the anti-colonial rhetoric of previous years, which as well as being based in the essential corruption of the colonial system also emphasized its resource extraction. Independence, and the rights of citizen therefore, also signalled control over national resources. As Benjamin Siegel has recently argued, the food control and rationing apparatus in India (and we might argue the same for Pakistan), served as 'a locus for managing and imagining the nation's food economy': the idea of public service tied up with the notion of 'responsibilities' for goods control, as well as 'rights' to those resources – the dual underpinning of the material bases of citizenship.[106] It was for this reason too, that food/supply-related corruption became such a powerful political issue following Partition.

As demonstrated by Krishnamachari's question in the Indian Constituent Assembly in late 1947 that opened this chapter, from the outset concerns were articulated not just in relation to people moving but what they might be taking with them when they travelled between Pakistan and India. And such concerns did not abate in the years that followed. To take just later one incident, Pakistan-bound passengers in 1949 protested vociferously about the searching of their baggage by Indian officials as

---

[105] *Dawn*, 28 February 1952.
[106] Benjamin Robert Siegel, *Hungry Nation: Food, Famine and the Making of Modern India* (New York: Cambridge University Press, 2018), pp. 88–9.

they journeyed by train across the Rajasthan border into Sindh, with similar complaints surfacing as a repeated refrain throughout this period.[107] As reactions to the issue of smuggling discussed above suggest, and as this chapter has underlined more broadly, fierce competition for scarce material resources such as foodstuffs, cloth and concrete marked the early postcolonial period in both India and Pakistan.

In our chosen localities of UP and Sindh, material shortages – within the wider framework of the economic austerity of the late 1940s and early 1950s – directly stimulated public discussion in the form of state rhetoric as well as stoking citizen complaint. Likewise, corruption, and how to limit if not to eradicate it totally, regularly dominated local headlines as the two sets of authorities tried to put a stop to this activity, deemed by many contemporaries to be against the national interest and hence 'unpatriotic'. In a similar fashion, anti-corruption campaigns, like anti-smuggling efforts – whether in Pakistan or in India – became methods of determining who belonged and who did not: in effect, as we have explored in this chapter, a citizen was increasingly deemed to be someone who placed the public good ahead of their personal ambition or needs.

---

[107] *Dawn*, 10 September 1949.

4   New Constitutions, New Citizens

In the September 1947 issue of *The Modern Review*,[1] published in Calcutta very soon after Independence and Partition, a short article entitled 'Nationality in the Indian Union' posed the question – from a legal perspective – as to 'what principle should decide the [sic] nationality in the Indian Union'. As its author Amarendra Nath Mukerjee pointed out, the Fundamental Rights Sub-Committee of the Indian Constituent Assembly was already framing the new country's draft nationality clause, and so for him this was precisely the right time to direct attention to a matter that 'seems to be the most essential factor in the political life of a person'.[2]

Interestingly, however, Mukerjee's article did not linger long on the legal tussle between the determining principles of *jus soli* and *jus sanguinis* but moved quickly to a question that obviously preoccupied him, that of the possibility of South Asian citizens holding a 'double nationality'. As he put it, 'If the Hindus of Sind [sic], the Sikhs of a part of the Punjab and the Hindus of East Pakistan are deprived of their Indian nationality because they happen to belong to those parts of the country which under most unfortunate circumstances form a different state (Pakistan), it would be doing a great injustice to them and alienating them for ever from their motherland'. Under the current 'peculiar circumstances' in which they were submitting to Pakistani nationality 'with reluctance and under pressure of circumstances', the desirable way forward would be to confer 'the benefit of Indian nationality' upon Pakistani Hindus, making

---

[1] *The Modern Review*, founded in 1907, carried essays on politics, economics, sociology, as well as poems, stories, travelogues and sketches, becoming 'the leading journal of the progressive Indian intelligentsia', Ramachandra Guha, 'A Mask That Was Pierced?, *The Hindu*, 24 April 2005, www.thehindu.com/mag/2005/04/24/stories/2005042400270300.htm (accessed December 2018).

[2] Amarendra Nath Mukerjee, 'Nationality in the Indian Union', *The Modern Review* 82, 3 (September 1947), pp. 203–4.

them concurrently subjects of Pakistan and India. But, significantly, for Mukerjee, there was no harm in granting this concession for, as he reminded readers of *The Modern Review*, 'We must not forget that the consent of the people is an essential factor in determining their national-ity at the present time': individual self-determination, or personal choice, lay at the centre of his argument. And so, while he conceded that creating provisions for the acquisition of Union nationality by Hindus in Pakistan might 'give rise to jarring claims', Indian law 'should not follow the beaten track'.[3]

It is now widely recognized by historians and political scientists that processes of exclusion as much as inclusion drive and shape the concept of belonging. Developments in the subcontinent from 1947 prove no exception to this rule. Determining nationality – and as a consequence who did or did not legally belong where – represented a central and consistent priority throughout the constitution-framing years that followed Independence and Partition in both India and Pakistan.[4] Anupama Roy in *Mapping Citizenship* has explored from a legal per-spective various moments in the history of India's citizenship laws and the twists and turns within them since 1947, showcasing the 'liminality' of the concept of citizenship, and how far the legal citizenship in India that emerged at the commencement of the Indian Republic in the context of Partition's fallout remained a contentious and contested issue.[5] According to Vazira Zamindar, bureaucratic and juridical acqui-sition of the term 'migration' proved particularly problematic in attempts to control and fix Partition-related displacement within the bounded limits of these two newly emerged hostile countries.[6] More recently, Joya Chatterji has highlighted the extent to which India and Pakistan followed similar trajectories in terms of citizenship formation while also pointing to where these diverged, challenging what she views as Zamindar's overemphasis on the role of the state and substituting this approach with greater acknowledgement of the impact of pressure from below.[7]

---

[3] Ibid.
[4] Sarah Ansari, 'Subjects or Citizens? India, Pakistan and the 1948 British Nationality Act', *The Journal of Imperial and Commonwealth History* 41, 2 (2013), pp. 285–312.
[5] A. Roy, *Mapping Citizenship in India* (New Delhi: Oxford University Press, 2010).
[6] Vazira Zamindar, *The Long Partition and the Making of Modern South Asia: Refugees, Boundaries, Histories* (New York: Columbia University Press, 2007).
[7] Joya Chatterji, 'South Asian Histories of Citizenship, 1946–1952', *Historical Journal* 55, 4 (2012), pp. 1049–71.

Acknowledging the direction of travel of recent historiographical discussion, this chapter takes as its starting point Chatterji's observation that 'the citizenship regimes of India and Pakistan shared remarkably significant ... symmetries',[8] and considers how far the processes involved in constitution-building and citizenship-making in both countries as well as their early experiments with democratic elections based on a universal franchise shed light on evolving notions of citizenship in postcolonial South Asia. Further, we explore the ways in which the concept of 'citizen rights' that were encapsulated within their post-Independence constitutions (1950 in the case of India and 1956 for Pakistan) chimed with the events and processes explored in Chapters 1–3 and what many ordinary Indians and Pakistanis at the time believed were their rights as 'citizens' to be. When deciding upon citizenship rights, both governments faced the common challenge of having to negotiate the dissonance between the agenda that they set from above and the way in which this agenda was interpreted and implemented from below. Rather than assuming that the two countries in constitutional terms moved – inexorably – in separate directions, we draw attention to similarities as well as differences between the processes at work in the decade following Independence, and thus to the degree of interconnectedness that operated despite the upheavals of 1947. In this context, a range of quotidian readings of constitutional rights emerged alongside more formal expressions of citizenship entitlement.

In contrast to earlier approaches that have viewed constitutions as 'canonical' documents located at the heart of processes of attempted consensus,[9] this chapter highlights the decentring processes of constitution-making as contingent practices, which can implicate ordinary subject/citizens, their experiences of governance and their multiple imaginaries of rights. One lens through which it looks at these developments is the range of responses to the new constitutions and other constitutional documents that were implemented in the decade following

---

[8] Ibid., p. 1051.
[9] For instance, the main work on India's constitution by Granville Austin, naturally places the formal drawing up of the document at the centre of its narrative. Since Austin's extensive and seminal work, there has been very little focus on the broader social implications of what he described as 'first and foremost a social document'. See Granville Austin, *The Indian Constitution: Cornerstone of a Nation* (New Delhi: Oxford University Press, 1999).

Independence, reactions that were often linked to notions about the allocation of and access to public goods. Another way that it investigates them is via India and Pakistan's early experiments with democratic elections, and other similar if not identical state-building efforts that drew on and invoked notions of citizenship and belonging. For, as we argue in what follows, the postcolonial state – whether Indian or Pakistani – did not simply engage with its citizens through formal political processes during this period of transition. Instead, official initiatives, such as national censuses, offered opportunities for its citizens alike to engage with the new – postcolonial – political reality taking shape across South Asia in these important transition years.

'New Constitutions'

Here comes the biggest republic of the world,
Prepare the throne for the 300 million people,[10]
The coronation is not of a king today.
It is of the people.[11]

India and Pakistan today are associated with markedly different reputations when it comes to their long-term democratic credentials. Despite the challenge to the post-1947 Nehruvian dream of a secular India posed by the recent success of Hindu nationalist parties and politicians, India's western-style parliamentary democracy – drawing on political 'credit' built up over the decades following Independence – continues to be celebrated by many onlookers as the largest democratic state, as well as the most successful by rates of participation, in the contemporary world. Pakistan, by contrast, earned itself a poor reputation for democracy thanks to the imposition of military rule that displaced civilian politicians at periodic intervals after 1947, earning it the label of a 'failing' if not 'failed' state (despite more recent elections resulting in relatively smooth handovers of power from one political party to another).

Constitutionally, too, India and Pakistan tend to be viewed as being poles apart. Both drew heavily on the same 1935 Government of India Act when it came to their constitutional agendas, but whereas India's 1950 Constitution remains in place after more than 70 years (albeit with hugely significant subsequent amendments), Pakistan's 1956 Constitution was abrogated within two years when the military seized power in 1958,

[10] A reference to the estimated population of the Indian Union in 1950.
[11] Extract from the poem entitled 'Vacate the Throne, for the People are Coming' (*Singhasan khaali karo ke janata aaati hai*) by Dr. Ramdhari Singh 'Dinkar' (1908–74), who wrote it on 26 January 1950, the day on which the new Indian Constitution became effective.

Figure 4.1 Indian leaders in the Constituent Assembly, Council House Library, New Delhi, 1947.
Photo by Hulton Deutsch/Corbis Historical/Getty Images

and thereafter a succession of civilian- and military-led administrations sought to re-mould Pakistan in different constitutional ways. This first section consequently explores the processes involved in constitution-building in India and Pakistan in the late 1940s and 1950s and how people living in them at the time viewed their own rights and responsibilities.

India and Pakistan began life as independent countries in August 1947 with a common legacy in the shape of two separate indirectly elected Constituent Assemblies (see Figure 4.1).[12] Originally established

---

[12] The idea for a Constituent Assembly of India was proposed in 1934 by M. N. Roy, pioneer of the Communist movement in India and an advocate of radical democracy. It became an official demand of the Indian National Congress in 1935. In 1939 Rajagopalachari had voiced the demand for a Constituent Assembly based on adult franchise, something that was eventually accepted by the British in 1940 when the Viceroy Linlithgow's August Offer included allowing Indians to draft their own constitution. Under the Cabinet Mission Plan of 1946, elections were held for the first time for the Constituent Assembly, with members elected by the provincial assemblies by a single transferable vote system of proportional representation in August that year. The total membership of the Constituent Assembly was 389: 292 were chosen by the provinces, 93 represented the Princely States and 4 were from the chief Commissioner Provinces of Delhi, Ajmer-Merwara, Coorg and British Baluchistan.

as one combined body in 1946, the institution split following the announcement of the Partition Plan on 3 June 1947, when representatives from Sindh, East Bengal, Baluchistan, West Punjab and the North West Frontier Province – territories more or less certain by then to be part of Pakistan – withdrew to form Pakistan's own separate assembly that met for the first time in Karachi on 10 August. In India, what remained of the original body reassembled on 14 August and assumed parliamentary authority, holding its first working session at the end of December. By January 1950, the Indian Constitution had been promulgated; it took until 1956 for its Pakistani equivalent to materialize. Both were contentious exercises in translating democratic hopes and expectations into political reality.

Until recently, a number of inter-related research paradigms have stalled the development of more socially nuanced accounts of South Asia's post-1947 constitutional processes.[13] As far as India is concerned, older 'constitutional histories', for instance, formed part of the empirical and structural studies of the colonial system that emerged during the 1960s and 1970s. Historians writing during this period tended to explore Indian politics as a Namierian-style response to shifting colonial jurisdictions, in which constitutional systems of dyarchy and provincial autonomy formed a proverbial steel frame.[14] From the 1980s, these were subsequently critiqued and effectively limited as an area for ongoing research by scholars from within the tradition of Subaltern Studies. Problems also emanated from another direction – namely the assumption that the enactment of its 1950 Constitution represented an end point in the fulfilment of India's freedom struggle.[15] As the 'logical [legal] conclusion' to decades of British imperialism, this foundational political text has thereby been made rather static in political and historical accounts. It has been represented as a document of rights, classifications and federated structures, embedded beneath India's fluid political realities, with its history one of constitution makers and the formal ends to which they were driven – in other words, the realm of politics from above. But, surprisingly, with the exception of the recent work of Rohit De, the 1950 Constitution that underpins India's brand of democracy does not

---

[13] The most prominent exception to this is Rohit De, *A People's Constitution: The Everyday Life of Law in the Indian Republic* (Princeton, NJ: Princeton University Press, 2018).

[14] Anil Seal, *The Emergence of Indian Nationalism: Competition and Collaboration in the Later Nineteenth Century* (Cambridge: Cambridge University Press, 1971); Peter Robb and David Taylor (eds.), *Rule, Protest, Identity: Aspects of Modern South Asia* (London: Curzon Press, 1978).

[15] Arvind Elangovan, 'The Making of the Indian Constitution: A Case for a Non-Nationalist Approach', *History Compass* 12, 1 (January 2014), pp. 1–10.

possess a serious or detailed historiography that explores its broader popular significance.[16] Studies such as the one by Granville Austin, dating from 1966 and extended in 2004, still dominate the literature, placing the 1950 Constitution firmly at the heart of independent India's legal history, and framing it as *the* canonical document embodying India's moment of national freedom and democratic institution-building.[17] As such, India's Constitution continues to be presented largely as a document that was the product of (changing) consensus, with little detailed sense of how its meanings were shaped or evoked by those outside the formal political processes of the state.

Studies of Pakistan's fluid constitutional arrangements have been similarly constrained. Owing to the fact that political agreement could not be reached until 1956, in large part because of the difficulties involved in reaching an agreement between the different 'constituencies' within the country, the process of constitution-making in Pakistan turned out to be particularly drawn out, dominating discussions at the federal level for nearly a decade following Independence. Unlike India where later constitutional amendments offered a way of making changes, successive Pakistani regimes chose (at least until the 18th Amendment of 2010) to rewrite the country's constitution afresh, whether we are talking about General Muhammad Ayub Khan's 1962 replacement constitution that provided for a presidential form of government – abolishing the office of prime minister and establishing a tier of electoral colleges starting with 80,000 Basic Democrats divided equally between the two wings of the country – or Zulfikar Ali Bhutto's 1973 revision that turned Pakistan into a parliamentary democracy but with executive power concentrated in the office of the prime minister. Hence, scholars with an interest in Pakistani political history have focussed mainly on what these successive constitutions reveal about the regimes that introduced them, and how they fitted into the broader power struggles of their time – again, a politics from above approach.[18]

Exploring processes of constitution-making in India and Pakistan in the late 1940s and 1950s alongside each other highlights common challenges in their parallel, if not identical, transitions from colonial rule to Independence. This approach also points to the important interactions taking place between developments at the political centre and popular

---

[16] Uday Mehta, 'Constititutionalism', in *Oxford Companion to Indian Politics*, eds. Niraja Jayal and Pratap Bhanu Mehta (New Delhi: Oxford University Press, 2010), pp. 15–27.

[17] Austin, *The Indian Constitution*; Granville Austin, *Working a Democratic Constitution: The Indian Experience* (Oxford: Oxford University Press, 2000).

[18] Imran Ahmad, '"Strategic Constitutions": Constitutional Change and Politics in Pakistan', *South Asia: Journal of South Asian Studies* 40, 3 (2017), pp. 481–99.

responses in both countries despite their different circumstances. That the two sets of processes were closely interlinked is clear, at least to the extent that what one enacted had consequences for the other, whether directly or indirectly or thanks to what was or was not incorporated in their respective new constitutional arrangements.

Let us turn first to the Indian side of the border, where the new Constitution was formally promulgated at the end of January 1950. For international observers it was clear that this constitutional document – containing 395 sections and incorporating 8 schedules – 'broke all previous records'.[19] Five sessions of the Constituent Assembly had been devoted to it, and in all 2,473 amendments had been moved, not to mention frequent debates behind the scenes. The Constitution, having been agreed, now had to be put into practice. And here what is particularly striking is the contrast between reporting on it prior to India's first general election in 1952 and reflections afterwards. Before 1952, the views of Patrick Gordon Walker, then British Secretary of State for Commonwealth Relations, epitomized the earlier response:

> The inauguration on the 26th January was, indeed, something of an anti-climax to the man in the street: for to him, in essence, the position remained what it had been since the transfer of power ... Some of the ideals seem impossible of fulfilment in any foreseeable future and almost ludicrously inapposite in the context of Indian poverty and backwardness.[20]

Walker, with a possible tinge of resentment, continued: 'it is one thing to write a constitution, another to make it work'. What was also noticeable for him in 1950 was the absence of specific protections for 'minorities' – for which he read Muslims – but equally he commented that it was 'satisfactory that so great a preponderance of authority has been granted to the centre'. There seemed to be a grudging recognition on his part that democracy 'may work' but equally that India had 'deeply rooted in its political practice the tradition of despotism', although, for British observers such as Walker, resistance to despotism remained an 'Anglo Saxon concept'.[21]

In many respects, the well-known projects of social justice contained within India's 1950 Constitution seemed somewhat hollow to contemporary observers, and were often reported as such at the time. During parallel celebrations in Kathmandu, the Indian Ambassador to Nepal, C. P. N. Singh, referred in his speech to a 'long war of Independence' led

---

[19] P. C. Gordon Walker, Secretary of State for Commonwealth Relations, March 1950, FO371/84239 UK National Archives (hereafter UKNA).
[20] Ibid.   [21] Ibid.

by the Congress as the greatest element in that achievement. For him, the Indian Republic stood for the 'fundamental human rights of man', while the idea of the 'secular state' would bind India in 'a homogenous unity to overcome religious, linguistic and provincial differences that enslaved us to foreign rulers'. As a result, in his view, their new constitution empowered Indians to oppose colonialism in all its forms around the world, as well as to denounce war as an instrument of policy and to bring about 'the renaissance of the ancient traditions and culture of Asia'.[22] On the other side of the world, in Washington, DC, the US Congress celebrated the nobility of the project, with the Congressional record suggesting that 'as partners in democratic faith, India and America can help meet the moral and material needs of mankind. The peoples of India and the peoples of America share a spiritual strength ... Together, India and America can make the four freedoms real for all races and nations'.[23] In the meantime, British government representatives lost few opportunities to express their doubts. At Republic Day celebrations organized by Indian embassy officials in Stockholm the same year, British reporters suggested that the National History Museum had been ransacked for specimens of Indian fauna – three peacocks, a cheetah and a gazelle. 'The Indian Minister, and still more Mrs Nehru, have lost no opportunity of impressing on anyone who cares to listen the merits of the ancient Indian democracy', reported the UK Ambassador, adding perhaps disappointedly, 'I cannot say that they have permitted themselves any generous tributes to British statesmanship in bringing the new Republic to birth'.[24]

The notion that the rights and freedoms guaranteed by its new constitutional framework were somehow too advanced for a country like India was not only held by western observers. Individual figures within the Congress organization itself, especially those occupying government roles, could be just as cynical concerning what they regarded as the precipitate creation of new freedoms, and hence some of them advocated renewed control over the Fundamental Rights that it included. This was evident at a regional level as well. In UP, its Chief Minister G. B. Pant certainly held this view as far as press freedoms were concerned. When it came to the tendency of UP newspapers to criticize public servants openly and to expose corruption scandals, Pant complained that 'Freedom of speech and expression guaranteed by the constitution is being

---

[22] Speech of C. P. N. Singh, FO371/84239 UKNA.
[23] Congressional Record, Senate, 26 January 1950, FO371/84239 UKNA.
[24] A. Lambert, 'Republic Day Celebrations in Stockholm: Publicity and Comment in the Press', 30 January 1950, FO371/84239 UKNA.

wantonly abused. Venomous and filthy attacks are being made from day to day against the central and state governments and ministers and officers holding responsible positions maliciously and in an extremely vulgar and indecent manner'.[25] In a 1951 note, entitled 'On some proposed amendments to the constitution of India', Pant suggested to Nehru that it might eventually be necessary for reasons of 'decency and morality' to amend Article 19 of the Constitution on freedom of speech by adding conditions regarding libel, defamation, slander and the contempt of court. After all, Clause II of Article 19(a) had already imposed restrictions on the exercising of this freedom. Unlike many other countries, Pant continued, where courts were permitted to intervene to decide the scope of police powers, this was not the case in India, where 'courts [were] powerless to question the propriety or reasonableness of a law restricting the freedom of speech or expression'. As Pant explained,

In other countries there are certain standards of public life which are usually adhered to and sound principles defining and limiting freedom of speech and expression have gradually evolved. Our constitution being only a year old, healthy traditions which normally develop in the course of time, have not yet developed.[26]

The amendment of Article 19 eventually became the subject of legislative enactment in the autumn of 1951, when the Indian government introduced the Press (Incitement to Violence) Bill, which provided scope for the authorities to take action against the publication, circulation or exhibition of 'objectionable matter'.[27] Journalists' organizations were furious and the press in UP criticized the bill for re-affirming some of the pre-Independence censorship powers of the Indian Press Emergency Powers Act.[28] The UP Working Journalists Union passed a resolution against the legislation, claiming that it continued the powers of the 1931 Act, and that the idea of 'objectionable matter' was too vague.[29]

---

[25] G. B. Pant to Nehru, 5 March 1951, Pant Papers, Reel 1 Nehru Memorial Museum Library (hereafter NMML).

[26] 'Note on Some Proposed Amendments to the Constitution', 5 March 1951, Pant Papers, Reel 1 NMML.

[27] 'Press Bill Is Introduced', *National Herald*, 1 September 1951.

[28] 'The Press Bill', *National Herald*, 8 September 1951. During the Second World War, the executive had exercised exhaustive powers under the Defence of India Act. Pre-censorship was reinforced, in the shape of the 1931 Press Emergency Powers Act and the 1923 Official Secrets Act. At the same time, the publication of all news relating to the Congress activities was declared illegal. The special powers assumed by the Government during the war ended in 1945.

[29] 'No Justification for Press Bill: UP Union Executive Urges Appointment of Commission', *National Herald*, 10 September 1951.

In relation to other issues, however, the UP government was able to claim that it was very closely following the Fundamental Rights as laid down in the Constitution. Pant argued firmly against any amendment to Article 31(4), which underpinned the redistribution of large landed estates via Zamindari Abolition, and was keen to show how this chimed in with notions of equality while still allowing for notions of discrimination:

Ours is a Republican constitution. The preamble of our Constitution declares to secure to all the citizens of the state equality of status and of opportunity ... Equality of persons is the fundamental on which our Constitution has been built ... it is another thing that sometimes discrimination is necessary in the interest of the collective interest of the community and in such cases it will not be correct to say that equality before the law or the equal protection of law has been denied ... Every individual has rights not absolute but in the context of collective rights of the community.[30]

But alongside circulating concerns about equality and justice, prior to January 1950, there was also more basic disquiet that was discussed at length a propos how the Constitution's subtle notions of secular rights would play out in reality. A resolution regulating communal organizations, for instance, had been passed by the Constituent Assembly on 3 April 1948, influenced by continuing communal tensions as well as Gandhi's still very recent assassination. Nevertheless, both at that time and later on, Nehru's administration acknowledged the difficulties of drawing 'a clear cut line between religious, cultural and social and educational activities (which may be termed non-political activities) and other political activities'.[31] The main challenge was that the Fundamental Rights soon to be conferred by the Constitution could render certain types of political activities justifiable even when they were pursued by communal organizations. To take just one example, if some of these Fundamental Rights were in practice denied to a particular community in a particular area, then its members might justifiably organize themselves for the purpose of asserting these entitlements and getting other communities to recognize them. This concern was in addition to the implicit 'communal' assumptions underlying the principle of provisions for 'depressed classes' that the Constitution contained.

   Doubts about the application of the Constitution, especially in relation to secularism, were exposed by responses to the election of P. D. Tandon – leading member of the right wing of the Congress who hailed from UP – as the party's president in 1950, in the process defeating the Sindhi

---

[30] Re: Zamindari and Article 31 HCM, note 2, 5/3/51, Pant Papers, Reel 1 NMML.
[31] 'Regulation of Communal Organizations', Min. of Home Affairs Ests F 60/220/48 NAI.

politician Acharya Kripalani[32] who was widely believed to be backed by Nehru. As we saw in Chapter 2, Tandon had been publicly urging the Indian authorities to adopt a tougher line on evacuee property, refugees and Pakistan more generally, resulting in fellow Congress members such as Rajagopalachari, by now the governor general, to express concern about the growth of a militant Hindu spirit within the party and how this might confront a militant aspect of Pakistani identity.[33] Karachi newspapers reacted to Tandon's election by suggesting that his victory was a clear indication of the growing strength of communalism within the Congress. According to *Dawn*'s leading article on 5 September that year, his appointment represented the first crack in the walls of Nehru's cabinet, and 'the biggest potential danger to the more sensible section of the Congress'.[34]

Despite such misgivings, it was still the case that the Fundamental Rights contained within the Indian Constitution were arguably more developed and held more promise than any modern constitution had previously offered. Furthermore, the creation of a republic that was to stay within the Commonwealth represented a change with far-reaching international consequences, not least for neighbouring Pakistan. Shortly following Independence, the UK Foreign and Commonwealth Office (FCO) was keen to gather news on the reaction among Pakistani diplomats to the declaration of the Indian Republic. At a toast given by the UK Ambassador to Afghanistan A. J. Gardiner in December 1949 celebrating the decision that the new Republic would remain part of the Commonwealth, he 'steer[ed] a narrow course' in response to the Indian Ambassador's speech. On the one hand, Gardiner plainly wanted to avoid offending Indians; on the other, in seeking to persuade Afghans that Britain had only grudgingly accepted the idea of a 'Republic' existing within the Commonwealth, he also 'had to avoid giving the Pakistanis the impression that the new Indian Constitution was regarded with such warm approval that Pakistan might, with no loss, follow India's example', and become a republic as well. Pakistani commentators, not unexpectedly, produced a different interpretation: the Kabul correspondent for *Dawn*, for instance, reported that the 'bubble of the Indian Republic was

---

[32] Jivatram Bhagwandas Kripalani (1888–1982), popularly known as Acharya Kripalani, was a Sindhi Congress politician prior to Independence, noted particularly for holding the presidency of the Indian National Congress during the transfer of power in 1947. Kripalani was supported by Nehru for election to the Congress presidentship in 1950, but was defeated by Patel's candidate P. D. Tandon.

[33] Acting UK High Commissioner Pakistan, 7 September 1950, FO371/84239 UKNA.

[34] Acting UK High Commissioner Pakistan, 5 September 1950, FO371/84239 UKNA.

pricked' by Gardiner's congratulating India for electing to remain a member of a Commonwealth that was still headed up by a monarch.[35]

Undoubtedly, therefore, tension in early high-level readings of the Indian Constitution was also directly related to the emerging reality of India and Pakistan's deteriorating relations. British diplomats, for whom the Indian decision to become a republic was 'regrettable', remained concerned that Pakistan would be 'infected by India', and that together these two South Asian countries might contaminate 'other members of the Commonwealth'.[36] The idea of India influencing decisions taken in Pakistan more broadly was also borne out by discussions on the latter's own constitutional developments, with Prime Minister Liaquat Ali Khan broadcasting to the nation in May 1949 that Pakistan might well change its relationship with the Commonwealth in precisely the same way that India had done. For external observers, it would be impossible for any government to remain in power in Pakistan if it did not emulate India in this respect.[37]

Throughout these early post-Independence years, tensions between India and Pakistan ran high, and were often reflected in a range of incidents centred around formal ceremonial moments. These connected diplomats to more everyday understandings of citizenship and belonging while highlighting the political distance that now separated the two countries. In Saudi Arabia, for instance, the Pakistan Consulate's enthusiastic celebration of Pakistan's first Independence Day in 1948 was marked by a speech that talked of Muslims having been 'obstinately denied their birth right' by India's leaders.[38] A year later, on the occasion of Independence Day in 1949, Indian policemen on duty at the flag-raising ceremony in Delhi insisted on seeing the identity card of the High Commissioner for Pakistan and those of his staff who were attending the anniversary celebrations. Not having the requisite document with him, the High Commissioner immediately left.[39] In 1949, anti-India riots occurred in Karachi on the anniversary of Independence, leading police officers to open fire on the crowd.[40] According to contemporary reports,

---

[35] UK Ambassador Kabul, 24 December 1949, FO371/ 84239 UKNA; *Dawn*, 5 February 1950.

[36] CRO to UK High Commissioner Pakistan, Telegram, 9 November 1950, FCO371/ 84258 UKNA.

[37] UK High Commissioner Pakistan to CRO, Telegram, 30 October 1950, FCO371/ 84258 UKNA.

[38] Enclosure to Jedda Despatch 140, 17 August 1948, address delivered by Mr. Shah Jehan Amir Kebir on the occasion of Pakistan Day at Pakistan Vice-Consulate on 14 August 1948, DO133/106 UKNA.

[39] F. K. Roberts, Telegram, 17 August 1949, DO133/106 UKNA.

[40] UK High Commissioner, Telegram, 17 August 1949, DO133/106 UKNA.

a large number of refugees had invaded the Indian High Commissioner's staff hostel and insisted that an Indian flag – hoisted by Indian clerks in the building – be taken down. The police contingent proved too small to cope with the protestors and so, following the ineffective use of tear gas, it resorted to firing, leading to fifteen casualties and one death. Moments of celebration in this way became occasions on which perceptions about the differences between India and Pakistan were exposed and reinforced, nationally and internationally.[41]

Pakistan's progress with constitution-making in the late 1940s and early 1950s proved slow as compared with India's, in large part because politicians and public alike became bogged down by the process of working out what its new identity as a place intended first and foremost for Muslims meant in constitutional terms, and also how the two wings of the country would work together. Jinnah's own rhetoric in the year before his death repeatedly emphasized the importance of the authorities maintaining law and order, rooting out corruption and treating minorities with 'absolute fairness'. His speech to the Pakistan Constituent Assembly, delivered on 11 August 1947 just before Independence, has often been held up as a guarantee of what minorities could expect in terms of personal religious freedom in this new Muslim-majority country, though Jinnah's critics also point to his readiness to manipulate religious sentiment when the need arose.[42] Provincialism, it seems, was a bigger worry for Jinnah in the immediate aftermath of Partition: speaking in particular to East Pakistanis but with provincial tendencies already visible in other parts of the country including Sindh, he warned Pakistanis that, 'As long as you do not throw off this poison in our body politic, you will never be able to weld yourself, mould yourself, galvanize yourself into a true nation'.[43]

Seven months after Jinnah died, the Pakistan Constituent Assembly passed the Objectives Resolution on 12 March 1949, which Liaquat Ali Khan described as 'the most important occasion in the life of this country, next in importance only to the achievement of Independence', and which UK observers regarded as a 'delicately balanced blend of Islamic terminology and western liberal principles'.[44] Contemporary discussion

---

[41] Inward Telegram to CRO, 16 August 1949, DO133/106.
[42] 'Muhammad Ali Jinnah's first Presidential Address to the Constituent Assembly of Pakistan (August 11, 1947)', in G. Allana, *Pakistan Movement Historical Documents* (Karachi: Department of International Relations, University of Karachi, n.d. [1969]), pp. 407–11, www.columbia.edu/itc/mealac/pritchett/00islamlinks/txt_jinnah_assembly_1947.html (accessed December 2018).
[43] *Speeches of Quaid-i-Azam Mohammad Ali Jinnah as Governor General of Pakistan* (Karachi: Sind Observer Press, 1948).
[44] 'Mullahs and Their Influence in Pakistan', 14 February 1951, DO35/3185 UKNA.

triggered by this 'historic' resolution – in particular how it addressed the 'Aims and Objects of the Constitution' – centred on the extent to which its aim was to establish Islam as the scaffolding for Pakistan's future constitutional arrangements, and consequently what the significance of this reality would be for non-Muslim minorities. Liaquat Ali Khan frequently emphasized that the 'so-called Ulamas [*sic*]' were misrepresenting what Islam would mean in practice within this framework, and it apparently became so 'fashionable' among government supporters, 'to attack the "mullah element" [with] slogans of "Down with Mullaism" … painted on thousands of walls in Karachi', that some years later Maulana Mohammad Akram Khan, member of the Constituent Assembly, reflected bitterly:

Yes, it is always the fault of the mullahs. If there is water shortage in Karachi, it is the fault of the mullahs; if Muslims fight among themselves, it is again the mullahs who are to blame. In short, whatever goes wrong mullahs are responsible for it.[45]

However, there was also criticism from a handful of Constituent Assembly members – articulated by the left-leaning Punjabi politician Mian Iftikharuddin – of the resolution's failure to guarantee more material forms of fairness and justice to Pakistani citizens whatever their religious affiliation. Despite repeated assurances that the state would observe the principles of democracy, and likewise fundamental rights such as freedom, equality, tolerance and social justice, Iftikharuddin warned that 'The fight in this country is not going to be between Hindus and Muslims. The battle in times to come will be between Hindu have-nots and Muslim have-nots on the one hand, and Muslim and Hindu upper and middle classes on the other'.[46]

All the same, broader issues of 'sovereignty', and who or what wielded it, lay at the heart of much of the debate promoted by the 1949 Objectives Resolution. Despite newspaper headlines, like those in *Dawn* that claimed that 'Sovereignty over the entire universe belongs to God Almighty alone', there proved to be little consensus among members of the Constituent Assembly or Pakistanis more generally.[47] As McGrath has pointed out, for the modernizers among them, the Objectives Resolution was 'a statement of morality, not a concrete prescription for the

---

[45] Constituent Assembly of Pakistan, Debates, Vol. 16, p. 483, 20 September 1954, cited in Keith Callard, *Pakistan: A Political Study* (London: George Allen & Unwin, 1957), p. 209.

[46] Grace J. Calder, 'Constitutional Debates in Pakistan I', *The Muslim World* 46 (1956), p. 43.

[47] *Dawn*, 2 March 1949.

operation of government'; at the same time, for many *ulama* and other religious leaders in the late 1940s Pakistan, it signalled 'the end of Jinnah's concept of a modern national state'.[48] Either way, despite stipulating that the state would exercise its powers 'through the chosen representatives of the people', the Constituent Assembly's assertion that this authority was delegated by God meant that religion occupied a very different position within constitutional debates in Pakistan to what it had done in India, where Nehru in the wake of Gandhi's assassination in early 1948 famously asserted that 'We are planning to create a Secular State, where one particular community or group or party will not be permitted to usurp the rights of another'.[49] But as Leonard Binder has argued, 'The real issue of the nature of an Islamic state was not yet joined, nor was it even clearly defined [... the Objectives Resolution] was in fact only an agreed formulation which both sides interpreted' according to their own priorities.[50]

The Basic Principles Committee,[51] established in March 1949 by the Governor General Khawaja Nazimuddin on the advice of Liaquat Ali Khan and tasked with preparing a more detailed constitutional framework, produced its initial interim report in the form of a draft section of the proposed constitution the following September.[52] Subsequent progress, however, proved to be slow, impeded by the infrequent meeting of the Committee during its twenty-month lifetime, and discussions were frustratingly opaque since 'all proceedings [of its sub-committees] were classed as confidential and although occasional statements were issued, they were brief in nature'.[53] Public impatience mounted alongside increasing anxiety, with even pro-government newspapers such as *Dawn* calling for clarity. The prime minister responded by arguing that the task demanded 'an unprecedented reconstruction in the realm of political thought and practice'.[54] In November 1949, it was announced that the work on fundamental rights was 'almost complete' and that the

---

[48] Allen McGrath, *The Destruction of Pakistan's Democracy* (Karachi: Oxford University Press, 1996), p. 71.

[49] *Times of India*, 1 February 1948. For a classic early appraisal of Indian secularism under Nehru, see Donald E. Smith, *India as a Secular State* (Princeton, NJ: Princeton University Press, 1963).

[50] Leonard Binder, *Religion and Politics in Pakistan* (Berkeley: University of California Press, 1963), pp. 150–4.

[51] The Basic Principles Committee had a president, 24 members, a steering committee and was itself subdivided into committee with responsibility for exploring Federal and Provincial Constitutions and Distribution of Powers; the Franchise; the Judiciary; and, later in 1952, Baluchistan States and Tribal Areas.

[52] 'Interim Report of the Basic Principles Committee of the Constituent Assembly of Pakistan', 17 November 1949, FO317/84258, UKNA.

[53] McGrath, *Destruction*, p. 74.   [54] *Dawn*, 18 December 1949.

constitution would be ready for 'enforcement' in the middle of 1951, to be followed by a new Parliament elected in 1952.[55] As Dr. I. H. Qureshi, Federal Minister and a Bengal member of the Constituent Assembly, explained in his presidential address to a gathering of political scientists in Lahore in December 1949, Pakistan faced a dilemma; in short, unless the people were entrusted with responsibility, they would never attain political maturity. This was a risk that Qureshi concluded had to be taken.[56]

In October 1950 Constituent Assembly members received another draft for consideration, though this was 'basically the [1935] Government of India Act with some of the amendments to that Act made by the Indian Independence Act, and with the Objectives Resolution as a preamble'.[57] East Pakistanis, many of whom by now were disenchanted with the political reality of being dominated by West Pakistani interest groups, opposed this interim document on the grounds that its contents represented 'a shameless conspiracy against [their] province [by the] power-drunk oligarchical ruling clique in Karachi [which sought] to impose a dictatorship under the camouflage of Islam'.[58] In November 1953, in protest at a discussion in the Constituent Assembly in support of Pakistan being made an Islamic Republic, 'Hindu members walked out, objecting to the general trend of the proceedings, and citing, specifically, violations of minority rights through the expected provision that the Head of State must be a Muslim'.[59] Meanwhile, on the other hand, widespread criticism of the draft was also voiced by 'mullahs and their friends in all parts of the country', who viewed the proposed constitution as too secular and western in character and objected to the Objectives Resolution being embodied only as a 'directive principle'.[60] Liaquat Ali Khan was accordingly forced to withdraw it in November 1950, though not before criticisms had also been voiced in West Pakistan. The *Pakistan Times*, known in the 1950s for its critical stance vis-à-vis the central government, echoed a broader mood when it cautioned against the over-centralization of state powers, something, it argued, that pointed to 'a suspicion of democratic methods and procedures'.

---

[55] *Dawn*, 25 November 1949.
[56] 'The Future Constitution', Presidential Address, Political Science Conference, Lahore, December 1949, in I. H. Qureshi, *Pakistan: An Islamic Democracy* (Lahore: Institute of Islamic Culture, n.d.), p. 10, cited in A. W. Burks, 'Constitution-Making in Pakistan', *Political Science Quarterly* 69, 4 (December 1954), p. 549.
[57] McGrath, *Destruction*, p. 74.   [58] *Pakistan Observer*, cited ibid., p. 76.
[59] Ardath W. Burks, 'Constitution-Making in Pakistan', *Political Science Quarterly* 69, 4 (December 1954), p. 560.
[60] 'Mullahs and Their Influence in Pakistan', 14 February 1951, DO35/3185 UKNA.

S. C. Chattopadhyaya, leader of the Hindu bloc, was quoted at the same time as commenting: 'This tramples on the principles of equal rights for all citizens and implies an inferior status for all non-Muslims'.[61]

Throughout this period of political transition, the kind of state that Pakistan's forthcoming constitution would create and the place of its citizens within the new constitutional arrangements figured as significant topics of discussion, inflected by awareness that developments across the border in India were proceeding at a faster pace. In January 1950, its timing neatly coinciding with the inauguration of the Indian Constitution, *Dawn* published a series of three linked articles, entitled 'Pakistan – Your State', in which the author – one Hamid Khalil – set out ideas about what constituted a citizen's civil liberties: 'Civil liberties form a part of the rights of citizenship that an individual commands as a citizen of a state. But then you may ask "what is a citizen" and what is meant by the rights of citizenship?' Khalil proceeded to answer his own question by explaining that while some civic duties were imposed by law, 'a good citizen realizes the highest freedom in discharging all the moral and legal duties of citizenship because true freedom implies the existence for every one of the opportunity to contribute out of the richness of one's own experience to the furtherance of the common good'. For him, a 'good' citizen was clearly not supposed to be a passive instrument at the hands of the government. Instead citizens 'should exert [themselves] to find out what is conducive to the welfare of the body politic of which [they are] a part'.[62]

Three years later, against the backdrop of the political crisis set in motion by the dismissal of the country's first Constituent Assembly in October 1954 by the Governor General Ghulam Mohammad, wider public reactions were revealing how ideas about citizenship could be viewed by Pakistanis at this time. The Assembly had been dismissed largely in response to proposed constitutional amendments that would have removed the governor general's power to replace the Cabinet and also nullified the use of PRODA proceedings against politicians charged with abusing their privileges.[63] A 'Cabinet of Talents' was duly appointed, headed up by the then Prime Minister Mohammad Ali Bogra, but also containing military generals (Ayub Khan, Iskander Mirza) and bureaucrats (Chaudhry Mohammad Ali, M. A. H. Isphani). The courts, to which opponents of Ghulam Mohammad's allegedly 'unconstitutional' action turned for support, proved unhelpfully divided in their

---

[61] *Pakistan Times*, 30 September 1950.   [62] *Dawn*, 8 January 1950.
[63] Ian Talbot, *A History of Modern South Asia: Politics, States, Diasporas* (New Haven and London: Yale University Press, 2016), p. 175.

judgements. In February 1955, the Sindh's High Court upheld the appeal filed by the Speaker of the Constituent Assembly Maulvi Tamizuddin Khan that the dissolution had been illegal on the grounds that the necessary power to do this had not been expressly conferred on the governor general. Moreover, there could be no working Cabinet without a working Assembly, since Cabinet members had to be Assembly members as stipulated in the 1935 Government of India Act. The Federal Court, however, while agreeing that there was no specific empowerment of the governor general that allowed him to take this action, overruled the earlier decision on a technicality, but also stressed that if the Constituent Assembly had performed its functions within a reasonable period then it would have dissolved itself by 1954: in effect, 'after eight years of its existence it had not given the country a constitution ... thereby rendering itself completely unrepresentative of and unresponsive to public opinion'.[64] The governor general's prerogative to intervene was permitted, albeit retrospectively, and a sixty-member 'constituent convention' was formed in May 1955 (elected by existing provincial assemblies) to ensure that any legislation was legally valid. Emergency powers also placed a 'blanket prohibition on all proceedings against the central government in connection with the dismissal of the first constituent assembly'.[65] Following 'painful negotiations', the constitutional bill was presented to members of this second 'Constituent Assembly' in early January 1956, who approved its contents, 670 proposed amendments notwithstanding, on 29 February. And finally on 23 March 1956 – nearly a decade after Pakistan's creation – its first Constitution came into effect.[66]

It did not take long for Pakistan's eagerly awaited constitution to attract criticism, however. In response to the fresh political crisis that was gripping both West and East Pakistan by the middle of 1956,[67] a *Dawn* editorial argued that 'it would be useless now for anyone to pretend that political stability has been achieved and that Pakistan is well set on the road to progress. Such hopes arose with the passage of the Constitution, and the high-sounding oaths, pledges and claims were taken by people on face value'. Instead, 'the Constitution has been

---

[64] Mushtaq Ahmad, *Government and Politics in Pakistan* (2nd ed., Karachi: Space Publishers, 1970), p. 31.

[65] Ayesha Jalal, *The State of Martial Rule: The Origins of Pakistan's Political Economy of Defence* (Cambridge: Cambridge University Press, 1990), p. 204.

[66] Ibid., pp. 213–4.

[67] G. W. Choudhury, 'The Constitution of Pakistan', *Pacific Affairs* 29, 3 (September 1956), pp. 243–52; UK High Commissioner, Karachi, Telegram, 26 May 1956, DO35/3407 UKNA.

reduced to a farce in less than two months, the people continue to be betrayed, and the world laughs'.[68] While *Dawn*'s editorial was far from neutral in its sympathies, as evidenced by its staunch support of the Muslim League as the political institution most likely to 'save' Pakistan and ensure the country's future, its criticism exposed wider popular frustration at the 1956 Constitution's failure to remedy the country's political instabilities: deploying the scientific language of medical diagnosis, the newspaper claimed that

the body-politic of Pakistan has been infected by such multiple viruses that the mere passage of a Constitution on paper has not proved an effective enough 'antibiotic' to cure it and restore it to normal health. Only the inherent strength of that body-politic – what physicians call the formation of adequate antibodies or disease-fighting organisms in the system itself – can help to conquer the disease.

While for *Dawn*, and those whose interests it represented, the Muslim League remained 'that rallying point round which healthy tissues will grow and multiply in the body-politic and give it again enough health and vitality to defeat and throw out eventually the pestilence with which it is now infected',[69] the editorial's criticism – as British observers commented – was 'an indication of the more open phase of manoeuvring into which Pakistan politics have passed since the bringing into force of the new Constitution'.[70]

Pakistan's first constitutional experiment proved to be extremely short-lived. Unlike the introduction of One Unit, which a year before had amalgamated the constituent parts of West Pakistan into a single province and which despite opposition survived intact until the break up and subsequent reconstituting of Pakistan in 1971, its 'democratic deficit' proved its downfall. As Paula Newberg's study of incomplete constitution-making stretching from the 1940s to the 1990s explains, by 1958, the 1956 Constitution had become an 'icon of political failure'[71]: in her words, it 'ushered in a short period of constitutional rule but the constitution's roots were also its shortcomings, which in turn compounded political instabilities across the country'. In return for the creation of a powerful presidency, limited parliamentary rule and little challenge to the writ of either the bureaucracy or the military, Pakistanis received a set of fundamental rights and judicial autonomy, at least in theory.[72] On 7 October 1958, following two and a half years of steadily

---

[68] *Dawn*, 24 May 1956.   [69] Ibid.
[70] UK High Commissioner to CRO, 26 May 1956, DO35/3407 UKNA.
[71] Paula Newberg, *Judging the State: Courts and Constitutional Politics in Pakistan* (Cambridge: Cambridge University Press, 1995), p. 71.
[72] Ibid., p. 69.

more unstable civilian politics and alarmed by the looming prospect of national elections, the military intervened and staged a successful coup. Newspapers the following day contained President Iskander Mirza's pronouncement justifying the imposition of martial law. In his view, 'the vast majority of the people no longer [had] any confidence in the present system of government', and Pakistan's integrity had been seriously compromised by the 'ruthlessness of traitors and political adventurers whose selfishness, thirst for power and unpatriotic conduct' could not be restrained.[73] Clearing up the mess created by civilian politicians was the order of the day, and some foreign observers even raised the suggestion that Pakistanis might be willing to put up with a military administration as long as it was reasonably 'clean' and 'efficient'.[74] All the same, many ordinary residents of Karachi, particularly those with refugee backgrounds, viewed 'Operation Cleanup' – launched by the city police to reduce serious crime in the aftermath of the military takeover – with grave misgivings, and stories of police brutality circulated widely in the city.[75]

As these constitution-building efforts in India and Pakistan – and reactions to them whether from Indians, Pakistanis or foreign observers – demonstrate, constitutions in the late 1940s and 1950s acquired huge symbolic as well as concrete significance for contemporaries, who often made sense of what they contained in terms of their own rights and responsibilities as citizens. Arvind Elangovan, in making his case for a non-nationalist approach towards the Indian Constitution, has maintained that by 'separating nation-making from constitution-making, the field of constitutional and political history' becomes 'a richer and more informative resource to understand the complex postcolonial developments in India'.[76] The same point could be made about the context within which Pakistan made (or failed to make) progress with regard to producing a constitution in the decade that followed Independence. And this also proved to be the case when it came to how India and Pakistan's new citizens flexed their constitutional muscles as voters going, or not going, to the polls over this same period.

---

[73] 'Martial Law Proclaimed', *Civil and Military Gazette*, 8 October 1958, cited in ibid., p. 71.
[74] UK High Commissioner, Despatch 20, 14 April 1958, DO35/8936 UKNA.
[75] Despatch 1206, 27 June 1958, 790D.00.6-2758, USNA. For more details on the impact of martial law on life in Karachi, see Sarah Ansari, *Life after Partition: Migration, Community and Strife in Sindh, 1947–1962* (Karachi: Oxford University Press, 2005), pp. 181–91.
[76] Elangovan, 'The Making of the Indian Constitution', p. 1.

'New Citizens'

Give way,
Listen to the thunderous roar of the chariot of time,
Vacate the throne, the people are coming.[77]

In *How India Became Democratic* (her detailed exploration of the preparations underpinning India's first general election over the winter of 1951–2) Ornit Shani argues that the preparation of electoral rolls on the basis of universal franchise, ahead of as opposed to following the promulgation of the Constitution, produced struggles for citizenship, often driven from below by Indians of modest means.[78] While tremendous administrative efforts went into the making of the universal franchise for the largest electorate in democratic history, the drawing up of the actual electoral rolls themselves informed the process of constitution-making from the ground upwards. From as early as November 1947, the Constituent Assembly Secretariat set in motion the preparation of draft electoral rolls on the basis of universal franchise, implementing the first constitutional promise to be fulfilled by the new Indian Republic, namely the principle that every adult citizen would have the right to vote, with the aim of holding of 'fresh general elections as early as possible after the new Constitution [came] into force'.[79] Moreover, during the actual preparation of the rolls, Indians – as Shani explains – conceived of their voting right as a basic constitutional guarantee, and hence various citizens' organizations were established in order 'to safeguard the right of franchise' that it promised.[80] Numerous other Indians meanwhile fought to get their names entered on the roll so as to ensure their voting rights as citizens.

Consequently, citizenship was directly identified from the outset with casting a vote, not an action that the vast majority of newly enfranchised Indians or Pakistanis had directly performed before Independence. Under the 1935 Government of India Act – the last piece in the colonial legal 'jigsaw puzzle' that subsequently shaped constitutional arrangements directly in India and Pakistan after 1947 – suffrage had been extended to a little more than thirty million people or about a fifth of the adult population, including a small number of women. Following Independence, elections – even when they did not take place – were extremely symbolic of the changed political postcolonial reality. This

---

[77] Dinkar, 'Vacate the Throne'.
[78] Ornit Shani, *How India Became Democratic: Citizenship and the Making of the Universal Franchise* (Cambridge: Cambridge University Press, 2018).
[79] Ibid., p. 91.   [80] Ibid., p. 64.

chapter's second section, therefore, builds on Shani's insights with respect to developments in India to explore further the parallel processes at work on the two sides of the new Indo–Pakistan border as people engaged, or sought to engage, with their new responsibilities as enfranchised citizens. At the same time, the authorities – in both countries – embarked on what seemed like a perpetual task of counting heads, often but not exclusively in preparation for the conducting of these elections. In different ways, early post-Independence exercises in number-crunching brought Indian and Pakistani citizens into closer proximity with the state at the everyday level, helping to embed notions of what citizenship entailed – at least in theory – from the perspective of both.

In the first Lok Sabha polls held between October 1951 and February 1952, India possessed around 176 million voters, out of an overall population of about 360 million. But following the relative lack of triumphalism between 1948 and 1950, political figures across the spectrum expressed doubts about the readiness of India's largely rural society for universal suffrage. None of this was lost on Sukumar Singh, author of *Report on the First General Elections of India, 1951–2*, who was the first Chief Election Commissioner. Eighty-five per cent of the electorate after all could neither read nor write. Each had to be registered and polling stations set up (see Figure 4.2). In addition, the size of the Indian general election was unprecedented at a global level. As one American observer, Richard Park, wrote, this all added up to 'a problem of colossal proportions'. There were to be c. 25,000 candidates across central and state assemblies for 4,500 seats (500 for the central parliament and rest for the provincial parliaments), and 224,000 polling booths, with two million steel ballot boxes, made from 8,200 tonnes of steel; 16,500 clerks were appointed to collate electoral rolls; 380,000 reams of paper used for printing the rolls; and there were 56,000 presiding officers, with a further 280,000 helpers and 224,000 policemen. Nehru himself travelled a total of 25,000 miles in all, criss-crossing the country on the Congress campaign trail. The voting stations were spread over more than one million square miles. In the case of remote hill villages, even bridges had to be specially constructed.

Many women did not wish to give their own names at the voting stations, preferring to be referred to as A's wife, or B's mother, which resulted in some 2.8 million women having to be struck off the list.[81] Yet, despite the high levels of illiteracy in India, the turnout was around 60 per cent (see Figure 4.3). Bombay – the city with the greatest density

---

[81] Ibid., p. 46.

Figure 4.2 Parliamentary elections, Delhi, January 1952.
Photo by Popperfoto/Getty Images

Figure 4.3 A queue of voters, India, January 1952.
Photo by Keystone-France/Gamma-Keystone/Getty Images

of polling stations – saw participation levels of c. 70 per cent, and in Travancore-Cochin as a whole, the level of participation reached nearly 80 per cent. Despite the often large distances involved and the inaccessibility of some villages, the turnout among rural voters living in vast constituencies (some of which had populations of 350,000 plus) was higher than in towns. Election symbols were used to help the illiterate – a bullock cart for one party, an elephant for another, a hut for a third.[82] Multiple ballot boxes, one for each party, were used to prevent mistakes by voters, and Indian scientists had developed an indelible ink to foil impersonation that involved the use of some 390,000 phials of ink. A documentary on the franchise and its functions and the duty of the electorate was shown in thousands of cinemas in 1951, and many more voters were reached through broadcasts from All-India Radio.[83] In UP alone, there were 12,000 polling stations and 50,000 booths. The voting itself eventually took place over four days and each of UP's fifty-one districts was split into four sectors with votes cast in rotation. It was estimated that around half of the state's total police force of 55,000 was engaged in the maintenance of law and order.[84]

There was an array of parties across the spectrum, albeit dominated by the Congress Party. Nehru's election speeches, delivered to around two million people at some 300 mass meetings, declared 'war on communalism', and made good mileage out of Congress's leadership of the freedom struggle and the party's links to Gandhi. In this sense, Congress very much relied upon 'reputation' as opposed to 'issues', for which the large-scale symbolic events between 1948 and 1951 were all the more crucial. Some of the other parties were drawn into this strategy, including the Socialist Party of Jayaprakash Narayan, which accused the Congress of deserting the ideals of older Gandhians, and the Hindu right-wing party, the Jana Sangh. The latter stood for the reunification of Pakistan with India, suspected India's Muslims to be a problematic minority and criticized the Congress for appeasing them. However, other parties, particularly those on the left, campaigned directly on socio-economic issues. The Scheduled Castes Federation, led by B. R. Ambedkar, accused the Congress of ignoring the predicament of India's poorest and most disadvantaged. The Communist Party of India (CPI) too had resurfaced after the initial post-Independence crackdown by the Indian

[82] Archibald Nye, 'The Indian Elections', Despatch 32, 20 February 1952, DO133/114 UKNA.
[83] Ibid.
[84] 'Police Arrangements in UP during Elections', *National Herald*, 13 September 1951.

authorities. And added to the list in the provincial elections were regional parties based on local languages and ethnicities. Posters and emblems were everywhere to be seen – in shops, on boards, on the old colonial statues and in Bengal a common practice was to paint 'Vote for Congress' on the backside of stray cows.[85]

Independent India may now be commonly viewed as one of the world's most participatory democracies, but this was not how its first general election was anticipated in 1951. Contemporary observer, Penderel Moon, for one, suggested that it was an 'absurd farce' watching 'millions of illiterate people registering their vote'.[86] Until the results of the Congress victory were known, even Nehru himself possessed doubts, fearing that the noise of propaganda would drown out quality debate, and lead to the selection of 'dumb' or 'dictatorial leaders'. Not only that, Congress also found itself having to work alongside the same bureaucracy against which Nehru had fought in the lead up to Independence in 1947. The new US Ambassador to India, Chester Bowles, also changed his view: from initially thinking that a country such as India would need a benevolent dictatorship for a period, he came to believe that illiteracy was no bar to 'intelligent voting'. Of the relatively small number (1,250) of election offences reported, a good proportion involved canvassing within one hundred meters of a polling station. And it was surmised that some of the offenders could have been bovine.[87]

As it turned out, election observers reported relatively little election fraud or what they labelled as 'corruption'. Shortly after the results were announced, Nehru was quick to point out to his UP colleague Pant that he had 'received a large number of fresh complaints about the elections' there. On talking to the Election Commissioner, it seems that Nehru had found the large and sprawling UP to have been 'the most problematic state'. Evidently, quotidian practices bound up in the polls there were quite unusual in some cases:

> One such remarkable complaint was that the UP Govt [*sic*] had not used the Godrej voting boxes, but instead boxes made locally through cottage industries. Many of them were falling apart, and the lid was coming off. Also, when opened, it was found that some of the voting papers were in tied bundles as though they had been put in together and not separately.[88]

There was, however, a much more significant development, namely an emerging politics of corruption/anti-corruption allegation centred on

---

[85] Nye, 'The Indian Elections'.   [86] Ibid.   [87] Ibid.
[88] Nehru to Pant, 9 February 1952, Pant Papers, Reel 1 NMML.

candidates themselves, mostly focussed around black market activities, but also involving accusations of nepotism and alleged association with communal organizations. Much of this political discussion developed through two processes: first, internal party political rivalry and a sense of degeneration within the Congress, and, second (though connected to the first process), a broader and more extensive popular politics of anti-corruption and civic protest that, as we have discussed in earlier chapters, had emerged in India in the years since Independence.

The Congress's many attempts to consolidate its power in India – from its original decision to 'cut off the diseased limb' (namely Pakistan) in 1947, to its use of state ceremony and spectacle – now paid off. It won these first elections comfortably. However, the 'first past the post' system did show that the party was not fully representative. Congress secured only about 45 per cent of the popular vote for the central parliament, but ended up with control of almost 75 per cent of the seats: the proportion in the state elections represented 42 per cent of the popular vote, which translated into 68 per cent of the seats. In eighteen out of twenty-two assemblies, Congress emerged with a majority.[89] But this provided some surprise victories, such as in Partition-afflicted areas of the Punjab and Bengal, and in Bombay. All the same, twenty prominent Congress ministers lost their seats, the party held only slender majorities in Hyderabad and Rajasthan, and possessed no overall majority in Travancore-Cochin, Orissa, Madras and PEPSU.[90] In some respects, therefore, the election outcome signalled key challenges for the party in the future, especially in relation to developments on its left. In others ways, the results threw up surprises, with, for instance, the almost total elimination of right-wing parties that had been initially buoyed up by popular opposition to the creation of Pakistan and by the accompanying demonization of Muslim minorities in North India.

The situation in Andhra in the south and UP to the north provide contrasting but related images of what India's first general election meant for many of its ordinary citizens. In the seven districts of Andhra that voted overwhelmingly for the CPI, the failure of Congress candidates was attributed to charges of corruption and importantly a failure to 'get out' to voters, especially women.[91] This response strongly reflected the kinds of discourses produced in both the national and regional newspapers focussed around popular disengagement from the Indian state, resulting from low-level administrative corruption, as explored in Chapter 2. Unquestionably, there was a great deal of fear within officialdom about

[89] Nye, 'The Indian Elections'.   [90] Ibid.
[91] V. C. Martin, 'Andhra Goes Communist', 16 February 1952, DO133/114 UKNA.

the relative scale of the left parties – especially the CPI in South Indian states and in Bengal. This was particularly the case in Travancore-Cochin, which later became Kerala, but also in Madras and Hyderabad.[92] Communist organizations and parties had been banned in Bengal from March 1948, and had been engaged in ongoing armed struggle in Hyderabad (which by the time of the elections had become part of Andhra Pradesh) right up to the eve of the poll itself.[93] In Hyderabad, the relative success of the CPI was directly related to one of the central problems of early postcolonial state governments in India – that of dissatisfaction with food procurement and rationing. For instance, about 45 per cent of the rural population of West Godavari in 1951 were landless labourers who received a ration of around 6 oz of rice through government shops, in stark contrast to cultivators and small landlords who were permitted to keep back paddy at 12 oz per adult.[94] Added to this, as the left-wing press warned on Independence Day that year, was frustration driven by police suppression of communists in the years following Partition, the apparent stalling of linguistic reorganization by the ruling Congress regime and a widespread sense of 'administrative corruption' linked as well to Congress governance.[95] The Praja Party only fared reasonably well in Madras, but the Socialist Party, another breakaway from the Congress, was limited to making a mark in Bihar.

In UP, meanwhile, the Socialists had proved to be a more significant force than the CPI and so had high hopes of electoral success, but in 1948 only around 5 per cent (12 out of 200) of Congress UP Assembly members moved over to their ranks.[96] By 1951, however, there had been significant defections among the rank-and-file Congress workers.[97] Most importantly, both the Socialists and disgruntled sections within Congress itself – as in the South   fed off the scandals surrounding everyday corruption. In the summer of 1951, to take one instance, there had been a series of exchanges in the UP Assembly during the lead-up to the elections, in particular focussed on a link between Congress ministers and sugar producers, in which the former received payments to use influence in cases brought against them. MLA Khan Chand Gautam claimed that the Civil Supplies minister had engaged in a kind of 'broker-age' and charged a levy on the sugar production of individual industrial-ists: for Gautam, this 'amounted to asking for a share in the excess prices

[92] G. E. Crombie to Young, 26 February 1952, DO113/114 UKNA.

[93] Taylor Sherman, *State Violence and Punishment in India* (London: Routledge, 2010), pp. 161–8.

[94] G. E. Crombie to Victor, 26 February 1952, DO133/114 UKNA.   [95] Ibid.

[96] A. C. B. Symon to Rumbold, 6 April 1948, DO133/128 UKNA.

[97] '300 Resign from Congress in Eastern UP', *National Herald*, 22 August 1951.

that the sugar manufacturers charged from the consumers ... Cases against some industrialists had been hushed up on receipt of contributions to the Congress funds, he charged'.[98] In an accusatory 1951 debate, Raja Ram Shastri (Socialist) threw doubt on whether the elections would be conducted fairly, arguing that government officials were already supporting the ministry in power, especially in court cases centred on corruption. Shastri then read out an official letter from the District Supply Officer of Rae Bareli addressed to the Halwais' (Sweetmakers) Association in which the District Supply Officer had told them that he would agree to distribution of the sugar quota through their association only if the District Congress Committee passed a resolution to that effect. 'What does it amount to', Shastri argued, 'except giving a free hand to the District Congress Committee to coerce the halwais? Does it not prove that the administration is acting as a tool of the party?'[99]

As the pre-election war of words intensified, Begum Aizaz Rasool, leader of the opposition, through the mechanism of an amendment to the Assembly's thanks to the address of the governor, regretted that no mention had been made to any measure that the government intended to take to eradicate widespread corruption and nepotism and the growing insecurity of life in rural areas. Nor had it introduced schemes to bring down the prices of consumer goods. Assembly member and veteran nationalist UP politician S. K. D. Paliwal then moved an amendment seeking to add twenty-one grievances of the public against the government – the main ones relating to food, cloth, houses, alleged police tyranny, unemployment, poverty, increasing cost of living and inadequate pay, and dearness allowance for lower-level government employees. Paliwal argued that in the Gorakhpur district of UP alone hundreds of people were unable to procure even shrouds for burial purposes and that growing unemployment was responsible for many cases of suicide in the state.[100] Accusations of corruption in supply and requisitioning were also linked to another controversy involving public clashes with the administration – in this case, what was described in the Assembly as the 'Hardoi Incident'. Here, a number of women in villages of the district had brought allegations of police rape in the summer of 1951. A police constable who then went to issue a court summons was beaten up and his gun snatched. On receipt of this information, thirty-six people were

[98] *National Herald*, 23 August 1951.
[99] 'Assembly Debates Governor's Address – Sharp Congress-Praja Party Exchanges', *National Herald*, 22 August 1951.
[100] 'Food Relief Urged for Eastern Districts – Discussion on Governor's Address in Council', *National Herald*, 23 August 1951.

arrested.[101] Paliwal remained consistent in his critique of the Congress over the months leading up to the election, arguing that the regime had failed in the areas of health, poverty and food security and communal relations, and was unable to establish either a welfare or a police state.[102]

Much of this politicking in the run-up to the first Indian general election was geared towards cross-party accusation about influence with the bureaucracy, and the sense in which the 'corruption' of the Congress leadership distanced it from the everyday lives of ordinary citizens. In a debate about possible deaths from starvation in north Garhwal linked to existing food policies, the Food Minister Chaudhury Charan Singh was asked to explain how permission had been given by the administration for a 300-strong dinner for the State Congress Committee, supplied with controlled foodstuffs. By contrast, the Food Commissioner had apparently refused to permit the organizers of the Kisan Mazdoor Praja Party Conference in Lucknow to entertain more than forty-nine people.[103] The sense of disillusionment of many was summed up by K. K. Malaviya who explained his resignation from the UP government with the following words in a speech in the Assembly:

The history of the past four years of Congress rule has been undoubtedly a history of creating problems instead of solving them. It is common knowledge that corruption and black marketing have unfortunately become the normal incidents of our social economy today. In meeting the bare necessities of life, lying and cheating have become inevitable for you and for me in the existing set-up ... It will be no exaggeration to say that Congress today stands very well-isolated from the people whom it aspires to serve ... Nepotism and jobbery have now become the warp and woof of its texture ... No state minister can be sure, today, of the prompt and ungrudging execution of Government programmes by many of those who have to do it ... A Minister of the state Government, who does not belong to the power group, must always be ready to be obstructed, thwarted and even slighted. The services have been made conscious of the precarious lot of such minister and outcastes. They can never be sure that of their orders being obeyed and carried out substantially.[104]

There was little doubt that the pre-election political environment in UP had encouraged forms of patronage, which prefigured sectional groups support for particular leaders. In Etawah, for instance, the working committee of the UP Momin Conference set up a committee for granting

---

[101] Ibid.
[102] 'Paliwal Asks People to Vote for the Praja Party', *National Herald*, 5 September 1951, p. 2.
[103] 'No Starvation Deaths – Gupta's Denial in Assembly', *National Herald*, 25 August 1951.
[104] 'Slackness and Corruption in State Services – Malaviya Gives Reasons for Resignation – Use of Govt. Machine for Party Cause', *National Herald*, 25 August 1951.

scholarships to students and publicly expressed confidence in Nehru. The conference concluded with a request to increase the government yarn quota.[105]

However, despite these claims of influence and the deterioration of India's principal political party, there was a sense in the final months before the election that exercising the vote was an exercise in rights assertion itself. The newspapers were filled with discussions of how to overcome the structural challenges of the electorate – illiteracy, the distances and extend of the electoral operation itself, and the problems of election expenses.[106] M. N. Roy, one of India's leading Communists from the 1920s onwards, argued in the press that, given the inexperience and illiteracy of the population, and the problems of corruption, it was likely that a range of independent candidates would be elected.[107] However, adversity during the electoral process was also turned into an opportunity to mobilize new and disadvantaged constituencies too. On 11 September 1951, over a dozen women's organizations, under the auspices of the Mahila Matadhikar Samiti (and Rameshwari Nehru[108]) urged the 'restoration' of voting rights to 'disenfranchised' women. Mrs. Durga Bal, MP, addressing the convention pointed out that nearly three million women had been struck off the electoral rolls due to defective enumeration as a result of which they were in imminent danger of being deprived of their rights. Mrs. Manmoham Sehgal proposed a resolution, seconded by Mrs. Sharda Bhargava, which placed on record this convention's

emphatic sense of protest against the manner in which millions of women of India have been summarily deprived of their just and legitimate rights of vote at the first general elections of free India. The Constitution of India guarantees franchise to every adult person but due to defective enumeration by the employees of the election departments of several states and negligence of their officers, the names of millions of women have been for no fault of theirs, declared invalid at the eleventh hour by an order of the Election Commissioner.[109]

Events unfolded differently in Pakistan. Unlike Indians, Pakistanis did not have the opportunity to take part in a general election until 1970, nearly two decades after Indians had first gone to the polls as full-fledged

[105] 'Momin Support for Nehru', *National Herald*, 7 September 1951.
[106] 'Election Expenses', *National Herald*, 16 September 1951.
[107] M. N. Roy, 'To Intelligent Voters', *National Herald*, Magazine Section, 16 September 1951.
[108] Rameshwari Nehru (1886–1966) was a social worker in colonial and post-Independence India. She was married to Brijlal Nehru, cousin of Jawaharlal Nehru.
[109] 'Restoration of Voting Right: Demand by Delhi Women's Delegation', *National Herald*, 12 September 1951.

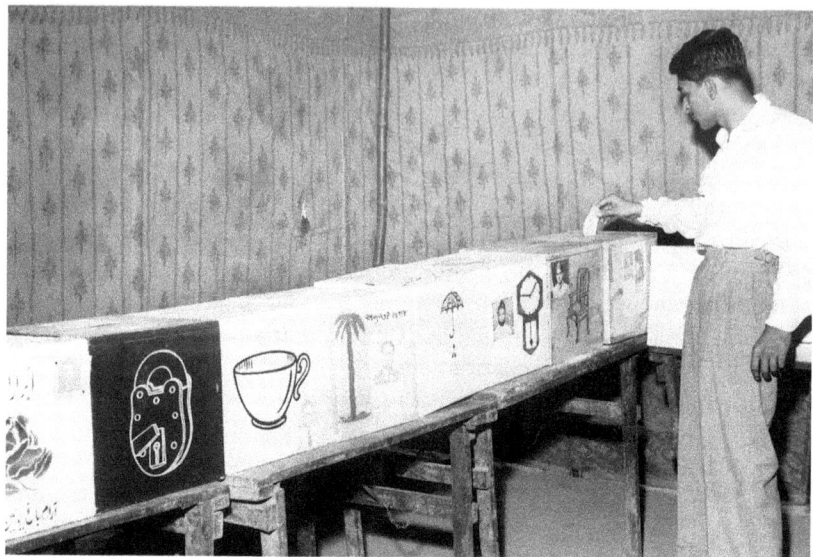

Figure 4.4 Local elections, Pakistan, December 1959.
Photo by Keystone-France/Gamma-Keystone/Getty Images

citizens. Direct comparisons with the experience of voting in India during the first ten years following Independence are consequently impossible to draw. At the same time, people in Pakistan spent much of the 1950s actively anticipating elections, and occasionally participated in them at a provincial or lower level (see Figure 4.4). So while the scale of Pakistan's tentative experiments in democratic participation was considerably smaller than their Indian equivalents, the significance invested in them in terms of hope and expectation was equally high. In many ways, therefore, the context was more similar on this side of the new border than is often acknowledged. For both the Pakistani state and its new citizens, simply preparing to vote was regarded as a 'rite of passage' as far as acquiring citizenship was concerned, with enormous emphasis placed on putting the necessary electoral 'scaffolding' in place: voter registration, for instance, assumed an enhanced meaning, particularly as it took place against the backdrop of the fallout from Partition's longer term demographic impact. All the same, while 'institution-building' on the scale demanded by the creation of a new state virtually from scratch was a slow and at times painful process, the challenges created by Partition offered some practical advantages in that this human 'emergency' provided opportunities for the newly created state to embed itself in the lives of its citizens, whether they were refugees or already living in the places that had geographically become Pakistan. Moreover, environmental crises such as severe flooding first in Sindh in 1948 and then in the Punjab in 1951 provided fresh opportunities for the state to promote itself in terms of its support for those affected by these natural disasters.

It was evident to observers in the years following Partition that the new Pakistani state had inherited a deficit when it came to the number of experienced staff required to fill its bureaucracy. Pakistan inherited only around 100 former ICS (Indian Civil Service) officers, of whom only a small fraction had any experience of working at the higher rungs of the administrative ladder: only 'one of them had been a joint secretary, and five or seven deputy secretaries in the government of undivided India'.[110] According to former US First Lady Eleanor Roosevelt, who visited Pakistan during her round-the-world trip in 1952, the 'wonderful people at the top in Pakistan' were 'handicapped by not having enough trained civil servants in the lower cadres'.[111] Competition between locals and refugees over who got what jobs within the new bureaucratic infrastructure, and with what terms of employment attached, caused repeated friction. When in November 1950, the Sindh Ministry changed its selection and promotion procedures, by no longer recognizing years of service in territory that was now in the Indian Union, many refugee government servants regarded this as a huge injustice, particularly since, for them, their 'experience and ability had proved an invaluable asset to the province [Sindh] during a period of national emergency [in the wake of Partition]'. In the words of a sympathetic newspaper editorial, fault lay primarily with provincial politicians: 'The rules governing the Permanent Services should have complete immunity against the evils of politicians' vagaries. The members of the Provincial Services should not be made to feel that their fate hangs in the balance every time there is a change in Ministerial setup. This will result in complete demoralisation of the services'.[112]

In India, as we have seen, the drawing up of electoral rolls was 'posited as ambitious and complex but, ultimately, a concrete technical and practical undertaking'.[113] It was a similar scenario in Pakistan. To judge from available records, the Pakistani state together with its civil servants spent a great deal of time from the late 1940s onwards trying to work out

---

[110] Liaquat Ali Khan's defence of Government decision to retain some British officials in key positions, *Constituent Assembly (Legislative) Debates, 1948*, Vol. I, pp. 279–80, cited in Ahmad, *Government and Politics in Pakistan*, p. 81.
[111] *Dawn*, 12 April 1952.   [112] *Dawn*, 10 April 1952.
[113] Ornit Shani, 'Making India's Democracy: Rewriting the Bureaucratic Colonial Imagination in the Preparation of the First Elections', *Comparative Studies of South Asia, Africa and the Middle East* 36, 1 (May 2016), p. 90.

who was living where and in what precise numbers as part of preparations for possible voting. From periodic headcounts throughout the 1950s driven by the need to quantify the whereabouts of displaced refugees in cities such as Karachi, to Pakistan's first national census in 1951, number-counting in this fluid context assumed political – nation-building – significance. According to one piece of expert advice received by the Indian authorities as early as October 1947, 'an electoral roll [was] a statutory document, while a census [was] a "useful inventory", and the implications of the two tasks [were] very different'.[114] But despite this distinction, which was also recognized by officials in Pakistan, the first national census in the latter which was announced in 1948 and carried out in early 1951, provided (with still no general election in the offing) an alternative way of projecting the role of the state alongside communicating the responsibilities associated with citizenship.

Studies on the purpose of censuses usually emphasize how far they enable the state to view and quantify society: for Benedict Anderson, in *Imagined Communities*, they represent the way in which the colonial state imagined its dominion.[115] But from the perspective of those being surveyed, particularly among populations with low literacy rates, the act of carrying out a census brings citizens face-to-face with the state as the representatives of the latter engage in recording the necessary information about the individual circumstances of the former. This was certainly what happened in Pakistan (and India too) in the early 1950s. With literacy low, the process of recording relied directly on volunteers – frequently praised for their 'patriotic' service[116] – taking the state along with its census questionnaires directly into people's homes.[117] In the case of the 1951 Pakistan census, some quarter of a million volunteers – comprised mainly of students, government employees, Muslim League workers and Muslim League National Census Guards – were deployed by the authorities, who divided the country into roughly 160,000 blocks, each containing approximately 100 dwellings, with 10 blocks making up a 'circle', and every ten circles a 'Charge'. These enumerators, as they were called, went from house to house with a supply of individual questionnaires, though not everyone had to answer all twenty-five

---

[114] Ibid., p. 88.
[115] Benedict Anderson, *Imagined Communities: Reflections on the Origins and Spread of Nationalism* (London: Verso, 1991 ed.), chapter 10, 'Census, Map, Museum', pp. 163–85.
[116] *Dawn*, 11 February 1951.
[117] Governor General Khwaja Nazimuddin was the first person to be counted, followed by those in Prime Minister Liaquat Ali Khan's household.

questions as people in rural areas were asked fewer than their counter-parts living in towns.

On 'Census Night' itself – 28 February – the streets of Karachi, for instance, were reported as completely deserted: 'a hush, ruffled only by gentle knocks and whispers of the enumerators, prevailed'.[118] Special police arrangements were in place for patrolling the streets during the voluntary curfew. By midnight, 3,000 enumerators, permitted to hire rickshaws at government expense, had spread throughout the city, charged with tracking down anyone who might have been left out of the count because they lacked a permanent lodging place. Similarly in Lahore, the hunt was on for the city's floating homeless population that usually spent its night on footpaths on in other places not on record with the municipal authorities. There were similar curfews in Dacca and Chittagong. According to contemporary reports, people living in rural areas proved easier to count; it was towns and cities that posed greater difficulties. In contrast to the so-called illiterates who apparently needed little persuasion to provide answers to the census questions, members of the urban intelligentsia posed more of a challenge to enumerators, with one 'Secretary to the Government [having] to be visited eight times at his house and office before his statement could be recorded'.[119]

All the same, the Pakistani authorities had to work hard to get the census taken seriously. Official rhetoric and public responses offer insight into wider processes at work in the late 1940s and early 1950s. Time and again officials repeated the message that for this 'corporate national job' to be successful, people would have to provide accurate information about themselves and their families.[120] Hence, addressing a public meeting in the Federal Capital on the first day of the operation (9 February 1951), Census Commissioner E. H. Slade, a British expert who had recently worked with displaced populations in post-war Germany, called for wholehearted public cooperation. Both he and the then Administrator of Karachi, Syed Hashim Raza, argued strongly that the census results were essential for planning how to build the new state:

Pakistan is still young and impressionable; its future plans and programmes are still on the anvil and its constitution still unshaped. We do not have to repair, renovate or demolish an old construction. We have to raise an altogether new edifice, a task which, although stupendous in itself, is less intricate and more

---

[118] *Dawn*, 10 February 1951.
[119] *First Census of Pakistan 1951: Administrative Report*, Part Two: The Reports of the Provincial Superintendents of Census Operations (Karachi: Government of Pakistan Press, 1953), chapter 14 'Sind', pp. 192–3.
[120] *Dawn*, 20 June 1950.

straight [*sic*]. Census results ... are destined to play a significant role in our future development schemes and in shaping a near-utopian society.[121]

Federal Minster of the Interior Khwaja Shahabuddin in a Radio Pakistan broadcast likewise drew attention to the census as an exercise in collective civic responsibility:

The gathering of all this information is a work that is being undertaken by a large body of unpaid workers. For the most part, they are the normal servants of the government who have to do this extra job as part of their already onerous duties but they have been reinforced by large numbers of non-official voluntary workers. To all these, Pakistan owes a debt of gratitude for their self-less labours.[122]

Shahabuddin went on to instruct his listeners as follows (though how many will have necessarily understood the English in which he was speaking is debatable):

Throughout most of Pakistan the month of February will see them very busily employed. When these gentlemen visit our homes ... we must treat them with courtesy and respect as men who are doing a vitally important job which will be of the greatest help to everybody. We must see that the information we give is to the best of our knowledge the real truth regarding the census questions. A census slip is to be made out for every person, young and old, man or woman, wherever they may be in Pakistan, and also for Pakistanis who at the time of the census happen to be abroad.

And the minister took similar pains to refute popular misconceptions that any information provided would be used to disadvantage individuals or that the census would arrive at a preconceived result: 'We are out to get at the truth whatever it may be ... and I am sure that the people of Pakistan and particularly the census officers will ensure that everyone is included once and only once, and that slips are not made out for non-existent people'. To the volunteer enumerators themselves, Shahabuddin drew their attention to the need 'for a tactful and friendly approach'; census officers, he explained, had 'to act with discretion and realise that the information with which [they were] entrusted by the citizen [had] to be an inviolable secret and disclosed to no one except the proper census authorities'.[123] Equally, the authorities appealed to all employers, businesses and offices, whose members of staff were acting as census officials, to excuse them from work and treat their absence as being 'on duty'.

---

[121] 'Social Significance of the Census', *Dawn*, 25 February 1951.
[122] *Pakistan Times*, 10 February 1951.
[123] Ibid. For a more detailed study of the carrying out of Pakistan's first census in Sindh, see Sarah Ansari, 'Pakistan's 1951 Census: State-Building in Post-Partition Sindh', *South Asia* 39, 4 (2016), pp. 820–40.

Organizing and administering direct elections at the provincial and municipal level, therefore, drew on the same combination of state rhetoric and citizen assistance, and, thus, provided officially endorsed opportunities for the state first to project and then to enact its recently acquired authority.

More generally, and in a similar fashion to the challenge facing Indian authorities in the run-up to the first election there, drawing up electoral rolls – whether at city, province or (optimistically as it turned out) national level – tested the Pakistan state's capacity to identify, verify and record those of its new citizens deemed eligible to vote. Elections were repeatedly postponed, often ostensibly because the authorities proved unable to carry out the necessary preparations in time, but also thanks, on many occasions, to official concerns about the elections' possible outcomes. In the case of Karachi Municipal Corporation (KMC) elections scheduled for April–May 1953, 400 enumerators – 200 male and 200 female – had begun the previous July to prepare the necessary electoral rolls. The deadline for preliminary lists of voters was the middle of December 1952. These were then made available for public scrutiny, and once any corrections had been made, the final version was prepared.[124] One problem reported early on – echoing a similar reluctance among Indian women – was shyness on the part of potential female voters who were not prepared to provide their names and ages even when approached by female enumerators.[125] And though this was only a municipal election, it was taking place in the federal heart of the new country, and so campaigners sought to rally voters by describing the Karachi polls as 'a test for the nation and not a reason for despondency and discouragement'.[126] But this heightened reality failed to live up to expectations. According to one contemporary report, 'perfection in the use of one of the major instruments of representative democracy – free elections fairly conducted – has not yet been attained in Pakistan, if the situation resulting from recent balloting for members of the Karachi Municipal Corporation is any indication'; after all the talk beforehand about fair and well-organized elections, 'in many wards, polling arrangements were not ready in time, and there [were] many complaints about mismanagement and inefficiency'.[127] Accounts of procedural maladministration produced a storm of protest, and appeals were made for re-polling in seven of the twenty-eight wards. Both independent

[124] *Dawn*, 2 July 1952.   [125] *Dawn*, 26 July 1952.

[126] US Embassy Despatch 950, 18 April 1953, 790d.00/4-1853 USNA.

[127] UK High Commission, Karachi, Review of Events in Sind, Karachi and Baluchistan, No. 9, 21 April–4 May 1953, DO35/5300 UKNA.

and Muslim League candidates complained that polling booths were either not in place or closed at the scheduled voting times.[128]

But for all the evident flaws and shortcomings associated with them, municipal elections were at least conducted in Karachi in the early 1950s, unlike in Lahore, Pakistani Punjab's largest city, where they had last been held as long ago as 1946. This lengthy delay prompted cynical reflections on Pakistan's democratic record in the years since Independence:

> In September [1951] it was announced that Corporation elections would be held early [in 1952]. [But] even at fag end of the year no one is certain when the promised elections will come. What is true of corporations of Lahore and Karachi is also true of a number of smaller municipalities and local boards. If provincial elections could be held in midst of other preoccupations, we do not see any reason why these elections should be postponed from year to year. It is idle to talk about the democratic role of local bodies when many of them do not even exist and many others are taken over by the Governments concerned.[129]

Nor did the larger-scale and better-known provincial elections that were held in Pakistan during the early 1950s prove, in practice, particularly effective attempts at state-building. As well as exposing the inability of local administrations to ensure that they were conducted fairly, they revealed frailties in the position of the ruling Muslim League, even though, unlike opposition political groups, the party was helped by its close relationship with the apparatus of the state. This advantage was clearly seen in West Punjab, wherein the run-up to Pakistan's first provincial election – held there in March 1951 – long-standing internal political rivalries divided the local Muslim League into two opposing camps. Supporters of Mian Mumtaz Daultana now lined up against those of the Khan of Mamdot, who had formed his breakaway 'Jinnah Awami Muslim League' as a direct challenge to League authority; and 'the party, the assembly and the administration were all split down the middle'.[130] Thanks to 'the shortage of housing, the high cost of rents as well as utilities and food, unemployment and undisguised favouritism in the allotment of property' that accounted for 'widespread opposition to anyone or anything associated with the central government', contemporary observers expected the League 'to be mauled in key urban centres'.[131]

With the votes counted, the League emerged victorious, though the low turnout of c. 30 per cent together with the party's unexpectedly clear

---

[128] US Embassy Despatch 982, 2 May 1953, 790D.00/5-253 USNA.
[129] *Dawn*, 1 November 1952.   [130] Jalal, *The State of Martial Rule*, p. 80.
[131] Ibid., p. 147.

margin of victory prompted widespread complaints that the elections had been 'a farce, a mockery and a fraud upon the electorates'. Critics claimed that more than fifty contestants had won seats precisely thanks to their relationship with public servants, and, in many eyes, these kinds of 'illegal tactics constituted a blot on the fair name of democracy'.[132] The subsequent Electoral Reform Commission Report recognized that 'Government servants by virtue of their position possess considerable influence'. This meant that they had to be

unequivocally directed to keep themselves altogether aloof from politics: they must not be allowed to canvass or otherwise interfere or use their influence in connection with or take part in elections to the legislative bodies, except by way of freely exercising their right to vote, and in this respect also they must be enjoined not to give any indication of the manner in which they propose to vote or may have voted.[133]

This apparent high moral stance, however, did not prevent the authorities themselves from playing a last-minute trump card the day before polling itself started. Bold newspaper headlines on 9 March announced that an attempted coup – the Rawalpindi Conspiracy – had been foiled. The alleged plot's purpose, Liaquat Ali Khan declared, had been 'to create commotion in the country by violent means'. Although newspapers refrained from explicitly calling on voters to support the ruling party at the polls, the implication of this apparent coincidence was clear: the nation having been placed in danger, Pakistanis (in this case Punjabis) needed to back the party that had averted the crisis, namely the Muslim League.[134]

Elections for the Sindh Legislative Assembly that were held in May 1953 surprised some contemporaries by the extent to which they appeared to be more 'fair and impartial' than many had expected. All the same, district local board polls, which had been scheduled for the end of March that year, were once more postponed on the grounds that 'two elections at about the same time' would overstrain the administration.[135] In the end, the Sindh provincial elections were themselves held also over a year late thanks to the imposition of governor's rule in December 1951, which had resulted in the postponement of elections scheduled for March 1952.[136] Election Commissioner Syed Hashim Raza (by now

---

[132] *Electoral Reform Commission Report*, 1956, p. 1, cited in Tahir Kamran, 'Early Phase of Electoral Politics in Pakistan: 1950s', *A Research Journal of South Asian Studies* 24, 2 (July–December 2009), p. 265.

[133] Cited in Ahmad, *Government and Politics in Pakistan*, p. 158.

[134] *Dawn*, 9 March 1951.

[135] UKHC, Karachi, Review of Events in Sind, Karachi and Baluchistan, No. 5, 24 February–9 March 1953, DO35/5300 UKNA.

[136] US Embassy Despatch 805, 4 January 1952, 790D.00/1-452 USNA.

Secretary of the Sindh Department of Education, Health and Local Self-Government) took personal responsibility for ensuring that the administration would perform its duty, in his words, 'honestly and impartially'. He toured the province to 'set the election machinery in gear', and instructed district officials 'in their duties during the polling'.[137] The following measures were put in place. First to help illiterate voters, each of the contending parties would receive 'election colours' to be used on ballot boxes. Indelible ink for obtaining thumb impressions which would last for at least twenty-four hours following voting would be used. Second, Gazetted officers, as far as possible, were to act as presiding officers at the elections, on the grounds that 'they would be less amenable to influence'. Ballot boxes would be sealed and only opened for counting in the presence of candidates or their election agents. And finally, government officials were to be instructed to remain strictly aloof from factionalism during the elections. In all, it was later calculated that these elections cost an estimated one million Pakistani rupees (in addition to the 900,000 rupees spent on preparing voters' lists), though of the 1,709,355 registered voters in the province, fewer than one-sixth (240,519) were women.[138]

But Sindh's close proximity to the federal capital Karachi meant that it was not only provincial politicians who entered the campaign fray there. Prime Minister Mohammad Ali Bogra, for instance, visited Upper Sindh in the week before the polls opened, addressing voters in Jacobabad, Sukkur, and other smaller towns and villages, while other members of his Cabinet as well as ex-ministers toured the province in support of the Muslim League cause.[139] The wider significance of local electoral politics had been underlined by recent developments in Sukkur in Upper Sindh, where the election of the former Speaker of the Sindh Legislative Assembly, Agha Bahruddin, to the presidency of its District Board the previous October in the face of opposition from supporters of former Sindh Chief Minister Khuhro (then awaiting the verdict of a PRODA corruption tribunal) had drawn attention to the extent to which local rivalries had become entangled with League politics.[140]

---

[137] UKHC, Karachi, Review of events in Sind, Karachi and Baluchistan, No. 5, 24 February–9 March 1953, DO35/5300 UKNA; UKHC, Karachi, Review of Events in Sind, Karachi and Baluchistan, No. 8, 7–20 April 1953, DO35/5300 UKNA.

[138] US Embassy Despatch 884, 26 March 1953, 790d.00/3-2653 USNA.

[139] UKHC, Karachi, Review of Events in Sind, Karachi and Baluchistan, No. 9, 21 April–4 May 1953, DO35/5300 UKNA.

[140] *Dawn*, 27 October 1952. To illustrate how tangled Sindhi politics was during the 1950s, a couple of years later, in July 1955, with his PRODA disqualification by then quashed and already re-appointed Chief Minister of Sindh, Khuhro was re-elected unopposed to the Sindh Legislative Assembly (SLA) in a by-election in Tando Adam-Shahdadpur constituency. According to an admittedly not very sympathetic press, four other

The key provincial election in terms of wider, all-Pakistan, political impact, however, was that of East Bengal in March 1954, whose results rippled, or perhaps more accurately ripped, across the country as a whole. This poll involved some twenty million voters, of whom around 85 per cent were illiterate and 50 per cent women, with the vast majority never having participated in any election before. Despite the rhetoric of the ruling provincial Muslim League ministry, which emphasized its expected victory, 'the ordinary man is made aware at every point of an administration and a political party which seem to him to be full of individuals who are personally corrupt and feathering their own nests at his expense'.[141] In the words of one foreign observer,

the Muslim League are sparing no effort on the organizational side to win this election. Controlling as they do the electoral machinery, the administration, the police and ample funds they stand a good chance of pulling it off – by hook or by crook … the fact is that the election is not 'free and fair' and the League commands infinitely greater resources of inducement, force and fraud than the United Front.[142]

These provincial elections exposed similar problems from a wider administrative perspective. In late January 1954, the date for polling originally set as 16 February was changed to 8 March. Prime Minister Mohammad Ali Bogra, arriving back in Karachi from a pre-election trip to East Pakistan, gave as the first reason for the postponement that the administrative arrangements were not complete on the grounds that the previous arrangements had not given 'sufficient time to the candidates and the electorate to do justice to the task'[143]: in his words, 'there was no use going to the polls to find that there were no ballot boxes'.[144] But he added that all contesting parties supported a later poll, primarily so as to give themselves more time to coordinate their campaigning. Civil servants, on the other hand, were hesitant about the need for delay:

candidates (including former SLA Speaker Mir Ghulam Ali Khan Talpur) had tried to stand but had been prevented from doing so by administrative action that had allegedly hustled them into official transport and then 'dumped them in the middle of the Sind desert'. UKHC, Karachi, Review of Events in Sind, Karachi and Baluchistan, No. 15, 15–28 July 1955, DO35/3501 UKNA.
[141] Deputy High Commission, Dacca, 'Report on East Pakistan Elections', (n.d. March 1954), DO35/5196 UKNA.
[142] Ibid.
[143] Pakistan Fortnightly Summary Pt II, No. 19, 3 February 1954, DO35/5196 UKNA; Deputy High Commission, Dacca, Fortnightly Report No. 3 for period ending 5 February 1954, DO 35/5298 UKNA.
[144] UKHC, Karachi, to Commonwealth Relations Office, 1 February 1954, DO35/5196 UKNA.

The only people who have been opposed to the idea of postponements were senior members of the administration in Dacca and the districts; this is for two reasons. First, their plans and organization are geared to the original date ... and so it is no easy thing in a country where communications are so difficult and administrative expertise so lacking to make the necessary last minute adjustment in these plans. Secondly, there has been a certain amount of concern about the violence and disorders at some of the election meetings up and down the province and the administration were worried about the possibility of this developing into something more serious if the campaign is prolonged. Since, however, the parties are for once unanimous the administration could cut very little ice.[145]

As the campaign progressed, foreign observers were convinced that the election was not going to be 'free and fair', as the Muslim League commanded 'infinitely greater resources of inducement, force and fraud than the United Front'. In the closing stages of the campaign, the League brought into play what it calculated to be two powerful weapons. The first of these was the East Bengal Electoral Offences Ordinances deployed on 20 February to lock up around 500 opposition party workers. The second was Fatima Jinnah, who carried out an eight-day tour of the province, using the 'immense authority of her name to ram home the Muslim League thesis that the continued stability, prosperity and even existence of Pakistan' required a League victory. According to a British report, 'Much [was] being made of the fact that this [was] the first time that Miss Jinnah [had] taken part in a provincial election in Pakistan and that accordingly she must be deeply convinced of the danger to the nation of a Muslim League defeat'.[146]

Following the United Front victory, the incoming provincial Chief Minister Fazlul Haq took pains to make it clear that he was satisfied with the service that bureaucrats were rendering his Ministry in East Pakistan. According to foreign observers, government servants there gave no sign of anxiety or insecurity.[147] All the same, the response back in Karachi was that the Constituent Assembly should proceed 'without interruption' from early April onwards with the task of framing the constitution, so that direct elections could be held within the following year.[148] By the end of May, however, the central Government citing serious local disturbances (according to some foreign observers, defeated Muslim Leaguers 'bent

---

[145] Deputy UK High Commission, Dacca, to UK High Commission, Karachi, 30 January 1954, DO35/5196 UKNA.

[146] Deputy UK High Commission, Dacca, Fortnightly Report 5 for period ending 5 March 1954, DO35/5298 UKNA.

[147] UKHC Karachi to Commonwealth Relations Office, 14 April 1954, DO35/5323 UKNA.

[148] Extract from DRUM 612, 6 April 1954, DO35/5196 UKNA.

on discrediting Mr Fazlul Huq's Government' may have been at work behind the scenes) had suspended the recently elected provincial ministry under Section 92A of the 1935 Government of India Act, 'for the minimum time necessary to restore law and order and public confidence in the Province'.[149] What must have helped to prompt this action were Huq's recent statements in Calcutta as regards 'the essential oneness of "India" and the common heritage of the two Bengals'.[150]

In the longer run, and once the 1956 Constitution had been promulgated, a key factor that prompted the army coup in October 1958 was the prospect of a general election outcome that might bring an East Pakistani-dominated government to power, upsetting the existing balance of power that had been firmly tilted in West Pakistan's favour since Independence.[151] In this context, the municipal elections that took place in Karachi in April 1958 were expected to be an important litmus test of public opinion, though in the event their results confirmed the faction-ridden nature of the city's politics and frustrations with mainstream politicians.[152] Back in December 1957, that is prior to the military takeover, Karachi's Chief Commissioner N. M. Khan had announced the dissolution of the city's elected council, on charges of 'mal-administration, mismanagement, nepotism and corruption'.[153] A district magistrate was duly appointed caretaker 'Municipal Commissioner', and the date for the elections set for after May 1958. These latest Karachi elections once again exposed the practical challenges involved in registering voters. On this occasion, the names of only about a quarter (c. 450,000) of the city's population were included in the rolls that were drawn up by the end of February. Pakistani nationality was still not a requirement of voter eligibility. Instead, the criteria were adulthood,

---

[149] India Fortnightly Summary Pt II, 25 May 1954, DO35/5323 UKNA.
[150] Peshawar Report 10, 21 May 1954, DO35/4323 UKNA.
[151] Jalal, *The State of Martial Rule*.
[152] These municipal elections highlighted the support among refugees for the religio-political organization, the Jamaat-i-Islami, which had shifted much of its activities to the city from the Punjab, following the anti-Ahmadi riots there earlier in the 1950s. For more details, see Ansari, *Life after Partition*, pp. 175–81. For a broader discussion of the Jamaat's activities during the 1950s, see Ali Usman Qasmi, *Ahmadis and the Politics of Religious Exclusion in Pakistan* (London: Anthem Press, 2014), and on the organization over the longer-term see S. V. R. Nasr, *The Vanguard of the Islamic Revolution: the Jamaat-i Islami of Pakistan* (London: I.B. Tauris, 1994).
[153] 'Text of Press Note issued by the Chief Commissioner of Karachi dissolving the Karachi Municipal Corporation', 15 January 1957, 790d.00/1-1557 USNA. These comments echoed those of an earlier Chief Commissioner who had dissolved the KMA in early 1954 on similar grounds of 'selfishness, corruption, absence of decorum and lack of civic pride'. See UKHC, Karachi, Review of Events in Sind, Karachi and Baluchistan, 30 December 1954–12 January 1955, DO35/3501 UKNA.

a minimum of one year's residence in the city and appearing on the electoral roll itself. This meant that people still living on footpaths were restricted from voting as they had no officially recognized fixed abode.[154] As sections of the press later commented, while the government's action to dissolve the KMC had been 'to the relief of two million exploited, harassed and despoiled citizens of Karachi', 'in the present democratic age [the] death of any democratic organization at the hands of Government cannot be considered proper', and it queried what 'method of action' over the longer run would be taken 'to reform the irregularities and make the Corporation a democratic organization'.[155]

Conclusion

Across South Asia, in the decade following Independence and Partition, citizenship remained a work in progress. In this context, voting – and equally not voting – came to represent the degree of assumed 'progress' that each country was making as far as turning people who had formerly being subjects under colonial rule into bona fide citizens was concerned. In India, as developments in UP and elsewhere demonstrated, the outcome of early democratic elections proved to be more successful than many observers had anticipated. In Pakistan, in Sindh as in other provinces, the deceptively simple act of casting a vote was less straightforward and arguably a far more frustrating process, but those elections that did take place there were well-supported at the popular local level at least. Either way, just as the everyday experiences of citizenship, movement and urban living were coming to define the structures of belonging, so too were similar processes taking place within the sphere of electoral politics. During the early post-Independence period, South Asia's populations were finding their own ways of adjusting to the exercise of newly won, if not necessarily exercised, citizens' rights. Indeed, reactions and responses on the part of ordinary Indians and Pakistanis illustrate two key trends taking place in the years immediately following the ending of British rule.

First, external observers, leading members of the main political parties, and ordinary citizens in both India and Pakistan tended to share similar assumptions that successful democracy was an inescapable dynamic of 'modernity', defined by the metrics of socio-economic development.

---

[154] See US Embassy Despatch 678, 7 February 1958, 790D.00/2-758 USNA.
[155] *Comment* (Karachi), 16 December 1957; *Anjam* (Karachi), 16 December 1957; *Nai Roshni* (Karachi), 16 December 1957, cited in UK High Commission Opdom 56, 8–15 July 1958, L/WS/1/1599 IOR BL.

South Asia's new states had, according to this contemporary analysis, only recently reached a level of preparedness for universal suffrage. It remained to be seen from the vantage point of the 1940s and 1950s whether low levels of literacy, poor transport and communications infrastructure, and the persistence of traditional social structures (such as caste in India) would undermine elections. That this set of assumptions was proved conclusively wrong by the effective exercise of the vote in India in 1951–2 indicates something important about the gulf between contemporary modernist ideas of state and the realities of its substructure. As Shani has explored, thanks to the numerous ongoing interactions between people and administrators over the preparation of electoral rolls, these years witnessed the rewriting of bureaucratic imaginations with respect to the franchise and voting rights, and helping the universal franchise to become a meaningful political order in which Indians would believe and to which they would become committed.[156] Even when elections failed to materialize in Pakistan, or those that were held did not keep to the original timetable, they were still keenly anticipated and the subject of much, often heated, discussion.

However, as this chapter has also shown, widely held public pessimism about corruption and government mismanagement, together with the continuing chaos of post-Partition urban life, did not necessarily or automatically result in cynicism about politics overall. Quite the opposite. So the second trend apparent by the early 1950s was that participation in and discussion about elections seemed to be enhanced by everyday controversies centred on governance. Elections observers across India in those same 1951–2 polls, for instance, pointed out that in some places, UP among them, incumbent regimes were particularly challenged around issues such as food supply, corruption, budget irregularities, black markets, and misallocation of permits and licenses. It was in these places, too, where turnout was often the highest. Moreover, this observation is strengthened by the fact that in across the region – as exemplified by developments in Sindh and UP – heightened electoral engagement was often linked to problems of real or presumed maladministration.

This pattern of engagement would tend to adjust traditional arguments in the political science literature, which concentrate on the role of electoral cliques as part of a 'Congress system' in India during the years under scrutiny. Undoubtedly, factional arrangements had become

[156] Ornit Shani, 'How India Became Democratic – Part IV', www.firstpost.com/india/how-india-became-democratic-part-iv-ornit-shani-responds-to-experts-comments-on-her-book-4402445.html (accessed December 2018).

more fully formed by the time of India's second general election of 1957, and election complaints files relating to UP show that these had become a key dynamic of Congress' candidate selection to constituencies. But, all the same, the first Indian general elections demonstrated that the promises of early postcolonial regimes formed the background to common reactions to the electoral process. And these, in turn, were directly linked to the recent experiences of migration, movement and displacement caused by Partition. What Atul Kohli has described as the 'crisis of governability' in the 1990s, with the rise of caste-based political parties,[157] accordingly had its preconditions in the early 1950s, and there was no sense in which this weakened the electoral process itself. Meanwhile in Pakistan, the encounter was different. There political messages delivered by voting results at the provincial level – in particular signalled by the 1954 polls in East Pakistan but echoed to varying degrees elsewhere – sounded a warning bell for the central authorities regarding popular political expectations, and so played their part in delaying the long-anticipated all-Pakistan elections after 1956. Even a municipal election, such as the one held in Karachi in 1958, only served to reinforce the reluctance of those controlling the Pakistani state to permit its citizens to exercise their voting rights at the highest level. Indeed, as this chapter has discussed more broadly, talk about constitutions combined with the conduct of South Asia's elections in the decade following Independence when viewed from a comparative cross-border perspective sheds valuable light on how quickly popular engagement in politics in both India and Pakistan came to be shaped by civic circumstances, often in relation to debates centred on access to public goods alongside the exercising of what people perceived to be citizens' rights.

---

[157] Atul Kohli, *Democracy and Discontent: India's Growing Crisis of Governability* (Cambridge: Cambridge University Press, 1991).

5   Women and Differentiated Citizenship in Postcolonial South Asia

In 1940, in a Central Legislative Assembly debate regarding women's continuing legal disabilities, the UP activist Hajrah Begum asked when 'men of India [would] realize that it is of no use asking a third party to play fair when they themselves are willing to close their eyes to all the wrongs the women suffer and have mental reservations when freedom is proposed for womanhood?' According to her, 'Indians would not gain Swaraj until they had set their own house in order and granted women legal equality'.[1]

With Independence, all adult women in India and Pakistan, like all adult men, gained equality in the form of the right to vote; universal suffrage was to be part and parcel of the new political arrangements, and central to what citizenship in both countries would now confer. The Indian National Congress and the Muslim League in preceding decades had deliberately made space for female participation in their activities, harnessing the words and deeds of women as a way of signalling the inclusivity of the 'nations' that they claimed to represent. Political inclusion, however, was something that women themselves had been striving to obtain from the turn of the twentieth century, and so, long before Independence was actually achieved, how and where women fitted into wider understandings about citizenship and belonging were the subject of debate and disagreement. After August 1947, women, whose involvement had been accepted as essential during the freedom struggle, needed to be included in what constituted the new 'nation'. But what role was deemed appropriate for women and what their rights in practice as citizens encompassed were questions that proved problematic for both countries in the years that followed.

---

[1] Quoted in Geraldine Forbes, 'The Indian Women's Movement: A Struggle for Women's Rights or National Liberation?', in *The Extended Family: Women's Political Participation in South Asia*, ed. Gail Minault (Delhi: Chanakya Publications, 1981), p. 63. For a more detailed exploration of specific developments in UP, see Visalakshi Menon, *Indian Women and Nationalism: The UP Story* (New Delhi: Shakti Books, 2003).

In independent India, part of the resistance that women's groups and their representatives mounted to their enduring second-class status, derived from the legacy of the colonial landscape in which women's rights had been ascribed an almost 'ethnicized' element of group rights. In Pakistan – not surprisingly in view of its religious raison d'être – competing rhetoric with respect to women's rights often hinged on different interpretations of Islam. As this chapter will explore, in both UP and Sindh – as in India and Pakistan more widely – the status of women as citizens was keenly contested, and women's movements on both sides of the border in the first decade following Independence were caught up in the search for ways of balancing universal notions of citizenship alongside female mobilization. Women's organizations in the late 1940s and early 1950s engaged with the idea of group rights, in the main, by juggling liberal universal notions of citizenship on the one hand and movements for grassroots feminist mobilization on the other. Likewise, this was also a question of scales of mobilization: the often-difficult relationship between local movements and regional, national or international ones was also part and parcel of the challenges faced by women more generally, not least around problems of representation.

Colonial Developments

For India and Pakistan alike, developments in the late 1940s and early 1950s need to be placed in the context of longer term developments in women's rights dating from the late colonial period, and in particular from the interwar years. Gender inequality had deep roots in colonial South Asia, with women frequently denied the same legal rights as men in matters of inheritance, property ownership and the guardianship of children. To improve the status of women, social reformers from the nineteenth century had campaigned for women's education and widow remarriage, as well as to end social practices such as *sati* and child marriage. In all of these efforts, as Geraldine Forbes has explained, education was regarded as essential in order to produce 'a "new [Indian] woman" with interests that went beyond the household'.[2] In the first instance, men belonging to religious reform movements often took the lead and carried out invaluable work in terms of extending the educational horizons of at least some women. But these initiatives also imposed limitations since the thinking behind them tended to envisage the home

---

[2] Geraldine Forbes, *Women in Modern India* (Cambridge: Cambridge University Press, 1996), p. 64.

as the primary area of female activity. Thus, again as Forbes has noted, such social reform effort 'was often tentative, facile, or nugatory', and tended not to challenge patriarchal norms.[3]

Gradually, however, improving access to female education gained increasing support among women themselves. Bodies representing Muslim interests, such as the Anjuman-i Khawateen-i Islam that was founded in Lahore in 1908, reflected this shifting outlook. The main focus of the All-India Muslim Ladies' Conference set up in 1915 was likewise the challenge of expanding women's education. Both organizations also advocated a measure of social reform, targeting *purdah* and polygamy for particular criticism. During the First World War, Indian women from across communities came to be more involved in political activity. In 1917, the Women's Indian Association (WIA) – whose founders included a number of European women, such as Annie Besant, Margaret Cousins and Dorothy Graham Jinarajadass, alongside Indians such as Raj Kumari Amrit Kaur who became Gandhi's secretary in 1919 and later helped set up the All-India Women's Conference (AIWC) for which she acted as secretary for many years – accentuated the need to educate women, organized local classes and discussion groups, and campaigned against child marriage and for female inheritance and voting rights. In this context, Gail Minault's pioneering work on Muslim women's lives has shown how between 1911 and 1924 – a period that witnessed growing Muslim political self-assertion – Muslim women started to become more directly involved in political action. Taking the example of Bi Amman (mother of the Ali Brothers who headed the Khilafat movement that linked up with Gandhi's non-cooperation drive launched in 1919) and other women involved in the Muslim Ladies' Conference, Minault's writings, along with those of Siobhan Lambert-Hurley, have underscored the importance of '*purdah* politics' in generating support for a self-conscious Muslim political constituency during these protest years.[4]

The emergence of new women's organizations after the First World War further enlarged the arena within which female activism could take place. Lobbying in favour of the Child Marriage Restraint Act that was

---

[3] Ibid., pp. 27–8.
[4] Gail Minault, *The Khilafat Movement: Religious Symbolism and Political Mobilization in India* (New York: Columbia University Press, 1982); Gail Minault, 'Sisterhood or Separatism: The All-India Muslim Ladies' Conference and the Nationalist Movement', in *The Extended Family: Women and Political Participation in India and Pakistan*, ed. Gail Minault (Delhi: Chanakya Publications, 1981), pp. 83–108; Siobhan Lambert-Hurley, 'Fostering Sisterhood: Muslim Women and the All-India Ladies' Association', *Journal of Women's History* 16, 2 (Summer, 2004), pp. 40–65.

passed in 1929 drew women from different religious communities together in forums such as the National Council of Women in India and the AIWC that had been established in 1925 and 1927, respectively. According to Forbes, this Act proved to be a consensus issue that provided national organizations with the opportunity to coordinate women belonging to different regions and communities. Moreover, when, in the late 1920s, elements within India's Muslim communities tried to get this legislation amended in order to exclude Muslim women from its provisions, Muslim AIWC members argued in its favour and refused to allow men to speak on their behalf.[5]

Scathing Western critiques of Indian social and cultural practices involving women, epitomized by Katherine Mayo's controversial *Mother India* that was published in 1927, helped to increase the space for liberal feminism within the broader nationalist movement.[6] Before then, the prevailing gender ideology in Indian nationalist circles was that women 'naturally' embodied the spiritual sphere of the nation, itself deemed superior to the West. This correlation produced a scenario, in which, as Mrinalini Sinha has argued, 'The burden of representing the inner and authentic realm of the nation in nationalist discourse' fell on the figure of the 'modern Indian woman'.[7] But the storm of protest over polemical writings such as *Mother India* generated greater legitimacy for middle-class women's involvement in overt political activity and more support from nationalist men for female emancipation, something that has led Sinha to conclude that in interwar India 'The discursive figure of the modern Indian woman, once the signifier of national cultural difference, was now rearticulated in the discourse of liberal feminism as the model for the citizen of a new nation-state'.[8] This 'nationalist resolution of the women question' allowed women to move beyond the confines of their homes 'without defying their traditional roles as wives and mothers and

---

[5] Geraldine H. Forbes, 'Women and Modernity: The Issue of Child Marriage in India', *Women's Studies International Forum* 2, 4 (1979), pp. 407–19.

[6] For an exploration of the massive international controversy that followed the 1927 publication of *Mother India*, which explains how it became a catalyst for far-reaching changes, including a reconfiguration of the relationship between the political and social spheres in colonial India and the coalescence of a collective identity for women, see Mrinalini Sinha, *Specters of Mother India: The Global Restructuring of an Empire* (Durham, NC: Duke University Press, 2006).

[7] Mrinalini Sinha, 'Refashioning Mother India: Feminism and Nationalism in Late-Colonial India', *Feminist Studies* 26, 3, Points of Departure: India and the South Asian Diaspora (Autumn, 2000), pp. 624–5.

[8] Ibid., p. 626.

devote themselves to the service of the nation'.[9] Involvement with national movements permitted Indian women to be more demanding of their political rights, shifting their role from a relatively passive to a more active one, even if nationalist constructions of 'new women' arguably resulted in new forms of subordination.[10]

As early as 1921, following the Montagu-Chelmsford constitutional reforms of 1919, provincial legislatures gave women voting rights based on property qualifications, beginning with Madras in South India. A decade later, in the wake of Gandhi's salt *satyagraha* of 1930 – that saw 17,000 women imprisoned for their involvement in the protest – the Congress promised to introduce universal adult franchise when it came to power. Then, following the 1932 Pune Pact between Gandhi and the leader of India's so-called Untouchables, B. R. Ambedkar, the main Indian parties succumbed to the principle of communal electorates and reserved seats, though representatives of the AIWC and WIA, led by Amrit Kaur, rejected the extension of this politics of separate representation to include women.[11] In a letter to Eleanor Rathbone, British independent MP and long-term campaigner for women's rights,[12] Muthulakshmi Reddi (the first woman legislator in India who was appointed to the Madras Legislative Council in 1927) famously argued that

The only way to bring the Brahmans, the women and the pariahs together on a common platform is by enfranchising the women and the depressed classes on equal terms with others. If the women and the depressed classes are given

[9] Rochona Majumdar, '"Self-Sacrifice" versus "Self-Interest": A Non-Historicist Reading of the History of Women's Rights in India', *Comparative Studies of South Asia, Africa and the Middle East* 22, 1&2 (2002), p. 22, in which Majumdar draws on Partha Chatterjee's essay, 'The Nationalist Resolution of the Women's Question', in *Recasting Women: Essays in Indian Colonial History*, eds. Kumkum Sangari and Sudesh Vaid (New Brunswick: Rutgers University Press, 1999), pp. 233–54.

[10] Srimati Basu, *She Came to Take Her Rights: Indian Women, Property and Propriety* (New York: State University of New York Press, 1999); Suruchi Thapar-Björkert, 'The Domestic Sphere as a Political Site: A Study of Women in the Indian Nationalist Movement', *Women's Studies International Forum* 20, 4 (1997), pp. 493–504; Leela Kasturi and Vina Majumdar, *Women and Indian Nationalism* (Delhi: Vikas Publication House, 1994).

[11] For an overview of the processes involved in extending the franchise to Indian women, see Mary E. John, 'Alternate Modernities? Reservations and Women's Movement in Twentieth Century India', *Economic and Political Weekly* 35, 43/44 (21 October–3 November 2000), pp. 3822–9.

[12] For more on Rathbone's life and work, see Susan Pederson, *Eleanor Rathbone and the Politics of Conscience* (London: Yale University Press, 2004).

freedom, power and responsibility, I am sure that they would very soon learn how to rectify the present social evil.[13]

Despite most women's leaders opposing the principle of separate electorates, the Government of India Act of 1935 introduced separate seats for women.[14] The legislation provided for the formal induction of women into the political process through an extended franchise allowing some six million women to vote for both reserved and general seats in the Council of State, the Central Legislative Assembly and the eleven provincial assemblies. Six seats were reserved for women out of a total of 156 Council of State seats, to be elected by male and female members of the provincial assemblies.[15] Similarly, 9 out of 250 seats in the Central Legislative Assembly were reserved for women, who were to be chosen by the female members of provincial legislatures. Seats were also reserved for women in the provincial legislatures, though these equated to less than 4 per cent of the total number.[16] In the 1937 provincial elections that followed soon after, 4.25 million women registered to vote, and some 917,000 actually participated.[17] In terms of outcomes, in the provinces out of 1,500 seats, 56 women were elected (41 to reserved seats, 10 to general seats and 5 were nominated). In addition, thirty women joined the Central Assembly.[18]

Alongside the political developments of this period, the distinctively British colonial proposal for communal representation, whether in terms of the franchise or more broadly, tended to mobilize women's groups in pursuit of more cosmopolitan definitions of rights before Independence had taken place. This can be seen in discussions in UP in the mid- to late

[13] Quoted in Gail Pearson, 'Reserved Seats: Women and the Vote in Bombay', in *Women in Colonial India: Essays on Survival, Work and the State*, ed. J. Krishnamurty (Delhi: Oxford University Press, 1989), p. 205.

[14] Aparna Basu, 'Women's Struggle for the Vote: 1917–1937', *Indian Historical Review* 35, 1 (January 2008), pp. 128–43; Barbara Southard, 'Colonial Politics and Women's Rights: Woman Suffrage Campaigns in Bengal, British India in the 1920s', *Modern Asian Studies* 27, 2 (March 1993), pp. 397–439; Azra Asghar Ali, 'Indian Muslim Women's Suffrage Campaign: Personal Dilemma and Communal Identity 1919–1947', *Journal of the Pakistan Historical Society* 47, 2 (April 1999), pp. 33–46; Rosalind Parr, 'Citizens of Everywhere: Indian Nationalist Women and the Global Public Sphere, 1900–1952' (unpublished PhD thesis, University of Edinburgh, 2018), pp. 82–108.

[15] These six seats were allocated to the provinces of Madras, Bengal, Bombay, Uttar Pradesh, Punjab and Bihar.

[16] Jana Matson Everett, *Women and Social Change in India* (New Delhi: Heritage, 1979); Laura Dudley Jenkins, 'Competing Inequalities: The Struggle Over Reserved Seats for Women in India', *International Review of Social History* 44 (1999), pp. 53–75.

[17] The electorate as a whole amounted to some thirty million or 12 per cent of India's adult population at the time.

[18] Jahanara Shahnawaz, *Father and Daughter: A Political Autobiography* (Lahore: Nigarishat, 1971), p. 152.

1930s that centred on possible reservations for women in government service. In 1935, the Reforms Department requested a list of services and posts that might be reserved 'for a particular sex' [women] in line with Section 275 of the new Government of India Act, which stated that 'A person shall not be disqualified by sex for being appointed to any civil service of, or civil post under, the Crown in India'.[19] The main focus of the ensuing discussion, however, was around how the provincial authorities would be able to evade the equality provisions. Far from interpreting this as a mechanism for improving women's employment in the services, the proposal seemed to be more about maintaining existing preserves for men. It was noted, for example, that the Civil (executive) Services, UP Police, UP Civil (judicial), *tahsildars* and *naib tahsildars* should continue to be 'reserved exclusively for men', since these posts called for 'considerable powers of physical endurance. Though officers in the Judicial Department [were] not called upon to perform duties in riots, in raids on gambling dens, in chasing dacoits, etc., their service require[d] continuity of work, which in the case of women [was] likely to be interrupted by marriage etc.'.[20] In 1936, this qualification turned into specific government orders regarding those posts that were ordinarily to be 'reserved' for men, and others that might be recommended to be set aside for women. The former included appointments to higher positions in the Medical, Public Health, Forest, Revenue, Finance, Judicial and Public Works departments, while among the latter were named principal and lecturers at the Women's Medical School in Agra; superintendents of medical aid to women, matrons and female warders in jails; inspectresses in the Cooperative Department; chief inspectresses of Girls' Schools, circle inspectress of Girls' Schools, PA to the chief inspector of Girls' Schools, lady principals of Girls' Schools, head mistresses of Government schools, and matrons in the Educational Department.[21]

The real problem facing the authorities, however, was that under the recent legislation, existing civil services rules were set to become ultra vires from 1936 onwards, and so to overcome this constraint the UP government suggested that a general order could stipulate that women were 'not eligible for services requiring great physical endurance, control

---

[19] *Government of India Act 1935*, Article 275, p. 173.
[20] 'Notes and Orders: Reservation of Services and Posts for a Particular Sex under Section 275 of the Government of India Act, 1935', Appointments Dept, Box 212, File 724/1935 UPSA.
[21] 'Note for Government Meeting Regarding Section 275 of the Government of India Act, 1935', C. W. Gwynne, 14/6/1936, Appointments Dept, Box 212, File 724/1935 UPSA; 'Reservation of Services and Posts for a Particular Sex under Section 275 of the Government of India Act 1935' UPSA.

of men, extensive touring, or involving danger'.[22] Harry Haig, UP governor in 1938, put forward an argument that would later be used to oppose legal reform that addressed women's rights in family property, marriage and divorce. In his view, Indian society was still far too conservative to countenance the increase of women's roles in public service:

The feminist movement has made such rapid progress in recent years that we may not be able to say so positively for much longer that women are not as capable as men in powers of endurance and in the performance of work which involves the control of large bodies of men. On the other hand public opinion in India is generally conservative and will probably for many years resent the intrusion of women in the various branches of public service. Apart from public opinion and the difficulty that must arise when women marry and have families would present in Government service a problem almost insoluble.[23]

The UP-approved list of recommended reservations for men in the late 1930s was extensive: all the top executive posts, including secretary to the governor, advocate general, Public Service Commission and secretary to the Upper House had to be filled by males, while the office establishment and staff attached to those posts could be taken up by women.[24] Haig went on to comment that 'opinion in India itself is opposed to sex equality in service and indeed to the employment of women at all in most services. In practice the exclusion of women is mainly secured by the simple expedient of not appointing them to services'. He was clearly concerned that if women performed better in competitive examinations, this would likely make it difficult to exclude them, but he concluded with a final observation, 'Section 275 of the Government of India Act seems to be a piece of interfering stupidity by the English feminists, and apparently involves us in various ridiculous processes'.[25]

The problem of female government employment was taken up in due course by the UP Congress Ministry. The two years (1937–9) of Congress rule in eight of India's eleven provinces was in many respects a phase of political and administrative reform, and prefigured much of what happened during the early postcolonial period. Possibly it did so, although in a largely negative sense, in the area of women's rights, establishing a pattern of largely symbolic recognition of gender equality as a means of maintaining certain inequalities. G. B. Pant, for one, pointed out in discussions on the issue that no specific order actually needed to be put in place, since change would happen naturally at the

[22] Ibid.
[23] Harry Haig, 16 June 1936, Appointments Dept, Box 212, File 724/1935 UPSA.
[24] Ibid.   [25] Ibid.

discretion of the Public Services Commission. In a remark that was later to epitomize how independent governments approached the implementation of constitutional rights, Pant added, 'Let us observe the principle of equality of sex, *at least in theory*. I know that this province is too conservative to outgrow age long prejudice at once' [emphasis added].[26]

But by the time of the Second World War, earlier cross-community consensus within the women's movement had been greatly undermined by the growth of communal politics, and all-India women's organizations were fast losing their 'universal' authority. Mobilizing women had become crucial to the Muslim League, whose leaders wanted to stimulate the political consciousness of Muslim women as a means of generating and legitimizing support for their cause. In 1938, for instance, Jinnah famously supported a resolution moved at the annual Muslim League session that argued for opportunities to enable women to participate in the development of the 'Muslim nation', and called for more Muslim women to take a direct part in nationalist activity: after all, 'no nation [could] make progress without the co-operation of its women. If Muslim women support[ed] their men as they did in the days of the Prophet of Islam, [the League] should soon realise [its] goal'.[27] Muslim women now took part in increasingly numbers in pro-Muslim League demonstrations in the run up to independence. According to David Willmer, the Muslim League needed its 'mothers of the nation', since women represented 'an obvious and distinct constituency which could be readily exploited for rhetorical purposes and politically mobilized to good effect'.[28]

Undoubtedly, women who ended up supporting the Muslim League did so for a range of reasons. Some simply followed the example set by menfolk in their families. But others responded more independently, with their resulting activism a reflection of the somewhat greater degree

---

[26] Note of G. B. Pant, Appointments Dept, Box 212, File 724/1935 UPSA.

[27] Riswan Ahmad, *'Sayings of the Quaid-i-Azam': Mohammed Ali Jinnah* (Karachi: Quaid Foundation and Pakistan Movement Centre, 1993), p. 105, quoted in Akbar S. Ahmed, *Jinnah, Pakistan and Islamic Identity: The Search for Saladin* (London: Routledge, 1997), p. 60.

[28] David Willmer, 'Women as Participants in the Pakistan Movement: Modernisation and the Promise of a Moral State', *Modern Asian Studies* 31, 3 (1996), p. 573. According to Willmer, the extent of female involvement in the Muslim League's campaign to secure a separate Muslim state can be explained by the fact that the idea of 'Pakistan' contained a special – 'surplus' of – meaning for Muslim women, with that the result that women and men in the run up to Pakistan's creation had different 'gendered' visions of what its future held. But, in his view, the general failure on the part of historians to acknowledge the complexities of female involvement has meant that alternative 'moral' meanings have been submerged by the dominant political narrative of the Pakistan movement, and, hence, the issue of how far processes of the so-called modernization were woven into the struggle for some kind of 'Pakistan' has tended to be overlooked.

of autonomy that was permitted by the unsettled political circumstances of the time. Either way, it would be hard to imagine that the latter interpreted 'Pakistan' – whatever this might subsequently mean in practice – as a place where their rights as females would not be safeguarded. Jinnah, after all, had taken a prominent part in the campaign to secure the passage of the Shariat Application Act of 1937, which targeted existing customary laws that deprived women of their inheritance rights with respect to immovable property. Besides, he had been an active supporter of the 1939 Muslim Dissolution of Marriage Act, which had reinforced awareness of the possibility of challenging existing interpretations of religious law in order to improve the relative position of women vis-à-vis that of men.[29] As illustrated by Dushka Saiyid's example of Azra Khanum, the Lahore College for Women student who called upon Muslim women to educate Muslim men in a speech delivered in November 1942, women supporters of the League were adamant that they should participate as equal partners. Political liberation and the liberation of women, for them, were intimately, and inextricably, intertwined.[30]

The picture was equally complicated from the perspective of mainstream Congress nationalism. In 1934 the AIWC had passed a resolution demanding a revised Hindu Code that would address the deficit in female rights by modifying the laws governing marriage and inheritance.[31] But a decade later, in wartime India, when faced with a choice between supporting or boycotting (as Congress was doing) a government investigation into women's 'legal disabilities', AIWC member Vilasini Devi Shenai argued forcefully against automatically prioritizing the nationalist struggle: as she reminded readers of the AIWC's 1944–5 annual report, 'Today our men are clamouring for political rights at the hand of an alien government. Have they conceded their wives, their own sisters, their daughters, "flesh of their flesh, blood

---

[29] For further comment on these two pieces of legislation, see Gail Minault, *Secluded Scholars: Women's Education and Muslim Social Reform in Colonial India* (Delhi: Oxford University Press, 1998), pp. 298–306; David Gilmartin, 'Customary Law and Shari'at in British Punjab', in *Shari'at and Ambiguity in South Asian Islam*, ed. Katherine Ewing (Berkeley: University of California Press, 1988), pp. 43–62; Lucy Carroll, '*Talaq-i-Tafwid* and Stipulations in a Muslim Marriage Contract: Important Means of Protecting the Position of the South Asian Muslim Wife', *Modern Asian Studies* 16, 2 (1982), pp. 277–8.

[30] Dushka Saiyid, *Muslim Women of the British Punjab from Seclusion to Politics* (Basingstoke: Macmillan, 1998), p. 91.

[31] Geraldine H. Forbes, 'Caged Tigers: "First Wave" Feminists in India', *Women's Studies International Forum* 5, 6 (1982), p. 352.

of their blood" social equality and economic justice?'[32] Developments
that unfolded in the late colonial period thus produced the context in
which the early post-independence governments of India and Pakistan
responded to the larger issues of women's legal rights and structures of
employment, particularly in the public sphere. They also helped to shape
the response among women in both states to issues linked with citizenship and the rights and responsibilities that this generated.

Post-1947 India

Turning first to India – which after Independence formulated its new
constitution on the basis of equality for men and women – the provision
of women's reserved seats was ended. But, to a great extent, the gulf in
India between the symbolism of rights and the realities of how these
were implemented was reflected in detailed and ostensibly far-reaching
legislative enactments relating to women's rights. As Eleanor Newbigin
has explored in relation to the creation of the modern Hindu legal
subject, the picture on paper at least was a fairly positive one, with a raft
of legislation, backed up by the promotion of an equal position for
women in the Indian Constitution, supported and sometimes initiated
by a powerful group of female politicians in the central and state assemblies.[33] Up to India's second general elections, held in 1957, these
initiatives included legislation that affected women's lives in a range of
ways: the Indian Nursing Council Act, 1947; attempts to pass Prohibition of Dowry Bills, 1951–8; Prevention of Food Adulteration Bills,
1952–60; the Punjab Municipal Act, 1952 (which addressed deficiencies
in public health bills with respect to regulating and licensing institutions
caring for women and children under 18); the Suppression of Immoral
Traffic in Women and Brothels, 1953; the Protection, Maintenance,
Custody, Education and Employment of Children, 1953 (an attempt to
regulate or abolish child labour); Dentists' Bills, 1953; the Drugs and
Cosmetics Bill, 1954; the Equal Pay for Equal Work, 1956–7 (which
lapsed); and Divorce or Judicial Separation, 1956.[34]

---

[32] AIWC Report 1944–45, All-India Women's Conference Library, New Delhi, cited in
   ibid., p. 352.
[33] Eleanor Newbigin, *The Hindu Family and the Emergence of Modern India: Law, Citizenship
   and Community* (Cambridge: Cambridge University Press, 2013). For an assessment of
   where personal law fitted into this process, see Eleanor Newbigin, 'Personal Law and
   Citizenship in India's Transition to Independence', *Modern Asian Studies* 45, 1 (2011),
   pp 7–32.
[34] J. K. Chopra, *Women in the Indian Parliament (A Critical Study of Their Role)* (New Delhi:
   Mittal Publications, 1993), pp. 34–5.

As had been recognized in the 1930s, one of the key areas for the promotion of women's rights after Independence was professional employment, since economic autonomy was rightly accepted by a range of women's groups as essential when promoting other kinds of rights. In mid-twentieth-century India, state employment was central to the notion of professional development, given the role that the state was expected to take in the larger development of the nation. But what is interesting and perhaps less frequently acknowledged is the extent to which refugee displacement played a direct role in widening opportunities for women within the infrastructure of the new everyday Indian state. This can be seen in relation to female police officers, even though, as reflected in the duties of a cadre of female police established in Delhi in 1949, their responsibilities were restricted to that of other women and children only. Hence, their duties included interrogating women suspects, accused and witnesses (particularly *purdah*-observing women); attending all searches and investigations in which women were present; looking after the welfare of women in police custody; assisting in the duties connected with disorderly houses; conducting the investigation of all cases of offences against women; helping with the control of demonstrations in which women took part; taking a central role in the recovery of abducted women; and dealing with juvenile offenders.[35]

The first female police force to be properly established in independent India operated in the UP hill station of Dehradun, specifically to help directly with the influx of refugees. Government officials there had received reports that displaced refugee families were inducing their womenfolk to 'forcibly occupy [the] vacated houses' of Muslims, which made it difficult for male police officers to handle this delicate and complex problem without the aid of female colleagues. Considering the urgency of this situation, sanction was accorded for the creation of the temporary posts of one subinspector and two head constables for Dehrudun.[36] But, for the most part, women's police forces in these years were only really tried out at an experimental level, and to deal with very particular kinds of 'social ills' and civic problems – viz. the establishing of 'a healthy social order' and in support of older legislation such as the Naik Girl's Protection Act 1929; the UP Minor Girls' Protection Act, 1929; and the UP Suppression of Immoral Traffic Act, 1933.[37] By

---

[35] B. N. Srivastava, 19 September 1952, 'Women Police: Recommendations of the PRC', Home Police A, Box 389, File 662/47 UPSA.

[36] Ibid.

[37] Note of 20 August 1956, 'Women Police: Recommendations of the PRC', Home Police A, Box 389, File 662/47 UPSA.

1957 when the fifth 'All-India Conference of the Association of Moral and Social Hygiene' was held, state governments more generally were requested 'immediately to constitute Special Police Squads for preventative and vigilance work and to recommend the appointment of women to all grades of Police staff in the squads which [would] work in close cooperation with social workers'.[38]

There were wider issues surrounding women's rights and security that were naturally more clearly articulated in the early post-Partition period as a result of new public questions about violence against women. Rolled into this too were debates about public morality. In the meetings of the Association for Moral and Social Hygiene in 1951, for instance, requests were made for special ministries for social welfare, ratification of the UN Convention against the immoral traffic in women and women members on the Central Board of Film Censors. Conference recommendations also called for the registration and annual licensing of rescue homes, widow homes and orphanages; stricter and more stringent enforcement of the Suppression of Immoral Traffic Act; the establishment of reception homes for women and children; and special courts set up by state and central governments to try cases of social vice, held in camera. A corps of women, they argued, should work especially on social vice and with trained social workers to deal with rescue and rehabilitation. The Conference also called for the passage of legislation modelled on the Undesirable Advertisements Act of West Bengal.[39]

Many of these efforts were driven by middle-class, urban women whose vision crossed international borders, but whose experiences were limited to an English-speaking milieu. They were also dominated by India's large cities and their hinterlands, with a disproportionately low representation from the north when looked at on a national, all-India, scale. The most important organization representing such women was the AIWC, founded in 1927 (see Figure 5.1).[40] Included among its office-holders in late 1948 were a member of the National Cabinet, an Ambassador, a national delegate to the UNO, a member of the Executive Committee of the Asian Relations Conference, a member of the Congress Working Committee and a governor of a province.[41] The key

---

[38] Note of 18 February 1957, 'Women Police: Recommendations of the PRC', Home Police A, Box 389, File 662/47 UPSA.

[39] 'Recommendations of the Second All-India Conference for Moral and Social Hygiene, 26 and 27 December 1951, 'Women Police: Recommendations of the PRC', Home Police A, Box 389, File 662/47 UPSA.

[40] For a detailed survey of the AIWC's origins and development, see Parr, 'Citizens of Everywhere', chapter 1.

[41] Sumant Mehta, 'As Others See Us', Roshni III, 11 (December 1948), pp. 34–5.

Figure 5.1 Meeting of the All-India Women's Conference,
December 1947.
Photo by Keystone/Stringer/Hulton Archive/Getty Images

AIWC office-holders from UP in the 1948–9 period were Lakshmi
N. Menon from Lucknow, who was editor of the organization's main
publication *Roshni*, and Hajrah Begum, who was representative of the
Lucknow Women's Association (and branch representative for UP).
Also involved in these early post-independence years were Molina Ghosh
from Allahabad (branch representative for Agra, UP) and Prakashvati
Yash Pal from Lucknow.[42] The total budget for the AIWC was modest –
around Rs. 30,000 per year, most of which was consumed by the cost of
producing AIWC publications.[43]

The AIWC possessed a very varied and uneven regional membership.
In UP – India's most populous state in 1949 – its membership totalled
894, with a predominance of women hailing from its western districts.
But Delhi's membership alone almost equalled that at 863, while
Bombay boasted 7,393. Other states were also better represented than

[42] All-India Women's Conference (hereafter AIWC), Institutional Papers, Reel
33 NMML.
[43] January 1948 Meeting of the Standing Committee held at the Lady Willingdon College
Hostel, Madras, AIWC Institutional Papers, Reel 33 NMML.

the north – Maharashtra had 6,607 members, Madras 1,465 and Andhra 7,740. The two UP sections, therefore, only had six and three Annual Conference delegates (for Agra and Oudh, respectively) out of a total number of 308.[44] In this sense, the AIWC did not have a membership that was directly related to, or reflective of, the demographics of India as a whole. The organization was quite self-aware of these limitations: in 1948, it admitted that the four branches in the Bombay region made up around 50 per cent of the total membership, and that there were some very large cities with no branches and villages were rarely reached. The organization needed 'to do more than pass resolutions and actually set up wards and other committees through India'.[45]

To a great extent, unlike many of the caste and community-based rights movements that began to develop over the same period and later, the AIWC's ideas about women's rights fitted squarely into a secular conception of universal rights of the citizen, as defined by India's forthcoming Constitution. In its September 1948 issue of *Roshni*, the lead article stated that

The Dominion of India is a secular state, says the Prime Minister [Nehru]. Nothing could be more agreeable to the progressive citizen. Nobody has so far raised a voice of protest. Then, we ask why are the people treated to privileges, concessions and reservations? In a secular democratic state there should be no place for caste, creed and sex distinctions. There could be only citizens and not communities.[46]

As such, the AIWC saw its role as squarely situated in the realization of such civic rights, on the basis of what it saw as universal democratic values. In this sense, it was especially concerned with the promotion of education as a means to the enjoyment or exercise of citizenship. In the lead-up to India's first general elections, the AIWC Presidential Address by Urmila Mehta argued that:

Adult franchise will have no meaning unless the entire people are educated to the minimum extent of being able to read and write … The Women's Conference can undertake this work on a nation-wide basis and assist the governments and other social bodies in this task, by organizing a network of literacy classes for women all over the country.[47]

---

[44] 'Allotment of Delegates to Branches for the Twenty First Session of the Conference in Gwalior – January 1949', AIWC Institutional Papers Reel 33 NMML.

[45] Mehta, 'As Others See Us', pp. 34-5..

[46] 'In the Light', *Roshni* III, 8 (September 1948), pp. 2–3.

[47] 'What the President Said: Extracts from Shrimati Urmila Mehta's Speech at the Opening of the 21st Session, Gwalior', *Roshni* IV, 2–3 (February–March 1949), pp. 7–12.

Added to this focus on education, the AIWC set out to have a very broad-based rights agenda. In September 1949, it changed the 'Aims and Objectives' section of its Constitution to reflect this goal. Its new six-point programme was ambitious:

(1) To work for a society based on the principles of social justice, personal integrity and equal rights and opportunities for all; (2) To secure recognition of the inherent right of every human being in the essentials of life such as food, clothing, housing, education, social amenities and security, in the belief that these should not be determined by accident of birth but by planned social distribution; (3) To support the claim of every citizen to the right to enjoy basic civic liberties; (4) To stand against all separatist tendencies and to promote greater national integration and unity; (5) To help women to utilize to the fullest the Fundamental Rights conferred on them by the Constitution of the Indian Union; and (6) To cooperate with peoples and organizations of the world for the implementation of these principles which alone can assure permanent international amity and world peace.[48]

As a body interested in the rights of women as independent professionals, one of the key AIWC campaigns of the early post-Independence period involved women's professional development and, once again, representation in government services in particular. This effort came to a head almost immediately after August 1947 in relation to the need to expand the intake of new recruits to the Indian Administrative Service (IAS) and Indian Provincial Service (IPS). In a four-column advertisement inserted into newspapers by the Dominion Ministry of Home Affairs, entitled 'Emergency Recruitment to the Indian Administrative and Police Services', the fifth clause stated that 'Women are not eligible for appointment to the IAS and IPS'. The AIWC immediately issued a protest, arguing that this limitation contravened the fundamental rights of equality guaranteed in the draft Constitution. Its mouthpiece publication *Roshni* reported that women were considered eligible to participate in the struggle for freedom, for the posts of governors and ambassadors, for ministerial jobs and as delegates to international conferences. But when it came to government service, they ended up having to be teachers or lapsing into domesticity: 'We would like to know if it is the policy and intention of the government of free India to condemn women to the position of women in countries where fascism once existed'. This was not the first time in history, *Roshni* continued, that 'a successful democracy [had] ignored the fundamental rights of its citizens. We have seen civil

---

[48] 'Proposed Changes in the AIWC Constitution: Changes to the Aims and Objectives', *Roshni* IV, 9 (September 1949), p. 4.

liberties threatened in the name of internal security, political opposition snubbed if not scotched in the name of unity'.[49]

Although the AIWC tended to lobby government by drawing direct parallels and comparison with international contexts, it still promoted the specific rights of women in particular areas of employment in India. The Standing Committee at the end of July 1948, for instance, called for an enquiry into salaries in areas of public services that directly affected women, for example teaching.[50] At the same meeting, regret was recorded at discrimination taking place against married women employees of the Postal and Telegraph Department of the Government of India, and it was decided to lobby the Government of India in order to get 'the invidious distinction abolished'.[51] The women's movement also focussed on the employment rights of women in general and how it varied across different states. The tendency to regard women as second-class citizens, the *Roshni* lead column wrote in August 1948, seemed to be worse in Madras, the only place that had not responded to the demand for equal treatment in the services. Recently, it continued, a Labour Inquiry Committee appointed under the chairmanship of R. S. Nimbkar[52] had investigated the wages of industrial workers and recommended equal wages for both sexes.[53] Maintaining a reach that linked local to national and international, the AIWC was able, somewhat uniquely, to adopt a critical stance regarding other larger questions in the suppression of civil rights across India. For example, following the decision of provincial governments in the summer of 1948 to round up communists, *Roshni* quietly took up the issue of the ordinance promulgated by the Central Provinces government, which deprived citizens of the right to personal freedom by taking away their right to apply for a writ of habeas corpus and allowed arrests without warrant.[54]

Nevertheless, despite the immediate post-Independence concern centred on education, the professions and government service, powerful longer term initiatives for the promotion of women's legal rights were also on the agenda, especially connected to lobbying in connection with the proposed Hindu Code Bill in the late 1940s and early 1950s. In its

---

[49] 'In the Light', *Roshni* III, 6 (July 1948), pp. 2–4.
[50] Minutes of the Standing Committee of the AICC held in Patna on 29, 30 and 31 July 1948, Item 8, AIWC Institutional Papers Reel 33 NMML.
[51] Ibid.
[52] R. S. Nimbkar was a member of the executive committee of the Bombay Workers and Peasants Party established in 1927, who was later elected to the All-India Congress Committee and helped to persuade it to make Congress an associate member of the League Against Imperialism. Later, in 1933, as one of the accused in the Meerut Conspiracy Case, he was sentenced to twelve years imprisonment.
[53] 'In the Light', *Roshni* III, 7 (August 1948), pp. 2–3.   [54] Ibid.

July 1948 Standing Committee meeting, Kitty Shiva Rao[55] reported that the AIWC had organized deputations to meet the prime minister and the law minister, Ambedkar, to impress upon them the urgent need to pass the Hindu Code by the time that the August Assembly session ended, so that it would not be postponed any further.[56] The AIWC was one of the few organizations at this time that publicly exposed the direct contradictions involved in the very act of creating a Hindu Code. As the April 1949 lead article in *Roshni* put it:

It is also a matter of immense surprise to us that the Constituent Assembly, having agreed to the fundamental rights of equality for men and women in all spheres of life, having agreed to the need for a National Civil Code in free India, the nation having also voted in favour of the Universal Declaration of Human Rights in the recent General Assembly of the United Nations, should now discuss the rather absurd question whether the daughter should have the same share in her father's estate as her brother![57]

As the first general elections approached, women's organizations, with the help of the AIWC, took more direct action in relation to the Code Bill debates. A deputation of several of them – including the AIWC, National Council of Women, Delhi Mahila Samaj and Congress Sewika Dal – saw Nehru and protested against what they described as 'the vivisection' of the Hindu Code Bill. The delegation pressed the prime minister on the importance of the inheritance part of the Code and wanted 'top most priority given to it'. Furthermore, it told Nehru that if the inheritance clause was not passed, women would be forced to challenge the validity of the present inheritance law in the Supreme Court, for it conflicted with the Fundamental Rights of the Constitution.[58]

There were direct attempts to persuade MPs by local branches of the AIWC on the issue – in January 1949, Kitty Shiva Rao suggested in an AIWC meeting

that unless you make an effort and urge on the member of the legislature representing your town or province the urgency of taking up this measure and asking him for his support, it will be difficult to get the Code through ... I am

---

[55] Kitty Shiva Rao (formerly Verstaendig) was the wife of Benegal Shiva Rao, journalist and a member of the Constituent Assembly of India who was then elected representative of the South Kanara constituency in the first *Lok Sabha*.
[56] Minutes of the Standing Committee of the AIWC held in Patna on 29, 30 and 31 July 1948, Item 8, AIWC Institutional Papers Reel 33 NMML.
[57] 'In the Light: The Hindu Code Bill', *Roshni* IV, 4 (April 1949), pp. 2–3.
[58] 'Women's Protest to Prime Minister', *National Herald*, 22 September 1951.

therefore requesting you to write without delay to the member presenting you and urge on him that he should support this measure.[59]

AIWC strategy was based on the strong belief that public campaigning alone would not be enough to advance the rights of women, since the true opinions of women were held in secret, and thus worked against an obligatory public face presented by many. As *Roshni* reported, 'many women after opposing the Code in public, would quietly confide in you that these opinions were those of the "*gharwalas*" [men-folk at home], their own opinions being in favour of such equal rights of inheritance being given to women, and guaranteed legally'.[60]

Roshni's May 1949 editorial described an address, made by women from Madras to the future first president of the Republic, Rajendra Prasad, in which they called on him to support the Hindu Code Bill. The fury with which *Roshni* reported Prasad's reply leapt off the page: 'We must take into account the views of not only the advanced people but also those who are not advanced', Prasad had responded, 'I am sure that if the provisions of the Code were explained to my wife, whom I consider to be a representative of the orthodox women of India, she would not accept them'. The editorial then took out its scalpel: 'It is unfortunate that Mrs. Rajendra Prasad should have been mentioned at all. We have no doubt that Dr. Rajendra Prasad's wife is the arbiter of his destiny; but is it fair, we ask, to put on her frail shoulders the responsibility of the happiness of millions of her sisters?' As *Roshni* continued: 'It is almost as if the father of the family should say, when a member is ill with some serious ailment, "We should not only take the opinion of the expert Medical Board, but also of those who know nothing of medicine or disease".' *Roshni* was in no doubt that the progressive women of India were 'more qualified to speak on the proposal than either Dr. Rajendra Prasad or his orthodox wife. And, of course, we are sure that the latter would express an opinion in our favour, if she were informed by one of her sex'.[61]

In its attempt to work below the larger public radars of legislative assemblies and national media, the AIWC also sought to pursue its objectives through more local movements. It was involved in the promotion of popular grassroots social movements across North India, and was especially prominent in relation to refugee and post-Partition groups. In its annual conferences for 1948 and 1949, the AIWC discussed the setting up of groups at the following annual conference organized around

---

[59] Kitty Shiva Rao to members of the Standing Committee, 10 January 1949, AIWC Institutional Papers, Reel 33 NMML.
[60] 'In the Light: The Hindu Code Bill', pp. 2–3.   [61] Ibid.

'1. Social affairs, including legal and health; 2. Education, including culture; and 3. Economic affairs, including food'. There were some direct statements regarding the problems of low-level corruption and supply – the Standing Committee, for instance, recorded in its minute that 'the AIWC views with alarm the exorbitant prices of food, cloth and fuel and other necessities of life and strongly condemns Government for not taking effective measures to prevent blackmarketeering and profiteering'. Another resolution passed by the 1948 meeting expressed concerns at housing shortages, and demanded the requisitioning of military barracks, the establishment of complete government control established over rent and building materials, the accelerated construction of building temporary tenements, and the punishment of people taking *pugree*.[62] It also put some of these social proposals into practice. For example, the Honorary Secretary was tasked to issue instructions to branches to cooperate with the government in combatting high prices by helping with fair price shops. Likewise, the AIWC sponsored a 'Skippo Van' in Delhi to help with refugees, while its counterpart vehicle in Bombay toured villages and dispensed anti-cholera vaccinations to adivasi communities.[63]

The AIWC made contact with an array of more local women's movements across India too, especially in relation to their core objectives. Members of the Standing Committee maintained correspondence with organizations such as Dharwar Mahamila Mandal (which opposed the Hindu Code Bill as reactionary), the Bombay Mahila Sangh and the Federation of University Women in India.[64] They worked with a number of other agencies to promote the interests of refugee children, by helping to run children's homes (at first in Orissa and Malabar) alongside the All India Save the Children Committee.[65] Later, the AIWC supported homes in UP too, specifically one in Allahabad that took in around 100 displaced refugee children. The central government remitted forty rupees per month for each child, including orphans, children of widows who could not support them and children of destitute persons who had no known relations.[66] Detailed accounts of the care provided in these

[62] Minutes of the Standing Committee of the AIWC held in Patna on 29, 30 and 31 July 1948, AIWC Institutional Papers, Reel 33 NMML.

[63] Ibid.

[64] Meeting of the Dharwar Mahamila Mandal, 4 September 1949; 'Federation of University Women in India. Fourteenth to Twenty First Annual Reports, 1940–1949', AIWC Institutional Papers, Reel 33 NMML.

[65] Kamaladevi Chattopadhyay to Miss Owen, 8 February 1949, Save the Children Correspondence, AIWC Institutional Papers, Reel 33 NMML.

[66] Manmohan Kishan to Kamalevi Chattopadhyay, 31 May 1949, Save the Children Correspondence, AIWC Institutional Papers, Reel 33 NMML.

homes made their way to the AIWC, including the account of one Sindhi boy, Tulsidas, who ran away, probably to Bombay, claiming that he wanted to find his mother. The Allahabad member of the All-India Save the Children Committee wrote that

The other Sindhi children tell me that this boy had a complete railway timetable written in Sindhi in his possession and he had told them from the very beginning that he would not remain here and would go away to Bombay.[67]

Interestingly, the Allahabad home – named the Swaraj Bhavan Children's National Institute – was set up to reflect some of the utopian visions of the new India, moving away from older colonial boarding schools, and placing a focus on volunteering and national service.[68]

Women's movements during these early post-Independence years in UP clearly recognized the particular role that as members of wider civil society they had to play in challenging low-level corruption and problems of food supply. In 1949, *Roshni* reported that

People openly say that they buy in the blackmarket and ignorant public opinion sympathizes. Only a high civic conscience and a sense of the urgency of the problem can have any effect. It is here that voluntary organisations, political parties and other public institutions have a part to play. They can try to convince people of the iniquity of selling or buying in the black market and, by helping to grow vegetables, tapioca etc. on an individual small-scale basis, increase the supplies of substitute foodstuffs to take the place of grain.

Changing eating habits was something described by *Roshni* as located principally in the woman's sphere, and hence it argued that women could play a role in decreasing families' reliance mainly on grains in the diet.[69] Moreover, the idea of self-help citizens' movements was proposed as a distinctive urban model by AIWC member Purnima Banerji, in her 'Citizens' Self Help Leagues'. Although never fully put into effect, this blue print involved saving food in large towns where there was rationing: 'Those who get together should do so with the specific purpose of helping each other and to emphasise self-reliance and voluntary effort'. This scheme was set up not as a means of minimizing large-scale national planning, but to prevent the emergence of a 'culture of blame' against a large machinery. Citizens' organizations would gain a bit more control over the fair price shops at controlled rates, and provide extra food

---

[67] Shyam Kumari Khan to Mithan Lam, Women's Section of Relief and Rehabilitation, 24 September 1949, AIWC Institutional Papers, Reel 33 NMML.

[68] See, for example 'Monthly Progress Report of the Activities of the Swarajj Bhavan Children's National Institute, for the Period 15 July to 15 August 1949, dated 20.8.49', AIWC Institutional Papers, Reel 33 NMML.

[69] 'In the Light', *Roshni* IV, 9 (September 1949), pp. 2–3.

through them. This would also, it was hoped, have an effect on tackling the problem of black markets. As Banerji argued, such initiatives 'would make a positive contribution in our city life and give birth to that intelligent spirit of co-operation among citizens which is the very life and spirit of the democratic method of living in the community'.[70]

Post-1947 Pakistan

In a similar fashion to developments taking place in India, the circumstances surrounding Partition allowed certain groups or 'classes' of Pakistani women to come forward to offer their support to the nation and its people. A large proportion of the work involved in recovering abducted women, for instance, fell to women themselves, particularly but not exclusively in relation to the Punjab. Likewise, rehabilitation efforts frequently involved women (see Figure 5.2). Partition in effect opened up new opportunities for active welfare work to Muslim women from privileged backgrounds, stimulating what Begum Raana Liaquat Ali Khan, wife of the prime minister and the founder (in 1949) of the All-Pakistan Women's Association (APWA), optimistically described as 'a social revolution, the like of which history has no parallel for [in terms of] the speed and non-violence with which it established itself and spread'.[71] At APWA's first meeting, resolutions were passed calling for free and compulsory primary education for women; a women's bureau to collect statistics on working women; maternity and child welfare centres; a college for nurses[72] and a prohibition on children begging. More generally, the meeting emphasized that Pakistani women, in their different ways, were expected by APWA to 'fight till the end' to defend the interests of the new state of Pakistan. On the one hand, the status of women had to be enhanced to enable Pakistan to claim to be a modern Muslim state. On the other hand, women's rights had to be articulated in ways that would not undermine the 'Muslim-ness', or Islamic identity, of the new state, since this had been the basis on which its creation had been

---

[70] Purnima Banerji, 'Citizens' Self-Help Leagues', *Roshni* IV, 9 (September 1949), p. 9.

[71] Kay Miles, *The Dynamo in Silk: A Brief Biographical Sketch of Begum Ra'ana Liaquat Ali Khan* (2nd ed., Karachi: All-Pakistan Women's Association, 1974); Deepa Agarwal and Tahmina Aziz Ayub, *The Begum: A Portrait of Ra'ana Liaquat Ali Khan, Pakistan's Pioneering First Lady* (New York: Viking, 2019).

[72] At the Annual conference of Trained Nurses Association of Pakistan in 1952, the Punjab Governor, I. I. Chundrigar referred to that fact that Pakistan had possessed only two trained nurses at time of Partition, and so it was 'a matter of national pride' that by the time of his speech the Association commanded a membership of 1,000 trained nurses (seven per million people compared with the then ratio of 1 to 300 in the UK). *Dawn*, 19 April 1952.

Figure 5.2 Fatima Jinnah (C-back row, silver-haired, clad in white),
sister of M. A. Jinnah, surrounded by women making clothes for
refugees, Governor House, Karachi, December 1947.
Photo by Margaret Bourke-White/The LIFE Picture Collection/Getty Images

supported and sanctioned.[73] As the Association's 'Life President',
Begum Liaquat Ali Khan repeatedly stressed that the primary duty of
Pakistani women was 'to work towards the defence, development and
betterment of the country ... this [was] not the time for [them] to sit
quietly in their homes. They [had] to come out of their homes to learn to
work and then teach others to do so'.[74]

Initially, a Pakistan Women's Volunteer Service (PWVS) was established to channel this involvement along constructive nation-building
lines. On the whole, its activities were not seen as particularly

---

[73] For the text of her inaugural speech when APWA was set up, see *Challenge and Change:
Speeches by Begum Ra'ana Liaquat Ali Khan*, ed. F. D. Douglas (Karachi: All-Pakistan
Women's Association, n.d.), pp. 1–4.

[74] Begum H. I. Ahmed, *Begum Ra'ana Liaquat Ali Khan* (Karachi: n.p., 1975), p. 34,
quoted in Khawar Mumtaz and Farida Shaheed, *Women of Pakistan: Two Steps Forward,
One Step Back?* (London: Zed Books, 1987), p. 51.

controversial, largely because, as Khawar Mumtaz and Farida Shaheed have argued, social welfare work was viewed as an extension of a woman's domestic role, and easier to accept. Praise was in consequence lavished on the good deeds performed by Pakistani women social workers, 'gallant ladies' without whose assistance, for instance, 'the stupendous task [of recovering abducted women] could not have been successfully tackled by the authorities'.[75] Large numbers of ordinary middle-class women involved themselves in the day-to-day tasks of organizing relief in refugee camps; collecting and distributing goods, clothing, medicines and money; running and helping in clinics and hospitals; and opening and operating medical dispensaries, schools and what were referred to as industrial homes. Female volunteers under Begum Liaquat's leadership established, among other initiatives, an employment exchange bureau, a 'lost and found' bureau, a marriage bureau, a widows' home and a home for abducted women. One task that they took on was to arrange the marriage of unattached women in refugee camps so that 'no woman left the camp single'. During an 'Abducted Women's Week' in February 1948, launched to promote greater public cooperation in the integration of these women into Pakistani society, *Dawn* reminded its readers of the precedent set back in the days of the Prophet Muhammad when men were encouraged to marry widows produced by war. It accordingly called on Pakistani men to cooperate with the Widow Remarriage Committee by taking as their wives lone women who had been casualties of Partition violence: as one *alim*-cum-refugee spokesman had announced, 'it is the obligation of the society, and if we fail to do our duty towards these unfortunate creatures, the consequences will be foul and cruel, giving rise to many "immoral and un-Islamic practices". Our society at large stands to suffer'.[76]

Another expression of female mobilization on behalf of the nation in the wake of Partition were the Pakistan Women's National Guard (PWNG) and the Pakistan Women's Naval Reserve (PWNR), both of which aimed to teach their members the basics of nursing and to train them in physical fitness and methods of defence. But while their duties also included an important element of social welfare work, the PWNG and PWNR were criticized within months of their formation for permitting women to march with their heads uncovered. The official response was a compromise in the form of a *duputta* (scarf) added to the uniform to provide for greater modesty. In time, the three battalions of the PWNG – consisting of c. 2,400 young women – was disbanded once it

---

[75] 'Refugees in Pakistan', 1948–49, DO142/438 UK National Archives (hereafter UKNA).
[76] *Dawn*, 12 February 1948.

was decided that it had served its purpose.[77] Uniforms remained a sore point, however. For one anonymous member of the PWNR who had her letter published in *Dawn* in December 1951, the rising cost (from Rs. 25 to Rs. 80) of buying her uniform ignored the impact of the austerity of the early 1950s on the Reserve's less affluent recruits. But worse for her, and reflective of the class divisions within it, was the fact that the behaviour of PWNR officers was 'always humiliating':

They look down upon us as if we are their personal servants. As you may be aware, most of [us] come from respectable and educated families. So far as I am concerned I do not remember a single occasion when I have been rebuked by my parents even, but here we are ridiculed and abused in a most discourteous manner. Incidentally, I may mention that the PWNR is a volunteer service and no member is paid any emoluments whatsoever. We have got certain other grievances of serious nature but I do not want to publicise them and would try to bring home those also to the authorities concerned on suitable occasions. I hope that the high ups in the navy will pay their immediate attention to these matters.[78]

Such social activism, however, did not take place in a vacuum. As our earlier chapters have shown, once Pakistan had come into existence, and the immediate confusion of Partition had passed, the country (like India) entered a period of intense nation-building debate as to its identity and what shape its institutions – constitutional, political and legal – should take. Indeed, the Objectives Resolution passed by the Pakistan Constituent Assembly in March 1949 set in motion intense discussion about the role of religion in the functioning of both state and society, and in the process raised questions in relation to what specific role women as 'citizens' ought to play. Intensive lobbying ensued, carried out by those who sought to protect and enhance women's rights as citizens by putting pressure on the state to intervene proactively on their behalf. And education, as before Independence, was often viewed as the key to meaningful future changes. In October 1948, for instance, Zeb-un-Nissa Hamidullah in her *Dawn* column featured the importance of female education (albeit not necessarily a western one) and the expansion of educational institutions as a necessary first step for women to be able to operate as full-fledged citizens within the new state of Pakistan.[79] She likewise placed stress on women abandoning *purdah* as the correct 'patriotic' practice for women as citizens to follow, asking,

---

[77] Mumtaz and Shaheed, *Women of Pakistan*, p. 52.   [78] *Dawn*, 29 January 1952.
[79] 'Thru' a Woman's Eyes', *Dawn*, 11 October 1948.

Should we, the women of Pakistan, continue to veil our faces and take a back seat, or should we cast aside the burqa [veil] and its restrictions and prejudices and step forward to claim our rightful place as equal partners of our men folk in the service of our nation? The task is not as easy as it may appear. Often it is not within our power to decide whether we should go veiled or not. Men have a great deal to say on the matter and as we are both socially and economically dependent upon them, their word is law in the majority of Pakistani households. The very fact that the more intellectual among the males are the more zealous supporters of our anti-purdah drive, while the most relentless opponents are generally uneducated, narrow-minded and reactionaries should encourage us to proceed with our fight ... For the nation to rise to its full stature, men and women must march side by side ... We should use our freedom not for social or moral excesses but in social services and intellectual pursuits. Even when we shed the veil, we should remain true Muslims at heart.[80]

Citizenship in Pakistan during these transition years, as in India, thus often ended up being framed in terms of personal responsibility and commitment to nation-building. But when it came to women's involvement in formal political processes, the situation in Pakistan differed in that women's organizations there tended to support the continued reservation of seats for women at both central and provincial level. During its protracted process of constitution-making, the two female members of the Pakistan Constituent Assembly – Begum Jahan Ara Shahnawaz and Begum Shaista Ikramullah – repeatedly demanded that 10 per cent of seats be reserved for women in the country's first two elections at least. Drawing on the political experience that they had themselves acquired before Independence, they argued that until conservative elements in Pakistan society were ready to accept women as politicians and legislators, reserved seats would still be needed to ensure the presence of women in politics and policy-making.[81]

The provision of separate seats for women, however, remained a controversial topic. In October 1952, at an All-Pakistan Local Bodies conference session, presided over by Begum Salma Tasadduq Hussain, 'great controversy was raised on the proposal to reserve seats for women on local bodies. Supporters of the proposal underlined the importance of the role which women of Pakistan were to play in the development of the country while those who were opposed to the proposal doubted whether Islam permitted women to take part in such activities'. Supporters of the proposals also pointed out the contribution that women had made to securing the state of Pakistan, and asked how many men had volunteered to rescue the estimated 40,000 abducted Muslim women as yet unrecovered. Eventually, it was agreed that separate representation should be

[80] *Dawn*, 20 January 1948.   [81] Shahnawaz, *Father and Daughter*, p. 248.

allowed for women on local bodies as a matter of principle, with 25 per cent of the total number of seats on city corporations reserved for them. As regards other local bodies, it was decided that a tenth of the seats should be set aside, but in any constituency where women candidates were not available empty seats should be filled by men. At this point, those present who were not in favour of the proposal staged a walk out in protest.[82]

Issues connected with what citizenship in practice meant for Pakistani women continued to surface regularly through this period, often linked to occasions when female activities challenged prevailing understandings about their 'proper' or acceptable role. In November 1951, following the assassination of Liaquat Ali Khan, for instance, trouble broke out at his *chehlum* (mourning) ceremony held in Karachi's Aram Bagh public park, during which 'certain women', accused of cutting the loudspeaker wires, had 'created rowdyism', including an alleged insult to the late prime minister's mother. Begum Wilayat Butt, treasurer of the Khawateen (women's) Muslim League, censored these protestors for their 'un-Islamic ways', and claimed that they were being used by 'a certain faction' in the League to prop up its waning influence; she warned them 'to behave decently and not spoil the good name of Muslim women or Almighty God [would] sooner or later chastise them'.[83] Another League worker, Begum Muhammad Hussain Khan, then sought to put the record straight:

As the facts have been misreported, I would like to present the truth for the information of the public. All that happened was that instead of offering Fateha [prayers], for which the meeting was called, some ladies tried to move a resolution of no-confidence against the Karachi Muslim League. Most of the ladies objected to it, saying that the sanctity of the occasion did not permit raising of such a question. They insisted that Fateha should be offered at the meeting, to which the movers of the no-confidence meeting were not agreeable. ... The report that [Liaquat's] mother or for that matter anyone else was insulted is absolutely false and baseless.[84]

In response, the Working Committee of the Karachi Khawateen Muslim League issued a statement in which it expressed surprise at Begum Muhammad Hussain's explanation, claiming that 'elements who had occupied the dais long before the scheduled time had come with the set purpose of creating disturbance in the meeting', including efforts made to disrupt proceedings by disabling the microphone, raising slogans and

---

[82] *Dawn*, 28 October 1952.   [83] *Dawn*, 4 December 1951.
[84] *Dawn*, 8 December 1951.

even throwing dust on the dais where Liaquat's mother had been seated.[85] That the wider religio-political environment was creating challenges was reflected that same month in an attempt in the Punjab Legislative Assembly to introduce a so-called 'Purdah Bill'. According to the independent MLA, Maulana Abdus Sattar Khan Niazi, the people of Pakistan had fallen 'under the spell of the false and deceptive values of the Western culture', and so his bill was aimed at stopping 'the growing danger of women casting off their veil with all its consequential evils' and restoring 'woman to the place reserved for her by Islam'. Abdul Waheed Khan (Muslim League member of the Assembly), who opposed the bill, argued that 'the disease which the mover wanted to eradicate' would not be 'cured' by introduction of a penalty. Rather the way to solve the problem was education and 'training people on right path'; and the motion was duly rejected.[86]

Lack of consensus about what being a citizen of a Muslim state meant for women was reflected in other developments taking place in Karachi in 1951–2. As Pakistan's federal capital, the city housed both politicians and top bureaucrats, precisely those men whose wives, daughters and sisters proved themselves to be stalwart supporters of APWA. But APWA, while claiming to speak for Pakistani women as a whole, was first and foremost representative of a particular class of Pakistani womanhood (in this sense, like the AIWA in India), a handicap that contemporaries recognized and about which they occasionally complained. Frustration at the so-called 'Big Begums' who dominated APWA became increasingly apparent, sometimes expressed individually, on other occasions reflected in the establishment of rival organizations.[87] Indeed, according to Ayesha Jalal, those women who concerned themselves with extracting concessions from the Pakistani state in the years immediately following 1947 belonged mostly to the dominant classes, and so, for Jalal, it was precisely their privileged background that ensured that APWA's demands would be neither too radical nor overly embarrassing for the authorities.[88]

In April 1952, a new women's organization, Bint-i-Pakistan – in a move that openly challenged APWA's authority – held its first meeting not in Karachi but in Lahore, where its main sponsor, the veteran activist

[85] *Dawn*, 15 December 1951.   [86] *Dawn*, 23 December 1951.
[87] 'Women and Politics', 25 October 1955, 350/10-251955 US National Archives (hereafter USNA).
[88] Ayesha Jalal, 'The Convenience of Subservience: Women and the State in Pakistan', in *Women, Islam and the State*, ed. Deniz Kandiyoti (Basingstoke: Macmillan, 1991), pp. 77–114.

Fatimah Begum,[89] was elected president. The meeting was attended by over 400 women 'representing various walks of life'.[90] As Fatimah Begum explained, Bint-i-Pakistan's main purpose was to enable poor women to take an active part in the development of Pakistan. Referring obliquely to APWA, she argued that existing women's organizations, thanks to being restricted to 'the wives of the high officials and the rich', did not offer opportunities to middle-class and poor women to better their social or economic standards. Bint-i-Pakistan, in contrast, committed itself to opening schools where education would be free and stipends provided to 'deserving girls';[91] and at a later press conference held in Karachi, she reiterated that its aims were 'to safeguard the rights of women and work for uplift of the masses in various parts of Pakistan'. A membership drive followed in the federal capital, and by July, the organization claimed a membership of c. 11,000.[92] Soon afterwards, other dissenting voices also surfaced in the city. At a local meeting of the 'Muslim Countries Women's Organisation' held in Karachi in August the following year, demands were made for improved local female representation, with delegates 'completely dissatisfied with allocation of three seats for women in the Karachi Municipal Corporation', demanding instead that they should enjoy adequate representation on basis of their population, with at least twenty-five seats given to them.[93] Meanwhile, female 'shyness' was blamed as the main difficulty faced by enumerators appointed by the Corporation to register voters for next municipal elections; women, it appeared, did not 'tell their names and ages when ... approached by lady enumerators'.[94]

All the same, the way in which female assertiveness with respect to their rights as citizens generated anxieties can be gauged from the violence directed against women during the Independence Day celebrations in different cities of Pakistan, including Karachi, in August 1952.[95]

---

[89] Fatimah Begum (1890–1958) was appointed general secretary of the Islamic Association of Women established in 1908, and was later the founding principal of Jinnah Islamia College for girls in Lahore. She was an active Muslim Leaguer who campaigned actively on its behalf in the 1940s. For more discussion of her activities during this period, see Dushka Saiyid, *Muslim Women of the British Punjab: From Seclusion to Politics* (Basingstoke: Macmillan, 1998), chapter 6 'Political Activism'.

[90] The meeting on 30 April also elected Begum Sikandara Babar as secretary and Begum Salma Tassaduq Hussain and Begum Bashir Ahmed as vice presidents. *Dawn*, 3 May 1952.

[91] *Dawn*, 20 April 1952.   [92] *Dawn*, 8 July 1952; *Dawn*, 16 July 1952.

[93] *Dawn*, 5 August 1952.   [94] *Dawn*, 26 July 1952.

[95] Nazimuddin's 1952 Pakistan Day speech emphasized the dangers of internal disorder over external attack, reiterating that while he was 'a firm believer in the principle of freedom of speech and the freedom of the Press', he was also 'against the misuse of these freedoms'. See *Dawn*, 17 August 1952.

The Karachi festivities, held in the Aram Bagh, had become customary for all large-scale public events, and drew up to 20,000 participants who listened to Urdu poetry and songs, as well as to speeches that were viciously anti-central government, anti-Nazimuddin (the then prime minister) and anti-Ahmadi. (This was the time of the anti-Ahmadi campaigns of the early 1950s.) The gathering was marred, however, by physical attacks on women by so-called *goondas* (thugs) and, in the context of wider debates over the place of religion in Pakistan's future constitutional arrangements, this violence focussed attention on women's disputed status as citizens within the new state.

On the evening of 14 August, women celebrating the national festivities in the city (as was also the case in Lahore and Rawalpindi) 'were manhandled in the most disgraceful manner. Burqas were removed forcibly ... but the police who were there did nothing' until around three hours had elapsed.[96] APWA's Working Committee swiftly passed a resolution strongly condemning the hooliganism involved, and religious groups were blamed for instigating the abuse.[97] A Goonda Act was then implemented in the province.[98] But Zeb-un-Nissa Hamidullah's column captured the wider disappointment and frustration caused by this incident, framing the abuse of women as a national disgrace:

Hundreds of my sex felt as I did, hundreds of us felt shamed and shaken to the very cores of our being by the shameless acts of goondaism [*sic*] directed against us on the night of our Independence Day. It seemed as though a dirty, hairy hand had come from out of the crowd and thrown a fistful of gutter filth upon our flag, besmirching its beauty and heaping humiliation upon us. Yet, this is the most poignant and ironic fact of all, that it should be on Pakistan Day itself that Pakistani men should so shame their women; and that the moment chosen should have been one when our patriotic pride was at its height.

Hamidullah was scathing in her criticism of what she regarded as barbaric deeds, and the particular men who had perpetrated them. But, as she went on, with growing public and private condemnation of the incident in the weeks that followed, 'we women found our hurt and humiliation dissolve – dissolve and completely melt away with the knowledge that the goondas who were responsible for these foul acts were not even entitled to be called Pakistanis. For they are the scum that is washed

---

[96] *Dawn*, 22 August 1952.   [97] 'Shameful', *Dawn*, 28 August 1952.
[98] 'Goonda Act promulgated in Sind (21 Oct)', *Dawn*, 22 October 1952. The act came into force with immediate effect, and empowered the authorities to detain people considered to be bad characters. By October, nearly 2,000 so-called goondas had been identified in the Hyderabad and Sukkur districts of Sindh.

up from the sea; flotsam from the wreck of undivided India washed upon our shore'.[99]

By no means did all *Dawn*'s readers agree with Hamidullah. One dissenting correspondent, Mujahid Saghir Ahmed, writing from Karachi, in effect blamed women themselves together with the negative effect of recent efforts to ban prostitution in the city. Ahmed, having held 'immoral women' responsible for the violence, then concluded by calling for education to be remodelled: 'We should see that our younger generation instead of roaming in streets [*sic*] gets proper education, healthy environments and good society so that they prove themselves in their coming years as respectable citizens of a free and progressive country, Pakistan'.[100] The same issue of the newspaper contained a lengthy report from Hyderabad (Sindh) on the likely impact of the Goonda Act on the province, detailing 'goonda' involvement in brothels and other antisocial activities and bemoaning the fact that 'girls passing on foot, in cars or other vehicles are stopped, harassed, insulted and often molested'.[101]

By the early 1950s, as discussions over Pakistan's future constitutional arrangements gathered pace, including the question of restructuring the political balance between the eastern and western wings of the country, the paucity of female involvement within its political decision-making process had become untenable for many female activists. A letter to *Dawn* from Begum Soghra Raza reflected the growing impatience that existed for improved female representation at the highest level, and emphasized that they had earned their reward through their support for the new state:

Muslim women did not in any way lag behind men in playing their part in the great Muslim nationalist movement which culminated in the establishment of Pakistan. Again during the last four years of our independent national existence, women have worked with the utmost zeal and energy to create general awakening and to promote the social, cultural and economic wellbeing of the people. Pakistan being a new state faced a host of problems concerning the uplift of its female population, it is imperative that women should have a more effective voice in the country's legislature. It is self-evident that points of view, needs and grievances can best be represented in the legislature by ladies who have worked among the generality of women and have gained experience of their problems.

Raza called on the Central Parliamentary Board of the Pakistan Muslim League to select at least one suitable 'lady candidate' for what were at the time six vacant Constituent Assembly seats.[102] But her pleas fell on deaf

---

[99] *Dawn*, 30 August 1952.   [100] *Dawn*, 3 September 1952.   [101] Ibid.
[102] *Dawn*, 9 October 1951.

ears, and by the time that the Assembly was dismissed in October 1954 there had been no increase in its female membership.[103]

One response to this apparent stalemate was APWA's growing emphasis on the need to cultivate what it termed 'responsible citizenship' among the nation's womenfolk. At its annual conference held in Sukkur in February 1954, members urged the Pakistani authorities to bring in experts from abroad to train a cadre of women in leadership to work in the field of not just social but political rights as well. Indeed, it could be argued that the Sukkur meeting marked the beginning of efforts to expand APWA's work from its emergency beginnings to the more enduring task of building up 'an active and intelligent public opinion on the side of a better life and a better nation'.[104] The Aga Khan, while on a visit to his many followers in Karachi the same month, added his voice to calls for women to play a more prominent role in Pakistani life. In a speech read out by his wife to a reception held in his honour by APWA, he called on women to ensure religious freedom by participating in communal Friday prayers. Mosques, in his view, needed to open their doors to women. After all a country was like a human body – men and women represented its lungs and both of them were needed to function properly.[105]

The mid-1950s saw no slackening in terms of public debate centred on the rights of women in Pakistan. Rather, women's legal rights in relation to marriage became the vehicle for wider discussions. One particular area of disquiet that surfaced was the question of polygamous marriages, and female activists again presented their arguments primarily in terms of what was best for the nation. In February 1954, in an open letter to Prime Minister Mohammad Ali Bogra, leading APWA organizer Begum Anwar Ghulam Ahmed spelt out in no uncertain terms what she regarded as the long-overdue need for reforming the country's marriage laws. Despite more women entering various professions, marriage continued to be their generally accepted 'career choice', and so, according to her, the

---

[103] Its dissolution on 24 October 1954 was closely bound up with fears among West Pakistani interest groups – politicians, bureaucrats and military alike – that, under Bogra's premiership, the constitutional formula that was taking shape was going too far in favour of East Pakistan. The proposed unification of West Pakistan into one unit, which was intended to create an artificial parity between it and the more populated eastern half of the country, had been rejected by the Muslim League's assembly party. There was, however, little chance of it being enacted under the existing political arrangements, hence the dissolving of the Constituent Assembly. See Ayesha Jalal, *The State of Martial Rule: The Origins of Pakistan's Political Economy of Defence* (Cambridge: Cambridge University Press, 1990), pp. 185–93.
[104] *Dawn*, 28 February 1954.   [105] *Dawn*, 7 February 1954.

gravest danger to the well-being of the Pakistani home, and by extension the nation, was the 'unintelligent operation' of existing marriage laws:

The woes of a large number of women – and the indignities they suffer (physical, mental and financial) at the hands of wayward husbands are appalling. Divorce and polygamy hang over the heads of Muslim women as an ever-present and disruptive menace. The erstwhile mistress of a home can, without reasonable cause, be turned into a destitute through an irresponsible divorce or reduced to a chattel in her own home by the husband contracting a second marriage.

Since, in Begum Ghulam Ahmed's view, the security of the home had to be preserved for the nation to develop and prosper, she urged the government to set up a commission, comprising eminent jurists as well as women's representatives, to produce recommendations on the reform of Muslim personal laws.[106] In a late 1954 column, Zeb-un-Nissa Hamidullah deliberately challenged women to take responsibility for the problem, particularly those second wives who considered themselves as progressive, educated and enlightened, and who consequently, in her view, were even more remiss than their polygamous husbands. As she reminded her readers, citizenship was not only about harnessing rights, it was about exercising responsibility too.[107] Such discussions set the scene for the public furore that was sparked a few months later by the polygamous marriage of Pakistan's prime minister, Bogra, which exposed the extent of dissent and disagreement over women's rights as equal citizens, not just between female activists and the state, but also between women and men, and among women themselves.[108] They also helped initiate the process that eventually resulted in the (radical for its time) reform of Muslim personal law under Ayub Khan in the shape of the 1961 Muslim Family Law Ordinances.[109]

Following the announcement of the wedding of Bogra to his Lebanese-born former social secretary Aliya Saddy in April 1955,[110] a large meeting was held in Karachi, attended by representatives from major women's organizations as well as a number of prominent social workers.

---

[106] *Dawn*, 18 February 1954.   [107] *Dawn*, 18 December 1954.

[108] The following account draws on Sarah Ansari, 'Polygamy, *Purdah* and Political Representation: Engendering Citizenship in 1950s Pakistan', *Modern Asian Studies* 43, 6 (2009), pp. 1421–61.

[109] Freeland Abbot, 'Pakistan's New Marriage Law: A Reflection of Qur'anic Interpretation', *Asian Survey* 1, 11 (January 1962), pp. 26–27; Sylvia A. Chipp, 'The Role of Women Elites in a Modernizing Country: The All-Pakistan Women's Association' (unpublished PhD dissertation, Syracuse University, 1970), pp. 170–4; Sylvia Chipp-Kraushaar, 'The All-Pakistan Women's Association and the 1961 Muslim Family Laws Ordinance' in *The Extended Family: Women and Political Participation in India and Pakistan*, ed. Gail Minault (Columbia: South Asia Books, 1981), pp. 263–85.

[110] Pakistan Fortnightly Summary, 1–14 April 1955, DO35/5285 UKNA.

President of APWA's Karachi branch, Begum Chaudhry Mohammad Ali,[111] took the lead, urging that women form a new body specifically charged with seeking to safeguard their legal rights. The meeting then called for a boycott of second wives, as well as the parents of such women and their relatives, and insisted that the prime minister treat both his wives with complete equality, including their participation in social functions, as Islamic justice dictated. The meeting presented its criticism in patriotic terms, insisting that the official status of 'first lady' should remain with Bogra's first wife Begum Hamida alone, on the grounds that 'she is a Pakistani [and] Pakistani women [would never] tolerate, leave alone recognize, a non-Pakistani as their "first" lady'.[112] Another gathering was then held under the joint auspices of various women's organizations, including the Karachi Khawateen Muslim League, the Anjuman-i Taraqqi-i Urdu, the Khawateen-i-Pakistan and the Khawateen-i-Anjuman-i-Tablighul Islam, at which a unanimous resolution was passed expressing resentment at the second marriages of some of the country's politicians, and demanding that the authorities pass a law to force polygamous husbands to accord equal treatment to all their wives.

To many of those who participated in these debates of the mid-1950s, it was very important that women, as equal citizens, should enjoy and benefit from the same legal rights as Pakistani men. Just as custom and social conservatism were believed to be preventing women from playing a full part in the political life of the nation, so these same factors were blamed for undermining their position in other ways. APWA itself addressed the question of the status of women, including the specific problems posed by polygamy, at a conference that it held in Karachi in February 1955. Although attendees expressed satisfaction that women in Pakistan possessed equal rights to men in the political field (at least as far as the right to vote was concerned), the meeting advised women to exercise their voting rights in such a way that 'really deserving' people were elected. It also called on the authorities to ensure that marital disputes in courts were resolved more quickly. With a female literacy rate of only 4 per cent, women were bound to remain ignorant of their rights. Hence, speakers demanded further educational provision for girls, including free schooling up to matriculation, irrespective of family income.[113]

---

[111] Begum Chaudhry Mohammad Ali was the wife of the then Central Minister of Finance, Chaudhry Mohammad Ali, who would later become prime minister himself following Bogra's dismissal (August 1955).

[112] *Dawn*, 16 April 1955.   [113] *Dawn*, 22 February 1955.

In April 1955, however, a separate 'League for the Rights of Women' was formed to spearhead protest against Bogra's marriage. Begum Chaudhry Mohammad Ali was chosen as its president. Subcommittees followed, with Begum Anwar Ghulam Ahmed appointed the chair of its committee on women and family laws.[114] APWA itself was divided over the issue. Instructed by Raana Liaquat Ali Khan that APWA should disassociate itself as an organization from the controversy, supporters of the agitation felt the need to clarify whether or not they were conducting the kind of personalized attacks for which they were now being criticized. According to one of the less elite campaigners, Arshia Alwi,

We the women of Karachi have formed a board which has decided to work independently. Our aim is to demand the Islamic rights of women in Pakistan (APWA as an association has not been working for our rights). ... Thousands of women have been ruined on account of second marriages, and women are suffering from misery and pain. ... The Nation expects all good actions from a 'Leader'. The example of a 'Leader's' life furnishes the Nation a model which the Nation should follow.[115]

Following the spread of the protest from Karachi to other Pakistani cities,[116] a five-member deputation representing the League for the Rights of Women met the prime minister on 10 May. As a result of their ninety-minute interview, Bogra issued a public assurance a few days later that he would continue to act fairly towards his first wife, who would be completely free to operate according to her own best interests at all times. He also promised that during his next 'First-of-the-Month' Radio Pakistan broadcast to the nation he would announce the establishment of a high-powered commission to consider the need for reforming the country's marriage and family laws and report back within six months of being constituted. On the grounds that their only objective had been to fight for the 'Islamic rights' of Pakistani women, the League's executive accepted the prime minister's offer.[117]

---

[114] Wife of the Secretary of the Interior and prominent APWA member, Begum Ghulam Ahmed, represented Pakistan at the United Nations in 1954 on questions affecting the status of women, see Pakistan Fortnightly Summary, 24 November–8 December 1954, DO35/5284 UKNA. By March 1955, she had been elected vice chair of the UN Status of Women Commission, see *Dawn*, 16 March 1955.

[115] *Dawn*, 20 May 1955.

[116] The Hyderabad (Sindh) branch of APWA, for instance, added its voice to the clamour on 26 April, urging women to launch a strong campaign to fight polygamy. *Dawn*, 27 April 1955.

[117] *Dawn*, 15 May 1955. According to Begum Liaqat Ali Khan, Bogra had apparently been prepared to divorce his first wife, but because this was not what his wife wanted – she wished to retain her security and status as a wife – so her supporters were forced to

When Pakistan's second Constituent Assembly was reconstituted later that same month, however, it contained no female members, and complaints not surprisingly ensued. The Muslim League's Khawateen Sub-Committee lost little time in signalling its obvious disappointment by strongly condemning 'the women MLAs of the Punjab who in spite of assuring the Muslim League Parliamentary Board did not vote for the official woman candidate'. Its members insisted on 'the principle of women voting for women within the party mandate, specifically when they are elected solely on women's votes'.[118] Begum Akhtar Hussain from Karachi likewise highlighted the problem, complaining that 'when the population is not fully represented in the true sense, the popularity of the Constituent Assembly must become doubtful. Women must have a voice in the law-making of their country, especially when the question of their rights is involved. If at the very outset they are ignored, how can they hope to get justice in matters concerning them?'[119]

A range of women's organizations added their voices to this criticism of Pakistani authorities. The Executive Committee of the League for the Rights of Women expressed its 'deep regret' at the absence of female representatives at the highest level; Begum Abdul Hafiz, General Secretary of the Women's Refugee Rehabilitation Committee, appealed to the new members of the Constituent Assembly to elect two female members (one representing East Pakistan, one representing West Pakistan); Begum Najma Jafari, convenor of the Anjuman-i Tahafuuz Huqooq-i Niswan, deplored in even stronger terms women's non-representation, and urged women of the country to come forward to fight for their democratic rights and the Professional and Business Women's Club likewise called for special provisions to ensure that women took their rightful place in the Assembly. A gathering of the representatives of women's organizations that was brought together in Karachi by Begum Haroon, APWA's acting president, cited Jinnah – 'let it not be said that women have lagged behind and failed to do their duty' – in support of its demand that the government rectify its error.[120]

The complete absence of women in Pakistan's second Constituent Assembly, together with developments in relation to the actual drafting of its forthcoming constitution, stimulated additional demands to male politicians to address female needs. A meeting of the 'Women's Rights Committee' held in Lahore in August 1955 called for 15 per cent representation for women in provincial assemblies and 10 per cent in

accept this compromise, see Mehr Nigar Masroor, *Ra'ana Liaquat Ali Khan: A Biography* (Karachi: All-Pakistan Women's Association, c. 1980), p. 83.
[118] *Dawn*, 26 June 1955.   [119] *Dawn*, 3 July 1955.   [120] *Dawn*, 8 July 1955.

the national Parliament. Its ten-point memorandum to Constituent Assembly members emphasized the importance of Pakistani women not suffering from any inequality in the future; as well as their right to vote being confirmed, they needed to participate in ways that would allow them an equal footing with men.[121] Women's groups thus lobbied hard to influence the content of the proposed constitution. As one activist later explained, their protest was just as much about protecting the rights that women already possessed as obtaining new ones: in Begum Jalil Asghar's words, 'rights [had been] won by [women] under the guidance of Quaid-i Azam [Jinnah] and Quaid-i Millat [Liaquat], and women [who constituted 47% of the country's population] under no circumstances [were going to] surrender them'.[122]

In late October 1955, a twelve-member delegation representing the 'United Front of Women for Freedom and Protection of the People's Rights', led by the veteran activist (and former president of the Muslim League's Women's Committee) Fatimah Begum, then submitted a six-part memorandum, or 'Manifesto and Charter of Women's Rights', to the central minister of law for inclusion in the country's future constitution. It demanded that all citizens without any discrimination of sex should be eligible for public posts and offices on the basis of merit and qualifications. It also called for more seats for women in the legislative assemblies; the ineligibility of the wives of high government officials for elections to the Legislative Assemblies or Parliament; and the establishment of separate divorce and juvenile courts in the country.[123] 'Big Begums' came in for considerable criticism. In what was described as a 'smouldering rebellion' against those women who professed to be leaders of the women's movements, a delegation of dissidents complained to the central Government's Law Minister, I. I. Chundrigar that while the 'Big Begums' always managed 'to have a photographer present when they make such gestures as distributing flood relief or organizing girls in uplift programmes', their efforts were in reality 'limited to a very few occasions, while effectively followed up by considerable newspaper publicity'.[124]

On 1 January 1956, the *Pakistan Times* asked whether or not the New Year would prove to be a happier one for women. Responding to its own question, the newspaper claimed that the need for an independent party for women was greater than it had ever been. Rather than operating as the appendage of existing parties, such as the Muslim League or the

---

[121] *Dawn*, 14 August 1955.   [122] *Pakistan Times*, 22 April 1956.
[123] *Dawn*, 25 October 1955.
[124] 'Women and Politics', 25 October 1955, 350.00/10-2555 USNA.

Awami League, women urgently required a separate political organization of their own, one that would be prepared to struggle for the full
realization of their basic rights. But while the *Pakistan Times* urged a
separate political voice for women, it categorically rejected separate
electorates: under no circumstances would these ever be acceptable to
the women of Pakistan since their impact, it warned, would only be to
marginalize them further in political terms.[125] By 9 January 1956, the
second Constituent Assembly, minus any direct female involvement, had
finished drafting Pakistan's constitutional document. Once its contents
became known, women activists were quick to decry them. Begum
Shahnawaz, among others, was 'surprised and pained that certain basic
rights for women [had] either been left out or nullified by [its] provisos'.
Ending discrimination on the grounds of sex had found no place in the
Constitution, nor had equal pay for equal work been mentioned. Instead,
she called on 'all the prominent women workers and women's organizations to protest strongly against these omissions'.[126]

During the last week of January, a large number of women representing a variety of different women's groups gathered, again in Lahore (by
now thanks to the introduction of One Unit, the capital of the recently
amalgamated single province of West Pakistan) rather than in the federal
capital Karachi, to discuss their constitutional rights.[127] The resolutions
that they passed exposed just how far these activists were conscious of
the draft Constitution's limitations from the point of view of how it
promoted (or failed to promote) women's rights. They also appealed
explicitly to the members of the Constituent Assembly whose job (or
responsibility), they pointed out, was to represent both sexes equally, and
so to ensure that Pakistani women secured basic rights of equality with
men. In their view, Article 5, which referred to all citizens being equal
before the law, was not specific enough and should have incorporated
direct acknowledgement of sexual discrimination. Article 43, which dealt
with the composition of the future National Assembly, similarly came
under fire. According to the wording of this section, 'for a period of ten
years from Constitution Day, ten seats in addition to those specified in
clause 1 – five from West Pakistan and five from East Pakistan – shall be
provided in the National Assembly for women who shall be elected from
women's territorial constituencies delimited for this purpose'. But in the

[125] *Pakistan Times*, 1 January 1956.   [126] *Pakistan Times*, 13 January 1956.
[127] The organizations that attended this Lahore meeting included Muslim League's
Women's Committee, APWA, Lahore Ladies Federation for Women's Rights,
Anjuman Muhajir Khawateen, Pakistan Christian League, Awami League Women's
Committee, Professional Women's Club and women members of the Lahore members
of the West Pakistan Assembly. See *Pakistan Times*, 26 January 1956.

eyes of its female critics, it lacked clarity as to whether women would vote for the 300 seats not earmarked specifically for them, or if and for how long their representation would be confined to just those ten female seats alone. Until and unless this point was clarified, these provisions, they feared, would remain vague and risked being subsequently interpreted either way.

On 2 March 1956, Pakistan's first Constitution was given its assent by the governor general, and three weeks later, on 23 March (Republic Day), it came into force. The Constituent Assembly simultaneously reorganized itself into the country's legislative body, or National Assembly, thus averting any immediate need for general elections in which women alongside men could have cast their vote. Female activists associated with the Pakistan Federation of Women's Rights expressed their disappointment openly. Women may have had their full voting rights confirmed, but they had been allocated the reserved seats that at least some activists had rejected; as Federation spokeswomen reminded politicians and the public, women did not require special privileges, only their fundamental rights as 'workers, housewives and citizens'. But their pleas, it seemed, had not been heeded: 'Our leaders have called upon us many times during the past eight years to play our full part in the life of our nation. We in turn now call upon our leaders to guarantee our rights'.[128]

Pakistani citizenship during this same period, as reactions to the 1956 Constitution highlighted, came to be differentiated along gender lines. As well as the provision that barred a woman (like a non-Muslim) from becoming head of state, citizenship legislation formulated in the early 1950s prohibited Muslim mothers who were married to foreigners or non-Muslim men from passing on their Pakistani citizenship to their children. This was in stark contrast to the way in which the children of Muslim men married to non-Muslim women were permitted to acquire Pakistani nationality. In effect, this legislation stipulated that 'legitimate' Pakistani nationals needed to be born to a father with an 'authentic' Muslim identity. Since children gained citizenship with all its attendant rights through their fathers, and not courtesy of their mothers, the 1951 and 1952 acts reinforced an explicit connection between fathers and national citizenship.[129]

---

[128] *Pakistan Times*, 22 April 1956.
[129] 'Pakistan Citizenship Act 1951', Government of Pakistan Press Information Department, Handout E. No. 1384, 14 April 1951, FO372/7105 UKNA; 24 April 1951, FO327/7089 UKNA; UK High Commissioner, Karachi, to Commonwealth Relations Office, 14 April 1952, DO35/3560 UKNA.

By mid-1956, it had become clear that women's organizations such as the Federation were not going to secure the kind of outcome for which they had been lobbying, either in relation to female representation in the country's legislative assemblies or as far as bold changes in the content of Muslim personal law were concerned. When the Rashid Commission, set up, as promised by Bogra, to investigate family law reform produced its report in June 1956, it did recommend that second wives were only permissible with official consent, and it advised the establishment of special matrimonial courts, proposing equal rights in divorce matters for men and women alike. But the Commission – which included two women (Begums Shahnawaz and Anwar Ghulam Ahmed) among its members – was unable to go as far as recommending the complete prohibition of polygamy that female activists had urged. Instead, the report represented, at least to those who gave it a warm reception, 'a sensible first step towards a society where monogamy would be the general rule'. In this way, Pakistan would be allowed to 'justify its name by reverting to the original dynamic, liberal and creative spirit of Islam'.[130]

Pakistani women by the middle of 1956 had acquired some acknowledgement of the need to strengthen their legal rights with respect to the state's marriage laws, but, in the view of contemporaries, Pakistani women remained second-class citizens as far as the political role that they were empowered to play in the life of the state. For these activists, nothing symbolized this continuing subordinate status more than the ten reserved seats that had been gifted to women by the 1956 Constitution, which, they believed, had conspicuously failed to address other equally pressing issues that disadvantaged female lives on a daily basis. On the other hand, what the debates of the mid-1950s underlined was that as long as Pakistani women, and their male supporters, presented their citizenship demands as being in the nation's interests – for the greater, national, good – there was space to call for more individual freedoms as Pakistani citizens, and blur the boundaries between their private and public lives.

Conclusion

In October 1958, the army seized power in Pakistan, and set about 'cleaning up the mess' that it blamed squarely on the civilian politicians whom it had displaced. But as others before it had done, the military sought to legitimize political intervention by harnessing the support of women for its programme of reform. In June 1959, when an austerity

---

[130] *Pakistan Times*, 25 June 1956.

drive was in full force, Begum Shaikh (wife of the Minister of the Interior General K. M. Shaikh) – who had anticipated the austerity campaign by launching her 'wear cotton' crusade some months earlier – set about increasing the membership of the Women's Volunteer Group (WVG) that she had recently established. Together with instructions 'prescribing simplified habits of dress and eating' announced by the director of the Bureau of National Reconstruction, Brigadier R. F. Khan, activities of the 'busy Begums' bolstered regime efforts to 'create a psychological atmosphere which [would] promote popular participation in nation-building activities'. At a press conference, Begum Shaikh set out the WVG's fundamental principles as follows:

(1) To encourage women to participate in the economic reconstruction of Pakistan; (2) To patronize and promote cottage industries and Pakistan-made products; (3) To observe simplicity in style of living – dress, diet, and entertainment; (4) To live frugally 'within our means'; (5) To save and invest; (6) To get rid of false standards and false values 'from our homes and our society'; and (7) To refuse to purchase anything smuggled or at the black market price.

The WVG also committed itself to campaigning against the lavish dowries that were 'so well established', particularly among middle- and lower-middle-class families.

The ladies of the WVG have also been working on their husbands, to judge from press reports. According to these reports, their husbands have been purchasing 'khaddar' [homespun] clothes in order to support the austerity drive launched by their good wives ... In a peculiar blend of Saville Row and the village spinning wheel, Begum Tazeem Faridi, another WVG stalwart and wife of A.R. Faridi of Burmah Shell, proudly announced to the press that her husband had ordered a khaddar dinner jacket.

The chances of the WVG campaign being successful, however, looked pretty low as far as contemporaries were concerned. According to a story doing the rounds in Karachi not long after the military take over, 'Begum Shaikh, having advised a group of college girls about the "wear cotton" campaign, asked for questions. One brave young lady stood up and reportedly asked, 'Tell me Begum Shaikh, were you wearing cotton when you trapped the General"?' Such attitudes, observers felt, were unlikely to be helpful, even if 'these groping efforts towards creating a public conscious and a sense of national duty' were a commendable 'new feature of life in Pakistan'.[131]

---

[131] Press Information Handout, 'Specific Measures to Promote Simple Living – An Appeal to All Patriots – Officials to Set Example', 11 July 1959, in US Embassy Karachi, Despatch 57, 16 July 1959, 890d.414/7-1659 USNA.

However, as this anecdote from 1959 highlights, regimes in power – whether in Pakistan or India, and civilian or military – deployed and called upon women, their organizations and their representatives, to rally behind campaigns framed as being in the national good. As citizens women were expected to contribute patriotically to the common cause. But this episode also underlines that Pakistani and Indian women – like the feisty college student who was prepared to pose an awkward personal question to one of the 'Big Begums' – could and frequently did also demonstrate an independence of spirit that challenged their status as differentiated 'second-class' citizens.

Women's movements in both India and Pakistan throughout these years faced common problems in demonstrating their representative status. In both cases, the largest groups engaged in debating issues of constitutional rights were mostly composed of highly educated, English-speaking women from elite backgrounds. But, again in both cases, these movements transformed the very bases of debate about substantive citizenship rights, since their claims and arguments cut across traditional citizenship paradigms. Evoking ideas of universal rights, they set out the particular struggles of women to acquire rights, and, in this sense, their activism encapsulated the ways in which citizenship during the early postcolonial period could be seen as a process of struggle, rather than a fixed or given category. Perhaps most importantly, these women and their movements were able to articulate a somewhat different vision of the Indian/Pakistani public in which the relationship between private and public life was based in patriarchal inheritance from the colonial period.

6 'Hidden Citizens' in 1940s and 1950s India and Pakistan

> If 80 persons unanimously call day as night,
> It is the duty of 20 to consider it as a truth.
> This is a democratic age, old man – a democratic age,
> We are all helpless.[1]

As our previous chapters have indicated, the achievement of Independence across South Asia in August 1947 brought with it the excitement of democracy in the shape of introduction of the universal adult suffrage, which now extended to all citizens irrespective of their class, gender or religious identity, at least on paper. But while Indians acquired an elaborate framework for their democracy in their 1950 Constitution, it took until the mid-1955s, eight years after Indians had won their political freedom, before specific citizenship legislation there was finalized and it was clear who qualified as a citizen and who did not. Pakistanis, in the meantime, framed their citizenship rules first in 1951 and then again in 1952 – that is, well before the country's first constitution came into existence albeit fleetingly in 1956 – but these were primarily concerned with regularizing the position of people migrating from India than addressing broader issues of civic inclusivity and belonging. What citizenship meant in places such as UP and Sindh, as elsewhere in India and Pakistan, remained work in progress, with certain groups more included than others when it came to how their rights as citizens were formulated in practice.

Moreover, notions of citizenship as they unfolded in both states presupposed certain exclusions. The latter – what we term here as 'hidden citizens' – were generated and shaped by common processes on both sides of the border, including the material predicaments of refugees and non-migrating minorities, which helped define inclusion and exclusion from full citizenship rights from an everyday perspective. This chapter,

---

[1] Extracts from English translation of an Urdu poem entitled 'Democracy' by Majeed Lahori, *Jang*, 19 May 1957, in 'Death of Pakistan Political Satirist', 12 July 1957, Despatch 36, 890D41/7-1257 United States National Archives (hereafter USNA).

thus, explores issues connected with citizenship and belonging during the late 1940s and 1950s, and in particular focusses on the differentiated realities involved for marginalized groups – religious minorities and economically marginalized groups, such as Dalits, tribal communities and *haris* (share-cropper peasants) – who were excluded, in a range of ways, from the 'mainstream' benefits of what being a citizen came to mean in both UP and Sindh during the early post-Independence years.

Religious Minorities in Sindh and UP

In Chapter 2, we touched on the predicament of Muslim communities in UP whose properties were declared forfeit to the state as 'evacuee property', whether or not they had actually migrated. If they were deemed to be intending to leave, then, as Vazira Zamindar has explained, their property could be reallocated to incoming refugees in compensation for what the latter had left behind in Pakistan.[2] Such experiences were mirrored to a large extent by those of non-Muslims in Sindh, who, in a similar fashion, found themselves losing out materially thanks to assumptions about where their loyalties – both present and future – lay in the transformed political realities after Partition. The experiences of minorities in both localities in the aftermath of Partition thus highlights how far citizenship was drawn into the debates of these years.

In relation to Pakistan, most studies of its remaining non-Muslim minorities have concentrated on developments in Bengal, and so have tended to gloss over the experiences of those still living in the western half of the country. This historiographical 'imbalance' stems to a great extent from the fact that it was East Bengal, later renamed East Pakistan, which retained the largest non-Muslim minority after Independence. In contrast, Pakistani Punjab – where the bulk of the cross-border migration and violence took place in the immediate run-up to and in the aftermath of Partition – lost most of its non-Muslims, with the exception of relatively small numbers of Christians[3] and the even smaller community of

---

[2] For poignant instances of this process at work, see Vazira Zamindar, *The Long Partition and the Making of Modern South Asia: Refugees, Boundaries, Histories* (New York, NY: Columbia University Press, 2007), chapter 4, 'The Economies of Displacement'.

[3] According to Symonds, 'There [were] still four hundred thousand [Christians] in the West Punjab' where some of them were reported to have suffered considerable hardship in West Punjab, at the hands of 'incoming Muslim refugees [who] complained that Christians had looted them in East Punjab' and took out their frustrations on them. However, the skilful leadership by S. P. Singha, former Speaker of the Punjab Assembly, improved their position, and they came to be included in a special reservation of five per cent of the positions in the Services for minorities in that province. They had no representation in the Constituent Assembly, however, and so, in his view, they not unreasonably asked for separate electorates to continue until 'the Muslim League as the

Parsis who did not leave. Importantly, however, the prevailing focus on the Punjab, from a Partition studies perspective, has obscured the fact that a larger proportion of non-Muslims stayed on in Sindh, as corroborated by the 1951 census, which showed that the province contained the lion's share of Hindus still living in West Pakistan. One district – Tharparkar, located in the southeast of Sindh on the border with India – even possessed a local majority of non-Muslims, mostly low-caste agriculturalists, who to this day eke out a fragile living from what are dry desert-like farming conditions. But it was in Sindh's urban centres, where under colonial rule propertied Hindus had tended to live and work as merchants, run their farming interests as absentee landowners or service the professions and the bureaucracy, that their position as a minority community emerged as a particularly sensitive issue. Cities and towns such as Karachi, Hyderabad, Sukkur, Shikarpur and Larkana – like their counterparts in UP – witnessed events that highlighted the new uncertainties, and the suspicions that were directed towards non-Muslims more generally. The right to hold, or hold on to, material assets thus became a key indicator of 'belonging' in this fraught and uncertain context.

Working out who had the right to what property as Indian and Pakistani citizens, and how to compensate for any property losses incurred thanks to Partition, took up a great deal of legislative and bureaucratic time in both countries in the late 1940s and throughout the 1950s. As early as September 1947, legislation in the form of the East and West Punjab Evacuee Property (Preservation) Ordinances, which was soon extended to Delhi, empowered custodians of refugee property to manage vacated premises until the final whereabouts of their owners had been decided.[4] The question of what to do with this property moved quickly from being a private to a public headache as disputes between the Indian and Pakistani authorities increasingly centred on the relative value of the evacuee property involved. In an attempt to reconcile competing interests, the Karachi Agreement of January 1949 signed by the two governments addressed the need for each state to reimburse the other for the immovable property left behind by departing refugees. But which areas were covered by this formula, whether or not it included the voluntary sale and exchange of property and when the cut-off point for when migration was deemed to have occurred remained matters of contention for bureaucrats and ordinary Indians and Pakistanis alike for decades.

national political body [was] substituted by one or more political organisations open to all communities'. See Richard Symonds, *The Making of Pakistan* (London: Faber & Faber, 1950), p. 99.

[4] Zamindar, *Long Partition*, p. 123.

As Pakistan's minister for refugees at that time described later, the situation was a hugely complex one, and would complicate relations between the two countries well into the 1950s and beyond:

India does not seem to have given expression to her real reasons for opposing a 'limiting' date [... because] it may be that India is thinking not of Hindu/Sikh evacuees but of Muslims still in the 'agreed areas' in India whose migration to Pakistan they wish to encourage ... for the imposition of a limiting date for migration would automatically limit the Muslim evacuee property in those areas to whatever has already been abandoned.[5]

Against this backdrop, the particular dilemmas facing Sindh's non-Muslim minorities are captured in reports sent through to Delhi by the first Indian High Commissioner stationed in Karachi, Sri Prakasa.[6] The regularity of his reports, particularly in the months immediately following Independence, was hampered by a lack of sufficient staff but also by the impact of communal flare-ups such as the one that took place in late January 1948 when recently arrived refugees from India attacked a party of Sikhs heading for ships to take them to Bombay, and then turned on local Hindus, resulting in around 200 deaths.[7] Although many observers were taken by surprise by the ferocity of this apparently unexpected attack, there had been a similar outbreak of trouble in nearby Hyderabad in mid-December which had killed some thirty people. In that city, too, violence had been linked to incoming refugees whose tales of their own sufferings back in India had triggered revenge attacks.[8] By the end of January, a further 40,000 Sindhi Hindus had left the province,[9] prompting Prakasa to explain to Delhi that

Circumstances here [Karachi] at the present moment are very very difficult and a good deal of my time, energy and attention is taken up by the problems concerning evacuation. I do not know where and when all this is going to end. You can imagine in what state of mind and body I must be at the present moment; and so if you do not receive as many reports as you desire you will surely understand and appreciate the reasons.[10]

---

[5] Proceedings of the Constituent Assembly of Pakistan, 6 April 1951, cited in ibid., p. 126.

[6] Sri Prakasa (1890–1971) was a long-standing Congress politician from UP, who served as India's first High Commissioner to Pakistan, based in Karachi from 1947 to 1949; he was then governor of Assam from 1949 to 1950, governor of Madras from 1952 to 1956 and governor of Bombay from 1956 to 1962.

[7] Despatch 18, 12 January 1948, 845.F.00/1-1248 USNA.

[8] Despatch 278, 29 December 1947, 845F.00/12-2947 USNA.

[9] UKHC, Karachi, Opdom 5, 15–21 January 1948, IOR L/WS/1/1599 British Library (hereafter BL).

[10] Commissioner for India in Pakistan, Karachi, to Secretary, Ministry of External Affairs and Commonwealth Relations, New Delhi, 30 January 1948, MEA/2-1, 48 – Pak I (Vol. I) National Archives of India (hereafter NAI). In response, Prakasa was reassured that

The perspective of the Indian High Commission was certainly not neutral with respect to the difficulties being faced by local Hindus, but its assessments shed valuable light on the communal situation in Sindh during this period:

The stress in current politics is on regarding Pakistan an [an] Islamic state where the minorities are as foreigners. This intolerance of non-Muslims is so widespread that even the Jews and Anglo-Indians are migrating. The Hindus continue to be terribly hated and no Gandhi cap or Khadhar [*sic*] clothes can be seen in the streets. All Hindus disguise themselves as Muslims wearing Jinnah caps to escape violence at the hands of hoodlums ... Not a single Hindu who has left Pakistan intends or dares to return back, while thousands of Muslims are going back to India.[11]

During the first half of March alone, the High Commission estimated that another 20,000 Hindus had left by sea for Bombay and the Kathiawar ports, with large numbers also crossing the land border between Sindh and Rajasthan. Further, 23,000 more awaited evacuation in camps set up in Karachi and Hyderabad and maintained at Government of India expense, while others clustered in unofficial camps that had emerged across the province in towns such as Sukkur and Shikarpur.[12]

In discussions with Prakasa, M. A. Khuhro, Chief Minister of Sindh, acknowledged that conditions had deteriorated to the extent that all remaining Sikhs needed to be evacuated, and he agreed that most Hindus should be allowed to migrate since it was becoming impossible to persuade them to remain. However, Khuhro undertook to make one more attempt to urge Sindhi Hindus to stay, and he was accompanied in late March on a tour of different districts in Sindh by Prakasa. The tour included three Bengali Hindu members of the Constituent Assembly (B. N. Dutta, R. Chakravarty and Shrichandra Chatterji), who similarly argued that it was against the interests of Sindhi Hindus to leave.[13] But in Prakasa's view, such efforts, however well-intentioned, were bound to be futile, for

any attempt on the part of the Authorities to keep them in Sind under the Essential Services Ordinance or by the introduction of the Permit System only

Delhi 'was well aware of the peculiar difficulties and handicaps under which you are working at present' and so would not 'expect regular fortnightly reports from you until the situation in Karachi eases', Ministry of External Affairs and Commonwealth Relations, New Delhi, to High Commissioner for India in Pakistan, Karachi, 9 February 1948, MEA/2-1, 48 – Pak I (Vol. I) NAI.
[11] Fortnightly Report for the period 1–15 March 1948, 16 March 1948, MEA/2-1, 48 – Pak I (Vol. I) NAI.
[12] Ibid.   [13] Ibid.

results in irritation and added suspicion [and gives rise to] widespread complaints of bribery and corruption ... The exodus is largely due to the fear complex operating in the mind of the Hindus that something may happen in the future which will either destroy them or result in loss of religion, honour or property

Hence, even those Hindus 'who promised Mr. Khuhro at his Larkana tour to stay in Sind probably did so because they could not disappoint the Premier ...; but as soon as [he] left, [they] again began to request for help in migration'. The kinds of problems that they reported included being robbed and molested by Muslim National Guards, the refusal by Muslims to pay debts and *batais* owed to them, false claims being lodged against Hindus and general bitterness shown by Muslims against Hindus coupled with indifference on the part of officials when it came to protecting local minorities.[14] At the same time, Prakasa admitted that what had turned out to be the hasty departure of leading Sindhi Hindus represented a massive blunder: their action, he felt, had deprived those who remained of leadership and support, and 'had [they] been braver, and had they stayed back with their humbler brothers, the Hindu community as a whole could have stood a much better chance to defend themselves [and] agitate to the Government for the protection of their rights'.[15]

Reports from Karachi to New Delhi detailed the difficulties being experienced by Hindus remaining in the province. For instance, one Trimbaklal Joshi owned a shop in Karachi. When he was forcibly dispossessed of it by two Muslims, the District Magistrate ordered his property to be returned to him, but it was immediately reoccupied, leaving Joshi without both his stock-in-trade and his household possessions. Similarly, Goverdhan Vazirani, an advocate and General Secretary of the Sindh Provincial Congress Committee, was arrested following his advice to fellow Hindus to migrate. The fact that he was brought in handcuffs to court was viewed as unnecessarily humiliating and, in the High Commission's words, 'smack[ed] of vindictiveness'. Finally, another Sindhi Hindu A. D. Khanna had ordered certain goods to be sent from Karachi to Delhi, but when he found out that they had not reached their destination, he tracked them down at Hyderabad Railway Station. There the stationmaster, according to a later statement by Khanna's father, insisted that the goods could only be exported to India if the sender was a Muslim, whereupon Khanna claimed to be one. When this representation was discovered to be untrue, Khanna was arrested along with a relation who had supported his story.[16] Some local Christians also experienced similar communal intolerance. In May 1948, reports

[14] Ibid.   [15] Ibid.   [16] Ibid.

claimed that when a Pakistan Olympic Games was held in the city, the Christian-owned company that had provided furniture for the event was not paid the hire charges nor allowed to remove the furniture once the games were over. With rumours circulating that government officials had described them as 'Christian dogs' who were not wanted in Pakistan, the incident created a sensation among local Christians, who were now thought to be the largest minority in Karachi.[17]

By May 1948, there were reports of a move among Hindus 'left behind' in Sindh to organize themselves either as a 'Sind Hindu League' since the INC had disaffiliated its units in Pakistan, or under a joint organization consisting of all local minorities. A Hindu conference was held at Larkana in July, and former Congress activists Holaram Keswani and Hundraj Kukhayal also toured the province to explain why a new political body was needed.[18] Some of the main grievances that dominated Sindhi Hindu calls for redress that were sent to the Government of Sindh (no longer headed up by Khuhro who was by then under investigation for maladministration and corruption) included the non-payment of rents by Muslim tenancies to Hindu landlords, the reduction of the rents of houses owned by Hindus to below market-letting values by rent controllers, 'deliberate and systematic' attempts on the part of lower ranking staff in the revenue and irrigation departments to describe all Hindu property in their records as 'abandoned' even when their owners still occupied it and the fact that temples and other religious buildings remained unprotected, thus allowing Muslim squatters to move in. Calls for the appointment of a custodian of evacuee property, however, continued to fall on deaf ears.[19] And critics latched onto a speech delivered by Liaquat Ali Khan in Hyderabad that June in which he stated that 'In Karachi, in Hyderabad, or in other places in Sind, all the business [had been] in the hands of Hindus. Only in trades like camel-cart driving and donkey-cart driving, Muslims had the monopoly. Though the grace of God, Muslims have now taken their legitimate place in the business and trade of Karachi'.[20]

Responses to difficulties faced by non-Muslims in Sindh, however, cannot be disentangled from the way in which the predicament of their

---

[17] Fortnightly Report for the period 1–15 May 1948, May 1948, MEA/2-1, 48 – Pak I (Vol. I) NAI.

[18] Fortnightly Report for the period 1–15 July, 25 July 1948, MEA/2-1, 48 – Pak I (Vol. I) NAI.

[19] Fortnightly Report for the period 15–31 May 1948, 8 June 1948, MEA/2-1, 48 – Pak I (Vol. I) NAI.

[20] Fortnightly Report for the period 1–15 June 1948, 16 June 1948, MEA/2-1, 48 – Pak I (Vol. I) NAI.

Muslim counterparts in places such as UP were discussed and how policy consequently took shape in India. Reports from the Indian High Commission in Karachi during this period underline this very clear and direct flow of information between the two locations explored in this study. In May 1948, for instance, Praskasa's office reported the following encounter between High Commission staff and a Muslim refugee newly arrived from UP. According to the latter, about 30,000 Muslim Rajputs and Meos from Delhi, Gurgaon, Alwar, Bharatpur and Mathura now wished to return to UP and neighbouring Rajasthan, but needed help from the High Commission. Much to their dismay, Prakasa 'politely dismissed' their request for assistance on the grounds that they 'would be better off in Pakistan where there was ample irrigated land, which would be given to them'. All the same, Prakasa admitted that he was 'surprised to learn from this gentleman that all these Muslims had definite information that their lands in India were not yet allotted to any Hindu refugees, and would be available to them if they [went] back'. As a consequence, the High Commissioner advised his superiors in Delhi that, as a matter of priority, 'the Government of India must immediately allot to the Hindu refugees the lands and houses vacated by the Muslims in the same way as Pakistan has allotted the lands and the houses of the emigrating Hindus', as this would be the 'most effective way of discouraging the return of these Muslims'.[21] By July, news about the impending Pakistani authorities' introduction of a permit system had been published in Karachi newspapers, even before the Indian High Commission had been officially informed. *Dawn*, in line with its pro-Pakistan credentials, marked this decision with a cartoon showing Muslims thanking but declining Prakasa's invitation to return to India; Prakasa, who complained that because the permit system had been introduced too suddenly it had taken Indian officials 'completely by surprise', responded by highlighting the 'crowds of Muslims' who were surrounding his office and asking for permits.[22]

Developments in UP highlight parallel tensions that increased during this period. A couple of years later, during discussions in the Indian Parliament on the 1950 Administration of Evacuee Property Bill, the Minister of State for Rehabilitation – Mohanlal Saxena – gave an undertaking that those persons who had migrated to Pakistan, but – significantly – had returned to India before 18 July 1948, would be

---

[21] Fortnightly Report for the period 16–30 April 1948, 1 May 1948, MEA/2-1, 48 – Pak I (Vol. I) NAI.

[22] Fortnightly Report for the period 1–15 June 1948, 16 June 1948, MEA/2-1, 48 – Pak I (Vol. I) NAI.

exempted from this law.[23] However, by the early 1950s, despite the apparently increasing liberalism of UP government policies towards Muslims returning to this region of India, the ground realities for securing rights to property remained very difficult. Chapter 2 has already explored the problems of Muslims as migrants/return migrants in the immediate aftermath of Partition. Perhaps the best indication of how Muslims managed 'belonging' in India in the early Independence period can be seen in popular and civic responses to events in Pakistan. One of the most important instances of this took place nearly three years following Partition: the precariousness of everyday life for many Muslims in UP was directly exacerbated by incidents of communal violence following the violence and subsequent exodus of Hindus from East Pakistan from March to May 1950. News of these events had a knock-on effect for a range of Muslim organizations across North India, and especially their perception of security. It also had direct repercussions for minorities living across the border in Sindh.

From August 1949, reports circulated in UP of attacks on Hindu villages in East Pakistan, particularly in the Barisal and Sylhet districts. Then in December, in retribution for an attack on policemen involved in the alleged rape of a suspected communist's wife, mass violence broke out in the Khulna district of East Bengal triggered by what appeared to be state-sponsored attacks on non-Muslims.[24] Over the next month, an estimated 30,000 local Hindus responded by migrating to India. In February 1950, a large-scale anti-Hindu procession in the East Bengal provincial capital Dhaka, protesting against an attack on a Muslim woman, prompted further attacks on Hindus in the city and surrounding villages. What followed through February were further incidents of violence in Barisal, Chittagong, Noakhali and Sylhet. In total, around 180,000 Hindu refugees made their way to India between February and May 1950 in reaction to the upsurge in violence.[25]

But despite the fact that the vast majority of East Pakistan Hindus still migrated less for reasons of direct violence and more due to a variety of quotidian forms of discrimination,[26] the response of Muslim organizations in UP was to publicly denounce the 'communal threat'. The arrangement of Muslim-led deputations and meetings represented in stark form a clear statement on Muslim belonging in the new

---

[23] *National Herald*, 14 March 1950.
[24] Joya Chatterji, *The Spoils of Partition: Bengal and India, 1947–1967* (Cambridge: Cambridge University Press, 2007), p. 112.
[25] Ibid.   [26] Ibid., pp. 111–3.

postcolonial Indian state. On 1 March 1950 in Lucknow, Phool Singh, MLA and secretary of the UP Provincial Congress Committee, suggested that batches of 'selfless workers' acceptable to the Pakistan Government should be sent to East Bengal to live among Hindus there and to influence Muslim opinion. Muslim divines, religious heads, *ulama* and 'former' Muslim Leaguers should, he argued, be selected.[27] Following from this, S. M. Ishaq Sambhali, member of the Provincial Congress Committee, issued a press statement in which he argued that the violence was a blot not just on Pakistan but also on Islam. His suggestion was that Indian Muslims, specifically, should champion, in popular movements, a condemnation of the violence across India:

The Muslims of the Bharat Republic should take a lead in the matter by holding mass meetings in every mohalla and every village, appealing to all the true believers of the world to censure these brutalities of the East Bengal goondas and the regrettable and reprehensible attitude of the East Bengal and Pakistan Governments.[28]

But such pronouncements of loyalty and protest by UP-based Muslim leaders and associations were not necessarily spontaneous expressions of support for the Indian Union. Rather, across the state, both high-level and more mundane threats to minorities also elicited similar declarations. In Saharanpur in western UP, for instance, a large meeting was held at the Bankhandi-Nath ground on 3 March at which lurid tales of arson, murder, kidnapping and looting perpetrated on Hindus in East Bengal were narrated. The state government was urged to take immediate and strong measures to check them, and Bishan Chandra Seth, general secretary of the Hindu Mahasabha, criticized the authorities for what he described as their 'weak-kneed' policy towards Pakistan.[29] In Banaras, the Mahasabha organized a procession through the main streets of the city, condemning the official response to events in East Bengal as 'weak'.[30]

At a more general but also routine level, anti-Muslim scares and attacks relating to Pakistan occurred in this period too. The 1950 Holi festival in UP, for instance, was marred by a number of riots and resulting casualties in cities such as Aligarh, Moradabad, Pilibhit and Bareilly.[31]

---

[27] *National Herald*, 2 March 1950.
[28] 'Indian Muslims Urged to Hold Protest Meetings', Ibid.
[29] 'Murder of Hindus in Pakistan: Citizens Urge Govt. to Take Strong Action', *National Herald*, 4 March 1950.
[30] *National Herald*, 6 March 1950.
[31] 'Eight Killed in Holi Incidents: Aligarh and Moradabad under Curfew', Ibid. In some cities, notably Kanpur, there was a deliberate attempt to make Holi an 'inter-communal' celebration. See 'Holi or Holocaust', *National Herald*, 15 March 1950.

In some cases, these led to pitched battles,[32] with one triggered by alleged firing from the house of a Muslim League leader.[33] In Agra, in early March, two 'Muslim visitors' were reported to be operating 'in the city under suspicious circumstances' and promptly arrested. The action was closely linked to migration, since 'The arrests followed inquiry by the police into the cause of departure of many Muslims to Pakistan during the last week. It was found that certain persons were moving about in Muslim localities persuading people to sell all their belongings'.[34] Public meetings in response to communal-related violence in East Pakistan also revisited some other Partition themes, notably the security of women. Six female MLAs in UP, including Purnima Bannerji, an honorary director of Relief and Rehabilitation in the state (women's section), and Begum Afzaz Rasool, leader of opposition in the upper chamber, offered their services to the West Bengal Provincial Congress Committee, so that they could specifically help women affected by the violence.[35]

But for many Muslim leaders in UP, it was not just a matter of shoring up security for their co-religionists in India, but rather these developments offered an opportunity to articulate a concept of civic rights for minorities on both sides of the border. To a great extent, as Taylor Sherman has argued for Hyderabad (Deccan), this was a narrow field of political expression,[36] but one in which some attempt was made to use the leverage of cross-border minority rights. In Lucknow, over twenty prominent UP Muslims issued a joint statement suggesting to the Government of Pakistan that the surest way to instil confidence amongst minorities was to allow them to participate in the administration of the country. The signatories, who included Chaudhary Haider Hussain, MP, Iqbal Ahmad, Maulana Bashir Ahmad, Dr. Abdul Hameed and Begum Habibullah, called on Karachi in the interests of three crore Muslims in India – almost one-third of whom were to be found in UP – to take prompt action to 'stop [communal] incidents':

The Government of Pakistan and East Bengal profess a tender corner for the Muslims in the Indian Republic. If there is the least sincerity in these professions the only way in which they can translate it into practice is to accord impartial

---

[32] The riot in Aligarh led to forty injuries and five deaths and had involved the collection of two mobs in Sultansarai and Atishbazar for a pitched battle on 4 March. *National Herald*, 7 March 1950.

[33] 'Towns in UP Return to Normal Conditions', Ibid.

[34] 'Pakistan Agents in City?', *National Herald*, 4 March 1950.

[35] 'UP Women MLAs Offer Services for Relief of East Bengal Refugees', *National Herald*, 9 March 1950.

[36] Taylor Sherman, *Muslim Belonging in Secular India: Negotiating Citizenship in Postcolonial Hyderabad* (Cambridge: Cambridge University Press, 2015), p. 143.

justice to the minorities in their own dominion. They have to be assured not only of the safety of their life and property but full civic right at a par with the majority.[37]

This idea of 'civic right' also drew upon a specific historical reading of Indo-Islamic culture as inherently cross-communal, building on a typically Nehruvian approach. The Chairman of the District Board in Saharanpur, K. R. Jamshed Ali Khan, released a public statement, which 'gave expression to the genuine feelings of ourselves and 70,000 Muslims of Saharanpur City'. He impressed on the Government of Pakistan 'in the name of humility and the noble teachings of Islam, that the inhuman and deplorable treatment meted out to non-Muslim minorities in East Bengal and other parts of Pakistan is not only a clear violation of international justice and laws but is also a disgrace to Islamic history, character and principles'.[38] Likewise, in Jhansi a meeting of about 300 Muslims at the Sipri Bazar Jama Masjid, with the Municipal Commissioner Dildar Khan in the chair, passed a resolution condemning the 'crimes and atrocities' committed on the minorities in East Bengal.[39] Further gatherings took place in big cities across the country,[40] and in many respects – for instance, one held in Lucknow on 19 March – produced calls for Muslim organizations to play a greater civic role in the life of the country.[41] This meeting, held at Ganga Prasad Memorial Hall in Lucknow, was initiated by an awareness that – as the veteran Congress Muslim leader Maulana Hasrat Mohani put it – 'Muslims [themselves] should realise that they have as much of a role to play in moulding the new order as any other community'.[42]

In the meantime, Indian Federal Minister for Home Affairs Vallabhai Patel indulged in the usual point scoring with Pakistan, but with a coercive nod to the idea of Muslim loyalty: if there was a government masterplan against minorities, he argued in a speech in Lucknow, this was happening in Pakistan, not in India where police actually fired on Hindu rioters. In Pakistan by contrast, he claimed, the police stood by while Hindus were killed; and while in his view the Karachi newspaper

---

[37] 'Pakistan Asked to Be Just to Hindus: Appeal in Interest of Muslims in India', *National Herald*, 4 March 1950.
[38] 'East Pakistan Urged to Realise Responsibility towards Minorities', *National Herald*, 11 March 1950.
[39] 'East Bengal Atrocities Condemned', *National Herald*, 13 March 1950.
[40] 'Bombay Muslims Appeal', *National Herald*, 11 March 1950.
[41] 'UP Muslims to Meet in Lucknow', ibid.
[42] The other supporters of and convenors of this 19 March meeting included Abdul Bari, Abdul Wahhab, Abdul Ghani Ansari, Abdush Shakoor, Muhammad Sami, Z. H. Lari, Zakir Ali, Muhammad Nazeer, Muhammad Farooq and Mufti Fakhrul Islam. 'Appeal to UP Muslims', *National Herald*, 15 March 1950.

Dawn had made too much of the Holi disturbances in UP, for the most part 'Muslims of this province are showing support to the India Union'.[43] Communal pressures on UP-based Muslims in cities such as Aligarh, Kanpur and Bareilly triggered a sizeable increase in refugee traffic into Sindh, crossing the border from Jodhpur, where by May 1950 it was estimated that an additional 230,000 migrants had arrived.[44]

The impact of these new arrivals on communal tensions in Sindh was reflected in an incident that took place in Jacobabad in Upper Sindh also in May 1950. According to contemporary observers, a fracas started following an altercation between 'a few newly-arrived refugees and some members of the minority community'. Shops were looted and one Hindu died from his injuries. When the police arrived, they too were attacked by refugees; the result was a 'dawn-to-dusk curfew', and when 'the barracks in which the refugees lived were searched, ... looted property worth Rs. 8000 was recovered'. Pakistan Minister for the Interior Khwaja Shahabuddin together with the Sindh Chief Minister Kazi Fazlullah travelled to the city with the aim of restoring 'confidence in the minority community', while Chaudhry Khaliquzzaman, president of the Muslim League, who was touring the province to investigate the 'refugee problem' in the light of wider cross-border developments, called on the Indian government to 'organize propaganda to persuade Muslim emigrants on their way to West Pakistan to return to their homes in the United Provinces [UP] and elsewhere'.[45] The extent of the awareness of the wider situation could be seen in Karachi's Urdu press, which placed a huge emphasis on the problems of minorities in India, with the plight of refugees and evacuee problems taking up more than half of the non-advertising newsprint that month.[46]

A month earlier, coinciding with or perhaps prompted by these upsurges in migration across the border from East to West Bengal, and in knock-on fashion between India and Sindh, Nehru and Liaquat Ali Khan had met in Delhi in April 1950 to discuss the treatment of minorities in their respective jurisdictions. This prime ministerial encounter resulted in the two governments agreeing in very considerable detail to guarantee the rights of minorities. On the one hand, both undertook to take steps against individuals or organizations who said or did anything that could be interpreted as an incitement to war. On the

---

[43] 'Patel's Rejoinder', *National Herald*, 14 March 1950.
[44] Sarah Ansari, *Life after Partition: Migration, Community and Strife in Sindh* (Karachi: Oxford University Press, 2005), pp. 127–8.
[45] UK High Commissioner, Karachi, to FCO, 9 May 1950, FO371/84241 UKNA.
[46] US Despatch 494, 25 May 1950, 890D.411/5-2550 USNA.

other, both conceded the right of people to migrate from one country to another and that detailed rules should be drawn up concerning the conditions in which they might move, what property they could take, how they might dispose of valuables and what instructions needed to be given to the customs authorities in both countries. These rules, which would cover the ownership of property of evacuees, included a clause that gave 'benefits to those who return to the country which they have left by the end of [1950], obviously intended as an inducement to those who [had] left in a panic to think again'.[47] In a statement to the Indian Parliament on 10 April, Nehru 'placed considerable emphasis on the assurances received from Liaquat and embodied in the agreement to the effect that minorities in Pakistan enjoyed full rights of citizenship and that this would be effectively enforced'.[48] Later, the provisions were expanded to include anyone who had come back on a permanent return permit before October 1952.

Clearly these unfolding events generated challenges that concerned Sindh and UP jointly, although in an uneven way. As quid pro quo for the decision to receive 'recent migrants' from UP in accordance with the Nehru–Liaquat agreement, the Pakistan Government committed itself to re-accepting 5,000 Hindus who had earlier migrated from Sindh between February and May 1950. But by mid-1954, the authorities had only approved twelve families and out of these, only one had actually returned. In contrast, some 24,000 Muslims had returned from Sindh to UP by then. Of these, however, over 9,000 were not formally eligible for repatriation, which immediately placed them in a vulnerable legal position.[49] The UP authorities had been discussing whether and how to restore property to Muslims who had migrated to Pakistan but later returned to India. In these circumstances, according to Section 16 of the Evacuee Property Act they required a certificate from Government of India, but the state authorities acknowledged that proceedings were likely to be protracted if all legal formalities were observed. Indeed, because of the large number of Muslims who were 'clamouring for restoration

[47] UK High Commissioner, Delhi, to UK High Commissioner, Karachi, Telegram, 8 April 1950, FO371/84253 UKNA.
[48] UK High Commissioner, Delhi, to UK High Commissioner, Karachi, Telegram, 10 April 1950, FO371/84253 UKNA.
[49] P. G. Zachariah, Dep. Secretary to Government to the Secretary to the Government of Uttar Pradesh, Lucknow, Home Dept. Police (C), 5 July 1954, Procedure to be followed for restoration of properties left by evacuees which have been declared to be evacuee properties, Relief and Rehabilitation, File 758/50, Box 36 UP State Archives (hereafter UPSA).

ends',[50] UP ministers suggested 'early restoration' under Section 49 of the Act. In the case of Shahjahanpur district, for instance, the local District Magistrate expressed fears that if poorer Muslim returnees were unable to reclaim their properties, they might turn to a life of crime.[51] But recovering property proved to be a difficult and protracted process. In April 1955 alone, more than 1,000 applications for the grant of a certificate were still pending with the various assistant custodians, with many cases awaiting detailed investigation by the police. Securing the necessary official certificate required the preparation of an application which asked for the name, parentage, caste, residence, date of migration, date of return, permit number and its date, the name of all persons interested in the property and details of the shares of each, and the facts on which the claim for restoration was based. By May 1954, the UP authorities had issued 3,383 certificates, worth c. 25 million rupees, and, in order to deal with the paperwork generated by the spike in applications, they had had to appoint three special officers at the level of district and sessions judge.[52]

Similar challenges faced minorities when it came to securing government employment. It was now especially difficult for Muslims who might formerly have been members of political organizations such as the Muslim League or others with vague links to Pakistan, to get a post in the UP civil services. As state records testify, regular checks were conducted on candidates' geographical origins, and claims of 'false name' used in recruitment, such as when an alleged conspiracy was unearthed in 1950.[53] The fact that information on potentially 'suspicious' links of candidates was collected largely in the localities meant that low-level power structures could lead to further exclusions.[54] Meanwhile in Sindh,

[50] V. V. Singh, DM Shahjahanpur to the Custodian, Evacuee Property, UP, Lucknow 3 November 1950, Procedure to be followed for restoration of properties left by evacuees which have been declared to be evacuee properties, Relief and Rehabilitation, File 758/50, Box 36 UPSA.

[51] Letter of DM of Shahhajanpur to RS Das, 19 February 1951; Procedure to be followed for restoration of properties left by evacuees which have been declared to be evacuee properties, Relief and Rehabilitation, File 758/50, Box 36 UPSA.

[52] Rup Chandra to R. S. Das, 13 April 1955, Procedure to be followed for restoration of properties left by evacuees which have been declared to be evacuee properties, Relief and Rehabilitation, File 758/50, Box 36 UPSA.

[53] Government of India, Ministry of Home Affairs – 10 August 1950. 'Possibility of Muslims Who Opted Finally for Pakistan Joining Service in the Indian Union under Assumed Names', 'Verification of Character and Antecedents of Candidates under State Employment' Appointments Box 295, File 1947/321 UPSA.

[54] Letter from the Deputy Commissioner Almora to the Chief Secretary to Government Uttar Pradesh, 27 August 1955. 'Verification of Character and Antecedents of Candidates under State Employment' Appointments Box 295, File 1947/321 UPSA.

the position of non-Muslim government servants highlighted challenges faced by those who stayed on in Pakistan.

It is clear that there was a symbiotic relationship between the politics of minority citizens on each side of the border between India and Pakistan. In India, and especially in areas that were pivotal to the Muslim migration to Pakistan such as UP, organizations of Muslims had to transform rapidly from giving support for institutions of communal particularity, to providing assertions of civic rights as part of a larger national project. In this, the importance of Islam to the idea of the Indian nation was repeatedly articulated: in UP's cities, especially those with a historic connection to Indo-Islamic culture in the north such as Lucknow, Muslims described themselves as pivotal to Indian identity and civic values. It was significant that such declarations took place largely at times of inter-ethnic conflict, when the 'symmetry' of minority politics on each side of the border seemed to justify specific expressions of popular support for citizenship rights. On the whole, however, the events of the first five years following Independence did little to counteract Muslim feelings of insecurity in UP. As Chapters 2 and 3 have already shown, tenure in government service could be vulnerable, and touring Congressmen found 'an all pervading sense of fear' among Muslims as a whole.[55]

In Sindh, there may have been relatively fewer specific non-Muslim claims articulated with respect to civic rights (certainly as compared with issues being raised by the representatives of Bengali Hindus in the Pakistan Constituent Assembly debates during this period); yet the press there still formed part of the larger cross-border discourse about the related lives of minorities on each side of the border. As the 1950s progressed, the number of Sindhi Hindus who left for good increased, with knock-on effects as far as the province's non-Muslim presence and profile was concerned. Those with business interests moved on, either to India where they settled in places such as UP or Bombay, or, alternatively, they departed for other parts of the world to become a permanent part of the long-established global diaspora of Sindhi merchant firms.[56] And while non-Muslims had continued to hold government posts in the province in the immediate years following Partition, this situation changed in relation to both pull and push factors. By the 1950s, their growing marginalization was reflected in the calculations of the Sindh

---

[55] This was the sense of Mohanlal Gautam in May 1950, as cited in Mushirul Hasan, *Legacy of a Divided Nation: India's Muslims from Independence to Ayodhya* (London: Routledge, 1997), p. 180.

[56] Claude Markovits, *The Global World of Indian Merchants 1750–1947: Traders of Sind from Bukhara to Panama* (Cambridge: Cambridge University Press, 2000).

Government when it published how it was to draw up seniority lists within the provincial civil service bureaucracy: any Hindu incumbents of government posts, it announced, were to be 'taken into consideration, confirmed, and then weeded out'.[57]

Dalit, Tribal and *Hari* Rights

Just as citizenship in India and Pakistan was, from the outset, seen as exclusionary and limited around religious minorities, other communities also sought to establish their relationship to each state, as 'marked' citizens. Dalits, *adivasi*s, 'denotified' (ex-Criminal) tribes in India and *haris* (share-cropper peasants) in Pakistan balanced their demands to rights via existing frameworks of universal rights, with claims for special recognition. Traditionally, historians of citizenship have tended to explore the claims of such communities in terms of 'group-differentiated' rights within citizenship paradigms.[58] In this section, we explore the tension between claims asserted on the basis of group identities with others articulated in terms of broader unmarked constitutional rights. Most importantly there were sometimes contradictions between the formal lobbying organizations and the activities of local grassroots movements, particularly in cities on each side of the border, and this could encourage such organizations to work outside traditional paradigms of civic rights. In the case of India, our argument operates alongside those of Ramnarayan Rawat that challenge previous assumptions about the assimilation of Dalit politics into the party politics of the Congress in the late 1940s.[59] In some cases, the spatial aspects of these groups' claims created problems for the assertion or rights, over and above the issue of social marginalization, not least because of the higher-level politics of tension between India and Pakistan.

---

[57] *Sindh Government Gazette*, 24 March 1955 (Karachi: Sindh Govt. Press, 1955), p. 206. For a fuller picture of the process of migration experienced by Sindhi Hindus, see Nandita Bhavnani, *The Making of Exile: Sindhi Hindus and the Partition of India* (New Delhi: Westland Tranquebar, 2014); Rita Kothari, *The Burden of Refuge: The Sindhi Hindus of Gujarat* (Hyderabad: Orient Longman, 2007); and Subhadra Anand, *National Integration of Sindhis* (New Delhi: Vikas, 1996). For more personal recollections, see the oral testimonies collected in Saaz Aggarwal, *Sindh: Stories from a Vanished Homeland* (Pune: Black-and-White Fountain, 2012).

[58] For instance, see Niraja Gopal Jayal, *Citizenship and Its Discontents: An Indian History* (Cambridge, MA: Harvard University Press, 2013).

[59] Ramnarayan Rawat, 'Partition Politics and Achuut Identity: A Study of the Scheduled Castes Federation and Dalit Politics in UP, 1946–1948', in *The Partitions of Memory: The Afterlife of the Division of India*, ed. S. Kaul (New Delhi: Permanent Black, 2001), pp. 111–39.

By the early 1950s, there was an established framework in UP, as in other states, for recognizing the rights of Scheduled Castes to government employment. This, of course, had its colonial antecedents in the struggles led by Ambedkar for statutory recognition of the separate political rights of 'Untouchables' or 'Depressed Classes' (to use the language of the interwar years). There were significant limitations to the implementation of these structures of representation in the services, which reflected what Jesus Chairez-Garza has described as a structural high-caste dominance in late 1940s Indian politics.[60] Overall, the UP government had a statutory requirement to reserve 10 per cent of all posts for Scheduled Castes and Tribes (SC/STs), although this was increased to 18 per cent in September 1952.[61] But, when exploring the various means by which these communities asserted their civic rights in the period under scrutiny, it is important to note that formal, state-driven measures had very little effect in bringing scheduled castes (SCs) into state employment. National debates on the failure to enhance recruitment among SC/STs in the early 1950s noted that a large proportion of posts were filled by promotion rather than appointment. Although communities themselves could prove that some members were well qualified, they were relatively unsuccessful in civil services entry tests. The Commissioner for Scheduled Castes argued that a separate exam should be prepared, but the Government of India opposed such an idea, drawing on Article 335 of the Constitution that argued that provisions for SC/STs should be consistent with the maintenance of the efficiency of administration.[62] Indeed, the UP government acknowledged in 1953 that its record in filling quotas in government service had been 'very poor'. Effectively, the system simply reinforced the predominance of low-status communities in the most menial government jobs. Divided into formal 'classes', there was a concentration of SC/ST representation in the bottom Class IV category, which included unskilled and irregular day rate workers. In fact, permanent security of employment at this level was not established until the early 1990s, via the efforts of the UP Class IV Employees Association.[63] In the 1950s, their situation was precarious, a

---

[60] Jesus Francisco Chairez-Garza, '"Bound Hand and Foot and Handed over to the Caste Hindus": Ambedkar, Untouchability and the Politics of Partition', *The Indian Economic & Social History Review* 55, 1 (2018), pp. 1–28.

[61] G.O. no. 2328/II-B 104 1952 dated 22 September 1953, Irrigation Department, Box 11, File 333/1952 UPSA.

[62] 'Debate on the Report of the Commissioner for Scheduled Castes and Scheduled Tribes for the Years 1952 and 1953', Home, CS (A), 67/54-CS (A) NAI.

[63] *State of UP v. Class IV Employees Association*, Laws (All) 1993-9-7, High Court of Allahabad, Judgement. See www.the-laws.com/Encyclopedia/Browse/Case?CaseId=303991165000 (accessed December 2018).

problem compounded by a total absence of higher-level bureaucratic representation. For instance, in the state's Irrigation Department in 1953, there were no SC appointees in Classes I and II, only 5 in Class III (1.5 per cent) and 107 in Class IV (12.25 per cent). In most departments of the state, there were between 5 and 9 per cent recruitment of SC/STs to Class IV posts, and usually around 0.5–1.5 per cent in Class III.[64]

From the 1940s, the UP authorities had attempted to guide bureaucratic recruitment with reference to what were, in that decade, described as 'Depressed Class' organizations. But it did so with some reluctance since there was a fear that reference to one organization would only lead to a number of other – competing – groups to come forward. For instance, in 1942, when discussing the disbursement of grants from the 'reclamation department' for low castes, the UP Adi Hindu Depressed Classes Association submitted a petition calling for a body to advise on grants.[65] While it was pointed out that there were already two such associations in the province, the advisory board was eventually agreed. But through 1943–4, the Pasi Mahasabha and the District Jatava Conference both sent further representations to government, claiming that their interests of their specific caste groups were not being met.[66] Additional efforts were made from early 1952 to increase the quota of SCs and STs applying for government posts, which involved identifying organizations and newspapers, and raising the upper age limit for applicants from twenty-eight to thirty-one.[67] This was, however, mediated through specific provincial-level associations – specifically, the All-India Harijan Sevak Sangh, the Scheduled Castes Welfare Association, the UP branch of the All-India Scheduled Castes Federation, based in Parmat Kanpur, under the presidentship of Tilak Chand Kuril, and finally, the UP branch of the Depressed Classes League, based in Lucknow and led by Ramanand Shastri.[68] Clearly, these lobbying groups had little

---

[64] 'Statement Showing Number and Percentage of Scheduled Castes Employees in Various Departments of Uttar Pradesh Government', in 'Annual Reports – Commissioner for Scheduled Castes and Scheduled Tribes', Irrigation (Establishments) Box 13, File 338-B/1952 UPSA.

[65] 'Special Meeting of the Executive Committee of the UP Adi Hindu Depressed Classes Association held on 27 June 1942', in Memorial of the Adi Hindu Depressed Classes Association. Harijan Sahayak, Box 4, File 1942/113 UPSA.

[66] 'Representation from the District Jatava Conference, Meerut, 2/3 June 1944', in Memorial of the Adi Hindu Depressed Classes Association. Harijan Sahayak, Box 4, File 1942/113 UPSA.

[67] 'Representation of Scheduled Castes in Public Services', Appointment (B) Box 28, File 159/1952 UPSA.

[68] H. K. Tandon to All Heads of Department, 24 February 1954 in 'Representations of Members of the Scheduled Castes in Services', Irrigation Department, Box 11, File 333/1952 UPSA.

practical effect in influencing the outcomes of government recruitment. Their function was formally limited to that of recommendation alone, and providing advice to applicants. Given (according to one Commissioner of Scheduled Castes) the lack of enthusiasm, even apathy, both within departments and among high-ranking officers to fill up quotas, their impact was minor.[69]

The legal rights of low-caste communities were also not so easily served from among their own communities, with very difficult recruitment into judicial services and the legal profession. One SC *vakil* (legal representative), Puran Chand, argued that the existing rule of three full years' service made it very difficult for SC candidates:

Knowing the scheduled caste lawyers in UP it can safely be said that no Scheduled Caste candidate can come within the four corners of these conditions ... I am probably the only Scheduled Caste candidate who has put in three years of actual practice at the Bar, but I would be exceeding the specified maximum age-limit by 1 year 5 months and 7 days.[70]

The corollary of this was that community organizations had to find alternative means to assert citizenship rights, via channels of political power and influence. Shortly after Independence, it was still difficult to directly lobby for one's community using the influence of a political party within the civil bureaucracy itself. Any individual engaged in what was officially defined as 'subversive activities' was banned from applying for posts,[71] yet in the mid-1950s the UP government admitted that in the area of bureaucratic appointments, influence was in any case wielded much more effectively via bribes.[72]

In a few cases, however, community organizations represented their rights very clearly through a connection of community activism and petitioning, sometimes around state-run industrial enterprises. In the first years following Independence, the Pasi Sammelan represented its demands for greater bureaucratic representation in the UP in regular meetings, featuring high-level Congress leaders.[73] These groups often worked through existing industrial policies of government too. The Uttar Pradesh Sanyukt Kori Mahasangh, for instance, held a mass meeting of community members at the Achutanand Park in Kanpur in late

---

[69] L. M. Shrikant, Extract from *Hindustan Standard*, 1 August 1952, in 'Representation of Scheduled Castes in Public Services', Appointment (B) Box 28, File 159/1952 UPSA.

[70] Puran Chand, Vakil, Collectorate Agra, to Premier UP Gov, 25/8/52 in 'Representation of Scheduled Castes in Public Services', Appointment (B) Box 28, File 159/1952 UPSA.

[71] 'Verification of Character and Antecedents of Candidates under State Employment', Appointments Box 295, File 1947/321 UPSA.

[72] Note of 17 November 1956, ibid.

[73] 'Kamishanari Paasi-Sammelan', *Aaj*, 6 January 1948.

December 1953, which resulted in a number of resolutions and proposals to the UP government, eventually produced an ornately printed
petition. Its contents included the insistence that only the Sanyukt Kori
Mahasangh could represent the community and that all other approaches
to government should be seen as 'individual'; that the Kori community
should be included on a recent government order recommending benefits to denotified communities; and that rural industrial help and land
should be provided for weaker or more vulnerable sections of the community. Most importantly, the petition set out its opposition to the UP
Weaver's Cooperative Association, which the petition recommended to
be replaced by a body representing handloom weavers. The petition also
opposed the actions of district industrial stores, which, it argued, were
working in the interests of other communities.[74] These claims for industrial advancement were placed alongside an appeal for greater political
representation too, which, the Kori representatives maintained, were
overshadowed by other communities. The 'low' status of Koris meant
that they were not fully represented in the Vidhan Sabha.[75]

This gulf between the language of rights and their quotidian implementation was illustrated in the case of forced labour and its prevention.
It was still the case in the few years after Independence that *begar* (forced
labour) was routinely extracted from Dalit communities. In fact, the UP
government issued a 'complaint form' to be circulated to all district
magistrates in 1947, which was to be used to record particular cases of
official use of 'free' labour. Information that came back found that in
many areas of the state *begar* continued to exist, but that its conditions
could be quite ambiguous.[76] Article 23(1) of the Indian Constitution
forbade forced labour except in the cases covered by Article 23(2) and
made contravention an offence, punishable under Section 374 of the
Indian Penal Code. But the communication of this framework was very
difficult. In a circular entitled the 'Abolition of Forced Labour', the
Ministry of Labour pointed out that

Reports received from some state governments show that the action taken by
them to give publicity to constitutional and legal provisions in regard to forced
labour has been restricted mainly to their publication in the English newspapers,
etc., or Press Bulletins. These are rarely read by villagers most of whom are
illiterate. I am to suggest that in so far as rural areas are concerned, [as well as the]

---

[74] Petition of the Kori Mahasabha, Kanpur, 27 December 1953, AICC Collection, PB 19
(1), Uttar Pradesh 1953 NMML.
[75] 'UP Handloom Weavers' Congress, Head Office Hathras', 31 December 1953, AICC
Collection, PB 19 (1), Uttar Pradesh 1953 NMML.
[76] Complaint from all DMS UP reg. Begar, Harijan Sahayak Department, Box 8 and 9,
File 175/48 UPSA.

distribution of leaflets in local languages, publicity may be given through local officials of the Revenue Department and District Public Relations Officers. It is further requested that the State Government may kindly consider giving publicity through the All-India Radio.[77]

In many cases, however, there was a dichotomy between organizations set up as official representatives of collective community groups, and the more grassroots manifestations of these same people. This was evident as far as rights movements of ex-Criminal Tribes – collectively funded in a number of welfare schemes in North India in the 1950s via the Vimukt Jati Sevak Sangh (VJSS) – were concerned. First, MPs complained in the mid-1950s that the distribution of welfare resources to the VJSS in Delhi was completely out of proportion to UP as a whole: there were fewer than 2,000 members of these communities in the city, compared to two million in UP, yet around 10 per cent of the funding was directed towards Delhi.[78] This imbalance was clearly supported by government's own admission that very little progress to date had been made on 'rehabilitation' programmes for ex-Criminal Tribes in the state. There were six settlements in UP which as late as the spring of 1950 were still pondering the implementation of the Criminal Tribes Enquiry Committee Report, in terms of how their day-to-day management should be decided.[79]

Second, and more troubling were accusations of the ill-treatment of community members, and embezzlement by the VJSS – an offshoot of the Servants of the People Society, and therefore, not an organization actually grounded in the politics of the groups involved. While officially headed by Algu Rai Shastri, P. D. Tandon and Rameshwari Nehru, most of the work of the VJSS was carried out by officers, such as the VJSS Secretary Bhagwat Singh. A grant of Rs. 88,000 had been dispersed to the organization to build a number of houses in Shahdara and Sansi Colony for ex-Criminal Tribes. The community to be housed, according the VJSS's own correspondence with the Government of India, were people who had been living in New Delhi railway station or at the Swatantra Mills. However, community members alleged that Bhagwat

---

[77] Copy of letter no. PL-17(49) dated December 24, 1951, from the Deputy Secretary to the Government of India, Ministry of Labour, New Delhi to All State Governments. Subject 'Abolition of Forced Labour', Increase in the number of carts and so on used by SDOs, Revenue B, Box 101, File 103B/1947 UPSA.

[78] L. M. Shrikant, Commissioner, 2.10.54, in Grant-in-aid for the Welfare of Ex-Criminal Tribes for the Year 1954–5 to the Vimukta Jati Sevak Sangh, New Delhi, MHA, Public-II, File no. 51/4/54-Public II NAI.

[79] 'Condition of Criminal Tribes in UP, Minister Admits Govt's Failure to Do Much. Prohibition to Be Enforced Gradually', National Herald, 16 March 1950.

Singh and other members of the VJSS management had misappropriated some of the funding, by working with a particular contractor in the city. In effect, the contractor, or so it was alleged, had used poor materials and had divided the unspent funds with the VJSS management.[80] A representative of the ex-Criminal Tribes wrote a long list of grievances, which included the use of loans as 'bribes' and misappropriation of funds.[81] Later, in 1955, the accusations extended to the keeping of 'girls for dancing'.[82]

Important here was the use of labour-specific organizational methods. Members of ex-Criminal Tribes represented themselves to the government via the Kasturba Nagar Co-Operative Multipurpose Society. In their petitions and appeals, they made free use of the same paradigms of citizenship rights seen in earlier years in the mainstream press. The Co-Operative representatives writing to the Home Minister in 1955 stated that they had 'listened to [his] speech and saw a flame of hope and success in it that we were also going to be counted among the free cityzens [*sic*] of free India after a slavery of countless years'.[83] In later letters, a similar sense of injustice and disempowerment in relation to educated elites characterized their correspondence with government officials:

Shri Purushottam Das Tandon, Mata Rameshwari Nehru and Shri Sewak Ram cannot work among us. They travel in cars. They think us slaves and the worst persons on the earth. They hate our children. They find bad smells in our small houses. They know to work out plans on papers and get money from the Government on our name and fill up their bellies.[84]

In much of the communication from this organization, Rameshwari Nehru was referred to as '*Mataji*' – a woman whose main task was to protect the interests of the social workers of the VJSS.

The idea that ex-Criminal Tribes faced specific problems in the early postcolonial period, in the context of limited rehabilitation policies, or the continuation of older policing cultures, extended into UP. In a State

---

[80] Jojinder Singh to K. N. Katju, 8 October 1954, Grant-in-aid for the Welfare of Ex-Criminal Tribes for the Year 1954–5 to the Vimukta Jati Sevak Sangh, New Delhi, MHA, Public-II, File no. 51/4/54-Public II NAI.

[81] 'Black Deeds of Office Bearers VJSS', 26 February 1955 in Grant-in-aid for the Welfare of Ex-Criminal Tribes for the Year 1954–5 to the Vimukta Jati Sevak Sangh, New Delhi, MHA, Public-II, File no. 51/4/54-Public II NAI.

[82] To SHO, 31 January 1955, ibid.

[83] Letter from Jojinder Singh, Secretary to the Kasturba Nagar Co-operative Multipurpose Society Ltd, to Kailash Nath Katju, 25 November 1954, Grant-in-aid for the Welfare of Ex-Criminal Tribes for the Year 1954–5 to the Vimukta Jati Sevak Sangh, New Delhi, MHA, Public-II, File no. 51/4/54-Public II NAI.

[84] Ram Chander et al. to Home Minister, 27 January 1955, ibid.

Assembly debate on the issue, Bhagwati Prasad Shukla discussed the alleged harassment of ex-Criminal Tribes by the police on the basis of reports that had been received, and suggested that the police should no longer be concerning themselves with implementing the Criminal Tribes Act. Chet Ram (Congress) claimed that 'backward classes' who could not assert themselves had been declared 'Criminal Tribes' and were now used as scapegoats for real miscreants. For him, the people of higher castes were more criminally-minded than the criminal tribes; freedom had been attained but not for the so-called Criminal Tribes.[85]

In a number of important cases in North India, the failures of state mechanisms to protect the rights of marginalized communities, and the superficiality of reform or rehabilitation programmes, encouraged lobbying groups to forego the normal mechanisms of civic organizations. Instead, in the lead up to the first general elections, Dalit, *adivasi* or denotified tribe bodies sought forms of political representation to further their specific rights. This was something that linked back strongly not only to the politics of the Scheduled Caste Federation (SCF) in the 1940s but also to smaller-level civic groups who attempted to get tickets, as 'Dalits', in Congress-dominated constituencies.[86] In the lead-up to the 1952 general elections in UP, a range of SC meetings in the state decided that the SCF should contest all SC seats, and some general ones, while reiterating faith in the leadership of Ambedkar. Many of these political meetings, however, were also cognisant of the connections between political representation and bureaucratic power: one such SCF meeting in Lucknow condemned the policy of the city's rationing authorities when it came to 'discriminating' between the federation and other political parties over the issue of ration permits around conferences.[87]

Across the border in Sindh, the position of SC communities and so-called criminal tribes is less easy to track in official archives as compared with developments in UP during this period. This is a great extent due to the twice-marginalized position of such groups which means that they seem to have been largely hidden from the historical record for the period following the creation of Pakistan. Not only were Sindh's Dalits members of a minority within Pakistan as a whole but they were also far smaller in size than East Pakistan's non-Muslim population, and hence for the late 1940s and 1950s, it was their counterparts in East

---

[85] '*National Herald*, 16 March 1950.
[86] For an instance of this process taking place in Western India during the same timeframe, see William Gould, Sarah Gandee and Chhara Dakxin, 'Settling the Citizen, Settling the Nomad: "Habitual Offenders", Rebellion and Civic Consciousness in Western India, 1938–1952', *Modern Asian Studies*, 2019, http://eprints.whiterose.ac.uk/144745/.
[87] *National Herald*, 11 September 1951.

Pakistan who have left more visible archival traces. As discussed earlier in this chapter, it was Sindh's urban, higher caste Hindus whose experiences following Partition are easier to track. By May 1948, the number of Sindhi Hindus remaining in the province was down to around 300,000 as compared with c. 1.5 million a year earlier. About half of these, contemporaries expected, were likely to stay on in Sindh. For some, this was because they possessed valuable property in the *mofussil* that was unlikely to be sold except at a loss, but most of them were poor and so could not hope for a better life elsewhere. The latter included Scheduled Castes, who were not expected to 'migrate as long as the embargo on the export of their cattle is not lifted, and who [anyway were] not assured of home and means of livelihood in India'.[88]

How Sindh's Scheduled Castes themselves regarded the new post-Independence political arrangements therefore remains to be explored, though in more recent decades, as our Epilogue will highlight, levels of activism increased substantially among groups such as the province's Kohli community. The emphasis in contemporary records is on developments in East Pakistan, where its provincial assembly's non-Muslim seats were officially divided between Caste Hindus, Scheduled Castes and Christian representatives. It is worth noting, however, that the second Pakistan Constituent Assembly deferred a decision on whether or not to opt for joint or separate electorates for minorities, transferring the matter to the provincial level to decide. The new West Pakistan Assembly, established following the introduction of One Unit in 1955, contained ten seats for non-Muslims but these were not subdivided or allocated to particular groups. According to Keith Callard, in debates on the issue in August 1956,

the only speakers against the motion were one Hindu, one independent member and the leaders of the Sind Awami Mahaz (G.M. Syed and Pir Ilahi Bakhsh). After four days of debates the matter was put to the vote, and the resolution in favour of separate electorates was carried by 129 to 10 ... Since the total membership of the Assembly was 310, a large proportion of MLAs either abstained or thought it prudent not to attend the session.[89]

As far as the so-called Criminal Tribes were concerned, there was one group in Sindh that had acquired notoriety during the war years, whose members did not have a SC identity, but who surfaced periodically as a subject of major concern immediately following Independence. These

---

[88] Fortnightly Report for the period 15–31 May 1948, 8 June 1948, MEA/2-1, 48 – Pak I (Vol. I) NAI.

[89] Keith Callard, *Pakistan: A Political Study* (London: George Allen & Unwin, 1957), pp. 250–1, citing *Dawn*, 7 August 1956.

were the Hurs, Muslim followers of an extremely influential local spiritual leader, the Pir Pagaro. Their activities during the war years – vari-
ously described as an 'uprising' or as a breakdown in law and order – had
resulted in martial law being imposed on the province (1942–3), the
detention of Hur families in guarded settlements (*lorhas*) and even the
execution of Pir Sibghatullah Shah II (in March 1943) on the charge of
waging war against the Crown.[90] Throughout the late 1940s and early
1950s, the authorities in the province continued to deal with the fallout
from this challenge, in the shape of gang members who were evading
capture and around 12,000 Hurs still living in concentration-style
camps. In May 1948, during discussions on how to check the smuggling
problem, the Sindh chief minister highlighted the need to curb Hur
activities in view of their recent lawlessness, and he blamed the continuing Hur 'menace' on 'a regular pernicious anti-Pakistan programme' by
'interested persons' who were largely responsible for 'vindictive Hur
attacks on peaceful Pakistanis in Hur areas'.[91] The Sindh authorities
decided to take up the matter with the Indian authorities, as 'Hur raiders
[had] found sanctuary in the border Rajputana states following their
release from Sind jails and [had been] making frequent incursions' into
the province from these strongholds.[92]

In December 1951, in an attempt to exert pressure from above, the
authorities decided to restore the *gaddi* (ancestral seat) to the eldest son
of the previous incumbent.[93] The new *sajjada nashin*, Pir Shah Mardan
Shah II,[94] promptly advised his Hur followers to abide by the law, calling
upon them to behave in a manner that would bring credit to him and the
shrine of his forbears. In the process, he expressed his gratitude to the
Sindh government, as well as the Government of Pakistan, for their
'generous gesture', and he was, he assured them, 'deeply mindful of his
duty by the State'.[95] Following the Pir's installation ceremony, which was
attended by 'thousands of Hurs including some from Bharati [Indian]

---

[90] For a detailed account of the origins of the Hurs and their activities in Sindh during the
British period, see Sarah Ansari, *Sufi Saints and State Power: The Pirs of Sind, 1843–1947*
(Cambridge: Cambridge University Press, 1992), chapters 3 and 6.
[91] *Dawn*, 21 May 1948.   [92] Ibid.
[93] 'Pir Pagaro's Gaddi to Be Restored to Eldest son', *Dawn*, 10 December 1951, p. 10.
[94] The new Pir, who had been sent for education to England by the authorities when his
father was executed, was influential in the early years of Pakistan's cricket development
in the 1950s. Before Pakistan's first tour of England in 1954 he had a grass pitch
constructed in his garden so that the Pakistan players, who had to play most of their
cricket at the time on matting pitches, could practise in something similar to English
conditions. He re-founded the Sindh Cricket Association, captained Sindh in the first-
ever match in the Quaid-e-Azam Trophy in November 1953 and captained a team under
his name against the MCC in 1955–6.
[95] *Dawn*, 14 December 1951, p. 5.

territory', it was acknowledged that the authorities had given [him] an opportunity 'to wean away his turbulent sect from a life of crime and lawlessness so that they [might] take their due place in the life of the country as loyal and law-abiding citizens'.[96]

Later in 1952, while the new Pir was attempting to persuade remaining Hur outlaws to lay down their arms,[97] the Sind Settlement Committee, which had been appointed by the Sindh authorities in 1950, issued a series of policy recommendations towards 'Criminal Tribes' in general, but particularly in relation to the Hurs. These included the abolition of Hur-guarded camps, with Hurs instead settled as far as possible in their original homes where 'free colonies' would be built for their speedy resettlement. The Committee further proposed that primary education for Hur children be made free and compulsory, and that secondary education scholarships be granted to Hur boys 'to serve as an incentive and turn their mind away from crime and fanaticism'. It also advised that the employment of Hurs should be encouraged by government and semi-government departments, a move that it hoped would 'bring back the lost faith among the Hurs'. As the report recognized, many Hurs had always possessed a nomadic lifestyle, and a large number had also been externed from Sindh thanks to what had happened during the period of martial law. In response, the authorities were urged to grant Hurs 'citizenship rights' and allot lands to them in various parts of the province.[98] Hur prisoners being held in Khairpur State[99] were released in June 1952, following meetings between the State's chief minister and the Pir, who had assured the Khairpur authorities that Hurs would 'not indulge in any anti-State activities and would behave as peaceful and law abiding citizens'.[100] By January 1953, news made the front page of *Dawn* that the last of the Hur outlaws to defy the Pir's orders had surrendered to the authorities. Muhammad Ali Narejo, who despite a prize on his head of nearly Rs. 10,000 had evaded capture for the previous seven years, was alleged to have been responsible for many murders and dacoities in Nawabshah and Tharparkar.[101] Land, however, remained a key challenge in Hur rehabilitation and absorption within mainstream society. As the Pir himself repeatedly pointed out in the early 1950s,

---

[96] At the time of the Pir's installation, official estimates put the Hur following at c. 1,500,000 persons in Pakistan and about 750,000 in India. *Dawn*, 5 February 1952.

[97] *Dawn*, 8 May 1952. [98] *Dawn*, 30 May 1952.

[99] This princely state formally acceded to the Dominion of Pakistan in October 1947, and was later merged into West Pakistan as part of the One Unit amalgamation process in October 1955.

[100] *Dawn*, 13 June 1952. [101] *Dawn*, 26 January 1953.

several thousand Hurs were leading lives without shelter or means of subsistence; the Pakistan Government had done nothing to return lands – over 100,000 acres confiscated by the British – to their rightful owners.[102] In his view, anti-Hur prejudice had not died away completely, and it eventually took until the 1960s for their rehabilitation to be recognized, helped by the active involvement of Hurs who took part in the brief war fought across the Sindh-India border in 1965.[103]

Land rights also proved central to another marginalized group in Sindh, its *haris* ('wielders of the plough', sharecropping peasants). A report produced by US embassy officials in the late 1950s pointed out that the social status of local Christians had declined thanks to the readiness of Punjabi Christian cultivators to take up sweepers' work in Sindhi cities and towns such as Hyderabad, Nawabshah and Sanghar: 'Christian cultivators [it was claimed] appeared to accept social inferiority and to conduct themselves as if the Muslims were a superior caste'. Indeed, this sense of inferiority, or so missionaries stationed in Sindh believed, was also proving a handicap to the work of the Sind Hari Committee and its leader Hyder Bakhsh Jatoi.[104] The Sind Hari Committee, which represented *hari* interests and dated back to the 1930s, led campaigns throughout the late 1940s and 1950s to improve the lot of landless agricultural workers in the province, and discussion about *hari* rights and the abolition of the prevailing *zamindar* system gripped the

[102] *Dawn*, 26 August 1952.

[103] *Dawn*, 8 July 1952. During the 1965 war between India and Pakistan, about 65,000 Hurs served in various fronts especially that of Sindh. While the Southern desert sector was a mere sideshow to the major battles fought in the Punjab and in Kashmir, the Indians had placed two divisions there with the aim of tying down Pakistani troops. Facing a shortage of troops and unable to divert any substantial forces from the Punjab and Kashmir sectors (from where the main Indian thrust had come), the commander of the Pakistan Rangers, Brigadier Khuda Dad Khan, turned to local help. Hurs apparently volunteered in droves. Given only basic training and light weapons, they fought alongside Rangers and regular army units, using their knowledge of the desert to help blunt the Indian offensive. But perhaps their most famous (and militarily important) action was the capture, though only briefly, of the Indian fort of Kishangarh, located several kilometres inside India. See https://defence.pk/pdf/threads/history-of-the-hurs-sindh.491945/ (accessed December 2018).

[104] 'Trip to Sind Area in Pakistan, April 1013, 1958', Despatch 983, 25 April 1958, 890D.413/4-2558 USNA. Jatoi towards the end of the Second World War had resigned as Deputy Collector in Sindh's provincial service in order to be able to champion the rights of Sindh's landless peasantry. While exact figures are not available, the number of members of the Sind Hari Committee are estimated to have ranged from 10,000 to 12,000 in 1947–8, reaching a peak at 15,000–16,000 in 1954–5. See Mahmood Hasan Khan, 'Sind Hari Committee, 1930–1970: A Peasant Movement?', World Employment Programme Research Working Paper (Geneva: International Labour Organisation, 1979), pp. 20–1.

province periodically during this period.[105] When (a different) 'Hari Committee of Enquiry', which had been tasked in early 1947 with investigating possible ways of reforming tenancy arrangements in the Sindhi countryside, recommended against the abolition of the *zamindar* system and the grant of full tenancy rights to the peasants in May 1948, a storm of protest ensued. For some contemporaries, the Committee of Enquiry's findings turned too much of a blind eye to the local imbalance of agrarian power, and thus ignored the rights of those in Sindh actually working the land.[106]

The Committee's Majority Report, which drew attention to the huge inequalities present in the Sindhi countryside, as well as the liabilities that flowed from this, did not lack sympathy for the *haris'* plight. By the late 1940s, *haris* made up more than 50 per cent of the province's total rural population of c. 3.6 million. As the report explained, not only did they pay half the produce of their efforts over to their *zamindar* but landlords typically deducted various levies (*abwabs*), which inevitably reduced the *haris'* share of any profit. And payment for guarding crops before harvesting, for weighing crops after they had been harvested, for lighting when the irrigation of crops took place at night and so on, were all paid for by *haris* who also had to provide bullocks and buy seeds. As tenants-at-will who could be dismissed at any time, this vulnerability was made still more precarious by the fact that since most contracts were oral they had no recourse to the law in the event of a dispute: as one contemporary put it, 'Government officials are beyond [the *hari*'s] reach, his landlord is the final arbiter of his fate'.[107] Furthermore, as the report continued:

Inwardly they [the *haris*] deplore the heavy extraction from their share of crops, the heavy infantile mortality, and the incidence of disease in their families, the loss of their bullocks by theft/disease, the shortage of essential domestic/consumer goods, their own illiteracy and lack of education, the heavy demands of social customs on their hard-earned incomes, and various other disabilities which are their present lot. Having no collective voice, they stoically endure these hardships imposed by the prevailing socio-economic system.[108]

---

[105] The origins of the Sind Hari Committee dated back to the 1920s and the formation of a 'Kisan Bureau', whose slogan was '*Hari hagdaar*' ('the *hari* deserves his rights'). The Bureau later turned into the Sind Hari Association, which in turn became the Sind Hari Committee in 1936. It mobilized mass protests across Sindh against the 1939 Bombay Tenancy Act that was adopted by the newly separated province, including a massive rally in Hyderabad in 1943, which helped to kick-start the investigations that resulted in the 1947–8 Hari Committee of Enquiry.

[106] UK Opdom 38, 6–12 May 1948, 12 May 1948, IOR L/PO/12/14 BL.

[107] *Civil and Military Gazette*, 10 June 1949.

[108] Report of the Government Hari Enquiry Committee 1947–48, Roger Thomas Papers, Mss Eur F235/282 BL.

Under these circumstances, it was surprising to sympathetic contemporaries that, having drawn so dismal a picture of conditions in rural Sindh, the Committee did not recommend reforms that critics believed would substantially improve the rights of people living and working there. Rather, it seemed to be saying that the problems of *haris* were either of their own creation or natural problems or government neglect, that *zamindar* was a friend of the *hari*, and consequently that land reforms were not just undesirable but represented a loss for the *hari*. One member of the committee, however, disagreed with the majority opinion. Muhammad Masud, a serving district officer (Collector of Nawabshah, who had won plaudits for his *hari* uplift work before Independence), stuck to his guns.[109] He refused to add his name to the final report, choosing instead to produce a 'Note of Dissent', as had originally been permitted, which was also presented to the authorities in July 1948. What Masud did not expect was for his opposition to be kept from the public.[110] In the words of British observers, 'the suppression by the Government of the minority report by one member of the Committee appointed to examine the agrarian question has attracted much attention'.[111] Even *Dawn* (which had little affection for the provincial authorities) commented approvingly on his stance:

[109] Muhammad Masud (1916–5), and later known as 'Masud Khaddarposh' and 'Masud Hari', was born in 1916 in Lahore; son of Dr. Ghulam Jilani, a *hakeem* and personal physician to the Shah of Iran, he graduated with a bachelor's degree from Government College Lahore after which he joined Law College, Punjab University, where he came first in the LLB examination in 1937. In 1941, he joined the Indian Civil Service and proceeded to Oxford for further education and training. Upon his return to India, his first posting as a Government Officer was in Ahmadnagar, Bombay Presidency; from there he was sent to Khandesh to work on the uplift of downtrodden Bhil tribes. His efforts there earned him the title of 'Masud Bhagwan'. In 1946, Masud was transferred to Nawabshah (Sindh) as Deputy Commissioner. In 1947, at the time of partition, he opted for Pakistan and continued at the same posting in Nawabshah. See http://pakistanprayers.blogspot.co.uk/2006/04/masud-khaddarposh-human-rights.html (accessed December 2018). In the run up to 1946 provincial elections, and knowing that he was a supporter of the idea of Pakistan, Congress politicians, afraid that his popularity among *haris* would swing votes in favour of the Muslim League, had mounted a campaign to get Masud transferred from Nawabshah, in response to which a Sindhi vernacular pro-League newspaper commented in October that year: 'Mr. Masud's only offence is that he helped the poor *haris* against the powerful *zamindars* and saved them from their oppression and tyranny. The Hindu Press has therefore moved heaven and earth against Mr Masud ... The Hindu Congress has turned against him because he is attacking the vested interests and the *zamindars* ... and the Congress is helping the vested interests ...', *Al Wahid*, 13 October 1948.

[110] M. Masud, 'Hari Committee Report Note of Dissent', Roger Thomas Papers, Mss Eur F235/650 BL.

[111] UKHC Opdom 104, 24–30 December 1948, L/PO/12/14 BL.

Mr Masud is believed to have expressed strong views on the existing disabilities of the *haris* and suggested far-reaching changes. There is a feeling among sections of the public that the Sind Ministry, whose parliamentary support is largely derived from *Zamindar* elements, may not only shelve the minority report of the Hari Committee but even withhold it from the public.

Similarly, the *Pakistan Times* (itself critical of the authorities for failing to meet the expectations of Pakistan's 'common man') commented in an editorial from May 1948 that

> The Note of Dissent ... draws its inspiration from Islamic history and traditions; and after a study of the conditions of Sind agriculture and review of land reforms in Western countries, it recommends the complete nationalization of land. The only justification for what time and money was spent on the Hari Committee seems to be this minority report.[112]

Masud – who wrote that the condition of the *haris* was deplorable, differences between landlord and tenant too severe and unfair and, therefore, land reforms absolutely necessary – called instead for the complete abolition of *zamindari* system, the expropriation of land from landlords with minimum compensation and that absolute ownership of land should be vested in the state. In the process, he located his argument squarely in the context of the post-Partition challenges facing Pakistan:

> The shortage of agricultural labour in Sind has been due to the existing insecurity of the tenant, this factor in turn has discouraged immigration, and now the shortage of labour has been accentuated by the exodus of about two lacs of Koli, Bhil and Mainghwar *haris* [non-Muslims]. Tharparkar district is threated with a big drop in the cultivated area this year and consequently a serious fall in food production as well as State revenues. The refugees could fill this gap, but they are prevented from settling in Sind by the complete insecurity of tenure and hostile surroundings. A situation such as this threatens the prosperity and productivity of the whole of Sind and in Sind's own interest more than anything else, it is necessary that a new approach should be made to the problem. By the expropriation of *zamindars* and the creation of peasant proprietorship Sind will not only solve the problem of its 20 lacs *haris* but also help the cause of refugee resettlement on a very large scale, which is the foremost problem of Pakistan.[113]

Protest against the withholding of Masud's Note of Dissent surfaced quickly, with pressure on the Sindh Provincial Muslim League and district League committees to pass resolutions demanding its publication. Students also agitated. Even the president of the All-Pakistan Muslim League, Chaudhry Khaliquzzaman, personally appealed to the

---

[112] *Pakistan Times*, 21 May 1948.
[113] Masud, 'Hari Committee Report Note of Dissent', p. 98.

Sindh governor, urging him to intervene to make the provincial government yield to public demand.[114] With a new Sindh chief minister in post (Yusuf Haroon) who lacked the customary landed connections, the Sindhi authorities finally published Masud's 'Note' in June 1949. As its opening statement made clear, it represented a full-bodied attack on the status quo: '[*Haris*] are human beings, and as such, rational animals and though they drudge like domesticated animals, they enjoy no privileges of rationality, nor any rights of human beings'.[115] From the perspective of local Communist Party activists, the problem of tenancy reform was one part of a bigger set of issues confronting people in Sindh:

The rise and fall of Ministers in Sind, the disastrous floods that could have been prevented, the practice of smuggling food grains across the Borders leading to food shortage in a surplus province, the bribery and corruption rampant in the administration, the bungling policy in settling refugees, the wide-spread chaos that is haunting the province, all these things are not accidental but form an integral part of the Zamindari system, and can only end with it.[116]

Included among the demands now made the Hari Committee were 'education to be made universal, free and compulsory', and 'new elections to be held on the basis of adult franchise'.[117] Indeed, a convention organized by *hari* leaders in Karachi in March 1949 highlighted this lack of representation:

How the voice of the Hari has been suppressed could best be judged from the fact that in the House elected under the present Constitution [the Sindh Legislative Assembly], 30 lakhs of Haris do not have one single representative in the Assembly whom they could call their own. The 30,000 Trade Union Workers of Sind have only one representative, Qazi Mujtaba … Not that Hari does not have a vote but what with the fear of the Zamindar and the canvasing for votes done on behalf of the Zamindars by mobilizing Pirs and Maulvies [*sic*]. How can the Hari exercise his vote freely, under these circumstances?[118]

At the end of the meeting, its president – flushed with excitement – declared that the *haris* were not prepared to give up the Red Flag: 'it was the flag of the oppressed [and] as long as exploitation continued, so long would the Red Flag be the symbol of their struggle against oppression'.[119]

---

[114] *Dawn*, 4 January 1949.   [115] Masud, 'Hari Committee Report Note of Dissent', p. 1.
[116] 'Hari Movement', *The Communist Party of West Pakistan in Action*, Published by the Deputy Inspector-General of Police, C.I.D., Punjab, Lahore (Lahore: Superintendent Government Printing, Punjab, 1952), p. 129.
[117] Ibid., p. 130.   [118] Abdul Khaliq Azad, 'Sind Haris on the March', ibid., p. 143.
[119] Ibid., p. 145.

In March 1949, a Sind Tenancy Bill had been published with the stated intention of regulating the rights and liabilities of tenants and landlords in the province.[120] At a government-sponsored joint 'Hari-Zamindar Conference' in April, *hari* representatives demanded hereditary rights to the land that they ploughed, with no time qualifications. They also wanted to substitute *batai* (crop sharing) with cash rents, and demanded the abolition of forced labour (*begar*).[121] In 1950, more than 15,000 peasants from across the province gathered in Karachi where they conducted a 'sit-in' outside the Sindh Legislative Assembly, and such was the strength of support that assembly members were not allowed to leave the building. In the event, though the Sindh Assembly passed tenancy legislation in 1950, its implementation was delayed, and by March 1951, the recently re-appointed Sindh Chief Minister M. A. Khuhro felt sufficiently confident to declare – much to the surprise of many of his contemporaries – that Sindh's *hari* problem only existed in 'some newspaper offices'.[122] According to press reports of his speech, 'what Mr Khuhro did not say [was] that he was determined to make his "poor zamindars" richer and the "rich hari" poorer'.[123] At a well-attended public meeting of Sindh *haris* held soon afterwards in Hyderabad, speaker after speaker criticized the Sindh Legislative Assembly, describing it as a body that represented only vested interests, while peasants who comprised the vast majority of the province's population remained completely unrepresented in it: 'Nothing short of the immediate dissolution of the Assembly and new elections on the basis of universal franchise would satisfy the peasants'.[124] All the same, as *hari* leader Hyder Bux Jatoi pointed out, 'in spite of 15 years of service of the Hari Committee for the cause of *haris*, [*haris* were] still at the mercy of *zamindars*, with no proprietary interest in the land'.[125]

In February 1952, a Hari Committee deputation, headed by Jatoi, presented its latest set of demands to the Sindh governor, Din Mohammad. These included proposed amendments to the Sind Tenancy Act, and rights for *haris* on land that they were presently cultivating.[126] In response, the governor assured *hari* representatives that they would not be hindered in their political work as long as it remained constitutional. The following day, Jatoi and his fellow *hari* leader, Abdul

---

[120] *Sind Government Gazette*, 3 March 1949.
[121] 'Haris Want Hereditary Rights in Land and Substitution of Batai System by Cash Rent', *Dawn*, 23 April 1949.
[122] *Dawn*, 28 March 1951.   [123] *Civil and Military Gazette*, 30 March 1951.
[124] *Civil and Military Gazette*, February 1951.
[125] *Civil and Military Gazette*, 30 March 1951.   [126] *Dawn*, 3 February 1952.

Kadir, reiterated their call for the abolition of *zamindari*, without compensation. But they were also careful to assure refugee agriculturalists of their 'fraternal feelings', and accused *zamindars* of creating differences between local *haris* and *muhajirs* (refugees).[127] In a conference held in Umarkot in July, reportedly attended by nearly 20,000 people and presided over by Faiz Ahmed Faiz, then Secretary of the All-Pakistan Confederation of Labour, the Sind Hari Federation once more issued its call for the abolition of the *zamindar* system without compensation and the 'allotment of land to toilers of the soil' on an equitable basis.[128]

A report on 'Muslim tribes' in Sindh compiled by US officials in 1955 underlined the continuing predicament of the province's *haris*. The Sind Tenancy Act may have represented a first step towards greater protection for their interests (by granting permanent tenancy rights [*harep*] as long as the same plot of land had been cultivated for three consecutive years), but in practice, 'according to the law, a *hari* [had to] apply for his *harep* rights, and due to unawareness of the law or fear of the landlord, not 5 per cent of the *haris* have gained [them] since the passage of the Tenancy Act'.[129] Furthermore, as another – earlier – report had pointed out, the legislation anyway contained loopholes that 'allowed the landholder to follow the letter if not the spirit of the law', which in the case of Sindh was 'emasculated by evasive language', and so the passage of the legislation there, rather than strengthening their rights, had led to the 'widespread eviction of tenants'.[130]

The creation of Pakistan, as reflected in developments in Sindh during the post-Independence period, heightened the significance of other kinds of identity that were not linked quite so directly to being or not being a Muslim. In the scramble for resources that Partition generated, dividing lines were often more complex than a simple 'Muslim' versus 'non-Muslim'. As demonstrated by the desire to integrate the Hur followers of the Pir Pagaro into mainstream society, and likewise the struggles concerning land rights by the province's exploited *haris*, discussion about material entitlement – in particular that on offer on the ground in what had become Pakistan – could be inflected by expectations about the impact of Independence on people's everyday lives and what over the longer run this meant for their position as equal citizens within the new state.

---

[127] *Dawn*, 4 February 1952.   [128] *Dawn*, 11 July 1952.
[129] 'Information on Sind Muslim Tribes, and Other Groups', Despatch 765, 23 May 1955, 350.00/5-2355 USNA.
[130] 'The Problem of Land Reform in Pakistan', 6 September 1951, 702.5/9-651 USNA.

Conclusion

As this chapter has explored, not only were certain communities in places such as UP and Sindh excluded from typical frameworks of citizenship rights in postcolonial India and Pakistan, but also the latter were sometimes established to marginalize them deliberately, requiring them to seek out alternative methods for lobbying government. Despite this, Muslims, Dalits and other groups of people in India still rallied around the presumed logic of legal rights contained within the 1950 Constitution, alongside the implications of affirmative action that were contained within its Fundamental Rights. Even though 'secularism' was not placed directly in the preamble of the Constitution until 1976, yet still there was a sense among Muslim leaders in UP, for instance, that Indian legislators were – in the main – striving for a multicultural plural society. The fragility of processes of secularization, however (for which, as Mushirul Hasan has argued, few strove in reality),[131] meant that moments of mass communal strife, especially during those involving cross-border tensions, could raise the spectre of a removal of rights, or an attack on the remnants of Indo-Islamic culture in India. This also meant that Muslims in India were required to devise careful and more strategically limited ways of promoting group rights.

In some ways, therefore, the normative and universal rights of citizens in both India and Pakistan were framed as forms of protection against communities that were unsettled and disadvantaged, perhaps marked as 'backward' or indeed sometimes as 'criminal'. This made the working (and prior to that, the working out) of differentiated rights very difficult. We might relate this unfolding reality to what Nivedita Menon describes as clashing moral universes of 'rights', which are ineffectively adjudicated by law.[132] For the most part, our excluded or 'hidden' citizens in both India and Pakistan devised alternative means for asserting or promoting rights – new kinds of lobbying organizations, alternative forms of petitions, sit-ins and other kinds of mass protest, through which to try to make their voices heard. In the lead-up to Independence, this tactic could involve unusual short-term strategic alliances, such as that between Ambedkar and the Muslim League in the late 1930s.[133] But in the main, after August 1947 and in the late 1940s and early 1950s, we see particular forms of associational politics emerging in the cities and countryside of

---

[131] Hasan, *Legacy of a Divided Nation*, p. 145.
[132] Nivedita Menon, 'State/Gender/Community: Citizenship in Contemporary India', *Economic and Political Weekly* 33, 5 (1998), pp. 3–10.
[133] Chairez-Garza, 'Bound Hand and Foot', p. 4.

UP and Sindh, which tied more general issues of food and civil supply, or government corruption, to specific questions of identity and belonging. Finally, we might likewise relate these activities to the very specific spaces and neighbourhoods of these places themselves, and the media used to report on them. Such 'hidden citizens', while being generally excluded from the normal frameworks of rights enjoyed by those with access to political influence, were beginning – as early as the first decade following Independence – to carve out new or reconfigured repertoires of politics in our specific locales within Pakistan and India.

Epilogue and Conclusion

On 26 December 2017 while attending a political function in Kukanur in Karnataka, the Union Minister Anant Kumar Hegde stated that the BJP would 'change the Constitution', and especially in relation to its references to 'secularism'.[1]

Call 1135 if anyone sees any sort of rigging/paid voters/snatching of NICs or any sort of UNFAIR proceedings on 25 July. Call this number immediately, be responsible, play your part as an *honest citizen.*[2] (emphasis added)

In *Boundaries of Belonging*, we have considered how far the rights of and the concepts surrounding the 'citizen' in both India and Pakistan, and the promotion of those rights, were affected by what was happening across the new border in the years following Independence and Partition. We have explored this at the state level, but also considered what it meant from the perspective of two localities, UP and Sindh, that came to be closely connected, thanks to the protracted impact of Partition on understandings about citizenship, rights and belonging across the subcontinent. And the connection continued, though the form taken by it has varied, as the second half of the twentieth century wore on. This relationship, we would argue, can be seen perhaps most clearly in the ways in which both new states subsequently managed the promises of 'universal' citizenship rights set against the realities of diverse and varied group claims upon them. In many ways, however, this tension is not easily captured in most general works on the concept of citizenship. The problem in much of the literature, as recognized by Will Kymlicka, is that 'most Western political theorists have operated within an idealized model of the polis in which

---

[1] Maya Sharma, '"We Are Here to Change the Constitution" Says Union Minister in New Controversy', *NDTV*, 26 December 2017, www.ndtv.com/india-news/we-are-here-to-change-the-constitution-says-union-minister-anant-kumar-hegde-in-new-controversy-1792197 (accessed December 2018).
[2] Advice to Pakistani voters during the general elections of July 2018, shared widely on social media. (NIC = national identity card.)

fellow citizens share a common descent, language and culture'.[3] Both India and (to a lesser extent) Pakistan shared this tradition but both also incorporated a statutory concept of differentiated or group rights, which has been implemented (in the case of India certainly) more clearly since the 1990s, and in Pakistan to different degrees at various points following its creation. This epilogue will summarize the main arguments of this book, following a survey of some of the contemporary outcomes flowing out of our period of focus in the mid-twentieth century.

There are pressing contemporary reasons for examining the immediate context in which constitutional experiments and ideas about citizenship and rights unfolded in South Asia in the late 1940s and 1950s. In recent decades, the constitutions of both countries have come under fresh scrutiny, connected in large part with ongoing challenges to the political status quo. In twenty-first-century India, citizens are exploring and critiquing their constitutional framework in new ways, as reflected in the proliferation of rights-based movements that have come to prominence since 2010, especially those centred on women, sexuality, ethnicity and anti-corruption. On the other hand, since 2014 and again in 2019, with the election victory of the Bharatiya Janata Party (BJP) in India, particular constitutional rights, and the legal frameworks that arise from them, have been subject to new contestations of its pluralistic representation of Indian society. In Pakistan, the state has been challenged in much the same fashion by well-supported citizens campaigns that range from those focussed on enduring problems of corruption and disadvantage to others that unequivocally oppose or defend the rights of minorities and women. Almost since their inception, though in ways that have varied by region and community, levels of popular engagement have generated legal activism, out of which civil society initiatives have emerged, often in particular localities, on both sides of the border.

Pivotal developments in South Asian politics now revolve around an array of issues-based movements that resonate with the discussions on citizenship and rights that took place following Independence. The growth of anti-corruption movements between 2005 and 2012 across the subcontinent, echoing those of the 1940s and 1950s, now push for the exposure of high-level political corruption and greater access for citizens to information on day-to-day administration. Particularly since 2012, in the case of India, women's security and debates about a possible Uniform Civil Code have become key battlegrounds for political parties across the spectrum, challenging the constraints on women's rights in

---

[3] Will Kymlicka, *Multicultural Citizenship: A Liberal Theory of Minority Rights* (Oxford: Oxford University Press, 1996), p. 2.

practice, while in Pakistan, supposedly woman-friendly legislation continues to fail to address the myriad problems that plague women's lives
there. From these social movements, an array of other rights agendas
have emerged – including environmental challenges and rights around
disability, themselves affected or implicated by the rapid globalization of
rights movements, as communications technologies have developed in
the twenty-first century.

Rights movements have, of course, transformed in response to the
changing nature of globalization, the weakening of the nation state
and the growth of transnational corporate power. Globalization consequently has limited but also created opportunities for human rights
movements that have been able to draw on frameworks such as the
United Nations Declaration of Human Rights.[4] This has led, in turn,
to what some scholars have described as 'transnational advocacy
networks'.[5] Counter-hegemonic movements originating largely from
the Global South have posed new challenges to national legal frameworks, as well as highlighted the need for multi-sited ethnography.[6] Since
the turn of the millennium, they have tended to converge in anti-
globalization citizens' movements operating on both the right and the
left of the political spectrum. These have implicated NGOs that,
although often synonymous with protest, have also sometimes helped
to channel and control protest movements, and justify the rolling back of
the welfare state.[7] India's Dalit movement and that of adivasis and
DNTs, for instance, has become more clearly international since the
1990s, with the global expression of rights. Conferences of the international Dalit diaspora have been formed since 1998 in Canada, Malaysia
and the UK,[8] while the United Nations Human Rights Commission has
made some interventions around the recognition of Dalit rights.

Interestingly, frequent reference to the early formative periods of
constitutional development is used to bolster contemporary politics and

---

[4] For a theoretical discussion of these expanding frameworks, see John A. Guidry, Michael
D. Kennedy and Mayer N. Zald, *Globalizations and Social Movements: Culture, Power and
the Transnational Public Sphere* (Ann Arbor: University of Michigan Press, 2000),
pp. 2–12.
[5] Boaventura de Sousa Santos and Cesar A. Rodriguez-Garavito, *Law and Globalization
from Below: Towards a Cosmopolitan Legality* (Cambridge: Cambridge University
Press, 2004).
[6] Ibid., p. 4.
[7] Marjorie Mayo, *Global Citizens: Social Movements and the Challenge of Globalization* (New
York: Zed Books, 2005), pp. 155–6.
[8] Vivek Kumar, *India's Roaring Revolution: Dalit Assertions and New Horizons* (Delhi:
Gagandeep Publications, 2006); B. V. Muralidhar et al. (eds.), *The Dynamics of Change
and Continuity in the Era of Globalization: Voices from the Margins* (New Delhi: Sunrise
Publications, 2009).

activism in today's South Asia.[9] In political debates in India, the significance of the 1950 Constitution continues to be most clearly articulated in the complex but ubiquitous reference to the legacy of B. R. Ambedkar, and the championing of differentiated rights. Even though the election of a right-wing Hindu nationalist government in 2014 and 2019 represented a fateful break from decades of Congress dominance in Delhi, Narendra Modi's BJP regime makes explicit rhetorical connections with the late 1940s/early 1950s Congress heyday, with the iconography of Vallabhai Patel celebrated in the form of a world record-breaking gigantic iron statue being the most obtrusive example.[10] In present-day Pakistan, the context may look different but the rhetoric can be remarkably similar, involving often a harking back to what Pakistan's early political leaders are deemed to have promised but failed to deliver. Power may have been transferred from one civilian government to another in the 2013 and 2018 general elections, but the public's trust in the democratic process remains low, and scepticism about the role of the military pulling political strings behind the scenes endures: as one newspaper columnist in 2018 explained, 'mimicking democracy and providing a façade of elections cannot develop a political dynamic including budgetary allocations to redress the long-standing grievances and deep-rooted disabilities of the people. Despite electoral swings and wobbles, such elections merely reflect and reinforce existing structures of repression and power, which are making Pakistan a political dystopia'.[11] A satirical piece in the run-up to the 2018 national polls similarly advised political leaders 'scampering' to gain the public's trust, 'Do not even worry about making any promises. If you can ridicule the other party's promises repeatedly then it will seem like you have an agenda. Better yet you can mask your political motives under a veneer of social causes'.[12]

---

[9] Vinay Sitapati, 'What Anna Hazare and the Indian Middle-Classes Say about Each Other', *Economic and Political Weekly* 46, 30 (23 July 2011), pp. 39–44.

[10] The monumental statue of Vallabhbhai Patel has been constructed facing the Narmada Dam, 3.2 kilometre away, on a river island called Sadhu Bet, in the Indian state of Gujarat. It is twice the size of the US Statue of Liberty in New York, costing nearly Rs. 3,000 *crore*. Most importantly, it has led to the displacement of a number of adivasi villages in the region. On 31 October 2018, the date of its inauguration, this resulted in a protest among adivasis and migrant workers. See, 'A Statue of Unity in a Gujarat Deeply Divided', *Live Mint* 31 October 2018, www.livemint.com/Politics/QnAJqGsmyuFTTwgjEYOWgN/Sardar-Patel-Statue-of-Unity-inauguration-Narendra-Modi.html (accessed December 2018).

[11] Ashraf Jehangir Qazi, 'Elections and Movements', *Dawn*, 5 May 2018, www.dawn.com/news/1405769 (accessed December 2018).

[12] 'How to Win the 2018 Elections', *The Herald*, 25 January 2018, https://herald.dawn.com/news/1153986 (accessed December 2018).

As we have explored in *Boundaries of Belonging*, from the early 1930s –
well before Independence – caste interest groups in places like UP had
begun to lobby government for special consideration in administrative
appointments, with direct reference to putative constitutional changes.
These differences and early applications of India's 1950 Constitution
allowed a number of rights organizations, especially Dalit and adivasi, to
evoke it as a 'bill of rights' in support of their struggles. Historians
and political scientists have rightly located in these earlier responses
the roots of local mobilizations that, over recent decades, have used the
Constitution and concepts of legal rights to challenge traditional caste
hierarchies.[13] While some have argued that the rise of caste-based party
politics threatens the ability of the state to govern,[14] more common has
been the suggestion that, since the electoral decline of the Congress,
democracy has instead been strengthened by the more widespread
participation of low-status and marginalized communities.[15] We would
argue that current ideas about a 'crisis of governability' are similarly
based in historically erroneous assumptions about state control and
political dominance occurring in the post-1947 South Asia: in particular,
that citizens' movements, structured in some cases around group and
ethnicized concepts of rights, were already subverting, challenging and
channelling state hegemony by the early 1950s, not just in India but also
in Pakistan.

However, as highlighted in our Introduction, it is only relatively
recently that historians have started to incorporate anthropological meth-
odologies for exploring the workings of the state, and citizen engagement
with it, in South Asia.[16] This methodological shift has accompanied –
even prompted – fresh theoretical and empirical reflections on the liminal
quotidian interactions between the state, its representatives and its
presumed citizens.[17] Not only does rethinking along these lines represent
the basis for a potential history of citizenship 'from below'; it also shapes

[13] See, for instance, Hugo Gorringe, *Untouchable Citizens: Dalit Movements and
Democratization in Tamil Nadu* (New Delhi: Sage, 2005); Christophe Jaffrelot, *India's
Silent Revolution: The Rise of the Lower Castes in North India* (New York: Columbia
University Press, 2003).
[14] Atul Kohli, *Democracy and Discontent: India's Growing Crisis of Governability* (Cambridge:
Cambridge University Press, 1990), pp. 3–5.
[15] Gorringe, *Untouchable Citizens*, pp. 22–3.
[16] C. J. Fuller and Veronique Benei (eds.), *The Everyday State and Society in Modern India*
(New Delhi: Social Science Press, 2000); Akhil Gupta, 'Blurred Boundaries: The
Discourse of Corruption, the Culture of Politics, and the Imagined State', *American
Ethnologist* 22, 2 (May 1995), pp. 375–402.
[17] See Yasmin Khan, *The Great Partition: The Making of India and Pakistan* (London: Yale
University Press, 2007); William Gould, *Bureaucracy, Community and Influence: Society
and the State in India, 1930–1960s* (London: Routledge, 2011); Jonathan Saha, *Law,*

and alters existing views of the state, in terms of how and how far the state's administrative and executive structures are contested, and produced, by various imaginaries of the 'public' that circulate and feed back into law making.[18] What applies to the administration applies even more so to judicial and electoral politics. Work on the law in India, for instance, has departed from its previous more traditional approaches towards the 1950 Constitution as a statement of rights and legal structures, viewing it instead as an edifice that provides the foundations for legal dispute, challenge and reinterpretation.[19] Its legal core now serves to empower various gendered political interests that reach back to the late nineteenth century,[20] but which were transformed by way of political devolution in the interwar years.[21] The common experiences bound up in India and Pakistan's immediate post-Independence elections (national in the case of India, at the provincial level and below in Pakistan) likewise underline how far the process of creating and implementing universal suffrage drove popular responses to constitutional change. Changes in historical scholarship on South Asia (and, more specifically, approaches to the state there) that have emerged since the turn of the twenty-first century – in the form of explorations of law, the everyday state, civil society, citizenship and democracy – have thus directly shaped the context for and content of our book.

In sanctioning what still remains probably the world's most intricate set of constitutional arrangements, India's early postcolonial rulers oversaw the drawing up and implementation of a document which, in due course, became the cornerstone of a range of different rights movements.

Disorder and the Colonial State: Corruption in Burma c.1900 (Basingstoke: Palgrave Macmillan, 2013).

[18] Joel S. Migdal, *State-in-Society: Studying How States and Societies Transform and Constitute One Another* (New York: Cambridge University Press, 2001); Joel S. Migdal (ed.), *Boundaries and Belonging: States and Societies in the Struggle to Shape Identities and Local Practices* (New York: Cambridge University Press, 2004); Michael Warner, *Publics and Counterpublics* (Cambridge, MA: MIT Press, 2002).

[19] Rohit De, *A People's Constitution: The Everyday Life of Law in the Indian Republic* (Princeton, NJ: Princeton University Press, 2018), pp. 1–25; Rohit De, 'Rebellion, Dacoity, and Equality: The Emergence of the Constitutional Field in Postcolonial India', *Comparative Studies of South Asia, Africa and the Middle East* 34, 2 (2014), pp. 260–78. This is also clear in work that has explored the quotidian (politically mediated) responses to East African constitutions. Devra C. Moehler, 'Participation and Support for the Constitution in Uganda', *Journal of Modern African Studies* 44, 2 (2006), pp. 275–308.

[20] Indrani Chatterjee, *Gender, Slavery and Law in Colonial India* (Delhi: Oxford University Press, 1999).

[21] Mrinalini Sinha, *Gender and Nation* (Washington, DC: American Historical Association, 2006); Eleanor Newbigin, *The Hindu Family and the Emergence of Modern India: Law, Citizenship and Community* (Cambridge: Cambridge University Press, 2013).

As a consequence, the 1950 Constitution can be viewed as a document that stated certain universal rights from the outset, but which also took into account the range of specific sectional groups whose social disadvantages required a degree of state intervention. Accordingly, India's constitutional framework did not necessarily generate a milieu of liberal 'benign neglect',[22] but (in theory at least) promoted systems of affirmative action, albeit hesitantly at first. Unlike most attempts at affirmative action elsewhere, however, these measures did not turn out to be temporary in nature or in practice; rather, they sought to address deep historical inequalities over an indefinite timeframe. The Indian approach in practice persisted despite the fact that the Nehruvian rhetoric of social equality focussed on standard 'universally held' ideas of citizens' rights within an idealized *polis* – what Ornit Shani and others have termed a 'Liberal' concept of citizenship.[23] The failure of the first Backward Classes Commission of 1953, in the end, was premised on the idea that 'backwardness' as a condition could not be entirely explained by caste, but rather as the limitations of modernity.[24] The clear expectation was that as Indian society transformed in the years ahead, so too would the inequalities of caste be reduced. Commission reporters argued that

[the] inferiority complex cultivated by the backward communities leads them to believe that they are, and will always remain, deficient in certain qualities, and therefore, they need the backing of reservation. Experience in the past proves that reservations come in the way of healthy emulation and those who learnt to depend on reservation are oftentimes not alert enough to improve their quality.[25]

In India, since the late 1970s, there has been a clear shift towards caste-based political challenges to the political status quo. Though the concept of 'scheduled castes and scheduled tribes' (SC/ST) that was reinforced in the Indian Constitution had its roots in earlier constitutional formulations, the idea of 'backward classes' (BCs) was not

---

[22] Nathan Glazer, *Affirmative Discrimination: Ethnic Inequality and Public Policy* (New York: Basic Books, Inc., 1975).

[23] Ornit Shani, 'Concepts of Citizenship in India and the "Muslim Question"', *Modern Asian Studies* 44, 1 (2010), pp. 145–73; Anupama Roy, *Mapping Citizenship in India* (Oxford: Oxford University Press, 2010); Filiz Kartal, 'Liberal and Republican Conceptualizations of Citizenship: A Theoretical Inquiry', *Turkish Public Administration Annual* 27–28 (January 2001), pp. 101–30.

[24] M. S. Srinivas (ed.), *Caste: Its Twentieth Century Avatar* (New Delhi: Penguin, 2000); Nomita Yadav, 'Other Backward Classes: Then and Now', *Economic and Political Weekly* 37, 44/45 (2–15 November 2002), pp. 4495–500; Christophe Jaffrelot, 'The Impact of Affirmative Action in India: More Political Than Socioeconomic', *India Review* 5, 12 (2006), pp. 173–89.

[25] Government of India, *Report of the Backward Classes Commission*, 3 vols. (Shimla: Government of India Press, 1955), p. viii.

reignited until the formation of the Janata government in India in 1977.[26] This coalition of opposition parties, which came to power on a wave of anti-Congress sentiment, set up the Mandal Commission in 1979 with a mandate to 'identify the socially or educationally backward classes' of India. Its 1980 proposals for 27 per cent reservations for BCs (which it estimated made up 52 per cent of India's total population) was eventually implemented, amid great controversy, in 1992 by the then minority Congress government.[27] From the mid-1990s, the Dalit movement proliferated into a range of different political and nongovernmental forums, managing to form ministries in some cases. Dalit movements such as Bahujan Samaj Party were especially successful in UP – one of the places on which *Boundaries of Belonging* has focussed – but a similar process was at work in other Indian states including Tamil Nadu (Viduthalai Chiruthaigal Katchi), Maharashtra (Republican Party) and Bihar (Lok Janshakti Party).

The contemporary political/electoral basis for the Dalit and adivasi movements emerging across India in the recent past, however, does not represent the full and arguably more complex historical picture of 'non-political' movements that have sprung from the grassroots. And it is these that connect back, more clearly, to the earliest historical developments of caste-based civic movements in the wake of Independence. These include, among others, the Backward and Minority Castes Employees Federation (BAMCEF) that has promoted a range of non-political social organizations at local levels, and the Bharatiya Dalit Panthers.[28] These groups are rather more like older pressure groups operating in earlier decades, working on lobbying administrations from below, rather than depending entirely on the patronage of leading Dalit parties. Many of the urban-based groups in UP cities such as Kanpur, Allahabad and Lucknow concentrate on conversion of Dalits to Buddhism, but in some cases (e.g. under the leadership of Dhaniram Panther) have also furthered the rights of Dalit state employees, and supported communities in 'getting work done' with the local administration.[29] In Western India too, grassroots Dalit movements, for example among Mangs, have been actively instrumental in campaigning against caste-based

---

[26] For the role of the courts in this process of recognition of Backward Class categories, see Marc Gallanter, 'Who Are the Other Backward Classes?', *Economic and Political Weekly*, 13, 43/44 (28 October 1978), pp. 1812–28.

[27] For the complete text of the Mandal Commission report, see *National Commission for Backward Classes: A Statutory Body under the Ministry of Social Justice & Empowerment*, www.ncbc.nic.in/User_Panel/UserView.aspx?TypeID=1161 (accessed December 2018).

[28] Nicolas Jaoul, 'Political and "Non-Political" Means in the Dalit Movement', in *Political Process in Uttar Pradesh: Identity, Economic Reforms, and Governance*, ed. Sudha Pai (Delhi: Pearson Longman, 2007), pp. 191–220.

[29] Ibid.

violence.[30] In this sense, perhaps just as durable as Dalit political representation, have been networks of Dalit employees in the administration – a pattern that was recognized in Dalit rights movements in early independent India.

One of the most prominent non-political rights movements to emerge in India alongside SC and ST organizations has been the Denotified Tribes Rights Action Group (DNT RAG), initiated in 1998 under the leadership of Ganesh Devi, Mahasveta Devi and Laxman Gaikwad, also involving a range of grassroots arts movements, including most prominently a street theatre and film-making group, Budhan Theatre. The latter, led by Dakxin Chhara Bajrange based in Ahmedabad, has, again since the early 2000s, consistently lobbied the authorities, especially around the differentiated rights of people whom this group self-categorizes as 'DNTs' in different states across India: some fall within the category of SC or ST while others are contained within official schedules of OBC. The DNT RAG have used street performance and protest campaigns to promote a particular vision of Indian citizenship which shines a spotlight on the historical injustice done to these adivasi groups in urban public spheres.[31] From the outset, it highlighted key instances of police brutality and custodial deaths,[32] most famously, the case of Budhan Sabar who died in police custody in February 1998 in West Bengal.[33] The DNT RAG claims to be unique – not quite an NGO, nor a pressure group on government, but more a movement – and it promotes a wide array of causes that all connect around the specific marginalization of ex-Criminal Tribe communities as Indian citizens. Rather than attempting to critique directly the fundamental assumptions of state power in relation to such marginal communities, the movement bases its activity on pragmatic Ambedkarite approaches to the role of the state in promoting group rights in today's India.[34]

[30] Suryakhant Whagmore, *Civility against Caste: Dalit Politics and Citizenship in Western India* (New Delhi: Sage, 2013), pp. 62–90.

[31] Caleb Johnston and Dakxin Bajrange, 'Street Theatre as Democratic Politics in Ahmedabad', *Antipode* 46, 2 (2014), pp. 455–76.

[32] See, for example Dilip D'Souza, 'De-Notified Tribes: Still "Criminal"?', *Economic and Political Weekly* 34, 51 (18–24 December 1999), pp. 3576–8.

[33] Ganesh Devy, 'For a Nomad Called Thief', in *Towards a Transcultural Future: Literature and Human Rights in a 'Post'-Colonial World*, eds. Peter H. Marsden and Geoffrey V. Davis (Amsterdam: Rodopi B.V., 2004), pp. 282–3.

[34] William Gould, Sarah Gandee and Dakxin Bajrange, 'Settling the Citizen, Settling the Nomad: "Habitual Offenders", Rebellion and Civic Consciousness in Western India, 1938–1952', *Modern Asian Studies*, http://eprints.whiterose.ac.uk/144745/, 2019. Its work feeds into a range of other regional lobbying organizations working for DNTs to promote a sub-quota of reservations: The DNT Adhikar Manch from Gujarat, the Lok Dhara from Maharashtra and the All Indian Od Welfare Sangh from Karnataka.

In Pakistan, the story of citizenship and rights has followed a somewhat different track, thanks to the changing nature and composition of society there since 1947. As far as the position of non-Muslims has been concerned, the creation of Bangladesh in 1971 meant that Pakistan was more than halved in size population-wise, and the majority (though by no means all) of its non-Muslims (Hindu Bengalis) faced the future as citizens of a different state. In what remained of Pakistan (its western wing), Zulfikar Ali Bhutto's Pakistan People's Party (PPP) government played the religion card as a way of reinforcing the shared identity of Pakistan's remaining citizens. The replacement 1973 Constitution declared Islam to be the state religion, even if the meaning attached to this was different to how it would be interpreted by the Islamization policies of General Zia ul Haq in the late 1970s and 1980s. The fallout from Bhutto's move, intended to see off his religio-political critics, included the creation of a new category of differentiated citizenship on the one hand, and added challenges for existing non-Muslim minorities on the other. The Ahmadiyya community, which had been targeted since the 1950s on the grounds of denying the finality of the Prophet Muhammad, was now declared constitutionally 'non-Muslim', its members (like others categorized as 'non-Muslim') excluded from the full, undifferentiated, benefits of citizenship. According to a 2011 report on Pakistan's minority communities which counted Ahmadis within this category,

It remains a cause for worry that the Pakistani state still expects key affirmations of citizenship, such as applying for a passport, to include a deliberate othering of Ahmadis, by disavowing them in a separate clause. While this clause has repeatedly come up for discussion for removal in Parliament, the religious lobby has been successful in silencing its critics. However, the notion that it is essential to sign an anti-Ahmadi clause on forms used for issuing or renewing passports is not entirely correct. A small, but growing number of citizens have reportedly refused to sign the clause, yet succeeded in obtaining a passport.[35]

Later under Zia and the regimes that followed, the position of Ahmadis became steadily more difficult. Efforts to reverse the marginalization of the Ahmadiyya community have proved ineffective, and its second-class status remains a feature of twenty-first-century Pakistani society and politics. More generally, accusations of blasphemy and vigilante reprisals have featured as a growing problem in Pakistan over the last two decades. High-profile cases include the murder of serving governor of Punjab Salman Taseer by a member of his police bodyguard in 2011 in revenge

[35] Mariam Faruqi, *A Question of Faith: A Report on the Status of Religious Minorities in Pakistan* (Islamabad: Jinnah Institute, 2011), p. 60, https://starfishasia.com/assets/Jinnah_Minority_Report20511-PDF.pdf.

for his support for Asia Bibi (a Christian woman sentenced to death in 2010 for blasphemy but controversially acquitted by the Supreme Court in 2018 on the grounds of material contradictions and inconsistent statements of the witnesses that the judges felt cast a shadow of doubt on the prosecution's version of facts),[36] the killing of Shahbaz Bhatti – Christian Cabinet member and outspoken critic of Pakistan's blasphemy laws – two months later and the arrest the following year of a Christian girl Rimsha Masih for allegedly burning pages from the Quran.[37]

In 2010, Pakistan ratified Article 27 of the International Convention on Civil and Political Rights (ICCPR), accepting the entitlement of minorities 'in community with the other members of their group, to enjoy their own culture, to profess and practice their own religion, or to use their own language'.[38] By then, however, Sindh, home to c. 95 per cent of Hindus still living in Pakistan, was already witnessing rising levels of tension and violence directed against the province's non-Muslims. General-turned-President Pervez Musharraf, meanwhile, had scrapped the controversial separate electorates introduced in 1980s by Zia according to which non-Muslims could only vote for candidates of their own religion to fill seats reserved for minorities in the national and provincial assemblies. But when Sudham Chand, a Hindu community leader who had led a local campaign in Sindh to oppose this system, was killed in broad daylight, Ramesh Lal, a member of the National Assembly, was prompted to comment that the restoration of the conventional electoral system was of little use if the minorities lacked security.[39] An All-Pakistan Minorities Alliance (APMA) was formed in 2002 in response to problems faced by minorities groups such as Christians, Ahmadis and Hindus. Other more specific organizations, such as the Pakistan Hindu Welfare Association (PHWA) and coalitions of Hindu *panchayats* (local councils of community elders) also became more active in local politics. But by the mid-2000s, frustrated at their lack of representation in the PHWA, a number of Dalit organizations had come together, including the Pakistan Dalit Forum, the Scheduled Castes Federation of Pakistan and the Pakistan Dalit Solidarity Network. Indeed, Dalit representatives

[36] On 4 January 2011, Taseer was assassinated at Kohsar Market in Islamabad by his bodyguard Mumtaz Qadri, who disagreed with Taseer's concerns about the implementation of Pakistan's existing blasphemy law.
[37] *Rimsha Masih v. Station House Officer*, Police Station Ramna, PLD 2013 Islamabad, www.ihc.gov.pk/Announcements/Judgements/Court1/W.P.%203172-Q-2012.pdf (accessed December 2018). Following her acquittal, Rimsha and her family were given permanent residency in Canada on humanitarian and compassionate grounds.
[38] Faruqi, *A Question of Faith*, p. 19.
[39] 'Hindus Feel the Heat in Pakistan', *BBC News*, 2 March 2007, http://news.bbc.co.uk/1/hi/world/south_asia/6367773.stm (accessed December 2018).

condemned the continuing reservation of seats as illegitimate on the basis that Musharraf's joint selection process did not differentiate sufficiently between caste Hindu and Dalit electorates.[40]

Political competition fuelled by competition for scarce resources, rather than religious difference, goes a long way towards explaining the rise in communal tension in Sindh. In Tharparkar, close to the border with India, around 80 per cent of its non-Muslims (who make up over half this district's population) are low caste or Dalit Meghwars, Kohlis and Bhils. Whenever there is drought, which has now become frequent thanks to the reduction in the flow of the Indus River and problems of salination, these agricultural workers travel to other districts that remain irrigated in search of food for themselves and fodder for their livestock. There, they are employed as temporary farm workers on the lands of powerful Muslim landlords. As Dalit rights activist Veerji Kohli explained in 2016, 'After a drought hits Thar Desert, these Dalits become internally displaced people. They walk hundreds of miles with their livestock, to find some employment as agricultural workers with a powerful Muslim landlord. But in many cases, work is forcibly extracted out of them; they are often not paid, and eventually, are pushed into bonded labour'.[41] Hindus in Sindh conventionally bury their dead, rather than cremating them (a choice usually attributed to the high costs

---

[40] Ghulam Hussain, 'Kohli-Peasant Activism in Naon Dumbalo, Lower Sindh: creating space for marginalized through multiple channels' (unpublished PhD thesis, Quaid-i-Azam University, Islamabad, 2014), p. 97. A notable exception to this pattern was the nomination of Pakistan's first Dalit woman senator, Krishna Kumari Kohli, by the PPP in March 2018. 'Born to a poor peasant, Jugno Kohli, in February 1979, Ms. Kohli and her family members spent nearly three years in a private jail owned by the landlord of Kunri of Umarkot district. She was a grade 3 student at the time when held captive. She was married to Lalchand at the age of 16, when she was studying in 9th grade. However, she pursued her studies and in 2013 she did masters in sociology from the Sindh University. She had joined the PPP as a social activist along with her brother [...] Ms. Kohli also actively participated and worked for the rights of downtrodden people of marginalized communities living in Thar and other areas'. See 'Pakistan Elects Its First Dalit Woman Senator', *The Hindu*, 5 March 2018, www.thehindu.com/news/international/krishna-kumari-kohli-pakistan-elects-its-first-dalit-woman-senator/article22923550.ece (accessed December 2018).

[41] Kohli was himself a bonded labourer in his childhood. After working with Mehergarh, an educational NGO, he started pursuing the cause of bonded labour and became a prominent human rights activist. But in 2017, he was arrested on charges of murder, something that he and his supporters vehemently denied, blaming the allegation on a dispute over land between Kohlis and local Muslims. According to a spokesperson for Mehergarh, Veerji had 'always resisted the feudal system' and 'when someone stands against the powerful feudal lords, he is bound to make enemies. A fake case has been registered against him for precisely this reason'. See 'Caste and Captivity: Dalit Suffering in Sindh', *Dawn*, 13 March 2016, www.dawn.com/news/1244684 (accessed December 2018).

involved in cremation), but while burial was often permitted in Muslim cemeteries in the past, more recently this practice has generated violent responses. Following the desecration of a Hindu grave in 2013, an official from the Pakistan Institute of Labour Education and Research (PILER)[42] commented that this incident was based on a 'political griev-ance' against the particular non-Muslim Bheel community involved, in particular because it had voted for a rival party in that year's general election.[43] Other controversies have included the kidnapping and con-version of young Dalit women, who are then married to Muslim men, often against their will. As a Hindu resident of Umerkot (Sindh) told Mariam Faruqi in 2011, 'Our temples are being vandalized and women being raped. Atrocities against us are increasing day-by-day. We won't get permanent jobs unless we convert to Islam. In Pakistan, we are subject to persecution and have to live our daily lives in fear'.[44]

Closely linked to the predicament of non-Muslims in Sindh has been the network of civil society organizations that have coalesced around the issue of land reforms. The Sindh Land Reform Movement (SLRM), comprising peasant groups and concerned NGOs, was formed in 2012 to challenge the 'virtual serfdom' of people working on the land in the province. At the time of the SLRM's founding, Sindh had the highest incidence of absolute landlessness, with 26 per cent or two million households falling into this category. As a result, debt-bondage was on the increase, with the precar-iousness of peasant livelihoods badly affected by widespread flooding across Sindh in 2010 and 2011. SLRM demands included the distribution of state land to 'bona fide' *haris* along the lines of proprietary legislation that was introduced in 2011 by the Punjab Government, with priority to be given to released bonded labourers and flood-affected people including women; and the issuing of formal land deeds to all rural residents, includ-ing *haris*, wage workers and sharecroppers. In particular, the SLRM called for an urgent review of the 1950 Sind Tenancy Act in order to bring it into line with current conditions in the Sindhi countryside, within the mean-time, steps were taken to compulsorily register all *haris*, establish *hari* courts and permit agricultural workers to form associations to conduct

---

[42] The Pakistan Institute of Labour Education & Research (PILER) was founded in 1982 by a group of concerned individuals from the trade union movement, academia and various other professions. In 1988, it established a formally designed research and training programme with regular workshops, courses and advocacy activities, http://piler.org.pk/ (accessed December 2018).

[43] 'Activists Protest against Desecration of Hindu Grave in Sindh', *Dawn*, 10 October 2013, www.dawn.com/news/1048799 (accessed December 2018).

[44] Sroop Chand Malhi, Hindu resident of Umerkot, Sindh, 2011, quoted in Faruqi, *A Question of Faith*, p. 2.

collective bargaining on their behalf.[45] Member organizations include the Pakistan Fisher Folk Forum[46], a registered civil society body formally founded in 1998 to work for the advancement of social, economic, cultural and political rights of fisherfolk and peasants more broadly in Pakistan, and the Bhangar Hari Sangat, which works to end the iniquitous practice of bonded labour in Sindh.[47] Across the border, in rural areas of India, landless labourer movements in Telangana led to the formation of Mahila Sanghams, which multiplied throughout the 1980s and 1990s. And in the north Indian hill areas of Garhwal and Kumaon, a forest protection drive developed over the same period – the Chipko movement.

Moving on to the theme of corruption, one of the most important ways in which the rights of the citizen was discussed in both India and Pakistan in the late 1940s and 1950s related to the idea of administrative and political venality. Then, the very notion of citizenship values was frequently juxtaposed to the idea of the defeat of 'old' colonial corruption on the one hand, and the need to maintain the values of 'national' service in the future, on the other. Patriotism was a core component of the anti-corruption rhetoric of those years. Discourses of corruption, accordingly, in the early postcolonial period, reflected both backwards and forwards in time. But if we accept that anti-corruption arises at particular moments when the idea of the citizen emerges in popular debate, then another such moment occurred much more recently in 2005, with the passage of the Right to Information Act in India. 'Right to Information' (RTI) movements in present-day India continue the much older tradition of investigations into local malfeasance and corruption, and have been built upon a particular notion of outdated bureaucratic practices. This can be seen, for instance, in the activities of workers' movements such as the Mazdoor Kisan Shakti Sangathan since the 1990s,[48] and in pressure for exploring public accountability using citizen activism, particularly around accessing public information.[49]

---

[45] 'Sindh Land Reforms Movement (SLRM) – A Civil Society Network', http://piler.org.pk/wp-content/uploads/2017/03/Sindh-Land-Reforms-Movement.pdf (accessed December 2018).

[46] Pakistan Fisher Folk Forum, http://pff.org.pk/ (accessed December 2018).

[47] Bhangar Hari Sangat, www.endslaverynow.org/bhandar-sangat (accessed December 2018).

[48] Rob Jenkins and Anne Marie Goetz, 'Accounts and Accountability: Theoretical Implications of the Right-to-Information Movement in India', *Third World Quarterly* 20, 3 (1999), pp. 603–22.

[49] Anne Marie Goetz and Rob Jenkins, 'Hybrid Forms of Accountability: Citizen Engagement in Institutions of Public Sector Over-Sight in India', *Public Management Review* 3, 3 (2001), pp. 363–83.

The notion of the 'citizen' that appears in these movements, especially since the launching of national-level protests, has linked the local with the national too, in ways that are not unlike those of the early years of independent India and Pakistan. Since 2005, most Indian political parties have included an anti-corruption plank in their manifestos and from 2012, a new political party was built explicitly on its agendas – the Aam Aadmi (Common Man) Party (AAP) – fixed on the idea of the 'ordinary' citizen. Arvind Kejriwal, its leader, styled himself as a 'common man' in his dress (the widespread customary use of a head-scarf) and in the party icon of the broom (with which to sweep the state clean). Kejriwal also expressed this 'common-ness' in his critique of the larger nexus between administration or politics and business. This latter critique, too, had its origins in the early post-Independence anti-corruption critiques within the Congress party. During both phases – the late 1940s/early 1950s and in contemporary India, as Jonathan Parry has argued – the very fact that anti-corruption protest surfaced, despite the apparent ubiquity of the phenomenon, suggests the long-standing internalization of citizenship values.[50] These values, as we have argued in *Boundaries of Belonging*, developed through the emergent phase of Indian and Pakistani citizenship, in which large-scale frameworks of civic values were key. These were also inherently relational ideas, in which contacts between citizens and the state (or '*aam log*' to coin the contemporary phrase) made repeated reference to minority communities belonging to the other state. In both places, importantly, they involved an implicit critique of the state, from a position of 'ordinariness' that connected back to a shared anti-colonial heritage. Since the 2000s, a range of NGOs have drawn on this heritage by critiquing levels of criminality in India's polit-ical institutions – the National Alliance of People's Movements, the Narmada Bachao Andolan and the Mazdoor Kisan Shakti Sangathan among others. In UP, one of the most important grassroots movements that picked up on this trend – Asha Parivar – was led by Sandeep Pandey and worked to extend the idea of ordinary citizenry questioning the actions of local governments through the RTI mechanism.[51] Most prom-inently, the pressure from Anna Hazare for a Jan Lok Pal (Ombudsman) Bill since 2009 has similarly drawn upon Gandhian ideas with which to critique the state at its base, albeit with authoritarian undertones.

---

[50] Jonathan Parry, 'The "Crises of Corruption" and "The Idea of India": A Worm's-Eye View', in *The Morals of Legitimacy*, ed. Italo Pardo (New York and Oxford: Berghahn Books, 2000), pp. 27–55.
[51] For more details on the work of Sandeep Pandey and Asha Parivar, see http:// ashaparivar.org (accessed December 2018).

Pakistan, like its neighbour, has huge problems with corruption, and this has prompted a range of local and national responses as in India. In 2011, for instance, there were protest actions that struck observers as closely resembling the tactics pursued by Hazare. In one case, Raja Jehangir Akhtar promised to undertake a fast-unto-death against corruption and high defence expenditure, while another human rights activist Ansar Burney launched a protest against terrorism and corruption. As press reporting observed,

Both … draw strength from the popular sentiment displayed in India against corruption. Demanding a Jan Lokpal Bill for Pakistan, Mr. Akhtar [had] decided to set his goalposts exactly the way Anna Hazare decides for his campaign. 'If Anna Saheb decides on a particular timeline and gives Parliament a certain number of days to enact the law, I will also do the same,' he said.

Striking a note of caution, however, commentators also expressed fears that anti-corruption movements of this kind were vulnerable to being hijacked by the religious right. As a 2011 blog entitled 'Let Us Build Pakistan' duly reminded its readers,

These surges are destined to fell prey in the hands of the far-right that seize the moment by hijacking the zeal. The most glaring example in Pakistan is the fate of the so-called movement for restoration of judiciary. The same judiciary that once was a beacon of hope has gone overboard in giving the clean chit to convicted terrorists and publically castigating the notion of secularism whilst undermining the supremacy of the elected Parliament. These lawyers who once were pioneers of the movement have been found showering roses upon a self-confessed killer.[52]

The 'killer' referenced here was Mumtaz Qadri, the guard-turned-murderer of Salman Taseer mentioned earlier, and the 'judiciary' were those lawyers who defended his violent actions. Pressure from lawyers, however, has proved particularly politicized in twenty-first-century Pakistan. The 'Lawyers' Movement', also known as the 'Movement for the Restoration of Judiciary' or the 'Black Coat Protests', was a popular mass protest initiated in response to Pervez Musharraf's suspension of the chief justice of the Pakistan Supreme Court Iftikhar Muhammad Chaudhry in March 2007. Following his suspension, the Supreme Court Bar Association (SCBA) declared Chaudhry's removal to be an assault on the independence of judiciary. The protest, which snowballed to include political parties that arguably jumped onto its bandwagon, culminated in a 'Long March' from Karachi to Islamabad in 2009, which

---

[52] 'Pakistan Keenly Watches India's Anti-Corruption Movement', *The Hindu*, 24 August 2011, www.thehindu.com/news/international/pakistan-keenly-watches-indias-anticorruption-movement/article2393164.ece (accessed December 2018).

eventually persuaded the PPP government to reinstate Chaudhry. Corruption, more generally, has become a convenient means of censuring political opponents, the most recent (at time of writing) senior politician to be convicted being former Prime Minister Nawaz Sharif who was sentenced in absentia by a Pakistani anti-corruption court in July 2018; a much earlier high-profile case was that of the imprisonment for corruption of Asif Ali Zardari between 1996 and 2004. Indeed, the reference to 'justice' (*insaaf*) in the name of Imran Khan's political party Tehreek-i-Insaaf points to the centrality of corruption and anti-corruption in public rhetoric and debate.[53]

The development of women's movements in South Asia, and in particular the influence of third-wave feminism as part of a global phenomenon from the 1970s, is too vast a subject to be explored here. All the same, it is possible to examine some of the long-term trends that emerged, specifically, from the popular and grassroots attempts to promote women's legal rights shortly after Independence in India and Pakistan. One of the most important periods of change in women's movements in both countries has been the development from the 1980s of what could be described as 'women's activism', focussed on political as well as social and religio-legal issues. Perhaps the most enduring area of rights demands revolved around the promotion in India of a Uniform Civil Code (UCC), following on from the inadequacies of the Hindu Code Bill, and also (as far as supporters of the Hindu right parties are concerned) continued customary practices exercised by Muslim Personal Law, such as *tin talak*.[54] This particular campaign, within which a range

---

[53] *'Saaf'* in Urdu means 'clean', sending additional subliminal messages perhaps about Imran Khan's purported mission to clean up Pakistani life.

[54] *Tin talak* allowed men to precipitately announce a divorce from a woman using the simple verbal utterance of 'I divorce you' three times. The practice was legally banned in Pakistan in 1961 with the introduction of the Muslim Family Law Ordinances under Ayub Khan. See Freeland Abbott, 'Pakistan's New Marriage Law: A Reflection of Qur'Anic Interpretation', *Asian Survey* 1, 11 (January 1962), pp. 26–32; Lucy Carroll, 'The Muslim Family Laws Ordinance, 1961: Provisions and Procedures – A Reference Paper for Current Research', *Contributions to Indian Sociology* 13, 1 (1979), pp. 117–43; Sana Khan, 'Women and State Laws and Policies in Pakistan: The Early Phase, 1947–77', *Proceedings of the Indian History Congress* 74 (2013), pp. 726–33; Matthew Nelson, 'Inheritance Unbound: The Politics of Personal Law Reform in Pakistan and India', in *Comparative Constitutional Traditions in South Asia*, eds. Sunil Khilnani, Vikram Raghavan and Arun Thiruvengadam (Delhi: Oxford University Press, 2012), pp. 219–46.

of complex sociolegal arrangements have been debated,[55] has led to the somewhat paradoxical theoretical 'alliance' between women's movements and the Hindu right – the latter also pushing for a uniform code, as part of its broader majoritarian programme. Such developments relate, historically, to the range of movements that were generated around the Muslim Women's (Right to Protection on Divorce) Bill, introduced in the Lok Sabha in 1986. In terms of the Constitution, there are also apparently conflicting provisions: on the one hand, Articles 14–15 suggest equality and non-discrimination, and Articles 25–28 protect religious freedom and cultural plurality; on the other, Article 44 suggests that the Uniform Code can be a Directive Principle of State Policy. Because of the means by which the Hindu right has used the UCC since the mid-1990s, many women's movements have abandoned their own demand for it.[56]

In Pakistan, Zia ul Haq's Islamization initiatives during the late 1970s and 1980s had an undeniably negative though differential impact on the lives, and status, of Pakistani women. While some strongly supported his reforms, many others protested at the inequality vis-à-vis men implemented by his regime's legal changes. Despite a handful of high-profile appointments, steps towards institutional-building for women's development (the establishment of a Women's Division in the Cabinet), a commission enquiry into the status of women in Pakistan and the inclusion of a chapter on 'women in development' in the country's Sixth Five-Year Plan (1983–8), women's rights declined overall during the Zia period. His government's promotion of *pardah* (female seclusion) imposed a more restrictive dress code on women operating in the public sphere, requiring them to cover their heads with a *duputta* (scarf). But the main focus for protest was the impact of Islamization on the country's penal code. The All-Pakistan Women's Association (APWA), still led by Begum Liaquat Ali Khan, together with the Women's Action Forum (WAF) – which attracted support from younger, arguably more radical but still mostly from elite families, urban-based and well-educated women – objected vociferously. WAF was set up in Karachi in 1981 in response to the first sentence of death by stoning and public whipping handed down to a couple under the 1979 Zina Ordinance, though many of its leading members had existing links to Shirkatgarh, the women's

---

[55] Werner Menski, 'The Uniform Civil Code Debate in Indian Law: New Developments and Changing Agenda', *German Law Journal* 9, 3 (2008), pp. 211–50.

[56] Flavia Agnes, 'The Supreme Court, the Media and the Uniform Civil Code Debate in India', in *The Crisis of Secularism in India*, eds. Anuradha Dingwaney Needham and Rajeshwari Sunder Rajan (Durham, NC: Duke University Press, 2007), pp. 294–9.

rights organization that had been formed in 1975 in response to the launch of the UN's Decade for Women (1975–85).

In many ways, Karachi's *Star* newspaper, until then known primarily for covering entertainment stories, became the voice of the women's movement, with leading female journalists such as Najma Babar and Najma Sadeque frequently reporting on women's rights and challenges to their political status on its pages. Though activists themselves rejected the claim, many people both inside and outside Pakistan regarded WAF as spearheading the challenge against Zia's policies. The new laws of evidence proposed in 1983 – 'Qanun-i-Shahadat (Law of Evidence) Order', according to which the evidence of one man would be equal to two women – were trenchantly rejected by women of all classes who took to the streets in protest and ended up badly beaten by police and tear-gassed during rallies such as those held in Lahore in February that year. Even though these actions did not lead to the total repeal of the Hudood Ordinances, they succeeded in bringing about a partial retreat on the part of the authorities, and acknowledgement of women's position as citizens within an Islamic state. In 1984 Zia's regime was forced to substitute its initial legislation with a different version that restricted Islamic rules regarding the unequal giving of evidence to financial and maximum punishment *hudud* cases only.[57]

In India, this period witnessed growing public perception about the divide between the legal enactment of women's rights and their implementation, a gulf that was most strongly seen in cases of dowry deaths and rape. Legal protections for women continue to be routinely transgressed around a wide array of rape categories: 'landlord rape' or violent forms of droit de seigneur; rape by men in positions of occupation authority; 'caste rape'; and class, police and army rape. The failure of formal legal mechanisms to remedy these problems led to a shift (again in the 1980s) from mass protests around legislative change, to the development of women's centres to assist in individual cases of social welfare and domestic abuse. The most well-known examples of this response was Saheli ('Beloved Friend'), the Delhi women's organization set up in

---

[57] Farida Shaheed and Khawar Mumtaz, 'Islamisation and Women: The Experience of Pakistan', *New Blackfriars* 71, 835, Special Issue: The World of Islam (February 1990), pp. 67–80; Asthma Jehangir and Hina Jilani, *The Hudood Ordinances: A Divine Sanction* (Lahore: Sang-e-Meel Publications, 2003); Afshan Jafar, 'Women, Islam and the State in Pakistan', *Gender Issues* 22, 1 (December 2003), pp. 35–55; Fawzia Afzal-Khan, 'Betwixt and Between? Women, the Nation and Islamization in Pakistan', *Social Identities: Journal for the Study of Race, Nation and Culture* 13, 1 (2007), pp. 19–29; Amina Jamal, 'When Are Women's Rights Human Rights in Pakistan?', in *Gender, National Security and Counter-Terrorism: Human Rights Perspectives*, eds. Margaret Satterthwaite and Jayne Huckerby (New York: Routledge, 2013), pp. 208–29.

1983 and extended to other cities, which hosted workshops, some of which also promoted women's creativity, association and discussion of political and social issues that concerned them.[58]

The significance of these later movements was how they triggered other, broader fronts for women's rights, both among Indian feminists and in specific areas of government activity. For instance, government-sponsored Mahila Mandals were rejuvenated as a result of the problems publicized by Chipko, and a range of other social agitations, such as anti-alcohol movements, were set up. In addition, the issues facing women overall were more clearly interconnected within these movements – linking the conditions of work to broader questions about the nature of women's role in families, levels of women's education and the role of children. These thematic networks operating in women's movements, we would argue, had already been implicit in much earlier manifestations of citizen's mobilizations centred around the rights of women in South Asia in the early post-Independence years. At different levels, we have also seen early forms of vernacularization taking place in the concept of rights of citizens, which foreshadowed later movements, particularly among women.[59] Other rights movements have learned from the experiences of the women's movement – for example, the disability rights movement. This did not manage to establish, however, the same kind of grassroots presence and internal lobbying compared to other movements, and instead was eventually driven by international pressure on the government to pass the Persons with Disabilities Act of 1995.[60]

In Pakistan the status of women similarly remains a highly contested issue. The Women's Protection Bill (WPB) of 2006 was an attempt to amend the heavily criticized 1979 Hudood Ordinance laws that still governed the punishment for rape and adultery in Pakistan. Critics of the Hudood Ordinance alleged that it made it exceptionally difficult and dangerous to prove an allegation of rape, and thousands of women had been imprisoned as a result. The 2006 WPB transferred a number of offences back from the Zina Ordinance to the Pakistan Penal Code (where they had been located before 1979), and removed whipping and amputation as punishments for adultery. In short, this law meant women

---

[58] Radha Kumar, *The History of Doing: An Illustrated Account of Movements for Women's Rights and Feminism in India, 1800–1990* (New Delhi: Kali for Women, 1993), pp. 143–5.

[59] Peggy Levitt and Sally Merry, 'Vernacularization on the Ground: Local Uses of Global Women's Rights in Peru, China, India and the United States', *Global Networks* 9, 4 (October 2009), pp. 441–61.

[60] Nilika Mehrotra, 'Disability Rights Movements in India', *Economic and Political Weekly* 46, 6 (5–11 February 2011), pp. 65–72.

would not be jailed if they were unable to prove rape, and it also allowed rape to be proven on grounds other than witness testimony, such as forensics and DNA evidence.[61] Other more recent 'female-friendly' legislation has included the Acid Control and Acid Crime Prevention Act and the Prevention of Anti-Women Practices Act, both passed in 2011.

In terms of women's political representation, the debates of the first decade after Independence still reverberate. With the advent of martial law in 1958, and the suspension of the 1956 Constitution, female suffrage on the basis of women's territorial constituencies was abolished. Then, under Ayub Khan's 1962 constitutional re-working, three seats for women in each of the two wings of the country (East and West Pakistan) were introduced for a period of ten years, though these, like the other 300 members of the National Assembly, were chosen indirectly by an electoral college made up of 'Basic Democrats'. Yahya Khan's Legal Framework Order of 1970 maintained the principle of reserved seats, this time with seven for women of East Pakistan and six for those in West Pakistan, and the same pattern continued under Zulfikar Ali Bhutto when Pakistan's 1973 Constitution included ten reserved seats for women. Later, in 1985, under Zia this total was raised to twenty. The occupants of these reserved seats, however, like their predecessors, were not elected directly but were chosen through a voting process conducted in the already-elected National Assembly.

After the 1988 elections, the constitutional provision, which sanctioned this affirmative action on the part of the state, lapsed. However, prior to elections in 2002 Musharraf revived reserved seats for women, returning the number to twenty. By the time of the 2008 polls, this total had been increased to sixty. In the meanwhile, though many Pakistani women experienced practical difficulties in exercising their right to vote due to family and/or community pressures, the number of women standing for general seats increased, with sixty-four candidates contesting in 2008, of whom approximately 25 per cent proved successful.[62] The inclusion of Pakistan 'hidden' transgender population in the 2017 census and the first-ever proposed transgender law were viewed by sympathetic supporters as positive developments, but minorities – women, non-Muslims and transgender people – continued to experience violent

[61] Martin Lau, 'Twenty-Five Years of Hudood Ordinances – A Review', *Washington and Lee Law Review* 64, 4 (2007), pp. 1291–314.
[62] Shahbana Shamaas Gul Khattak and Akhtar Hussain, 'Women Representation in Pakistani Legislatures: A Study of the 2002, 2008 and 2013 General Elections', *South Asia Survey* 20, 2 (2016), pp. 191–205.

attacks, discrimination and government persecution, with human rights organizations criticizing the Pakistani authorities for failing to provide adequate protection for these citizens and their rights.

As this epilogue has underlined, while the political frameworks operating in India and Pakistan have not been identical, there are parallels between the developments that challenge the working of democracy in India and the 'failed state' narrative that dominates assessments of the challenges faced by twenty-first-century Pakistanis. Unlike India, however, Pakistan had 'ideology' in the form of religion as the official rationale for its creation: as Tahir Kamran has argued, while Jinnah's ambition for Pakistan was based on the principle of 'one nation, one culture, one language', in reality 'the repetitive expression of the Hindu as the other', together with the emphasis on one particular language Urdu, was tightly woven into Pakistani identity and politics from the outset, generating huge challenges for those Pakistani citizens who did not fit this patriotically approved national template.[63] However, the presumed knock-on negative effects of this 'collective failure' have demonstrated, according to Ian Talbot, that 'language and religion, rather than providing a panacea for unity in a plural society, have opened a Pandora's box of conflicting identities'.[64] Again, unlike India, whose 1950 Constitution remains intact (despite a succession of amendments that have rewritten large amounts of what it originally contained), Pakistanis – should they ever wish to do so – can pick and choose from three Constitutions and a 'Legal Framework Order' when it comes to framing their current demands for political reform. With Pakistan now a very different territorial space compared to when it was created, it is the 1973 Constitution (rather than its 1956 forerunner) that has been the focus of discussion since the turn of the twenty-first century.[65] In particular, the 18th Amendment passed during Asif Ali Zardari's PPP presidency in April 2010, which among other changes removed the power of the president to dissolve Parliament unilaterally, also rebalanced the relationship between

---

[63] Tahir Kamran, 'Islam, Urdu and Hindu as the Other: Instruments of Cultural Homogeneity in Pakistan', in *Composite Culture in a Multicultural Society*, eds. Bipen Chandra and Sucheta Mahajan (Delhi: Pearson, 2007), p. 97.

[64] Ian Talbot, *Pakistan: A Modern History* (London: C. Hurst and Co., 1999), p. 1.

[65] For modifications of the 1973 Constitution up to 2012, see http://na.gov.pk/uploads/documents/1333523681_951.pdf (accessed December 2018). Sadaf Aziz, *The Constitution of Pakistan: A Contextual Analysis* (Oxford: Hart Publishing, 2018).

centre and provinces.[66] For Shahid Javed Burki, writing in 2010, there was little doubt that

the 18th Amendment [was going to have] a profound impact on the way the country is governed and its economy is managed. If the federating – the provinces – receive additional powers as a result of the abolition of the concurrent list put into the 1973 constitution by its framers, it will mean transferring large amounts of economic authority to the provinces.[67]

Whether its critics view it quite so optimistically over a decade later is debatable.[68]

As the first quotation at the start of this epilogue suggests, there have also been recent suggestions in India that changes to the Constitution are not beyond the pale, in the context of a regime that is transforming all manner of state institutions. The key political pressure, since the election of Narendra Modi's BJP government and the significant denudation of Congress authority in 2014, has been the repeated questioning of the 'secular' basis of the state. This is felt perhaps nowhere more strongly than in UP itself, especially following the election in March 2017 of the BJP hardliner, Yogi Adityanath, on a platform against the 'appeasement' of Muslims, and the need to 'crack down' on caste-based politics and 'corruption'. In his election speeches, Adityanath used the undiluted rhetoric of the Rashtriya Swayamsevak Sangh (RSS): 'I will not stop until I have turned India and UP into a Hindu *Rashtra* [state]'; calling for the installation of Hindu deities in Muslim mosques; the building of the 'world's largest' statue of Lord Ram; and claiming in 'post-truth' fashion that thanks to 'pseudo-secularism' Hindus are in demographic decline.[69] Just as in the early post-Independence years, there is now not much ambiguity in parts of UP that Muslims are expected to live, largely, as second-class citizens under fear of their security. The results have been the wider acquiescence in lynchings of Muslims, especially around the

---

[66] Other new features that were introduced into the Pakistan Constitution included the following: the North-West Frontier Province was renamed Khyber-Pakhtunkhwa; the ban on third-time prime ministership and chief ministership was lifted; and suspending the constitution was now made tantamount to high treason.

[67] Shahid Javed Burki, 'The 18th Amendment: Pakistan's Constitution Redesigned', Institute of South Asian Studies, National University of Singapore, Working Paper No. 112, 3 September 2010, www.files.ethz.ch/isn/120842/ISAS_Working_Paper_112_-_Email_-_The_18_Amendment_06092010121427.pdf (accessed December 2018).

[68] See 'Questions about 18th Amendment', 9 February 2017, https://pakobserver.net/questions-about-18th-amendment/ (accessed December 2018).

[69] Harsh Mander, 'Yogi Adityanath Is as Much a Creation of the So-Called Secular Parties as of the Sangh', *Scroll.in*, 21 March 2017, https://scroll.in/article/832292/adityanath-is-as-much-a-creation-of-the-so-called-secular-parties-as-the-sangh-parivar (accessed December 2018).

issue of cows and the work of butchers. Arguably, parties of all complexions have benefitted from both the rhetoric of 'secularism' (rather than its serious implementation),[70] and the strategic use of communal violence.[71] However, we have suggested, from India's first decade, the same need for new kinds of political repertoires by marginalized ethnic and religious groups in India when lobbying the state indicates the long-term fragility of Indian secularism's constitutional basis.

Ethnicity with its linkages to provincial identity and language, rather than caste divisions, has proved to be one of Pakistan's most exposed 'Achilles heels'. This was demonstrated most dramatically in the developments that led to East Pakistan becoming Bangladesh in 1971, but ethnic tension has also characterized relations between communities, and between provincial and federal political leaders in provinces of former West Pakistan. In Sindh, friction between the various communities brought together in the province by Partition was made more complicated by the internal southwards migration of Punjabis and Pashtuns seeking employment there. Sindhis (who even before Independence had been sensitive to the presence of outsiders in 'their' province) saw themselves as increasingly marginalized from power (whether in relation to civilian politics, the sway of the bureaucracy or the dominance exercised by the military), and they associated Urdu-speaking migrants – *muhajirs* – as well as other migrant communities living in 'their' province with the priorities and plans of the country's increasingly Punjab-dominated federal authorities. Many Sindhis had quickly come to believe that their language and the cultural heritage that went with it were under threat. In the early 1970s, language turned into a dangerous bone of contention, echoing earlier resentment of Urdu in East Pakistan in the 1950s and 1960s. In July 1972, the provincial PPP ministry, led by Mumtaz Ali Bhutto, introduced the 'Teaching, Promotion and Use of Sindhi Language Bill', which made Sindhi into the province's sole official language: alongside Urdu Sindhi was made a compulsory subject for school pupils up to Class 12. This legislation also raised the prospect of government employees having to learn Sindhi within a stipulated period and so it challenged Urdu's (by then) established place in government offices and the law courts. Urdu speakers took to the streets to protest vehemently in defence of their linguistic interests and, as one Urdu

---

[70] Ibid.

[71] Ibid. State governments have done little in UP, for example around the resettlement and rehabilitation of Muslims following severe rioting in Muzaffarnagar in September 2013. See also Steven Wilkinson, *Votes and Violence: Electoral Competition and Ethnic Riots in India* (Cambridge: Cambridge University Press, 2006).

newspaper sarcastically remarked on its front page, if the authorities wanted to bury Urdu, then they really needed to do it in style (*Urdu ka janaza hai zara dhoom se nikle*). In riots that followed, lives were lost and properties torched in urban centres where Urdu-speaking *muhajirs* lived, such as Karachi, Hyderabad, Sukkur, Mirpurkhas, Nawabshah and Larkana. Pro-Sindhi activists belonging to G. M. Sayed's Sindhi nationalist movement, Jiye Sindh Mahaz (Long Live Sindh Movement) joined the fray, making bonfires of Urdu newspapers and defacing portraits of the national – Urdu-writing – poet, Iqbal. Sindh Sujag Jathas ('Sindh Awakening Squads') carried Jiye Sindh's message into rural areas. From a Sindhi nationalist perspective, there were clear parallels between Sindh's position and events in East Bengal that had resulted in the drama of Bangladesh's bitterly fought secession.[72]

This 'ethnic' unrest was eventually contained, but in 1973 *muhajir* fears were again raised by the introduction of a new federal quota system for government employment, which split Sindh's share of just less than 20 per cent into two parts – rural (11.4 per cent) and urban (7.6 per cent). As Sindhis largely fell into the first category and *muhajirs* into the second, many Urdu speakers believed that this measure threatened all-important access to government jobs, even though this was a sector of (secure) employment within which they had been arguably over-represented since Pakistan's creation. By the end of 1970s, around 50 per cent of the inhabitants of Karachi were Urdu speakers, with a further 13 per cent speaking Punjabi, and only around 7 per cent speaking Sindhi.[73] By 1981, Urdu speakers accounted for 61 per cent of Karachi's population. That number-crunching continues to dominate politics in Sindh was highlighted by the long-awaited 2017 national census, which its critics believed severely under-counted the city's population as a tactic to preserve the ruling Pakistan Muslim League – Nawaz (PML-N) power base ahead of general elections to be held in 2018. Farooq Sattar, chief of Muttahida Qaumi Movement (MQM) that had ruled Karachi and urban Sindh for decades, termed the early results 'a great injustice': 'The census has been rigged If we are counted less, then our seats in parliament will remain the same [instead of being

---

[72] For more discussion about *muhajir* responses to political developments in Sindh politics, see Oskar Verkaaik, *Migrants and Militants: Fun and Urban Violence in Pakistan* (Princeton, NJ: Princeton University Press, 2004); Nichola Khan, *Mohajir Militancy in Pakistan* (London: Routledge, 2012); and Laurent Gayer, *Karachi: Ordered Disorder and the Struggle for the City* (London: C. Hurst and Co., 2014).

[73] It should be added, however, that many of the city's pre-Partition inhabitants had actually spoken Kutchi, a language claimed as a dialect by both Gujarati and Sindhi.

increased]', he told reporters in Karachi.[74] Add to this, ongoing debates about the rights of long-settled Afghan refugees, and the connections between ethnic identity and citizenship in twenty-first-century Pakistan appear even more complex.

So, to sum up, in *Boundaries of Belonging* we have explored how, despite the violence and displacement of Partition, and in some cases because of it, societies in newly independent India and Pakistan alike articulated a popular politics of citizenship. Ideas of belonging, however, were not generally expressed through texts comprising coherent ideologies, but rather via direct and active engagement with different forms of political and civic life, some of which we have set out through the course of this book: engagement with large-scale state ceremonies of symbolic import-ance, refugee rehabilitation, property and housing, the control and movement of goods and food supplies, the exercise of voting and the promotion of specific group rights. Alongside the topics that we have investigated in *Boundaries of Belonging* there are others, such as those relating to business and finance, religious foundations, labour practices, education and new publishing or intellectual enterprises, which we have deliberately not pursued, but which suggest that our chosen modes of civic assertion were not the only important forms in this period of transition and 'nation-building'. Our focus has also been primarily on urban contexts, and on themes in which the relationship between regions on each side of the border was direct and explicit, since we argue that this inter-regional/international relationship was crucial to the substantive formation of citizenship ideas in both countries. Overall, we believe that our inter-regional study presents a number of new ways of thinking about citizenship in South Asia.

First, we have considered how far the rights of and the concepts surrounding the 'citizen' in both India and Pakistan were affected by what was happening across the new border in the years following Independence and Partition. Since the idea of the citizen presupposed association with a nation state, it was always articulated in relation to other spaces beyond the boundaries of that state, especially those places that had mutually symmetrical meanings for citizens in both places. We have found, therefore, not just similarities between cities in Sindh and

---

[74] 'Census Sparks Political Row over Growth in Major Cities', *The News*, 29 August 2017, www.thenews.com.pk/latest/226860-Census-sparks-political-row-over-growth-in-major-cities (accessed December 2018).

UP, but also mutually constituted ideas about, and movements surrounding, the 'citizen'. For instance, as Chapters 2 and 3 explored, both
localities experienced a range of popular protests around the problems of
food and civil supply or rationing in the late 1940s and early 1950s. But
these widespread concerns were strongly related to commonly held ideas
about bureaucratic changes brought about by Partition-related migration, by problems of international corruption (not least smuggling) and
by questions surrounding minority enjoyment of resources, among
groups associated with the 'other' state.

Second, given that the framework for *Boundaries of Belonging* has been
about the inter-relationship of specific places on each side of the Indo-
Pakistan border, in which citizenship was not necessarily expressed in a
textual discourse, but by forms of action and engagement, the level of the
locality has been our main focus. Prioritizing this approach has allowed
us to begin to re-think the spatial scales of citizenship's everyday meanings, exploring not simply ideas of rights/belonging to nations, but also
how ideas about the relations between particular cities or regions and
their respective nations played out. Our new citizens, whether Indian or
Pakistani, constantly navigated these spatial scales, and, in many ways,
the very differences between promises issued from the centre and the
realities of the locality could shift, colour and even undermine some of
the formal principles of citizenship as these took shape. For instance, we
looked at the promises of new supposedly responsive public services and
servants at a national level, and the realities of engagement with the
administration in particular locations. We also examined the very specific
problems of refugees and housing at the level of an individual city or
town, alongside the larger politics of bilateral international agreements
about rehabilitation. In our later chapters, we similarly explored connections between local rights movements, especially for women, and their
links to larger national and international themes regarding the political
rights of women. We have considered another dimension of scale too. In
our specific discussion of developments taking place in UP and Sindh,
we have sought to extend, again spatially, the correlation between
Partition's conditions and citizenship outcomes, and take this beyond
engaging with the immediate spheres of Partition violence, principally
the Punjab and Bengal. This regional extension for us is crucial for
considering the wider resonance of the mid-twentieth-century processes
of decolonization taking place across South Asia as a whole, albeit by
focussing on one specific intersection of regions.

Third, it follows from this configuration of citizenship that rights
associated with it were in no sense 'certain' or 'a given', and, importantly,
that this uncertainty could change over time. As a number of exclusions

have shown globally, in relation to Commonwealth/postcolonial communities in European countries, or with respect to migrants from other states who have formed minorities in their new homes, 'citizenship' was socially differentiated in terms of its attendant securities. It was never fully determined. As we have highlighted throughout *Boundaries of Belonging*, some communities – such as Muslim groups in UP and Hindus in Sindh – were repeatedly or intermittently excluded from the full and unambiguous enjoyment of rights, or expressions of belonging to the nation, whether in India or in Pakistan. This broad theme has certainly been explored elsewhere in the immediate, messy aftermath of Partition,[75] but our book addresses these differentiated insecurities of citizenship at a more mundane and 'unremarkable' level, in everyday life courses and struggles that were not immediately connected to Partition itself.

Fourth, as *Boundaries of Belonging* highlights, the interconnection between India and Pakistan during the late 1940s and 1950s was seen perhaps most unambiguously in the ways in which both states subsequently managed the promises of 'universal' citizenship rights set against the realities of diverse and varied group claims on them. In many ways, however, this tension is not easily captured in most general explorations of the concept of citizenship. This is because few studies in historical literature have attempted to make sense of how citizenship is enacted in day-to-day movements to claim, critique and protect rights in political action. All the same, there have been attempts to draw out the problem of India's implementation of 'liberal' citizenship rights, and the effects of 'closure', to deploy Anupama Roy's term, of such rights in reality for certain minorities.[76] In a more recent work, India's Constitution is presented as having 'imbrications in everyday life', in ways that have led to the constant reinterpretation of the document.[77] For us, however, the notion of the citizen is not always explicitly stated. Rather it is often indirectly articulated in struggles for resources and the symbolic capital of 'belonging'. In attempting to explore these complex social histories of the emerging citizen in two interconnected sites, we find that there were meaningful gaps between the political statement of rights and their enjoyment or implementation in practice – from the legal position of women, to the administration of resource distribution, and the maintenance of secularism. It is in this gap, and debates about it, that the wide array of citizens' movements that we have encountered here mostly appear – the movements of women, caste or adivasi organizations, or

---

[75] Vazira Zamindar, *The Long Partition and the Making of Modern South Asia: Refugees, Boundaries, Histories* (New York: Columbia University Press, 2007).

[76] Roy, *Mapping Citizenship*.   [77] De, *A People's Constitution*, pp. 4–5.

religious minorities, for instance, were all anchored in a similar set of critiques regarding the state's promise to implement universal rights and the ultimate shortcomings of the formal processes surrounding that ambition.

Last but not least, we hope that *Boundaries of Belonging* will encourage rethinking about the changing modes of active popular citizenship, which were shaped by forms of political engagement in both states in the late 1940s and 1950s. In the first five years following Independence, both new states faced comparable public complaints regarding governance, which were to some extent inter-related. Again, this was partly a result of the fact that many of the complaints about corruption related to war-time provisioning, black markets and evacuee property. In both UP and Sindh, however, everyday problems of governance did not create a sense of fatalism about political redress, or undermine popular belief in the importance of representation, even though factional politics quickly mapped onto the patronage networks of resource allocation. Accusations of corruption/maladministration and the like did not hinder Indians and Pakistanis from exercising, or seeking to exercise, their democratic rights. And the fact that virtually the opposite has been the case in more recent decades tell us something interesting about the idea of a 'crisis of governance' in the region more generally. In a larger sense, we argue that some popular movements took the concept of civic assertion into their own hands, emulating what sociologists have seen in other contexts of mass displacement – namely, innovative and makeshift citizenship responses to rapidly changing circumstances.[78]

What this citizenship complex shows is that written bills of rights, expressed in the form of national constitutions, are living documents in ways that are perhaps different in our two states, especially when compared to other contexts. Most written constitutions are incomplete, continually amended and reworked; there is nothing usual here as far as India and Pakistan are concerned, though clearly their respective constitutional 'stories' have not been identical. But, at the same time, the Indian and Pakistani constitutions possess very specific and contingent meanings for different communities, not least in India, where some groups simultaneously employ strategies drawing on its constitution's fundamental principles and promises of rights to particular defined categories of citizen. Moreover, the recourse to constitutional documents for promoting or defending rights is currently of great urgency in both states, not least because of inherent political threats to their content, or

---

[78] James Holston, *Insurgent Citizenship: Disjunctions of Democracy and Modernity in Brazil* (Princeton, NJ: Princeton University Press, 2009).

because of their political fragility. In the case of Pakistan, this has been based on a certain form of majoritarianism that pivots largely on the balance (or imbalance) between provinces, and their relationship to the centre, at times inflected by religion. In the case of India, it is related to different expressions of majoritarianism, sometimes based in caste or alternatively its denial, and sometimes founded on the inherent weakness of secularism within the state, as the demonization (or simple marking) of religious minorities intermittently becomes the key process in creating the normative citizen and broader understandings of political 'belonging'. Either way, in twenty-first-century South Asia, citizenship and rights remain as central to contingent understandings and continuing debates about what it means to belong to a place as they proved to be in the decade following Independence and Partition.

Glossary

aam aadmi	ordinary man
aam log	ordinary people
abadgar	constructor, developer
abwab	agricultural levy
adivasi	original (tribal) inhabitant
alim	(pl. *ulama*), a learned man, typically a man learned in Islamic legal and religious studies
anjuman	association (Muslim)
Anjuman-i Khawateen-i Islam	Association of Muslim Women
Anjuman-i Tahafuuz Huqooq-i Niswan	Association for the Protection of Women's Rights
Anjuman-i-Taraqqi-i-Urdu	Association for the Advancement of Urdu
Arya Samaj	Hindu social reform movement
Awami Mahaz	People's Front
badmash	criminal
bania	Hindu merchant
batai	crop sharing
begar	forced labour
begum	honorific title for a Muslim woman
bhai-bandi	(lit. fraternity) nepotism
Bhil	Scheduled Tribe in India and Pakistan
bidi	cigarette
Bint-i-Pakistan	daughter of Pakistan
chehlum	Muslim mourning ceremony
chhatank	measurement of weight, c. 50 grams
crore	10,000,000
dargah	shrine of a religious figure, usually Sufi-connected
Dar-ul-Ulum	religious seminary (Muslim)

dharamshala	building devoted to religious or charitable purposes, especially a rest house for travellers
Dharma Chakra	wheel of cosmic order
Dharwar Mahamila Mandal	Women's organization
duputta	scarf
Eid ul Azha	important stage in the annual Hajj or pilgrimage to Mecca
Eid ul Fitr	celebration marking the end of Ramadan
Eidgah Maidan	ground where communal Eid prayers are held
fateha khawani	condolence prayer meeting (Muslim)
gaddi	(lit. seat, throne) Sufi shrine
gharwalas	menfolk in the home
godown	warehouse
goonda	thug
gurdwara	Sikh place of worship
halwai	sweetmaker
haq/haqdaar	rights
harep	permanent tenancy rights
hari	sharecropper peasant
Harijan	'Children of God', Gandhian term for Dalit communities
Harijan Sevak Sangh	Harijan Service Union
Hindi Sahitya Sammelan	organization devoted to the spread of the Hindi language
Hindu Mahasabha	right-wing Hindu nationalist movement and political party
Holi	Hindu festival
hudud	(lit. borders, boundaries, limits) refers to punishments that under Islamic law (*Shariah*) are mandated and fixed by God
Hukumat-i-Pakistan	Government of Pakistan
insaaf	justice
Jamiat-i-Muhajireen	Refugee Council
Jamiat-ul-Ulama	Council of Theologians
Jatava	Scheduled Caste group in UP
jus sanguinis	'right of blood', heritable citizenship
jus soli	'right of the soil', birthplace-defined citizenship
kanungo	local revenue officer

khadi	homespun cloth
Khaksars	militant Islamic volunteer movement based in Punjab and UP
Khawateen	womankind
Khawateen-i-Anjuman-i-Tablighul Islam	Women's Association for the Spread of Islam
Khawateen-i-Pakistan	Women of Pakistan
Kisan Mazdoor Praja Party	Farmers' and Peasants' Citizen Party
Kori	Scheduled Caste group in UP, weavers
lakh	100,000
Lok Sabha	Lower House of the Indian Parliament
lorha	guarded settlement
maund	measurement of weight, c. 37 kilos
Mahila Matadhikar Samiti	Women's Suffrage Conference
Mahila Samaj	Women's Society
Mahila Sangh	Women's Union
Mataji	mother
maulvi	honorific religious title given to Muslim religious scholar
mazar	tomb
mofussil	parts of a country outside an urban centre; rural areas
mohalla	neighbourhood of a town or city
muhajir	one who migrates, a refugee (pl. *muhajirin*); in the context of South Asia someone from India who settled in Pakistan after Partition
Muharram	first month of the Islamic calendar
naib	deputy
paan	preparation combining betel leaf with areca nut widely consumed throughout South Asia for its stimulant effects
panchayat	council
Pasi	Dalit community, mostly agriculturalists
pir	Sufi master who leads disciples along his spiritual path
pugree	interest-free security deposit given by a tenant to a landlord
purdah	female seclusion

Qanun-i-Shahadat	Law of Evidence
qasbah	small town
qawwali	singing of Muslim devotional songs, often inducing ecstasy among listeners
Quaid-i-Azam	'Great Leader'
Quaid-i Millat	'Leader of the Nation'
Ramadan (Ramzan)	Muslim month of fasting
rashtra	state
Rashtriya Swayamsevak Sangh (RSS)	militant right-wing Hindu nationalist volunteer movement
saheli	*beloved friend* (female)
sajjada nashin	(lit. 'one who sits on the carpet'); head of *pir* family and/or guardian of a Sufi shrine
Sansi	ex-criminal tribe community
Sanyukt Kori Mahasangh	Kori Community Joint Federation
Satyagraha	non-violent resistance
Seva Dal	volunteer movement linked to the Congress
Sewika Dal	women's movement linked to the Congress
shirkatgarh	lit. a place of participation
swaraj	self-rule
sir	land that is owned directly by the landlord, and which is cultivated by the landlord, or by employees and/or tenants
tahsildar	revenue officer
Tehreek-i-Insaaf	Justice Party
tin talak	triple utterance for Muslim divorce
ulama	pl. of *alim*
vakil	legal representative
Vidhan Sabha	State Assembly
vimukta jati	ex-criminal tribe
Vimukt Jati Sevak Sangh	Ex-Criminal Tribe Service Union
zamindar	landowner, especially one who leases his land to tenant farmers
zamindari	system under which zamindars hold land
zindabad	long live!

Bibliography

Primary Sources

Government Records

The British Library (BL), London
Political Records (L/PO)
Public and Judicial Records (L/PJ)
War Staff Papers (L/WS)

National Documentation Wing (NDW)
Pakistan Ministry of Interior

National Archives of India (NAI), New Delhi
Ministry of External Affairs
Ministry of Home Affairs

United Kingdom National Archives (UKNA), Kew
Dominion Office Records (DO)
Foreign and Commonwealth Office Records (FCO)
Foreign Office Records (FO)

United States National Archives (USNA), Maryland
US Embassy Pakistan Files

Uttar Pradesh State Archives (UPSA), Lucknow
Appointments Department
General Administration
Harijan Sahayak Department
Home Police Department
Irrigation Department
Relief and Rehabilitation
Revenue

Manuscripts

The British Library (BL), London
Roger Thomas Papers

National Archives of India (NAI), New Delhi
P. D. Tandon Papers

Nehru Memorial Museum and Library (NMML), New Delhi
All India Congress Committee Papers
All-India Women's Conference Papers
G.B. Pant Papers
Mridula Sarabhai Papers

Newspapers and Contemporary Publications

Aaj (Banaras)
Al Wahid (Karachi)
Constituent Assembly (Legislature) Debates (1948–1949)
Chicago Tribune (Chicago)
Civil and Military Gazette (Lahore and Karachi)
Dawn (Karachi)
Gazette of Pakistan
'Hari Movement', The Communist Party of West Pakistan in Action, Published
    by the Deputy Inspector-General of Police, C.I.D., Punjab, Lahore
    (Lahore: Superintendent Government Printing, Punjab, 1952)
The Hindu (Delhi)
Jang (Karachi)
Leader (Allahabad)
Manchester Guardian (Manchester)
*National Commission for Backward Classes: A Statutory Body under the Ministry
    of Social Justice & Empowerment*, available at www.ncbc.nic.in/User_Panel/
    UserView.aspx?TypeID=1161 (accessed July 2018).
National Herald (Lucknow)
Official Report of East Bengal Legislative Assembly, Vol. III (1949)
Pakistan Times (Lahore)
The Pioneer (Lucknow)
Report of the Backward Classes Commission, 3 vols. (Shimla: Govt. of India
    Press, 1955)
Report of the Government Hari Enquiry Committee 1947–48 (Karachi: Sindh
    Govt. Press, 1948)
*Report of the State Committee Appointed to Examine the Question of the Retention
    in Public Places of Statues of the British Period and Other Relics* (Bombay:
    Govt. of India Press, 1961)
Roshni (Lucknow)

Sindh Government Gazette (Karachi: Sindh Govt. Press, 1955)
The Statesman (Delhi)
The Times (London)
Times of India (New Delhi)
Times of Karachi (Karachi)
Vartman (Kanpur)

Published Primary Sources

Challenge and Change: Speeches by Begum Ra'ana Liaquat Ali Khan, ed. F. D. Douglas (Karachi: All-Pakistan Women's Association, n.d.).
Collected Works of M. K. Gandhi (Ahmedabad: Government of India Publication Division, 1973).
Pakistan Movement Historical Documents, ed. G. Allana (Karachi: Department of International Relations, University of Karachi, n.d. [1969]).
Report of the State Committee Appointed to Examine the Question of the Retention in Public Places of Statues of the British Period and Other Relics (Bombay: Govt. of India Press, 1961).
Selected Works of Jawaharlal Nehru (New Delhi: Oxford University Press, 1994).
Speeches of Quaid-i-Azam Mohammad Ali Jinnah as Governor General of Pakistan (Karachi: Sind Observer Press, 1948).

Secondary Sources

Abbot, Freeland, 'Pakistan's New Marriage Law: A Reflection of Qur'anic Interpretation', *Asian Survey* 1, 11 (January 1962): 26–32.
Abrams, Philip, 'Notes on the Difficulty of Studying the State [1977]', *Journal of Historical Sociology* 1, 1 (1988): 58–89.
Afzal-Khan, Fawzia, 'Betwixt and Between? Women, the Nation and Islamization in Pakistan', *Social Identities: Journal for the Study of Race, Nation and Culture* 13, 1 (2007): 19–29.
Aggarwal, Saaz, *Sindh: Stories from a Vanished Homeland* (Pune: Black-and-White Fountain, 2012).
Agnes, Flavia, 'The Supreme Court, the Media and the Uniform Civil Code Debate in India', in *The Crisis of Secularism in India*, eds. Anuradha Dingwaney Needham and Rajeshwari Sunder Rajan (Durham: Duke University Press, 2007): 294–315.
Ahmad, Imran, '"Strategic Constitutions": Constitutional Change and Politics in Pakistan', *South Asia: Journal of South Asian Studies* 40, 3 (2017): 481–99.
Ahmad, Mushtaq, *Government and Politics in Pakistan* (2nd ed., Karachi: Space Publishers, 1970, 1st ed., 1959).
Ahmad, Riswan, *'Sayings of the Quaid-i-Azam': Mohammed Ali Jinnah* (Karachi: Quaid Foundation and Pakistan Movement Centre, 1993).
Ahmed, Akbar S., *Jinnah, Pakistan and Islamic Identity: The Search for Saladin* (London: Routledge, 1997).

Ahmed, Feroz, 'The Rise of Muhajir Separatism in Pakistan', *Journal of Asian and African Affairs* 1, 2 (December 1989): 97–129.

Ali, Azra Asghar, 'Indian Muslim Women's Suffrage Campaign: Personal Dilemma and Communal Identity 1919–1947', *Journal of the Pakistan Historical Society* 47, 2 (April 1999): 33–46.

Anand, Subhadra, *National Integration of Sindhis* (New Delhi: Vikas, 1996).

Anderson, Benedict, *Imagined Communities: Reflections on the Origins and Spread of Nationalism* (London: Verso, 1991).

Ansari, Sarah, *Sufi Saints and State Power: The Pirs of Sind, 1843–1947* (Cambridge: Cambridge University Press, 1992).

'Partition, Migration and Refugees: Responses to the Arrival of *Muhajirs* in Sind after 1947', in *Freedom, Trauma, Continuities: Northern India and Independence*, eds. D. A. Low and H. Brasted (Armisted: Sage, 1998): 91–105.

Life After Partition: Migration, Community, and Strife in Sindh, 1947–1962 (Karachi: Oxford University Press, 2005).

'Polygamy, Purdah and Political Representation: Engendering Citizenship in 1950s Pakistan', *Modern Asian Studies* 43, 6 (2009): 1421–61.

'Everyday Expectations of the State during Pakistan's Early Years: Letters to the Editor, Dawn (Karachi), 1950–1953', *Modern Asian Studies* 45, 1 (2011): 159–78.

'Subjects or Citizens? India, Pakistan and the 1948 British Nationality Act', *Journal of Imperial and Commonwealth History* 41, 2 (2013): 285–312.

'Police, Corruption and Provincial Loyalties in 1950s Karachi, and the Case of Sir Gilbert Grace', *South Asian History and Culture* 5, 1 (2014): 54–74.

'At the Crossroads? Exploring Sindh's Recent Past from a Spatial Perspective', *Contemporary South Asia* 23, 1 (2015): 7–25.

'Identity Politics and Nation-Building in Pakistan: The Case of Sindhi Nationalism', in *State and Nation-Building in Pakistan: Beyond Islam and Security*, eds. Roger D. Long, Yunus Samad, Gurharpal Singh and Ian Talbot (London: Routledge, 2015): 285–310.

Appadurai, Arjun, 'The Production of Locality', in *Modernity at Large: Cultural Dimensions of Globalization* (Minneapolis: University of Minnesota Press, 1996): 178–200.

Applegate, Celia, 'A Europe of Regions: Reflections on the Historiography of Sub-National Places in Modern Times', *American Historical Review* 104, 4 (1999): 1157–82.

Austin, Granville, *The Indian Constitution: Cornerstone of a Nation* (1st ed., Oxford: Clarendon Press, 1966; New Delhi: Oxford University Press, 1999).

Working a Democratic Constitution: The Indian Experience (Oxford: Oxford University Press, 2000).

Axel, Keith, 'Anthropology and the New Technologies of Communication', *Cultural Anthropology* 21, 3 (2008): 354–84.

Azad, Maulana Abul Kalam, *India Wins Freedom: The Complete Version* (New Delhi: Stosius Inc., 1988).

Banerjee, Sukanya, *Becoming Imperial Citizens: Indians in the Late-Victorian Empire* (Durham, NC: Duke University Press, 2010).

Basu, Aparna, 'Women's Struggle for the Vote: 1917–1937', *Indian Historical Review* 35, 1 (January 2008): 128–43.

Basu, Srimati, *She Came to Take Her Rights: Indian Women, Property and Propriety* (New York: State University of New York Press, 1999).

Bhasin, Kamla and Ritu Menon, *Borders and Boundaries: Women in India's Partition* (New Delhi: Kali for Women, 1998).

Bhavnani, Nandita, *The Making of Exile: Sindhi Hindus and the Partition of India* (New Delhi: Westland Tranquebar, 2014).

Binder, Leonard, *Religion and Politics in Pakistan* (Berkeley: University of California Press, 1963).

Blom Hansen, Thomas and Finn Stepputat (eds.), *States of Imagination: Ethnographic Explorations of the Postcolonial State* (Durham, NC: Duke University Press, 2001).

Brass, Paul R., 'Muslim Separatism in United Provinces: Social Context and Political Strategy before Partition', *Economic and Political Weekly* 5, 3–5 (January 1970): 167–86.

Brennan, Lance, 'Government Famine Relief in Bengal, 1943', *The Journal of Asian Studies* 47, 3 (1988): 541–66.

Burki, Shahid Javed, 'The Eighteenth Amendment: Pakistan's Constitution Redesigned', Institute of South Asian Studies, National University of Singapore, Working Paper No. 112 (3 September 2010).

Burks, Ardath W., 'Constitution-Making in Pakistan', *Political Science Quarterly* 69, 4 (December 1954): 541–64.

Butalia, Urvashi, *The Other Side of Silence: Voices from the Partition of India* (London: C. Hurst & Co., 2000).

Calder, Grace J., 'Constitutional Debates in Pakistan I', *The Muslim World* 46 (1956): 40–60.

Callard, Keith, *Pakistan: A Political Study* (London: Allen & Unwin, 1957).

Cantwell Smith, Wilfred, 'Hyderabad: Muslim Tragedy', *Middle East Journal* 4, 1 (January 1950): 27–51.

Carroll, Lucy, 'The Muslim Family Laws Ordinance, 1961: Provisions and Procedures – A Reference Paper for Current Research', *Contributions to Indian Sociology* 13, 1 (1979): 117–43.

'Talaq-i-Tafwid and Stipulations in a Muslim Marriage Contract: Important Means of Protecting the Position of the South Asian Muslim Wife', *Modern Asian Studies* 16, 2 (1982): 277–309.

Casey, Edward S., *The Fate of Place: A Philosophical History* (Berkeley: University of California Press, 1997).

Chairez-Garza, Jesus Francisco, '"Bound Hand and Foot and Handed Over to the Caste Hindus": Ambedkar, Untouchability and the Politics of Partition', *The Indian Economic & Social History Review* 55, 1 (2018): 1–28.

Chandavarkar, Rajnarayan, *History, Culture and the City* (Cambridge: Cambridge University Press, 2015).

Chatterjee, Indrani, *Gender, Slavery and Law in Colonial India* (New Delhi: Oxford University Press, 1999).

Chatterjee, Partha, 'The Nationalist Resolution of the Women's Question', in *Recasting Women: Essays in Indian Colonial History*, eds. Kumkum Sangari and Sudesh Vaid (New Brunswick: Rutgers University Press, 1999): 233–54.

Chatterji, Joya, *The Spoils of Partition. Bengal and India 1947–1967* (Cambridge: Cambridge University Press, 2007).

'South Asian Histories of Citizenship, 1946–1970', *The Historical Journal* 55, 4 (December 2012): 1049–71.

Chattha, Ilyas, 'Competitions for Resources: Partition's Evacuee Property and the Sustenance of Corruption in Pakistan', *Modern Asian Studies* 46, 5 (2012): 1182–211.

Chipp, Sylvia A., 'The Role of Women Elites in a Modernizing Country: The All-Pakistan Women's Association' (unpublished PhD dissertation, Syracuse University, 1970).

'The All-Pakistan Women's Association and the 1961 Muslim Family Laws Ordinance' in *The Extended Family: Women and Political Participation in India and Pakistan*, ed. Gail Minault (Columbia, SC: South Asia Books, 1981): 263–85.

Chopra, J. K., *Women in the Indian Parliament (A Critical Study of Their Role)* (New Delhi: Mittal Publications, 1993).

Choudhury, G. W., 'The Constitution of Pakistan', *Pacific Affairs* 29, 3 (September 1956): 243–52.

Cooper, Frederick, *Citizenship between Empire and Nation: Remaking France and French Africa, 1945–1960* (Princeton: Princeton University Press, 2014).

Corbridge, Stuart, René Véron, Manoj Srivastava and Glyn Williams (eds.), *Seeing the State: Governance and Governmentality in India* (Cambridge: Cambridge University Press, 2005).

Cresswell, Tim, *Place: A Short Introduction* (Oxford: Oxford University Press, 2004).

Das, Suranjan, *Kashmir & Sindh: Nation-Building, Ethnicity and Regional Politics in South Asia* (London: Anthem Press, 2001).

De, Rohit, 'Rebellion, Dacoity, and Equality: The Emergence of the Constitutional Field in Postcolonial India', *Comparative Studies of South Asia, Africa and the Middle East* 34, 2 (2014): 260–78.

A People's Constitution: The Everyday Life of Law in the Indian Republic (Princeton: Princeton University Press, 2018).

Debs, Mira, 'Using Cultural Trauma: Gandhi's Assassination, Partition and Secular Nationalism in Post-Independence India', *Nations and Nationalism* 19, 4 (October 2013): 635–53.

Deepa, Agarwal and Tahmina Aziz Ayub, *The Begum: A Portrait of Ra'ana Liaquat Ali Khan, Pakistan's Pioneering First Lady* (New York: Viking, 2019).

Devy, Ganesh, 'For a Nomad Called Thief', in *Towards a Transcultural Future: Literature and Human Rights in a 'Post'-Colonial World*, eds. Peter H. Marsden and Geoffrey V. Davis (Amsterdam: Rodopi B.V., 2004): 281–90.

Dhulipala, Venkat, 'Rallying the Qaum: The Muslim League in the UP, 1937–1938', *Modern Asian Studies* 44, 3 (2010): 603–40.

Creating a New Medina: State Power, Islam, and the Quest for Pakistan in Late Colonial North India (Cambridge: Cambridge University Press, 2015).

D'Souza, Dilip, 'De-Notified Tribes: Still "Criminal"?', *Economic and Political Weekly* 34, 51 (18–24 December 1999): 3576–8.

Elangovan, Arvind, 'The Making of the Indian Constitution: A Case for a Non-Nationalist Approach', *History Compass* 12, 1 (January 2014): 1–10.

Everett, Jana Matson, *Women and Social Change in India* (New Delhi: Heritage, 1979).

Falzon, Mark-Anthony, *Cosmopolitan Connections: The Sindhi Diaspora, 1860–2000* (Leiden: Brill, 2004).

Faruqi, Mariam, *A Question of Faith: A Report on the Status of Religious Minorities in Pakistan* (Islamabad: Jinnah Institute, 2011).

Forbes, Geraldine H., 'Women and Modernity: The Issue of Child Marriage in India', *Women's Studies International Forum* 2, 4 (1979): 407–19.

'Caged Tigers: 'First Wave' Feminists in India', *Women's Studies International Forum* 5, 6 (1982): 525–36.

Women in Modern India (Cambridge: Cambridge University Press, 1996).

Freitag, Sandra B., 'South Asian Ways of Seeing, Muslim Ways of Knowing: The Indian Muslim Niche Market in Posters', *Indian Economic and Social History Review* 44, 3 (2007): 297–331.

Fuller, C. J. and Veronique Benei (eds.), *The Everyday State and Society in Modern India* (London: C. Hurst & Co., 2001).

Gallanter, Marc, 'Who Are the Other Backward Classes?', *Economic and Political Weekly* 13, 43–44 (29 October 1978): 1812–28.

Gayer, Laurent, *Karachi. Ordered Disorder and the Struggle for the City* (London: C. Hurst & Co., 2014).

Gellner, David W. (ed.), *Borderland Lives in Northern South Asia* (Durham, NC: Duke University Press, 2013).

Gilmartin, David, 'Customary Law and Shari'at in British Punjab', in *Shari'at and Ambiguity in South Asian Islam*, ed. Katherine Ewing (Berkeley: University of California, 1988): 43–62.

Glazer, Nathan, *Affirmative Discrimination: Ethnic Inequality and Public Policy* (New York: Basic Books, Inc., 1975).

Goetz, Anne Marie and Rob Jenkins, 'Hybrid Forms of Accountability: Citizen Engagement in Institutions of Public Sector Over-Sight in India', *Public Management Review* 3, 3 (2001): 363–83.

Gorringe, Hugo, *Untouchable Citizens: Dalit Movements and Democratization in Tamil Nadu* (New Delhi: Sage, 2005).

Gould, William, *Hindu Nationalism and the Language of Politics in Late Colonial India* (Cambridge: Cambridge University Press, 2010).

Bureaucracy, Community and Influence: Society and the State, 1930s–1960s (London: Routledge, 2011).

Gould, William, Taylor C. Sherman and Sarah Ansari, 'The Flux of the Matter: Loyalty, Corruption and the "Everyday State" in the Post-Partition Government Services of India and Pakistan', *Past & Present* 219, 1 (2013): 237–79.

Gould, William, Sarah Gandee and Dakxin Bajrange, 'Settling the Citizen, Settling the Nomad: 'Habitual Offenders', Rebellion and Civic Consciousness in Western India, 1938–1952', *Modern Asian Studies* (2019), http://eprints.whiterose.ac.uk/144745/.

Greenough, Paul R., *Prosperity and Misery in Modern Bengal: The Famine of 1943–1944* (New York: Oxford University Press, 1982).

Guidry, John A., Michael D. Kennedy and Mayer N. Zald, *Globalizations and Social Movements: Culture, Power and the Transnational Public Sphere* (Ann Arbor: University of Michigan Press, 2000).

Gupta, Akhil, 'Blurred Boundaries: The Discourse of Corruption, the Culture of Politics, and the Imagined State', *American Ethnologist* 22, 2 (May 1995): 375–402.

   Red Tape: Bureaucracy, Structural Violence, and Poverty in India (Durham: Duke University Press, 2012).

Hasan, Mushirul, 'The Khilafat Movement: A Reappraisal', in *Communal and Pan-Islamic Trends in Colonial India*, ed. Mushirul Hasan (New Delhi: Manohar, 1985): 1–16.

   Legacy of a Divided Nation: India's Muslims since Independence (London: C. Hurst & Co., 1997).

Holston, James, *Insurgent Citizenship: Disjunctions of Democracy and Modernity in Brazil* (Princeton: Princeton University Press, 2009).

Hussain, Intizar, *Basti* (1979), English Translation, available at www.columbia.edu/itc/mealac/pritchett/00litlinks/basti/chapter_05.html (accessed December 2018).

Irfani, Suroosh, 'Pakistan: Reclaiming the Founding Moment', *Viewpoints Special Edition: The Islamization of Pakistan, 1979–2009* (Washington: The Middle East Institute, 2009).

Islam, M. Mufakharul, 'The Great Bengal Famine and the Question of FAD Yet Again', *Modern Asian Studies* 41, 2 (2007): 421–40.

Jafar, Afshan, 'Women, Islam and the State in Pakistan', *Gender Issues* 22, 1 (December 2003): 35–55.

Jaffrelot, Christophe, *India's Silent Revolution: The Rise of the Lower Castes in North India* (New York: Columbia University Press, 2003).

   'The Impact of Affirmative Action in India: More Political than Socioeconomic', *India Review* 5, 12 (2006): 173–89.

   The Pakistan Paradox: Instability and Resilience (London: C. Hurst & Co., 2015).

Jalal, Ayesha, *The Sole Spokesman: Jinnah, the Muslim League, and the Demand for Pakistan* (Cambridge and New York: Cambridge University Press, 1985).

   The State of Martial Rule: The Origins of Pakistan's Political Economy of Defence (Cambridge: Cambridge University Press, 1990).

   'The Convenience of Subservience: Women and the State in Pakistan', in *Women, Islam and the State*, ed. Deniz Kandiyoti (Basingstoke: Macmillan, 1991): 77–114.

Jamal, Amina, 'When Are Women's Rights Human Rights in Pakistan?', in *Gender, National Security and Counter-Terrorism: Human Rights Perspectives*, eds. Margaret Satterthwaite and Jayne Huckerby (New York: Routledge, 2013): 208–29.

Jaoul, Nicolas, 'Political and 'Non-Political' Means in the Dalit Movement', in *Political Process in Uttar Pradesh: Identity, Economic Reforms, and Governance*, ed. Sudha Pai (New Delhi: Pearson Longman, 2007): 191–220.

Jayal, Niraja Gopal, *Citizenship and Its Discontents: An Indian History* (Cambridge, MA: Harvard University Press, 2013).

Jehangir, Asma and Hina Jilani, *The Hudood Ordinances: A Divine Sanction* (Lahore: Sang-e-Meel Publications, 2003).

Jenkins, Laura Dudley, 'Competing Inequalities: The Struggle Over Reserved Seats for Women in India', *International Review of Social History* 44 (1999): 53–75.

Jenkins, Rob and Anne Marie Goetz, 'Accounts and Accountability: Theoretical Implications of the Right-to-Information Movement in India', *Third World Quarterly* 20, 3 (1999): 603–22.

John, Mary E., 'Alternate Modernities? Reservations and Women's Movement in 20th Century India', *Economic and Political Weekly* 35, 43–44 (October–November 2000): 3822–9.

Johnston, Caleb and Dakxin Bajrange, 'Street Theatre as Democratic Politics in Ahmedabad', *Antipode* 46, 2 (2014): 455–76.

Juge, Tony S. and Michael P. Perez, 'The Modern Colonial Politics of Citizenship and Whiteness in France', *Social Identities: Journal for the Study of Race, Nation and Culture* 12, 2 (2006): 187–212.

Kamran, Tahir, 'Islam, Urdu and Hindu as the Other: Instruments of Cultural Homogeneity in Pakistan', in *Composite Culture in a Multicultural Society*, eds. Bipen Chandra and Sucheta Mahajan (New Delhi: Pearson, 2007): 93–122.

'Early Phase of Electoral Politics in Pakistan: 1950s', *A Research Journal of South Asian Studies* 24, 2 (July–December 2009): 257–82.

Kartal, Filiz, 'Liberal and Republican Conceptualizations of Citizenship: A Theoretical Inquiry', *Turkish Public Administration Annual* 27–28 (January 2001): 101–30.

Kasturi, Leela and Vina Majumdar, *Women and Indian Nationalism* (New Delhi: Vikas Publication House, 1994).

Khan, Adeel, *Politics of Identity: Ethnic Nationalism and the State in Pakistan* (London: Sage, 2004).

Khan, Mahmood Hasan, 'Sind Hari Committee, 1930–1970: A Peasant Movement?', World Employment Programme Research Working Paper (Geneva: International Labour Organisation, 1979).

Khan, Nichola, *Mohajir Militancy in Pakistan* (London: Routledge, 2012).

Khan, Sana, 'Women and State Laws and Policies in Pakistan: The Early Phase, 1947–77', *Proceedings of the Indian History Congress* 74 (2013): 726–33.

Khan, Yasmin, *The Great Partition: The Making of India and Pakistan* (London: Yale University Press, 2007).

'The Ending of an Empire: From Imagined Communities to Nation States in India and Pakistan', *The Round Table* 97, 398 (2008): 695–704.

'The Ending of an Empire: From Imagined Communities to Nation States in India and Pakistan', in *The Iconography of Independence: Freedoms at Midnight*, eds. Robert Holland, Susan Williams and Terry Barringer (London and New York: Routledge, 2010): 47–56.

'Performing Peace: Gandhi's Assassination as a Critical Moment in the Consolidation of the Nehruvian Secular State', in *From Subjects to Citizens: Society and the Everyday State in India and Pakistan, 1947–1970*, eds. Taylor

Sherman, William Gould and Sarah Ansari (Cambridge: Cambridge University Press, 2014): 64–89.

Khattak, Shahbana Shamaas Gul and Akhtar Hussain, 'Women Representation in Pakistani Legislatures: A Study of the 2002, 2008 and 2013 General Elections', *South Asia Survey* 20, 2 (2016): 191–205.

Khuhro, Hamida (ed. and intro.), *Documents on Separation of Sind from the Bombay Presidency* (Islamabad: Islamabad Islamic University, 1982).

Kohli, Atul, *Democracy and Discontent: India's Growing Crisis of Governability* (Cambridge: Cambridge University Press, 1990).

Kothari, Rita, *The Burden of Refuge: The Sindhi Hindus of Gujarat* (Hyderabad: Orient Longman, 2007).

Kudaisya, Gyanesh, *Region, Nation, "Heartland": Uttar Pradesh in India's Body Politic* (New Delhi: Sage, 2006).

A Republic in the Making: India in the 1950s (New Delhi: Oxford University Press, 2017).

Kumar, Radha, *The History of Doing: An Illustrated Account of Movements for Women's Rights and Feminism in India, 1800–1990* (New Delhi: Kali for Women, 1993).

Kumar, Vivek, *India's Roaring Revolution: Dalit Assertions and New Horizons* (New Delhi: Gagandeep Publications, 2006).

Kymlicka, Will, *Multicultural Citizenship: A Liberal Theory of Minority Rights* (Oxford: Oxford University Press, 1996).

Lambert-Hurley, Siobhan, 'Fostering Sisterhood: Muslim Women and the All-India Ladies' Association', *Journal of Women's History* 16, 2 (Summer 2004): 40–65.

Lau, Martin, 'Twenty-Five Years of Hudood Ordinances: A Review', *Washington and Lee Law Review* 64, 4 (2007): 1291–314.

Lee, Benjamin and Edward LiPuma, 'Culture of Circulation. The Imaginations of Modernity', *Public Culture* 14, 1 (2002): 191–293.

Legg, Stephen, *Prostitution and the Ends of Empire: Scale, Governmentalities and Interwar India* (Durham, NC: Duke University Press, 2014).

Levitt, Peggy and Sally Merry, 'Vernacularization on the Ground: Local Uses of Global Women's Rights in Peru, China, India and the United States', *Global Networks* 9, 4 (2009): 441–61.

Lister, Michael and Emily Pia, *Citizenship in Contemporary Europe* (Oxford: Oxford University Press, 2008).

Madhok, Sumi, 'Five Notions of Haq: Exploring Vernacular Rights Cultures in South Asia', London School of Economics, Gender Institute New Working Paper Series, ed. Wendy Sigle-Rushton, Issue 25 (November 2009).

'Rights Talk and the Feminist Movement in India', in *Women's Movements in Asia: Feminisms and Transnational Activism*, eds. Mina Roces and Louise Edwards (London: Routledge, 2010): 224–42.

Madhok, Sumi, Anne Philips and Kalpana Wilson (eds.), *Gender, Agency and Coercion* (London: Palgrave, 2013).

Majumdar, Rochona, '"Self-Sacrifice" Versus "Self-Interest": A Non-Historicist Reading of the History of Women's Rights in India', *Comparative Studies of South Asia, Africa and the Middle East* 22, 1–2 (2002): 20–35.

Markovits, Claude, *The Global World of Indian Merchants 1750–1947: Traders of Sind from Bukhara to Panama* (Cambridge: Cambridge University Press, 2000).

Masroor, Mehr Nigar, *Ra'ana Liaquat Ali Khan: A Biography* (Karachi: All-Pakistan Women's Association, c. 1980).

Massey, Doreen, 'A Global Sense of Place', in *Space, Place and Gender*, ed. D. Massey (Minneapolis: University of Minnesota Press, 2004): 146–56.

Mayo, Marjorie, *Global Citizens: Social Movements and the Challenge of Globalization* (New York: Zed Books, 2005).

McGarr, Paul M., 'The Viceroys Are Disappearing from the Roundabouts in Delhi: British Symbols of Power in Post-Colonial India', *Modern Asian Studies* 49, 3 (2015): 787–831.

McGrath, Allen, *The Destruction of Pakistan's Democracy* (Karachi: Oxford University Press, 1996).

Mehrotra, Nilika, 'Disability Rights Movements in India', *Economic and Political Weekly* 46, 6 (5–11 February 2011): 65–72.

Mehta, Uday, 'Constitutionalism', in *Oxford Companion to Indian Politics*, eds. Niraja Jayal and Pratap Bhanu Mehta (New Delhi: Oxford University Press, 2010): 15–27.

Menon, Nivedita, 'State/Gender/Community: Citizenship in Contemporary India', *Economic and Political Weekly* 33, 5 (1998): 3–10.

Menon, Visalakshi, *Indian Women and Nationalism: The UP Story* (New Delhi: Shakti Books, 2003).

Menski, Werner, 'The Uniform Civil Code Debate in Indian Law: New Developments and Changing Agenda', *German Law Journal* 9, 3 (2008): 211–50.

Migdal, Joel S., *State-in-Society: Studying How States and Societies Transform and Constitute One Another* (New York: Cambridge University Press, 2001).

   (ed.), *Boundaries and Belonging: States and Societies in the Struggle to Shape Identities and Local Practices* (New York: Cambridge University Press, 2004).

Miles, Kay, *The Dynamo in Silk: A Brief Biographical Sketch of Begum Ra'ana Liaquat Ali Khan* (2nd ed., Karachi: All-Pakistan Women's Association, 1974).

Minault, Gail, 'Sisterhood or Separatism: The All India Muslim Ladies' Conference and the Nationalist Movement', in *The Extended Family: Women and Political Participation in India and Pakistan*, ed. Gail Minault (New Delhi: Chanakya Publications, 1981): 83–108.

   Secluded Scholars: Women's Education and Muslim Social Reform in Colonial India (New Delhi: Oxford University Press, 1998).

Mitchell, Timothy, 'The Limits of the State: Beyond Statist Approaches and Their Critics', *American Political Science Review* 85, 1 (March 1991): 77–96.

Moehler, Devra C., 'Participation and Support for the Constitution in Uganda', *Journal of Modern African Studies* 44, 2 (2006): 275–308.

Mukerjee, Amarendra Nath, 'Nationality in the Indian Union', *The Modern Review* 82, 3 (September 1947): 203–4.

Mumtaz, Khawar and Farida Shaheed, *Women of Pakistan: Two Steps Forward, One Step Back?* (London: Zed Books, 1987).

Muralidhar, B.V., G. Stanely Jaya Kumar, Vivek Kumar and Tenepalli Hari (eds.), *The Dynamics of Change and Continuity in the Era of Globalization: Voices from the Margins* (New Delhi: Sunrise Publications, 2009).

Naregal, Veena, *Language Politics, Elites and the Public Sphere: Western India under Colonialism* (London: Anthem Press, 2002).

Nasr, S. V. R., *The Vanguard of the Islamic Revolution: The Jamaat-i Islami of Pakistan* (London: I.B. Tauris, 1994).

Nelson, Matthew, 'Inheritance Unbound: The Politics of Personal Law Reform in Pakistan and India', in *Comparative Constitutional Traditions in South Asia*, eds. Sunil Khilnani, Vikram Raghavan and Arun Thiravengadam (New Delhi: Oxford University Press, 2012): 219–46.

Newberg, Paula, *Judging the State: Courts and Constitutional Politics in Pakistan* (Cambridge; Cambridge University Press, 1995).

Newbigin, Eleanor, 'Personal Law and Citizenship in India's Transition to Independence', *Modern Asian Studies* 45, 1 (2011): 7–32.

The Hindu Family and the Emergence of Modern India: Law, Citizenship and Community (Cambridge: Cambridge University Press, 2013).

Orsini, Francesca, *The Hindi Public Sphere 1920–1940: Language and Literature in the Age of Nationalism* (New Delhi: Oxford University Press, 2009).

Pandey, Deepak, 'Congress-Muslim League Relations 1937–1939: The Parting of the Ways', *Modern Asian Studies* 12, 4 (1978): 629–54.

Pandey, Gyanendra, 'Encounters and Calamities: The History of a North Indian Qasba in the Nineteenth Century', in *Subaltern Studies III: Writings on South Asian History and Society*, ed. Ranajit Guha (Oxford: Oxford University Press, 1984): 231–70.

'Partition and Independence in Delhi: 1947–1948', *Economic and Political Weekly* 32, 36 (6–12 September 1997): 2261–72.

Parr, Rosalind, 'Citizens of Everywhere. Indian Nationalist Women and the Global Public Sphere, 1900–1952' (unpublished PhD thesis, University of Edinburgh, 2018).

Parry, Jonathan, 'The 'Crises of Corruption' and 'The Idea of India': A Worm's-Eye View', in *The Morals of Legitimacy*, ed. Italo Pardo (New York and Oxford: Berghahn Books, 2000): 27–55.

Pearson, Gail, 'Reserved Seats – Women and the Vote in Bombay', in *Women in Colonial India: Essays on Survival, Work and the State*, ed. J. Krishnamurty (New Delhi: Oxford University Press, 1989): 199–217.

Piliavsky, Anastasia, 'A Secret in the Oxford Sense: Thieves and the Rhetoric of Mystification in Western India', *Comparative Studies in Society and History* 53, 2 (April 2011): 290–313.

Potter, David, *India's Political Administrators 1919–1983* (Oxford: Oxford University Press, 1986).

Purushotham, Sunil, 'Internal Violence: The "Police Action" in Hyderabad', *Comparative Studies in Society and History* 57, 2 (2015): 435–66.

Qasmi, Ali Usman, *Ahmadis and the Politics of Religious Exclusion in Pakistan* (London: Anthem Press, 2014).

'A Master Narrative for the History of Pakistan: Tracing the Origins of an Ideological Agenda', *Modern Asian Studies*, https://doi.org/10.1017/S0026749X17000427, Published online: 18 October 2018.

Raghovan, Pallavi, 'The Making of South Asia's Minorities: A Diplomatic History, 1947–1952', *Economic and Political Weekly* 51, 21 (May 2016): 45–52.

'The Making of the India–Pakistan Dynamic: Nehru, Liaquat and the No War Pact Correspondence of 1950', *Modern Asian Studies* 50, 5 (2016): 1645–78.

Rahman, Tariq, 'Language and Politics in a Pakistan Province: The Sindhi Language Movement', *Asian Survey* 35, 11 (November 1995): 1005–16.

Ravinder, Kaur, *Since 1947: Partition Narratives among Punjabi Migrants of Delhi* (New Delhi: Oxford University Press, 2007).

Rawat, Ramnarayan, 'Partition Politics and Achuut Identity: A Study of the Scheduled Castes Federation and Dalit Politics in UP, 1946–48', in *The Partitions of Memory: The Afterlife of the Division of India*, ed. S. Kaul (New Delhi: Permanent Black, 2001): 111–39.

Retsikas, Kostas, 'Being and Place: Movement, Ancestors, and Personhood in East Java, Indonesia', *Journal of the Royal Anthropological Institute* 13 (2007): 969–86.

Richardson, Tim and Ole B. Jensen, 'Linking Discourse and Space: Towards a Cultural Sociology of Space in Analyzing Spatial Policy Discourses', *Urban Studies* 40, 1 (2003): 7–22.

Robb, Peter and David Taylor (eds.), *Rule, Protest, Identity: Aspects of Modern South Asia* (London: Curzon Press, 1978).

Roberts, Joanne, 'From Know-How to Show-How? Questioning the Role of Information and Communication Technologies in Knowledge Transfer', *Technology Analysis and Strategic Management* 12, 4 (2000): 429–43.

Robinson, Francis, *Separatism among Indian Muslims: The Politics of the United Provinces' Muslims, 1860–1923* (Cambridge: Cambridge University Press, 1974).

Roy, A., *Mapping Citizenship in India* (New Delhi: Oxford University Press, 2010).

Roy, Haimanti, *Partitioned Lives: Migrants, Refugees, Citizens in India and Pakistan, 1947–65* (New Delhi: Oxford University Press, 2012).

Roy, Srirupa, *Beyond Belief: India and the Politics of Postcolonial Nationalism* (Durham, NC: Duke University Press, 2007).

Royle, T., *The Last Days of the Raj* (London: Michael Joseph Ltd., 1989).

Rumi, Raza, *Delhi by Heart: Impressions of a Pakistani Traveller* (New Delhi: HarperCollins India, 2013).

Saha, Jonathan, *Law, Disorder and the Colonial State: Corruption in Burma c.1900* (Basingstoke: Palgrave Macmillan, 2013).

Saiyid, Dushka, *Muslim Women of the British Punjab from Seclusion to Politics* (Basingstoke: Macmillan, 1998).

Santos, Boaventura de Sousa and Cesar A. Rodriguez-Garavito, *Law and Globalization from Below: Towards a Cosmopolitan Legality* (Cambridge: Cambridge University Press, 2004).

Seal, Anil, *The Emergence of Indian Nationalism: Competition and Collaboration in the Later Nineteenth Century* (Cambridge: Cambridge University Press, 1971).

Sen, Uditi, 'Dissident Memories: Exploring Bengali Refugee Narratives in the Andaman Islands', in *Refugees and the End of Empire: Imperial Collapse and Forced Migration during the Twentieth Century*, eds. Panikos Panayi and Pippa Virdee (London: Palgrave McMillan, 2011): 219–44.

    Citizen Refugee: Forging the Indian Nation after Partition (Cambridge: Cambridge University Press, 2018).

Sen, Uditi, 'Refugees and the Politics of Nation Building in India, 1947–1971' (unpublished PhD, University of Cambridge, 2009).

Sengupta, Debjani, *The Partition of Bengal: Fragile Borders and New Identities* (Cambridge: Cambridge University Press, 2015).

Shaheed, Farida and Khawar Mumtaz, 'Islamisation and Women: The Experience of Pakistan', *New Blackfriars* 71, 835, Special Issue: The World of Islam (February 1990): 67–80.

Shahnawaz, Jahanara, *Father and Daughter: A Political Autobiography* (Lahore: Nigarishat, 1971).

Shani, Ornit, 'Making India's Democracy: Rewriting the Bureaucratic Colonial Imagination in the Preparation of the First Elections', *Comparative Studies of South Asia, Africa and the Middle East* 36, 1 (May 2016): 83–101.

    How India Became Democratic: Citizenship and the Making of the Universal Franchise (Cambridge: Cambridge University Press, 2018).

Sherman, Taylor C., 'The Integration of the Princely State of Hyderabad and the Making of the Postcolonial State in India, 1948–56', *Indian Economic & Social History Review* 44, 4 (2007): 489–516.

    State Violence and Punishment in India (London: Routledge, 2010).

    'Migration, Citizenship and Belonging in Hyderabad (Deccan), 1948–1956', *Modern Asian Studies* 45, 1 (2011): 81–107.

    Muslim Belonging in Secular India: Negotiating Citizenship in Postcolonial Hyderabad (Cambridge: Cambridge University Press, 2015).

Siegel, Benjamin Robert, *Hungry Nation: Food, Famine and the Making of Modern India* (New York: Cambridge University Press, 2018).

Sinha, Mrinalini, 'Refashioning Mother India: Feminism and Nationalism in Late-Colonial India', *Feminist Studies* 26, 3 (Autumn, 2000): 622–44.

    Specters of Mother India: The Global Restructuring of an Empire (Durham, NC: Duke University Press, 2006).

    Gender and Nation (Washington: American Historical Association, 2006).

    'Historically Speaking: Gender and Citizenship in Colonial India', in *The Question of Gender: Joan W. Scott's Critical Feminism*, eds. Judith Butler and Elizabeth Weed (Bloomington: Indiana University Press, 2011): 80–101.

Sipe, K. R., Karachi's Refugee Crisis: The Political, Economic and Social Consequences of Partition-Related Migration (unpublished PhD, Duke University, 1976).

Sitapati, Vinay, 'What Anna Hazare and the Indian Middle-Classes Say About Each Other', *Economic and Political Weekly* 46, 30 (23 July 2011): 39–44.

Smith, Donald E., *India as a Secular State* (Princeton: Princeton University Press, 1963).

Southard, Barbara, 'Colonial Politics and Women's Rights: Woman Suffrage Campaigns in Bengal, British India in the 1920s', *Modern Asian Studies* 27, 2 (March 1993): 397–439.

Srinivas, M. N., *Caste: Its Twentieth Century Avatar* (New Delhi: Penguin, 2000).

Stamp, Dudley, 'Philatelie Cartography: A Critical Study of Maps on Stamps with Special Reference to the Commonwealth', *Geography* 51, 3 (July 1966): 179–97.

Svensson, Ted, *Production of Postcolonial India and Pakistan: Meanings of Partition* (London and New York: Routledge, 2013).

Symonds, Richard, *The Making of Pakistan* (London: Faber and Faber, 1950).

Talbot, Ian, *Pakistan: A Modern History* (London: C. Hurst & Co., 1999).

'Punjabi Refugees' Rehabilitation and the Indian State: Discourses, Denials and Dissonances', *Modern Asian Studies* 45, 1 (2011): 109–30.

A History of Modern South Asia: Politics, States, Diasporas (New Haven and London: Yale University Press, 2016).

Tan, Tai Yong and Gyanesh Kudaisya, *The Aftermath of Partition in South Asia* (London: Routledge, 2000).

Thapar-Björkert, Suruchi, 'The Domestic Sphere as a Political Site: A Study of Women in the Indian Nationalist Movement', *Women's Studies International Forum* 20, 4 (1997): 493–504.

Van Horn Melton, James, *The Rise of the Public in Enlightenment Europe* (Cambridge: Cambridge University Press, 2001).

Verkaaik, Oskar, *Migrants and Militants: Fun and Urban Violence in Pakistan* (Princeton: Princeton University Press, 2004).

Warner, Michael, *Publics and Counterpublics* (Cambridge: MIT Press, 2002).

Whagmore, Suryakhant, *Civility against Caste: Dalit Politics and Citizenship in Western India* (New Delhi: Sage, 2013).

Wilkinson, Steven, *Votes and Violence: Electoral Competition and Ethnic Riots in India* (Cambridge: Cambridge University Press, 2006).

Willmer, David, 'Women as Participants in the Pakistan Movement: Modernisation and the Promise of a Moral State', *Modern Asian Studies* 31, 3 (1996): 573–90.

Yadav, Nomita, 'Other Backward Classes: Then and Now', *Economic and Political Weekly* 37, 44–45 (2–15 November 2002): 4495–500.

Yuval-Davis, Nira, 'Belonging and the Politics of Belonging', *Patterns of Prejudice* 40, Special Issue: 'Boundaries, Identities and Borders: Exploring the Cultural Production of Belonging' (2006): 197–214.

Zamindar, Vazira, *The Long Partition and the Making of Modern South Asia: Refugees, Boundaries, Histories* (New York: Columbia University Press, 2007).

Index

For EU product safety concerns, contact us at Calle de José Abascal, 56–1°,
28003 Madrid, Spain or eugpsr@cambridge.org.

www.ingramcontent.com/pod-product-compliance
Ingram Content Group UK Ltd.
Pitfield, Milton Keynes, MK11 3LW, UK
UKHW020432240426
470322UK00017B/471